Sport and Exercise Psychology

The new edition of *Sport and Exercise Psychology* asks four fundamental questions that get to the heart of this flourishing discipline:

- What inner states influence how people think, feel and behave?
- How can people manage or self-regulate their own inner states?
- How can sport and exercise psychology professionals help people manage their inner states?
- Is sport psychology just a placebo effect?

Taking an applied perspective that bridges the gap between sport and exercise, the book answers these questions by covering the key topics in the field, including confidence, anxiety, self-regulation, stress and self-esteem. There are also chapters on the role of music in performance, imagery and exercise addiction.

Each chapter is written by an expert in that field and includes a range of features illustrating specific issues, either within the research literature or in their practical application.

This is a comprehensive and engaging overview of an evolving discipline and will be essential reading to any student of sport and exercise psychology. It will also be of huge interest to athletes and coaches seeking an accessible understanding of the role of psychology in sport.

Andrew M. Lane is a Professor of Sport Psychology at the University of Wolverhampton, UK. He has authored more than 200 peer-refereed journal articles, edited books and is a regular contributor to print, radio and TV media.

Topics in Applied Psychology

Series Editor: Graham Davey, Professor of Psychology at the University of Sussex, UK, and former president of the British Psychological Society.

Topics in Applied Psychology is a series of accessible, integrated textbooks ideal for courses in applied psychology. Written by leading figures in their field, the books provide a comprehensive academic and professional overview of the subject area, bringing the topics to life through a range of features, including personal stories, case studies, ethical debates and learner activities. Each book addresses a broad range of cutting-edge topics, providing students with both theoretical foundations and real-life applications.

Clinical Psychology
Second Edition
Graham Davey

Educational Psychology
Second Edition
Tony Cline, Anthea Gulliford and Susan Birch

Work and Organizational Psychology
Second Edition
Ian Rothmann and Cary Cooper

Sport and Exercise Psychology
Second Edition
Andrew M. Lane

Health Psychology
Second Edition
Charles Abraham

Criminal Psychology
Second Edition
David Canter

Sport and Exercise Psychology

Topics in Applied Psychology

Second edition

Edited by
Andrew M. Lane

 Routledge
Taylor & Francis Group

LONDON AND NEW YORK

Second edition published 2016
by Routledge
27 Church Road, Hove, East Sussex BN3 2FA

and by Routledge
711 Third Avenue, New York, NY 10017

Routledge is an imprint of the Taylor & Francis Group, an informa business

First edition published by Hodder Education 2008

British Library Cataloguing in Publication Data
A catalogue record for this book is available from the British Library

Library of Congress Cataloging in Publication Data
Sport and exercise psychology : topics in applied psychology/edited by
    Andrew M. Lane – Second edition.
    pages cm
    1. Sports – Psychological aspects. 2. Exercise – Psychological aspects.
    I. Lane, Andrew M. (Andrew Michael).
    GV706.4.S76 2015
    796.01′9 – dc23
    2015003038

ISBN: 978-1-84872-224-8 (hbk)
ISBN: 978-1-84872-223-1 (pbk)
ISBN: 978-1-31571-380-9 (ebk)

Typeset in Bembo and Univers
by Florence Production Ltd, Stoodleigh, Devon, UK

Printed in the United Kingdom
by Henry Ling Limited

Contents

Contributors to the second edition

Chris Beedie, Aberystwyth University, UK

Tracey Devonport, University of Wolverhampton, UK

Michael J. Duncan, Coventry University, UK

Alexei Y. Egorov, Eötvös Loránd University, Budapest, Hungary

Emma L. J. Eyre, Coventry University, UK

Abby Foad, Canterbury Christ Church University, UK

Christopher Fullerton, University of Wolverhampton, UK

Andrew Friesen

Kate Hays, English Institute of Sport, UK

Philip Hurst, Canterbury Christ Church University, UK

Costas I. Karageorghis, Brunel University, London, UK

Andrew M. Lane, University of Wolverhampton, UK

Andrew P. Lane, Cardiff Metropolitan University, UK

Attila Szabo, Eötvös Loránd University, Budapest, Hungary

Dave Smith, Manchester Metropolitan University

Owen Thomas, Cardiff Metropolitan University, UK

Richard Thelwell, University of Portsmouth, UK.

Mark Uphill, Canterbury Christ Church University, UK

Caroline Wakefield, Liverpool Hope University, UK

Neil J. V. Weston, University of Portsmouth, UK

Series preface

Psychology is still one of the most popular subjects for study at undergraduate degree level. As well as providing the student with a range of academic and applied skills that are valued by a broad range of employers, a psychology degree also serves as the basis for subsequent training and a career in professional psychology. A substantial proportion of students entering a degree programme in psychology do so with a subsequent career in applied psychology firmly in mind, and, as a result, the number of applied psychology courses available at undergraduate level has significantly increased over recent years. In some cases, these courses supplement core academic areas, and in others they provide the student with a flavour of what they might experience as a professional psychologist.

The original series of *Texts in Applied Psychology* consisted of six textbooks designed to provide a comprehensive academic and professional insight into specific areas of professional psychology. The texts covered the areas of *Clinical Psychology, Criminal and Investigative Psychology, Educational Psychology, Health Psychology, Sport and Exercise Psychology* and *Work and Organizational Psychology*, and each text was written and edited by the foremost professional and academic figures in each of these areas.

These texts were so successful that we are now able to provide you with a second edition of this series. All texts have been updated with details of recent professional developments as well as relevant research, and we have responded to the requests of teachers and reviewers to include new material and new approaches to this material. Perhaps most significantly, all texts in the series will now have back-up web resources.

Just as in the first series, each textbook is based on a similar academic formula that combines a comprehensive review of cutting-edge research and professional knowledge with accessible teaching and learning features. The books are also structured so they can be used as an integrated teaching support for a one-term or one-semester course in each of their relevant areas of applied psychology. Given the increasing importance of applying psychological knowledge across a growing range of areas of practice, we feel this series is timely and comprehensive. We hope you find each book in the series readable, enlightening, accessible and instructive.

Graham Davey
University of Sussex, Brighton, UK
August 2014

Introduction

It has been a pleasure to act as editor for the second edition of *Sport and Exercise Psychology: Topics in Applied Psychology*. I enjoyed the process of editing the first version because I managed to recruit a group of authors who were not only experts but also enthusiastic. And the good news is that many of the authors from the first version of this book have revised and updated their chapters. There are several new chapters in the current version. Over the last 5 years, I have been working as part of a research group called 'Emotion Regulation of Others and Self'. The group was formed as the result of a research grant from the Economic and Social Research Council. During this time, I have been working with psychologists from a different area of application to sport and exercise, including neurological, social, clinical and occupational. It has been an enriching experience. Even within psychology, there are different definitions and different ways of working. Learning to accept this approach is a healthy way to approach work. Of course, there will be differences in emphasis between different areas of psychology, just as any two people will differ in their interpretation of evidence. Even a pint glass containing 300 ml of water is half full or half empty, depending on your perspective. We can see the water and so can assess just how much water is in the glass. We can't see thoughts and feelings in the same way, and psychologists' methods of capturing such inner states simply add further potential for differences in opinion.

Students studying sport and exercise psychology quite rightly are looking for correct answers – answers that will help them obtain their qualification, and answers that could guide their professional development as they begin their careers. The ability to consider the evidence, judge the appropriateness and robustness of the methods and be able to see the applicability of theory or previous research to the interpretation of future events requires a degree of wisdom. Reflection in professional practice is such a useful skill to employ, and producing this book has been an enjoyable journey for me as editor.

Many sport and exercise psychology textbooks are organized by dividing sport/exercise and individual/team into different sections. I considered this approach, but decided against it. I take the view that both sport and exercise psychologists are interested to some degree in behaviour change. Sport psychologists might focus on improving the quality of performance and use measures such as winning or finish time as markers of behaviour, whereas exercise psychologists might use the act of doing exercise as a marker, with less emphasis on the performance itself. Both share the feature of attempting to alter behaviour. Both sport and exercise psychologists are concerned with the well-being of the athlete. Of course, in sport psychology, the well-being of the athlete is often presented as a secondary goal to athletic achievement, but this does not differ hugely from an exerciser who ties well-being with completing an exercise session.

The book is organized in four parts, each with a question that hopefully will prompt curiosity in how they can be answered:

- The first question is, 'What inner states influence what people think and feel and how they behave?' It includes four chapters examining mood and emotion, self-confidence, anxiety and self-esteem.
- The second question, 'How can people manage or self-regulate their own inner states?', looks at how people manage these inner states or their intentions to achieve goals.
- The third question is 'How can sport and exercise psychology professionals help people manage their inner states?' In this section, we examine some commonly used techniques.
- The fourth and final part is a single, thought-provoking chapter called 'Beliefs versus reality, or beliefs as reality? The placebo effect in sport and exercise'. In this chapter, we are asked to reflect on our knowledge of the mechanisms proposed to explain intervention work. For scientists, thinking about how we should answer this question is fundamental to our work.

All the chapters are interesting and brought to you by world-leading researchers. The book has been enjoyable to put together, and I hope it will prove to be essential reading.

Professor Andrew M. Lane
February 2015

What inner states influence what people think and feel and how they behave?

1 Mood and sport performance

Andrew M. Lane

CHAPTER SUMMARY

Anecdotal quotes from athletes, coaches and fans report that playing and watching sport are emotional experiences. Watching Team GB win medal after medal during the summer Olympics of 2012 seemed to improve the mood of the nation. Yet, just 2 years later, England was feeling a sense of despair when the soccer team crashed out of the 2014 World Cup. The relationship between success and good and bad moods seems relatively straightforward on the face of it. Success brings happiness, and failure brings misery. Extending this thinking, does it also follow that feeling happy brings success, and feeling miserable brings failure? Listening to interviews with athletes and coaches alike, we hear evidence that sounds as though it supports this assumption. What is clear is that an inability to get it right mentally is cited by athletes and coaches as a reason for failure.

Amid the anecdotal evidence, the aspiring sport psychologist will be calling for an examination of evidence from scientific studies, and studies have focused on examining relationships between mood and performance. Researchers have taken measures of happiness and misery, examined how people performed and then correlated the two. If the above link between happiness and good performance held, then the researchers would find that happy performers were successful and miserable athletes failed. If we presume that the studies reported in the literature confirmed these ideas, then the extension would be to develop interventions to improve performance by making people happier, or worsen performance by making people feel miserable. And so, if that is the case, then sport psychologists should proceed to intervene at will! That is not the case, as the scientific basis for their work does not present such a clear view. Sport and exercise psychologists still believe that mood plays an important role in performance, and researchers continue to develop theories and methods to help identify meaningful relationships.

Sport and exercise psychology is a science, and practitioners base their work on evidence gathered from scientific studies. Evidence has to be gathered using rigorous methods, and, by the term rigour, I mean that the methods used are impartial and unbiased, and another researcher could reproduce them. One study finding that mood state X predicts performance is interesting, but 100 studies confirming this would provide a far more persuasive argument. The applied value of research is the extent to which it can say to a practitioner, if you do intervention X, it will have these effects, and be able to specify what those effects are. With reference to mood, we need to know the relationship between mood and performance, and so this chapter will focus on research that has investigated these two questions:

- *'Does mood predict performance?' (see Terry, 1995; Lane, 2007a); and*
- *'If I want to perform well, how should I feel?' (see Lane, 2012; Lane et al., 2012).*

In this chapter, I will focus on whether mood can predict performance: that is, if mood states assessed before competition predict performance. Fortunately, our task is made easier because a plethora of studies have examined mood–performance relationships. Unfortunately, the evidence base is not clear. Evidence indicates that mood–performance relationships are strong in some studies and weak in other studies. I will examine these studies and offer arguments to make sense of the literature.

LEARNING OUTCOMES

When you have studied this chapter, you should be able to:

1. Evaluate mood–performance relationships reported in the literature and be aware of factors that influence this relationship
2. Evaluate the conceptual model of Lane and Terry (2000) by examining studies that have tested it and describe the revised conceptual model proposed by Lane (2007a)
3. Be aware of ethical issues that might be relevant in either the research or practical application of mood and performance

ACTIVITY 1.1

What mood states do I feel when I perform well? And what mood states do I feel when I perform badly? How do these states differ?

The aim of this activity is to examine whether your mood differs when you performed successfully in comparison with when you performed poorly. The method used to do this is seemingly simple and designed to help you explore what thoughts and feelings occurred when performing. Remember, this is a retrospective approach to assessing your moods, and how you remember you felt could be different from what you felt at the time. The aim of the exercise is to illustrate the fact that a great deal of measurement of mood depends on self-report. Engaging in the activity and thinking carefully about whether you can identify your thoughts and feelings should illustrate the difficulties researchers and practitioners

TABLE 1.1 Identifying moods you felt when performing at your best

What to do?	Examples	Your go
1 To start with, I want you to think carefully about when you performed very well in a competition. It's up to you how you define very well. This could be achieving a personal best, winning or a sense that you performed your best; it's up to you. Try to use a recent experience, but, if you have not competed recently, then think back to a time when you performed well; the more recent the better, as these experiences are fresh in your mind, but go back to an experience where your moods were intense and you remember how you felt, and remember it well	A distance runner: 'Last weekend when I did a Personal Best' A soccer player: 'My best performance was in a game when I marked their best; I restricted her to just a few touches'	
2 Now remember how you felt before the competition started, consider how you felt physically, what were you thinking about and what emotions did you experience?	'I felt nervous, really nervous – constant loo stops but I felt positive and excited – I just wanted to get started' 'I felt up for the game; I was feeling full of energy'	
3 Write down all the moods you can recall experiencing. Use single words such as nervous, calm, excited, downhearted, happy, sad, vigorous or tired	'Excited', 'nervous', 'a little apprehensive', 'active'	
4 Write a sentence to capture what you felt	'I was excited because I thought I would perform well' 'I was sad because I knew I would not meet my expectations'	

TABLE 1.2 Identifying moods you felt when performing at your worst

What to do?	Examples	Your go
1 To start with, I want you to think carefully about when you performed very poorly in a competition. It's up to you how you define very poorly	A distance runner: 'Last weekend when I felt I slowed down when I was tired – but I think I could have gone faster and I feel bad about myself now' A soccer player: 'My worst performance was in a game when I should have been concentrating on player X and I lost concentration in the game – my nerves were everywhere and I did not know what to concentrate on and then boom: 1 nil down and it's down to me!'	
2 Now remember how you felt before the competition started, consider how you felt physically, what were you thinking about, and what emotions did you experience?	'I felt nervous, really nervous – constant loo stops; I wanted the event to be over – horrible' 'I felt so tired; I kept thinking, why do I feel like this, why now?'	
3 Write down all the moods you can recall experiencing. Use single words such as nervous, calm, excited, downhearted, happy, sad, vigorous or tired	'Downhearted', 'guilty', 'tired', 'grumpy'	
4 Write a sentence to capture what you felt	'I wanted to perform so well and when the day came I felt a wave of intense misery; I wanted to escape from these thoughts and feelings'	

face. It is hoped that you will get a sense that this is not an exact science, and that scores on the self-report scale or descriptions that come in qualitative accounts depend heavily on the extent to which you can accurately say how you felt.

A very poor performance

Go through the same four-point procedure you used above, but this time think of a time you performed very poorly. Remember, how you define poor is up to you, but it should represent a performance when you performed below expectations.

I suspect your list will contain a mixture of pleasant and unpleasant emotions. For example, athletes can feel excited (pleasant) and nervous (unpleasant) before an important competition. Athletes usually feel a number of intense emotions.

There are not right or wrong mood states to feel, and sometimes athletes, and people in general, tend to think pleasant emotions (happiness, excitement) always help you perform better, and unpleasant emotions (anxiety, anger, sadness) get in the way of good performance.

The difficulty people have is that many people appear to perform very well when feeling anxious, or find happiness is not overly useful before competition. The idea is that anxiety tells you, 'This is important, concentrate or you will fail', and this type of message helps you get ready for performance, and that's not a bad way to feel. Happiness can send the message, 'All is well'. This is OK, but in sport, there are so many uncertain factors that it might not be wise to be overly happy; feeling happy is arguably a good thing if the athlete has a clear idea of what is required, however much he or she can do that. Feeling happy might not be a good thing if it signals complacency.

This exercise is useful, as it acts as a warm-up to the research questions that psychology literature has attempted to answer.

LEARNING OUTCOME 1

Evaluate mood–performance relationships reported in the literature and be aware of factors that influence this relationship

Mood and performance: the evidence

'Has the iceberg melted?'

The mood–performance relationship has been researched extensively. A search on the database SPORT DISCUSS using the keyword 'mood' reveals more than 1,000 articles accessed.

Mood research in sport has concentrated on an examination of the iceberg profile (see Figure 1.1; Morgan, 1980). Mood researchers tend to use the Profile of Mood States (POMS: McNair *et al.*, 1971) or versions of the POMS such as the Brunel

ACTIVITY 1.2

Go back to those emotions listed for Activity Box 1.1. Pay close attention to unpleasant emotions, such as feeling angry. Based on your experiences, have you performed well when feeling angry? Or did you perform badly when feeling angry? It's possible you have done both. Anger is a powerful emotion.

Consider how you might try to control your thoughts and actions when feeling very angry. What do you do? By writing these experiences down, you will start to learn about how you experience mood, how you control mood states that could hamper performance, or how you psyche yourself up to perform successfully.

Situation when you were very high	Outcome on performance	Reflection
Example		
'I was cut up in a race; I think it was deliberate as I had to slow down and she gained a few metres on me. I felt rage searing through me'	'I felt strong and felt I could run through walls and so I surged by. The trouble was that there was still 600 m to go and I did not hold on'	'I wish I could have had that surge at 200 to go and then I would have had that extra kick when others also needed to dig deep'
Your go . . .		
1		
2		
3		

Mood Scale (BRUMS) (Terry *et al.*, 1999). The method that the majority of research that has examined mood is self-report. Self-report requires people to introspect on how they are currently feeling or have felt in the past. The POMS and its versions assess six psychological states: anger, confusion, depression, fatigue, tension and vigour. Morgan (1980) proposed that the POMS was the 'test of champions', based on evidence showing scores on the POMS could be used to predict performance. Examination of whether successful performance was associated with an iceberg profile provided the impetus for a great many of the studies that followed.

By 1995, there was considerable debate as to whether POMS scores could be used to inform sport psychologists on which athletes would succeed and which athletes would not. Three review articles were published in 1995 with very different conclusions

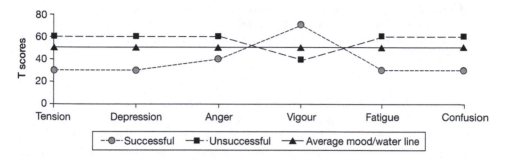

FIGURE 1.1 The iceberg profile: successful (iceberg) and unsuccessful (inverse iceberg) athletes, as proposed by Morgan (1980)

Source: Morgan, 1980

being reached, even though they reviewed largely the same set of studies. In a narrative review, Renger (1993) found that elite athletes did not uniformly report an iceberg profile. Renger also reported that non-athletes showed an iceberg profile. It must be remembered that researchers at the time expected elite athletes to show an iceberg profile, and thus it was deemed interesting for researchers to report when they did not. As a consequence, Renger argued that the POMS was a poor tool for distinguishing elite from non-elite athletes, or for distinguishing athletes from non-athletes. Using the evidence presented, Renger has clear evidence to support his conclusions.

In a second review article, this time a meta-analysis, Rowley *et al.* (1995) found that POMS measures accounted for approximately 1 per cent of the variance in performance. With 99 per cent of performance variance unexplained, Rowley *et al.* suggested that researchers 'abandon the POMS'. They argued that, despite more than 200 studies published, evidence was so equivocal that a more fruitful line of investigation lay elsewhere. Hence, Rowley *et al.*'s conclusion is consistent with Renger's – the POMS is not an overly useful tool.

To summarize these two studies (Renger, 1993; Rowley *et al.*, 1995), both are critical of the utility of the POMS. In contrast, a second review of mood literature in 1995, by Peter Terry, reached a different conclusion. Terry (1995) suggested that the mood someone is currently feeling is likely to influence what they think and what they do. He started to point out some of the methodological and theoretical gaps in the literature that needed to be addressed. In terms of methodological issues, he argued that mood should be assessed by examining how someone feels 'right now'. In the reviews published in 1995, many studies did not even report whether they assessed current mood ('right now') or a memory of mood ('How have you been feeling over the past week?'). He also argued that performance should be measured using the quality of a single performance, rather than a number of performances. For example, assess how you performed in a single race, rather than a series of races over the course of a season. Therefore, the method would be as follows:

- Assess mood states – how are you feeling at the moment?
- Measure performance – that is, the quality of a single performance, for example the time taken to complete 100 m.

- Correlate the scores on the scale used to assess pre-competition mood and the measure of performance used (e.g. finish time, or a self-rated performance, for example on a 1–10 scale, where 1 = poor performance and 10 = outstanding performance).

Research that has used a design such as this has had some success predicting performance. Terry (1995) used the POMS to monitor athletes preparing for World and Olympic competitions. In a series of studies, he reported that POMS could discriminate athletes who performed to their own expectation: that is, after the performance, it indicated that the quality of performance was either at or better than expectation or below expectation. Terry reported some impressive figures, including 100 per cent prediction in rowing and 71 per cent prediction in bobsleigh.

APPLYING THE SCIENCE 1.1

In the 1970s, there was a suggestion that scores on the POMS could be used to select athlete teams. Although there were some impressive results on the predictive effectiveness of POMS scores, it was too easy fake a good mood. Terry (1995) used scores on the POMS as a way of helping athletes identify states that they felt helped performance. As data were collected as part of scientific support, athletes and teams reporting unpleasant and dysfunctional moods could speak to the sport psychologist. Professor Terry has developed a fabulous and free online resource that allows athletes to monitor their own mood states.[1]

Returning to Rowley et al.'s (1995) and Renger's (1993) studies, Terry (1995) outlined methodological reasons to explain an inconsistent mood–performance relationship. Terry considered why mood states might predict performance and demonstrated that mood is an effective predictor of performance under certain conditions. In terms of methodological issues, Terry argued that mood states predicted performance in cross-sectional studies when a self-reference measure of performance was used, and when participants had similar levels of skill and fitness. He argued that mood has a subtle influence on performance, and that the research design needs to account for this. Beedie et al. (2000) conducted an updated meta-analysis to test Terry's proposals. Beedie et al. went to some lengths to unpack why Rowley et al. managed to come to a different conclusion.

'A tale of two questions'

Terry (1995) argued that mood is an effective predictor of performance when certain conditions are met. He emphasized the commonly understood point, among psychologists and laypeople alike, that mood states are transitory in nature and so vary. Research shows that the mood states experienced the day before competition differ from those immediately before competition, with an increase in the intensity of emotions such as anxiety and excitement (Lane, 2012; Lane *et al.*, 2012). Terry (1995) questioned the logic of using mood to compare elite athletes with non-elite athletes or to compare mood states of athletes with those of non-athletes. A research design to compare mood states of different groups in different situations effectively treats mood states as though they are stable or as though mood is relatively permanent. A wealth of evidence demonstrates that mood states change. For example, research shows exercise people start an exercise class in an unpleasant mood and finish the session reporting that they feel pleasant emotions (Berger and Motl, 2000; Lane and Lovejoy, 2001).

In their theoretical paper, Lane and Terry (2000) went to great lengths to explain what might seem a trivial point: that is, how the response time frame used influences the nature of the response. A reader could be led to believe it is a trivial point, because the actual response time frame has not been commonly reported in the literature (Lane and Terry, 2000). It was common for researchers to say that they used the POMS and not say whether someone reported that this was how they were feeling over the past week, past year or right then.

Lane (2007a) describes a hypothetical situation that could characterize the methods used to answer this question. He indicated that many studies posted a copy of the POMS questionnaire to the athlete. The athlete received the questionnaire in the mail and was asked to complete the POMS using a 'past month' response time frame – that is, think back over the previous month and provide a single score that summarizes these feelings. However, no consideration of situational factors was involved. The athlete completed the POMS, indicated his/her level of athletic ability and posted this information back to the researcher. Consider the following example to illustrate the problem as reported by Lane (2007a). Athlete A, who is a club-level athlete, receives the POMS in the post on a day when he also receives an enormous gas bill (negative mood). Athlete B, who is an elite athlete, receives the POMS in the post on a day when he receives a huge tax rebate (positive mood). If both complete the POMS when they receive it, Athlete A should report a negative mood, and Athlete B should report a positive mood. If we compared mood with performance, it would show that elite athletes report more positive mood states than non-elite athletes. Clearly, mood states were influenced by what was in the post. If the researchers do not know the situation in which the measure was completed, then they will not know what factors influenced mood at the time of completion. Given the number of factors that influence mood, what might be more surprising is that mood has predicted performance in some studies. The following section offers further methodological limitations of some of the early research.

How you ask the question shapes the answer you receive: a case for looking at the response time frame

Mood states vary from situation to situation (Lane *et al.*, 2011). Therefore, researchers should use a response time frame of 'how do you feel right now?' to assess the transient nature of mood. The POMS has two principal response time frames: 'How have you been feeling over the past week, including "today" and "right now"?' A great deal of mood research used the 'past week' response time frame, or did not specify the response time frame used. Lane and Terry (2000) highlighted problems with using a 'past week' response time frame. Consider the issue through the following example that is contained in Table 1.3. Both athletes report the same score for anger scores over the

TABLE 1.3 Anger scores using different response time frames

Day	Anger score on the BRUMS (raw score from 0–16)	
	Person A	Person B
Monday	0	6
Tuesday	0	0
Wednesday	0	0
Thursday	0	0
Friday	0	0
Saturday	1	0
Sunday (today: How do you feel right now?)	4	0
How have you been feeling over the past week, including today?	2	2

past week; however, one athlete is feeling angry at the time of testing, whereas the other athlete is recalling feelings of anger from memory.

The key point is that mood states are transitory, and research that explores mood–performance relationships should ideally assess mood *during competition*. However, this is difficult, and ethically inappropriate, as this could interfere with an athlete's performance. The most appropriate time to collect mood data is approximately 1 hour before competition, using the response time frame 'How do you feel *right now?*'. Mood researchers should seek to capture the mood states experienced before competition and so should not use the 'past month' response time frame, which assesses memories of mood across multiple situations. Taking psychological state assessments 1 hour before competition is the standard approach in anxiety research (see Martens *et al.*, 1990) and should be applied to mood (see Lane, 2007a). Many of the studies in the meta-analysis by Rowley *et al.* (1995) do not report the response time frame used, which is a major limitation of the early work in this area.

Mood and team performance

Terry (1995) argued that mood states have a relatively subtle influence on performance. Researchers need to design studies that acknowledge this effect size and include appropriate controls. It is unrealistic to expect mood states to predict team performance if we assess an individual's mood (and not the team's) and analyse performance by win/loss. For example, a soccer goalkeeper performing in a negative mood may perform badly but not concede any goals, owing to good performances from the surrounding defenders, or they may concede three goals, but their team scores four. It is also unrealistic to expect mood states to predict objective measures of performance in cross-sectional research where participants are heterogeneous in terms of skill and ability. Consider the following example to illustrate this point.

Two track athletes are competing in a 100-m race. Athlete A, an elite sprinter with a personal best time of 10.00 s, reports a negative mood before the race. Athlete B, a club sprinter with a personal best time of 11.00 s, reports a positive mood before the

ACTIVITY 1.3

Measurement issues

Both Person A and Person B have the same mood profile for the past-week response time frame. Athlete A is angry at the time of testing, and Athlete B is not, and the mood states currently being experienced will be more influential than mood states stored in the memory in terms of their relation with behaviour in this situation. However, anger scores are identical for the past-week response time frame, and so using this time frame leads to an unclear measure, as the individual could be angry at the time of testing or recalling a memory of a mood, and these affect behaviour and cognition differently. If both people are exposed to the same set of frustrations, Person A is more likely to respond in an angry manner, as he/she is currently angry.

With reference to your own mood states, consider which would affect your behaviour more:

1   feeling angry immediately before performance?
2   feeling angry during the week and having a memory of feeling angry?

same race. If both athletes run the race in 10.5 s, and no consideration is given to the relative quality of their performances, then results would indicate no relationship between mood and performance. Contrastingly, if the same elite athlete is compared with another elite athlete, with the same personal best, who reports a positive mood before the present race and runs it in 10.00 s, the result would suggest that mood and performance are related. It is, therefore, important to develop a self-referenced

ACTIVITY 1.4

Anger and/or performance relationships

Think carefully about when you have played your sport. What goals did you set for yourself? What standard of performance would you have been happy with? Now, imagine yourself playing in a competition and try to remember how you felt. Write down the emotions you felt and rate these emotions as 'a little', 'somewhat', 'moderately' or 'very much so'. Think of how well you performed. Rate whether you performed to expectation or underperformed. Performing to expectation should be related to positive mood states, and underperformance should be associated with negative mood states. It might be that you experienced anger and anxiety when performing successfully. We will look at the nature of anger and anxiety later in the chapter.

measure of performance to detect the relatively subtle influence of mood on performance (see Terry, 1993). Using the example of the elite and club sprinters cited above, a self-referenced measure of performance – for example, comparing current performance with previous performance – would show that the elite athlete under-performed and the novice athlete performed above expectation, and this is reflected by variations in mood.

Mood and performance in elite athletes

Research that has investigated mood and performance relationships in elite samples and uses a self-referenced measure usually shows significant relationships. Elite athletes tend to be similar in terms of skill and fitness levels, whereas non–elite athletes vary greatly in the amount of training conducted. It is reasonable to expect that training and physiological fitness will have a stronger relationship with performance than mood. With reference to the two athletes described above, Athlete A is almost always likely to beat Athlete B, regardless of mood states, as physiological factors will be more salient than psychological factors. However, if Athlete A races another athlete with the same personal best, psychological factors such as mood tend to predict variances in performance. Terry (1995) reported some impressive figures for mood performance research. He found that 100 per cent of performers were correctly classified as either successful or unsuccessful in rowing (Hall and Terry, 1995), 92 per cent of performers were correctly classified in karate (Terry and Slade, 1995), and 71 per cent of performers were correctly classified in bobsleigh (Terry, 1993).

POMS research: 'The baby and the bathwater' (Lane, 2007a)

Lane (2007a) described the state of affairs for prospective mood researchers considering starting a project in 1995. He argued that students planning to study mood would be

---

APPLYING THE SCIENCE 1.2

Meta-analysis results of Beedie *et al.* (2000)

Question: Can mood predict athletes of different levels of achievement, or do elite athletes have a monopoly on good mood?
Answer: No. The mean ES was 0.10, suggesting that the relationship between mood and achievement was minimal. This finding concurs with the 1 per cent of variance of performance that could be explained by variations in mood found by Rowley *et al.* (1995).

Question: Can mood states predict performance when assessed shortly before competition?
Answer: Yes. A mean ES of 0.31 indicates that mood measures assessed before a single performance have some predictive validity. However, this is not an overly strong relationship. Further, the research design is not experimental, and, therefore, we cannot infer causality.

unclear on how to investigate mood–performance relationships, given the inconsistent evidence presented in the literature. Two research articles attempted to address this confusion. Beedie *et al.* (2000) conducted two meta-analyses, with each analysis producing vastly different results. The first meta-analysis summarized findings from studies that sought to link mood and athletic achievement by comparing the mood responses of elite and non-elite athletes. The value of this research question is questionable: that is, we would not expect the mood of an elite athlete and a club athlete to differ in any predictable way. The overall effect size (ES) was very small, a finding consistent with the previous meta-analysis by Rowley *et al.* (1995). The second meta-analysis completed by Beedie *et al.* included studies that examined the relationship between pre-competition mood and subsequent performance. This is arguably a more productive line of enquiry, given that we would expect an athlete's mood to influence her/his performance.

Beedie *et al.* concluded the following from their meta-analysis:

- Vigour was associated with good performance, whereas confusion, fatigue and depression were associated with poor performance.
- Anger and tension were associated with good performance in some studies and poor performance in others.
- Effects were very small for the debilitative effects of fatigue.

LEARNING OUTCOME 2

Evaluate the conceptual model of Lane and Terry (2000) and evidence that has examined this model, and describe the revised conceptual model proposed by Lane (2007a)

Why do mood states predict performance?

The nature of mood: development of a theoretical model with a focus on depression

After identifying that mood states can predict performance, researchers continue to pose the question, 'Why do mood states predict performance?'. What is it about the nature of mood that influences performance? If mood states influence performance, how can intervention strategies lead to enhanced mood states before competition (see Karageorghis, this issue; Thelwell, this issue)? Turning to theoretical perspectives on the nature of mood, Lane and Terry (2000) developed a conceptual model around the mood states assessed in the POMS. A theory should offer a clear definition of what the construct is and what it is not. A surprising feature of mood research in sport and exercise was the absence of a definition in the literature. Few authors offer a definition.

To address this limitation, Lane and Terry (2000) offered a tentative definition of mood as, 'a set of feelings, ephemeral in nature, varying in intensity and duration, and usually involving more than one emotion' (p. 16). Lane *et al.* (2005a) recently acknowledged a limitation of this definition, in that emotion and mood are defined by each other (see Uphill, this issue, for further discussion). Lane *et al.* accepted that measurement issues drove their early definition of mood. Lane *et al.* used definitions of mood and emotion from the general psychology literature.

Lazarus (2000) offered the following definition of emotion as:

> an organized psycho–physiological reaction to ongoing relationships with the environment . . . what mediates emotions psychologically is an evaluation, referred to as an appraisal, of the personal significance for the well-being that a person attributes to this relationship (. . . relational meaning), and the process.
>
> (p. 230)

Parkinson et al. (1996) proposed that, 'mood reflects changing non-specific psychological dispositions to evaluate, interpret, and act on past, current, or future concerns in certain patterned ways' (p. 216).

Beedie et al. (2005) discuss issues related to mood and emotion distinctions; these discussions are extensive, and the interested reader is referred to this work. A key part of the definition forwarded by Lane and Terry (2000) involved demonstrating the transient nature of mood and arguing that mood–performance research in sport should assess mood states before competition, using the right-now response time frame (see Beedie et al., 2011).

Lane and Terry (2000) explored the nature of each mood state assessed in the POMS. They offered a definition of the nature of each construct, identifying its antecedents and correlates and describing its relationship with performance. After exploring the nature of each mood state in the POMS, Lane and Terry proposed that depressed mood should have the strongest influence on sport performance. Depressed mood is characterized by themes such as hopelessness, sadness and feeling miserable. Sport performance requires athletes to persevere in the face of adversity, drawing on personal resources to maximize their potential – in other words, depression is the antithesis of the mindset needed to bring about optimal performance. However, the meta-analysis results of Beedie et al. indicate a weak relationship between depression and performance.

In an attempt to address the issue of weak depression–performance relationships, data from several published studies were re-analysed (see Lane, 2007a, for a review), focusing on the depression scores. Following a close inspection of raw scores for depression, a pattern emerged that indicated that the modal score for depression from athletes close to competition was reported as zero for all items. Around 50 per cent of athletes report zero for all items in the depression scale, and, therefore, depressed-mood data have variance for only half the participants in the sample. As performance scores would vary in all participants, around 50 per cent of data would show a zero correlation. The result of this is that the overall correlation would be weak (see Lane et al., 2005b, for a discussion on how the range in data influences the size of a correlation coefficient). Quite simply, correlation results tend to increase when the variance in data is large. Lane and Terry (1999) reported that only 39 per cent of athletes from a sample of 1,317 athletes reported a depressed mood score of 1 or more on a 16-point scale. Depressed-mood data dichotomize into two groups: a no-depression group and participants scoring 1 or more on the depression scale. Lane and Terry (2000) labelled this group the depressed-mood group.

A second key issue regarding the nature of mood–performance relationships concerned inconsistent results for anger and tension (Beedie et al., 2000). Anger/tension was associated with successful performance in some studies (Cockerill et al., 1991; Terry and Slade, 1995) and with unsuccessful performance in other studies (Morgan, 1980). Lane and Terry (2000) hypothesized that anger and/or tension can be either facilitative or debilitative of performance, depending on interactions with depressed mood. Lane and Terry proposed that individuals in a depressed mood tend to direct feelings of anger internally, leading to suppression, self-blame and, ultimately, performance decrements (Spielberger, 1991). Similarly, such individuals tend to transfer tension into feelings of threat and worry, also leading to performance decrements. Conversely, in the absence of depressed mood, the arousal component of anger and tension can play a functional role by signalling the need for positive action (see Lane, 2007a, for a review). Specifically, anger is likely to be expressed outwardly, directed at the source of the original frustration (or displaced towards another object or person), and may be channelled productively into determination to succeed; symptoms of tension are more likely to be interpreted as indicating a readiness to perform and be seen as facilitative of performance.

Lane and Terry (2000) proposed four main hypotheses:

- The first hypothesis is that anger, confusion, fatigue and tension will be higher, and vigour will be lower, among athletes experiencing depressed mood.
- The second hypothesis is that interrelationships among anger, confusion, fatigue, tension and vigour will be stronger for athletes experiencing depressed mood.
- The third hypothesis is that vigour will facilitate performance, and confusion and fatigue will debilitate performance, regardless of the presence or absence of depressed mood.
- The fourth hypothesis is that anger and tension will be associated with debilitated performance among individuals reporting symptoms of depression, whereas anger and tension will show a curvilinear relationship with performance among individuals reporting no symptoms of depression.

Review of Lane and Terry's model

Lane (2007a) reported the seventeen studies that tested the Lane and Terry (2000) model. All seventeen studies provided strong support for the hypothesis that participants in the depressed mood group would simultaneously report higher scores for anger, confusion, fatigue and tension, but lower vigour scores. The mean ESs (Cohen's d) for these mood dimensions were in the moderate-to-large categories: anger: $M = .85$, $SD = .25$; confusion: $M = .93$, $SD = .25$; fatigue: $M = .79$, $SD = .37$; tension: $M = .61$, $SD = .27$; and vigour: $M = .51$, $SD = .34$. In terms of mood–performance relationships, the results lend support for the switching effect for anger and tension. Anger and tension were positively related to performance in the no-depression group and negatively related to performance in the depressed-mood group. The switching effect was significant for both anger and tension, but was clearly greater for anger. Vigour showed a moderate-positive relationship with performance in both groups, whereas confusion and fatigue showed weak-negative relationships. These findings support the notion that depressed mood moderates mood–performance relationships for anger and tension, but not for confusion, fatigue and vigour, as hypothesized by Lane and Terry (2000).

When viewed collectively, studies testing Lane and Terry's model offer reasonable support for the central hypotheses (see Mellalieu, 2003, vs Lane *et al.*, 2005a, for a

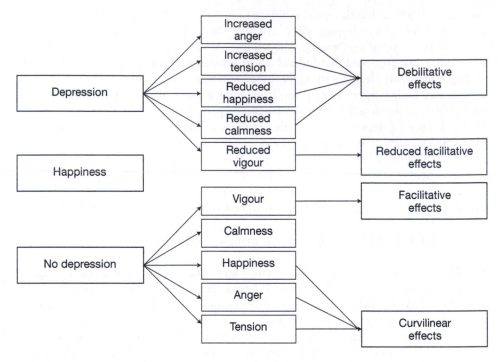

FIGURE 1.2 Revised conceptual model of mood and performance

Source: Lane, 2007a

detailed discussion of the utility of the model). The model may represent a plausible theoretical explanation for the apparently contradictory findings highlighted in previous reviews of the mood–performance research. Second, the model provides testable hypotheses relevant to the POMS, a measure that, despite much controversy, is still widely used by researchers and applied sport psychologists.

Although the conceptual model has arguably advanced POMS-based research, Lane *et al.* (2005a) highlighted that the POMS assesses a limited range of mood states (see Figure 1.2). The revised model included calmness and happiness and removed confusion. Confusion was removed because it is more of a cognitive state than a mood state. Confusion is arguably a manifestation of a mood disorder, rather than a mood state itself. The decision to include a greater number of positive mood states stems from applied work in which mood state responses were monitored among biathletes training at altitude (Lane *et al.*, 2003). Given the proposed influence of depressed mood, special attention was given to its detection. Self-reported happiness data helped detect maladaptive responses to training. Athletes reported high scores on the happiness scale and simultaneously reported zero on the depressed-mood scale. When an athlete was not coping with training successfully, happiness scores deteriorated, and fatigue scores increased. As happiness scores gradually deteriorated, the athlete started reporting some symptoms of depressed mood. Depressed mood was accompanied by confusion and anger. It appeared that happiness offered an early indicator to a possible rise in depression symptoms. Reductions in happiness over time could be used to monitor effective adaptation. Calmness was included, not only to increase the range of positive mood states, but also as it could offer insight into the nature of tension and anger when experienced in the absence of depressed mood. It is argued that, if athletes are using anger and tension to motivate behaviour, and are in control of these states, athletes should report feeling calm, angry and tense.

The revised model focuses on the influence and interaction between pleasant mood states, unpleasant mood states and performance. Happiness is proposed to show a curvilinear relationship with performance. It is argued that happiness is associated with the superficial processing of information, which can have negative performance effects (Sinclair and Mark, 1992). Happiness is also proposed to increase the accessibility of positive material in the memory and, according to Hirt *et al.* (1996), often leads to the recall of sufficient information to fill cognitive capacity, thereby debilitating performance through attentional overload. By contrast, happiness could be linked with high self-efficacy and, therefore, associated with enhanced performance through similar mechanisms. As a result, it is argued that two additional hypotheses should be included. The first is that happiness will show a curvilinear relationship with performance; the second is that calmness will show facilitative performance effects.

LEARNING OUTCOME 3

Ethical issues – discussion of ethical issues that might be relevant in either the research or practical application of mood and performance

Lane (2007b), in his chapter 'Developing and validating psychometric tests for use in high performance settings', described and discussed ethical issues when testing athletes in high–performance settings (see also Lane *et al.*, 2011). I indicated that a prospective

---

BEYOND THE FRONTIER

Recent research in conjunction with BBC Lab UK[2] and partners from the Emotion Regulation of Others and Self (EROS) Research Group[3] has produced a project titled 'Can you perform under pressure?'. The online project has gathered data on mood–performance relationships from 60,000 people. Former Olympian Michael Johnson narrated the project, and it involved each participant receiving personalized feedback. The project also investigated the effects of intervention strategies designed to improve performance. Although results are still being analysed, the concept of providing self-help online assessment and helping to teach people to regulate their own mood states is one that will grow. Peter Terry's resource moodonline[4] offers a similar resource. I suggest that the development of online materials and self-help materials will grow as technology advances. Our study will provide a solid evidence base on moods that people associate with best and worst performance. Future research should be intervention led, with interventions based on a solid theoretical and evidence base.

research methodology that is sensitive to the range of psychological states experienced by individuals performing under stress needs to be developed for such a purpose. It is important to recognize that the act of data collection intrudes on the typical preparation of individuals in such situations. The act of completing a psychological inventory can make participants aware of how they feel. For example, asking a soccer penalty taker how anxious he/she feels before shooting could raise anxiety, as the researcher has made the participant sensitive to how anxious they are feeling. What could follow from this is that the player, who is likely to have experienced anxiety previously, will make self-regulatory efforts to reduce anxiety. Theoretically, researchers do not wish to change the construct they are seeking to assess, and, if such research has damaging effects on participants beyond the benefits of conducting the research, then the study is unethical. Research teams need to consider the research skills of data collectors and investigate the extent to which asking the question leads participants to become aware of how they are feeling, and possibly engaging in strategies to change how they feel.

CONCLUSIONS

Athletes commonly report that emotional states influence thoughts and behaviour during competition. Research that has used appropriate methods has found support for the notion that mood states influence performance. A great deal of research has investigated whether mood states of athletes are different from the mood states of non-athletes, or whether elite athletes have a better mood than non-elite athletes. I have argued that there is no theoretical basis for this research question, and that it is not surprising that mood–performance relationships are weak. Lane and Terry (2000) developed a conceptual model for mood–performance relationships that emphasized the importance of depressed mood in interpreting POMS scores. Terry *et al.* (1999) developed a valid and internally reliable scale for assessing athletes before competition, and thus, between the studies, theoretical and methodological issues were clarified. Lane (2007a) reviewed studies that have tested Lane and Terry's model and found support for the switching effect for anger–performance relationships.

KEY CONCEPTS AND TERMS

Definition of mood

Lane and Terry (2000) defined mood as 'a set of feelings, ephemeral in nature, varying in intensity and duration, and usually involving more than one emotion' (p. 16).

Parkinson *et al.* (1996) proposed that, 'mood reflects changing non-specific psychological dispositions to evaluate, interpret, and act on past, current, or future concerns in certain patterned ways' (p. 216), a definition used in Lane *et al.* (2005a) in response to issues raised by Mellalieu (2003).

Definition of emotion

Lazarus (2000, p. 230) defined emotion as:

> an organized psychophysiological reaction to ongoing relationships with the environment . . . what mediates emotions psychologically is an evaluation, referred to as an appraisal, of the personal significance for the well-being that a person attributes to this relationship (. . . relational meaning), and the process.

Iceberg profile

This is a mood constellation characterized by above-average vigour and below-average anger, tension, confusion, depression and fatigue.

Meta-analysis

This is a method of re-analysing data that seeks to answer a similar research question.

Lane and Terry's (2000) conceptual model

This is a theoretical model based on the mood states assessed by the POMS, in which depression is proposed to moderate relationships with performance for anger and tension. In the presence of depression, anger and tension are linked with poor performance, whereas, in the absence of depression, anger and tension can be helpful for performance.

RECOMMENDED FURTHER READING

Books and book chapters

Lane, A. M. (2007). *Mood and Human Performance: Conceptual, measurement, and applied issues.* Hauppauge, NY: Nova Science.

Parkinson, B., Totterdell, P., Briner, R. B. and Reynolds, S. (1996). *Changing Moods: The psychology of mood and mood regulation.* London: Longman.

Journals

Beedie, C. J., Terry, P. C. and Lane, A. M. (2000). The profile of mood states and athletic performance: Two meta-analyses. *Journal of Applied Sport Psychology, 12,* 49–68.

Beedie, C. J., Terry, P. C. and Lane, A. M. (2005). Distinguishing mood from emotion. *Cognition and Emotion, 19,* 847–78.

Beedie, C. J., Terry, P. C., Lane, A. M. and Devonport, T. J. (2011). Differential assessment of emotions and moods: Development and validation of the emotion and mood components of anxiety questionnaire. *Personality and Individual Differences, 50,* 228–33.

Lane, A. M. (2012). I want to perform better: So how should I feel? *Polish Psychological Bulletin*, *44*(2), 130–6.

Lane, A. M., Beedie, C. J. and Devonport, T. J. (2011). Measurement issues in emotion and emotion regulation. In Lavallee, D., Thatcher, J. and Jones, M. (eds) *Coping and Emotion in Sport*, pp. 255–71. London: Wiley.

Lane, A. M., Beedie, C. J., Jones, M. V., Uphill, M. and Devonport, T. J. (2012). The BASES expert statement on emotion regulation in sport. *Journal of Sports Sciences*, *30*(11), 1189–95. (Based on the BASES expert statement.)

Lane, A. M., Beedie, C. J. and Stevens, M. J. (2005). Mood matters: A response to Mellalieu. *Journal of Applied Sport Psychology*, *17*, 319–25.

Lane, A. M. and Lovejoy, D. J. (2001). The effects of exercise on mood changes: The moderating effect of depressed mood. *Journal of Sports Medicine and Physical Fitness*, *41*, 539–45.

Lane, A. M. and Terry, P. C. (2000). The nature of mood: Development of a conceptual model with a focus on depression. *Journal of Applied Sport Psychology*, *12*, 16–33.

Mellalieu, S. D. (2003). Mood matters: But how much? A comment on Lane and Terry (2000). *Journal of Applied Sport Psychology*, *15*, 99–114.

Rowley, A. J., Landers, D. M., Kyllo, L. B. and Etnier, J. L. (1995). Does the Iceberg Profile discriminate between successful and less successful athletes? A meta-analysis. *Journal of Sport and Exercise Psychology*, *16*, 185–99.

Terry, P. C. (1995). The efficacy of mood state profiling among elite competitors: A review and synthesis. *The Sport Psychologist*, *9*, 309–24.

SAMPLE ESSAY QUESTIONS

1 Sport psychology should 'abandon the POMS'. With reference to theory and empirical evidence. discuss this proposition.

2 Terry (1995) proposed that mood states predict performance when certain methodological conditions are met. Describe and evaluate these methodological conditions with reference to theory and research.

3 The POMS offers an overly narrow conceptualization of mood. Discuss this finding with reference to Lane and Terry's conceptual model of mood–performance relationships (2000).

4 Critically evaluate Lane and Terry's conceptual model (2000). Use theory and research to support your ideas.

NOTES

1 www.moodprofiling.com/index.php
2 www.bbc.co.uk/compete
3 www.erosresearch.org

REFERENCES

Beedie, C. J., Terry, P. C. and Lane, A. M. (2000). The profile of mood states and athletic performance: Two meta-analyses. *Journal of Applied Sport Psychology, 12,* 49–68.

Beedie, C. J., Terry, P. C. and Lane, A. M. (2005). Distinguishing mood from emotion. *Cognition and Emotion, 19,* 847–78.

Beedie, C. J., Terry, P. C., Lane, A. M. and Devonport, T. J. (2011). Differential assessment of emotions and moods: Development and validation of the emotion and mood components of anxiety questionnaire. *Personality and Individual Differences, 50,* 228–33.

Berger, B. G. and Motl, R. W. (2000). Exercise and mood: A selective review and synthesis of research employing the profile of mood states. *Journal of Applied Sport Psychology, 12*(1), 69–92.

Cockerill, I. M., Nevill, A. M. and Lyons, N. (1991). Modelling mood states in athletic performance. *Journal of Sports Sciences, 9,* 205–12.

Hall, A. and Terry, P. C. (1995). Predictive capability of pre-performance mood profiling at the 1993 World Rowing Championships, Roundnice, the Czech Republic. *Journal of Sports Sciences, 13,* 56–7.

Hirt, E. R., Melton, R. J., McDonald, H. E. and Harackiewics, J. M. (1996). Processing goals, task interest, and the mood–performance relationship: A mediational analysis. *Journal of Personality and Social Psychology, 71,* 245–61.

Lane, A. M. (2007a). *Mood and Human Performance: Conceptual, measurement, and applied issues.* Hauppauge, NY: Nova Science.

Lane, A. M. (2007b). Developing and validating psychometric tests for use in high performance settings. In Boyar, L. *Psychological Tests and Testing Research,* pp. 203–13. Hauppauge, NY: Nova Science.

Lane, A. M. (2012). I want to perform better: So how should I feel? *Polish Psychological Bulletin, 44*(2), 130–6.

Lane, A. M., Beedie, C. J. and Devonport, T. J. (2011). Measurement issues in emotion and emotion regulation. In Lavallee, D., Thatcher, J. and Jones, M. (eds) *Coping and Emotion in Sport,* pp. 255–71. London: Wiley.

Lane, A. M., Beedie, C. J., Jones, M. V., Uphill, M. and Devonport, T. J. (2012). The BASES expert statement on emotion regulation in sport. *Journal of Sports Sciences, 30*(11), 1189–95. (Based on the BASES expert statement.)

Lane, A. M., Beedie, C. J. and Stevens, M. J. (2005a). Mood matters: A response to Mellalieu. *Journal of Applied Sport Psychology, 17,* 319–25.

Lane, A. M. and Lovejoy, D. J. (2001). The effects of exercise on mood changes: The moderating effect of depressed mood. *Journal of Sports Medicine and Physical Fitness, 41,* 539–45.

Lane, A. M., Nevill, A. M., Bowes, N. and Fox, K. R. (2005b). Investigating indices of stability using the task and ego orientation questionnaire. *Research Quarterly for Exercise and Sport, 76,* 339–46.

Lane, A. M. and Terry, P. C. (1999). The conceptual independence of tension and depression. *Journal of Sports Sciences, 17,* 605–6.

Lane, A. M. and Terry, P. C. (2000). The nature of mood: Development of a conceptual model with a focus on depression. *Journal of Applied Sport Psychology, 12,* 16–33.

Lane, A. M., Whyte, G. P., Godfrey, R. and Pedlar, C. (2003). Adaptations of psychological state variables to altitude among the Great Britain biathlon team preparing for the 2002 Olympic Games. *Journal of Sports Sciences, 21,* 281–2.

Lazarus, R. S. (2000). How emotions influence performance in competitive sports. *The Sport Psychologist, 14,* 229–52.

McNair, D. M., Lorr, M. and Droppleman, L. F. (1971). *Manual for the Profile of Mood States.* San Diego, CA: Educational and Industrial Testing Services.

Martens, R., Vealey, R. and Burton, D. (1990). *Competitive Sports Anxiety Inventory-2.* Champaign, IL: Human Kinetics.

Mellalieu, S. D. (2003). Mood matters: But how much? A comment on Lane and Terry (2000). *Journal of Applied Sport Psychology, 15,* 99–114.

Morgan, W. P. (1980). Test of Champions: The iceberg profile. *Psychology Today, 14,* 92–108.

Parkinson, B., Totterdell, P., Briner, R. B. and Reynolds, S. (1996). *Changing Moods: The psychology of mood and mood regulation.* London: Longman.

Renger, R. (1993). A review of the Profile of Mood States (POMS) in the prediction of athletic success. *Journal of Applied Sport Psychology, 5,* 78–84.

Rowley, A. J., Landers, D. M., Kyllo, L. B. and Etnier, J. L. (1995). Does the Iceberg Profile discriminate between successful and less successful athletes? A meta-analysis. *Journal of Sport and Exercise Psychology, 16,* 185–99.

Sinclair, R. C. and Mark, M. M. (1992). The influence of mood state on judgement and action: Effects on persuasion, categorisation, social justice, person perception, and judgmental accuracy. In Martin, L. L. and Tesser, A. (eds) *The construction of social judgement,* pp. 165–93. Hillsdale, NJ: Erlbaum.

Spielberger, C. D. (1991). *Manual for the State-Trait Anger Expression Inventory.* Odessa, FL: Psychological Assessment Resources.

Terry, P. C. (1993). Mood state profile as indicators of performance among Olympic and World Championship athletes. In Serpa, S., Alves, J., Ferreira, V. and Paulo-Brito, A. (eds) *Proceeding of the VIIIth ISSP World Congress of Sport Psychology,* pp. 963–7. Lisbon: ISSP.

Terry, P. C. (1995). The efficacy of mood state profiling among elite competitors: A review and synthesis. *The Sport Psychologist, 9,* 309–24.

Terry, P. C. and Slade, A. (1995). Discriminant capability of psychological state measures in predicting performance outcome in karate competition. *Perceptual and Motor Skills, 81,* 275–86.

Terry, P. C., Lane, A. M., Lane, H. J. and Keohane, L. (1999). Development and validation of a mood measure for adolescents: POMS-A. *Journal of Sports Sciences, 17,* 861–72.

2 Sport confidence

*Kate Hays, Andrew P. Lane
and Owen Thomas*

CHAPTER SUMMARY

One of the most consistent findings in the peak performance literature is the significant correlation between high levels of confidence and successful sporting performance (Feltz and Lirgg, 2001). Many great athletes attribute successes to a strong sense of self-belief. This is illustrated in the following quote from a British modern pentathlon Olympic medallist:

> *When you're confident on the piste you get your distances much better . . . When you're not confident in what you're doing you tend to be more timid in your movement and the thing with fencing is, once you go for a move you've just got to go for it . . . as soon as you hesitate it's too late, they've hit you.*
>
> *(Hays et al., 2009, p. 1192)*

Although most athletes believe that confidence is critical to performance, even the most successful athletes can be vulnerable to wavering levels of belief. Given such anecdotal importance, it is perhaps unsurprising that the study of confidence has figured prominently in the sport psychology research literature. This chapter will explore Vealey and Chase's (2008) revised model of sport confidence. It will focus on the mechanisms through which confidence is proposed to influence performance and discuss the relative stability of confidence. Additionally, there will be a strong emphasis on the application of recent sport confidence research to applied settings, particularly in relation to the sources and types of sport confidence, and the assessment of sport confidence.

LEARNING OUTCOMES

When you have studied this chapter, you should be able to:

1 Describe and evaluate Vealey and Chase's (2008) revised model of sport confidence
2 Identify some sources and types of sport confidence reported by athletes
3 Explain and evaluate confidence profiling as an assessment technique in sport
4 Be aware of the ethical issues that might be relevant in the measurement and application of sport confidence

LEARNING OUTCOME 1

Describe and evaluate Vealey and Chase's (2008) revised model of sport confidence

In 2008, Vealey and Chase updated Vealey's (2001) integrative model of sport confidence to include the most recent conceptual and theoretical findings. The revised model (see Figure 2.1) was developed to provide a framework from which meaningful extensions to the sport confidence literature could be expanded and sport confidence-based interventions could be designed. In line with earlier literature, sport confidence was defined as, 'the degree of certainty individuals possess about their ability to be successful in sport' (Vealey, 2001, p. 556).

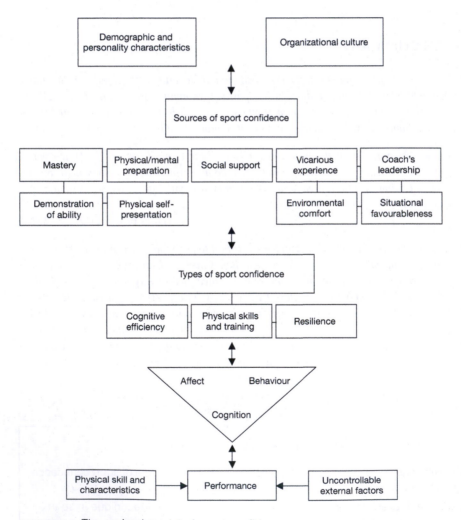

FIGURE 2.1 The revised model of sport confidence

Source: Vealey and Chase, 2008. Reprinted with permission

Fundamentally, the most significant revision within Vealey and Chase's (2008) model related to the multidimensional nature of sport confidence. To elaborate, although early sport confidence research had proposed sport confidence as a multidimensional construct, whereby different types of sport confidence may exist, Vealey *et al.*'s (1998) and Vealey's (2001) sport confidence models only incorporated performers sources of sport confidence (i.e., the sources of information athletes use to derive confidence from). Consequently, their models did not illustrate the multidimensional nature despite referring to it. However, emerging research (e.g., Hays *et al.*, 2007; Vealey and Knight, 2002) has shown that athletes can be confident in multiple types of beliefs rather than just being confident or not confident (uni-dimensional). For example, a rugby player might be confident about their ability to tackle effectively and carry the ball, but might not be confident about their ability to get into the right positions on the pitch. In summary, Vealey and Chase's revised model included allowance for the multidimensional nature of belief, through the recognition that sport confidence incorporated an athlete's types of sport confidence (i.e. what they are confident about), as well as their sources of sport confidence (i.e. what they base their types of sport confidence upon).

The revised model (Vealey and Chase, 2008) indicated that an individual's demographic and personality characteristics (e.g. age, gender, attitude) and the organizational culture of the sport (e.g. competitive level, motivational climate, goals and structural expectations of sport programmes) might impact upon how a performer develops their sport confidence. Further, hypotheses in the model proposed that an individual's sport confidence shares a bidirectional relationship (as indicated by the two-way arrow) with their affect, behaviours and cognitions (ABCs). That is, what an athlete thinks and feels and how they behave can impact upon their sport confidence belief, and, inversely, sport confidence can influence how athletes think, feel and behave. Together, an athlete's sport confidence and their ABCs continuously interact to influence performance, which is also proposed to have a reciprocal effect on these factors. Additionally, within the model, performance was also suggested to be influenced by an athlete's physical skills and characteristics, as well as uncontrollable external factors (e.g. weather, officials' decisions). In summary, Vealey and Chase (2008) emphasized that sport confidence (i.e. types and sources of sport confidence) is important to an athlete's sense of well-being and athletic performance, and that this is proposed to occur through three mediating processes:

1 affect;
2 behaviour; and
3 cognition.

Affect

Sport confidence has consistently been associated with pleasant emotions, such as enjoyment and happiness, whereas a lack of confidence has been associated with unpleasant emotions, such as anxiety, worry and depression (e.g. Hays *et al.*, 2009). Confidence has also been identified as a moderating factor in the interpretation of pre-competition anxiety symptoms. These propositions seem to accord with reports of athletes performing exceptionally well when they are feeling both anxious and confident. Conversely, performers who experience high anxiety without the accompanying feelings of confidence may suffer performance decrements (Jones and Hanton, 2001).

Behaviour

High levels of sport confidence have also been linked to productive achievement behaviours such as increased effort and persistence (e.g. Hays *et al.*, 2009). Research suggests that athletes set challenging goals and exert maximum effort in the pursuit of their goals, but only if they believe they have a reasonable chance (expectation) of success (Bandura, 1997). Thus, athletes who are high in confidence are likely to succeed owing to their productive achievement behaviours.

Cognition

Confident individuals have also been found to be more skilled and efficient in using the cognitive resources necessary for sporting success (Vealey, 2001). For example, Hays *et al.* (2009) found that confident individuals possessed an ability to retain an appropriate competition focus, either directed to the task or, when appropriate, the outcome. In contrast, when athletes were low in confidence, they reported an ineffective focus, such as being distracted by negative thoughts and, therefore, unable to concentrate on the task at hand. This is highlighted by a British Olympic diving medallist talking about his least confident career moment:

> I was a lot more negative than I would normally be, I was a lot more distracted by other athletes and what they were doing. Normally I follow a routine and I just stick to that and concentrate on it, but this time I was following my routine but I wasn't buying into it as I normally do.

In contrast, when describing his competition focus during his most confident career moment, this same athlete stated:

> [I was focused on] Me! And that was it. I ignored everyone else, I was just following my routines, being aware of the crowd but not being distracted by it, not thinking 'oh who's doing what? Where am I? What's the scoreboard saying?' All the kind of distractions which I was distracted by before. Just focusing on me and what I was doing.

> (Hays *et al.*, 2009, 1189)

Finally, confidence has been found to influence the coping processes of athletes. More specifically, athletes who possess a strong belief in their ability have reported being able to peak under pressure and cope successfully with adverse situations during competition (Cresswell and Hodge, 2004).

LEARNING OUTCOME 2

Identify the sources and types of confidence utilized by athletes

Vealey *et al.* (1998) proposed that athletes rely on sources of confidence influenced by their specific sporting context. Psychometric evidence, obtained from more than

500 high-school and collegiate athletes from a variety of sports, identified nine sources of confidence. These were:

1   mastery (i.e. mastering or improving personal skills);
2   demonstration of ability (i.e. exhibiting skills or demonstrating superiority to opposition);
3   physical/mental preparation (i.e. optimal physical and mental preparation);
4   physical self-presentation (i.e. an athletes' perception of his/her physical self);
5   social support (i.e. positive feedback and encouragement from coaches, teammates and/or friends);
6   vicarious experience (i.e. seeing someone else perform successfully);
7   coach's leadership (i.e. an athlete's belief in the coach's skills in decision-making and leadership);
8   environmental comfort (i.e. feeling comfortable in the competitive environment); and
9   situational favourableness (i.e. the athlete perceives something has happened in the sporting situation to increase his/her chances of success).

Beyond the identification of sources of sport confidence, Vealey et al. (1998) also sought to identify which sources were the best predictors of sport confidence levels. In accordance with previous research (e.g. Gill, 1988; Jones et al., 1991), athlete characteristics and the organizational culture of competitive sport were found to influence the development and manifestation of confidence in athletes. For example, gender differences highlighted that social support was a more important source of confidence for female athletes than for males. Physical self-presentation was also identified as more important for female college athletes than males; however male and female high-school athletes reported that physical self-presentation was the least important source of their confidence, emphasizing the influence of organizational factors (i.e. collegiate and high-school culture).

From their findings, Vealey et al. (1998) proposed that the stability of confidence over time might be a function of the sources upon which individuals base their confidence. For example, as a result of female athletes placing a greater importance upon uncontrollable sources, such as physical self-presentation, females' confidence beliefs were suggested to be more fragile than males'. Interestingly, the notion that confidence levels may vary as a function of gender is a relatively consistent finding in the research literature (e.g. Lirgg, 1991). Overall, Vealey et al. (1998) indicated that higher levels of sport confidence were generally associated with confidence derived from more controllable sources, such as physical/mental preparation, rather than uncontrollable sources (e.g. environmental comfort and physical self-presentation). Consequently, by further examining the antecedents of confidence in different athlete groups, we might achieve a better understanding of the way in which organizational culture and individual differences influence the development and stability of sport confidence. Moreover, since Vealey et al.'s (1998) preliminary sources of sport confidence were founded upon perceptions of high-school and collegiate athletes, they cannot readily be generalized to other athlete groups, therefore further research with additional populations was needed.

In an attempt to address this line of enquiry, Hays et al. (2007) identified nine sources of confidence salient to world-class athletes: preparation, performance accomplishments, coaching, innate factors, social support, experience, competitive advantage, self-awareness and trust. Where the preliminary sources of sport confidence identified by Vealey *et al.* (1998) were based upon a review of literature and deductions by the investigators, the sources of sport confidence reported by the world-class athletes in Hays *et al.*'s (2007) investigation were allowed to emerge inductively through qualitative interviews.

Allowing participants (in this case, world-class athletes) to respond to open-ended questions ensures that one can understand the world as seen by them. Indeed, this approach resulted in the identification of additional sources of sport confidence not highlighted by Vealey *et al.* (1998). For example, all athletes identified preparation as an important source of their sport confidence. However, responses were categorized into physical, mental and holistic preparation, rather than the global physical/ mental preparation reported by Vealey *et al.* (1998). To elaborate, a holistic approach to preparation for competition included video analysis, vision training, nutritional advice, arranging hotels and transport, and getting treatment (i.e. massages) when needed. Furthermore, physical preparation included responses pertaining to effort, good physical training/condition, training programme and skill repetition, whereas mental preparation referred to the use of several mental training strategies. Evidence of progressive performance accomplishments and the use of training logs, which enabled the athletes to look back over the months of hard training that they had done, further facilitated the athletes' feelings of confidence associated with the preparation source of confidence (see Hays *et al.*, 2007, for an example).

Akin to the findings of Vealey *et al.*'s (1998) study, gender variations were evident in the sources of sport confidence identified by the world-class athletes in Hays *et al.*'s (2007) study. For example, male athletes seemed to focus more on competition outcomes, whereas female athletes identified good personal performances as a source of their confidence. These gender findings, although subtle, might be used to inform goal-setting interventions. Specifically, world-class athletes might be encouraged to identify and focus on the aspects of their competition that facilitate their confidence (i.e. performance for females and outcome for males). In addition to possible gender differences in goal orientation, male and female athletes derived confidence from

RESEARCH METHODS

Given that Hays *et al.*'s (2007) study was exploratory in nature they adopted a qualitative method using an open ended semi-structured interview process. This format meant that the lead author asked open ended questions (e.g. talk to me about what you are confident about; where does your confidence come from?) and followed an interview guide but allowed the natural flow of the interview to determine the specific questions asked (e.g., Patton, 2002). The interviewer also used clarification (e.g., what do you mean by performance?) and elaboration (e.g., tell me more about that source) probes to ensure a strong understanding of all areas (e.g., Patton, 2002). Consequently, by the time the interview had concluded each participant had been asked the main questions from the guide.

ACTIVITY 2.1

Comparison of sources of sport-confidence with non-elite and elite athletes

Using the table below list the sources that emerged in Hays *et al.*'s (2007) research in the left hand column. Then, in the middle column list the sources from Vealey *et al.*'s (1998) study that relate/overlap to the sources that emerged in Hays and colleagues' work. In the right hand column describe any similarities and/or difference between the source frameworks that are provided by both pieces of research.

Sources of sport confidence identified by athletes at different skill levels		
Hays et al. *(2007)*	Vealey et al. *(1998)*	Similarities and differences

their coach in different ways. Females were found to derive confidence primarily from their coach's encouragement, positive feedback/reinforcement and compliments. In contrast, male athletes tended to derive confidence from a belief in their coach's ability to establish an appropriate training programme.

As noted previously, the significant update within Vealey and Chase's (2008) revised model of sport confidence related to the notion of the multidimensional nature of sport confidence and, specifically, the addition of types of sport confidence (i.e. what performers are confident about). The model included three types of sport confidence, based upon Vealey and Knight's (2002) work: Sport Confidence in *Physical Skills* and Training (e.g. an athlete's belief or degree of certainty that they have the abilities to execute the physical skills necessary to perform successfully), Sport Confidence in *Cognitive Efficiency* (e.g. an athlete's belief or degree of certainty that they possess the abilities mentally to focus, maintain concentration and make effective decisions to perform successfully) and Sport Confidence in *Resilience* (e.g. an athlete's belief that they can regain focus, overcome doubts and bounce back from performing poorly). Although interesting and a novel addition, Vealey and Knight's (2002) research is yet to be published in full in the academic literature. Moreover, it was conducted with high-school and collegiate athletes, and, thus, generalizations to other athletic samples are perhaps limited. These issues prompted further research in this area.

An additional line of enquiry within Hays *et al.*'s (2007) study related to understanding the types of sport confidence salient to world-class athletes. Importantly,

ACTIVITY 2.2

The influence of gender upon the sources of sport confidence

Using the information from Vealey *et al.*'s (1998) and Hays *et al.*'s (2007) studies, complete the table below by identifying the sources of sport confidence that would strengthen female athletes' confidence and state the sources that would enhance male performers sport confidence beliefs. In the final column of the table below think about and then write down specific examples of the sources related to males and female in a sport of your choice. An example is provided for both males and females to help you get started.

	Sources of sport confidence that would strengthen confidence	How might you apply this to a sport and activity of your choice?
Female sport performers	Example. Personal performances.	Provide positive feedback to a female runner about her performance.
Male sport performers	Example. Focus on outcome (performance related)	Recall a footballers previous successful penalty kicks to enhance their belief.

athletes could distinguish between where they derived their confidence from (i.e. sources of sport confidence) and what they were confident about (i.e. types of sport confidence) without difficulty, thus providing a solid conceptual foundation for the existence of different types and sources of sport confidence. Male and female athletes identified four types of sport confidence: skill execution (e.g. passing, good technique), achievement (e.g. outcomes or targets), physical factors (e.g. physical attributes such as speed, strength) and psychological factors (e.g. ability to deal with stress or nerves). Two additional types were found to be heavily influenced by gender. For example, superiority to opposition was reported by six of the seven male athletes and only one of the seven female athletes interviewed. Furthermore, tactical awareness was only reported by two male athletes. These findings are consistent with the prediction that

ACTIVITY 2.3

Identifying the types of sport confidence

Think of a time in sport when you have been highly confident, what types of things were you confident about? List all the things you were confident about in the first column of the table below. Then describe each type in the second column to clarify what you mean by the type. This description should help you identify how the type relates to the types of sport confidence that Vealey and Knight (2002) and/or Hays *et al.* (2007) reported. Note down the similarity using the specific terms for each type in the final right hand column. Again, we have provided you with an example to help you on your way.

Type of sport confidence	Description of this type	Similarity with previous research
Example: Putting top spin on a tennis forehand	Believing in my ability to create top spin on my forehand shots	SC-Physical skills and training (Vealey and Knight, 2002), Skill Execution (Hays *et al.*, 2007)

athlete characteristics (i.e. gender) can influence athletes' sport confidence (i.e. types) contained within Vealey and Chase's (2008) revised model.

It was evident that the sources of confidence identified by world-class athletes within Hays *et al.*'s (2007) study might influence the types of confidence they possess. For example, one male rugby world cup winner suggested that his preparation (e.g. 'knowing we'd done the work, we knew we were stronger') allowed him to be confident that he was superior to his opposition (i.e. type of sport confidence). It would seem logical, then, to view types of sport confidence as evidence-based belief systems grounded in athletes' sources of sport confidence. Thus, for an athlete to develop a robust sense of sport confidence, they would, perhaps, be best advised to derive their types of confidence from several sources, as one Olympic medallist highlighted:

> As I grew up I was told that I was naturally a great athlete. That gave me confidence but when I lost why couldn't I just turn it around? Because that bubble had burst, I hadn't won . . . So the confidence has obviously got to be coming from lots of places otherwise it's very easily broken just by not winning once.
>
> (Hays *et al.*, 2007, p. 449)

To further explore the relationship between confidence, performance and athletes' ABCs, Hays *et al.* (2009) conducted a study with world–class athletes. Specifically, they carried out qualitative interviews with fourteen sport performers (seven males, seven females), to examine the effect that confidence played upon an athlete's affect, behaviour and cognitions. Consistent with substantial anecdotal evidence and empirical research, results revealed that all athletes associated feeling confident with successful sporting performance, and, when experiencing low levels of sport confidence, the athletes tended to underperform. Furthermore, in support of the predictions contained within Vealey and Chase's (2008) revised model of sport confidence, Hays *et al.* (2009) found that high sport confidence was associated with positive thinking, an appropriate competition focus (e.g. on the task or the outcome) and effective decision-making. In contrast, low confidence was linked with negative thinking, distracted thought patterns and a lack of effort and persistency at a task. From an applied perspective, these findings are particularly pertinent, given that athletes in Hays *et al.*'s (2007) study perceived strategies designed to enhance sport confidence were ineffective when implemented in the pressurized environment of world-class sport competition. Athletes reported that, if they were not feeling confident going into an important competition, they were seemingly unable to raise their confidence levels once they were there. This highlights the importance of helping athletes to develop *and* maintain their confidence in competition preparation phases, rather than solely trying to increase confidence levels.

A further, important aim of Hays *et al.*'s (2009) investigation was to identify the factors responsible for debilitating world-class athletes' confidence. Participants identified several aspects that caused them to reduce or lose their confidence. Poor performances, poor preparation, coaching, and illness/injury emerged as factors responsible for debilitating athletes sport confidence. Interestingly, these factors were seemingly related to the sources from which their confidence stemmed. For example, preparation, performance accomplishments and coaching have been identified as the primary sources of sport confidence used by world-class athletes (Hays *et al.*, 2007). This evidence would seem to support Vealey *et al.*'s (1998) earlier suggestion that the stability of confidence over time maybe a function of the sources upon which performers base their confidence. Gender also seemed to influence the stability of the athletes' sport confidence. For example, the male athletes identified injury/illness as the primary debilitative factor affecting their confidence. In contrast, females reported poor performances, poor preparation, coaching, and pressure and expectations as the primary factors responsible for reducing their levels of confidence.

BEYOND THE FRONTIER: FUTURE RESEARCH INVESTIGATING THE STABILITY OF CONFIDENCE OVER TIME

The relative stability of confidence has been a consistent theme within the literature (e.g. Vealey *et al.*, 1998; Hays *et al.*, 2007, 2009) and has consequently been cited throughout this chapter as an important theme. For example, Hays *et al.* (2007) suggested that it is important to help athletes develop *and* maintain their confidence beliefs in pre-competition periods. Furthermore, Vealey and Chase (2008) noted that developing resilient, enduring and robust confidence beliefs is important to help overcome possible setbacks. However, there is a lack of research in this area. Most recently, Thomas *et al.* (2011) have explored the construct of robust sport confidence and attempted to define this particular phenomenon. Additionally, underpinned by Vealey *et al.*'s (1998) suggestion that changes in sources of sport confidence may impact upon how beliefs are developed, Kingston *et al.* (2010) examined the importance of the sources of sport confidence in a 6-week period leading up to competition in a group of elite male and female sport performers. Findings from this study indicated that the importance placed upon demonstration of ability, physical/mental preparation, physical self-presentation and situational favourableness increased as competition approached. Gender differences were also noted, demonstrating that female athletes perceived mastery, physical self-presentation, social support, environmental comfort and coach's leadership as more important than male performers did during the 6 weeks leading up to performance. These findings, together with the extant literature, suggest that attributing greater importance to, and deriving confidence from, controllable sources such as mastery and protecting these sources over time may help to create stable levels of sport confidence during the pre-competition period. However, future research needs to explore the relationship between the sources, types and confidence debilitating factors in more depth. Additionally, the models predictions that athlete characteristics and organisational factors influence sport confidence should be examined in terms of their impact over the temporal nature of performers beliefs and not just assessments at one point in time as is the case in most previous research within this domain (e.g. Hays *et al.*, 2007; Magyar & Duda, 2000; Magyar & Feltz, 2003; Vealey *et al.*, 1998).

Summary of sport confidence research

The positive relationship between high confidence levels and successful sporting performance is well documented (see Feltz and Lirgg, 2001, for a review). On examination of the processes and mechanisms underlying confidence effects, high sport confidence is associated with emotional control, effective competition behaviours and effective competition focus. In contrast, low sport confidence is associated with negative affect, ineffective competition behaviours and an inappropriate competition focus. Furthermore, strategies employed by the athletes to enhance low feelings of sport confidence have been found to be ineffective in the context of world-class sport competition (Hays *et al.*, 2007).

Taken collectively, evidence suggests that protecting and maintaining high sport confidence levels in the lead-up to competition are desirable. As research has shown that the factors responsible for debilitating an athlete's sport confidence are associated with the sources from which they derive their confidence, the most successful interventions might involve identifying an athlete's particular sources and types of confidence and ensuring that these are intact during competition preparation phases. Specifically, given Kingston *et al.*'s (2010) findings, underpinned by Vealey *et al.*'s (1998) initial work, deriving confidence from more controllable sources of sport confidence, such as mastery- and preparation-based sources, during the build-up to an important competition may be more conducive to enduring beliefs. Nevertheless, since demographic and organizational factors influence the sources and types of sport confidence utilized by athletes, and impact upon the factors responsible for debilitating their confidence levels, these aspects need to be considered when one is assessing the confidence of sport performers and determining how to develop appropriate interventions to enhance their confidence.

LEARNING OUTCOME 3

Explain and evaluate confidence profiling as an assessment technique in sport

Measuring confidence in sport

Several inventories have been developed to measure sport confidence. For example, Vealey (1986) developed dispositional (trait) and state (situational) measures of sport confidence, named the Trait Sport Confidence Inventory (TSCI) and the State Sport Confidence Inventory (SSCI), respectively. Both the TSCI and the SSCI assess sport confidence as a uni-dimensional construct and, therefore, combine types of sport confidence within one score. However, as recent research has provided evidence for the existence of different types of sport confidence (e.g. Hays *et al.*, 2007), in addition to information relating to sources, more recent sport confidence measurement instruments have advocated that sources and types of sport confidence should be assessed independently.

Vealey *et al.* (1998) developed the Sources of Sport Confidence Questionnaire (SSCQ) to measure the nine sources of confidence within their model. The SSCQ is, at present, the only validated questionnaire designed specifically to assess athletes' sources of sport confidence. However, other researchers have questioned some aspects of validity and reliability of the scale (see for example, Magyar & Duda, 2000; Magyar and Feltz, 2003; Wilson, Sullivan, Myers & Feltz, 2004). Further, the validation of the SSCQ was based upon high-school and collegiate athletes, and, therefore, generalizations to other athlete groups are limited (e.g. samples such as the world-class performers used in Hays and colleagues' research; Hays *et al.*, 2007, 2009). Consequently, demographic and organizational factors need to be considered when one is assessing sport performers' confidence. Finally, within Vealey and Knight's (2002) investigation, they attempted to operationalize the three types of sport confidence they identified (i.e. SC physical skills and training, SC cognitive efficiency, SC resilience) through the development of the Sport Confidence Inventory. This measurement tool attempts to quantitatively assess the three types. However, as noted previously, this inventory has not been published in a full validated article, and, consequently, there are concerns over its conceptual viability.

Towards practical confidence assessment measures

To address some of the limitations associated with adopting nomothetic measures (i.e., measures used with large sample groups that produce quantitative data and help to generalise findings) in applied sport psychology practice, Vealey and Garner-Holman (1998) proposed that more idiographic approaches to measurement (i.e. measurements generally associated with individual cases rather than groups) should be adopted. Eliciting information that is important to the performer, in contrast to using tests or questionnaires that plot the performer against predetermined axes, is in accordance with personal construct theory (PCT; Kelly, 1955).[1] The performance profile (Butler, 1989) is a natural application of Kelly's PCT (1955) and enables the performer to construct a picture of him- or herself, rather than forcing him or her to respond to fixed measures (see Weston, this issue).

Hays *et al.* (2010) adapted performance profiling to create an assessment of sport confidence for use within an applied context. In contrast to traditional nomothetic measures developed to assess athletes' sport confidence in research settings, Hays *et al.*'s (2010) confidence profiling technique provides a measurement of sport confidence from the athletes' perspective. Specifically, this method encourages each athlete to give an accurate account of their sources and types of confidence, and also to identify the factors that debilitate their confidence levels. Hays *et al.* (2010) explored this technique with seven athletes and incorporated three accredited sport scientists specializing in sport psychology with the British Association of Sport and Exercise Sciences to help reflect on the application of the process. Overall, their findings demonstrated the versatility of the confidence profiling technique when used to attain an in-depth assessment of the athletes' sport confidence (i.e. sources and types of sport confidence). In summary, this more idiographic approach to the measurement of sport confidence allows the confidence needs of athletes to be assessed at the individual level regardless of demographics, sport classification or competitive status.

LEARNING OUTCOME 4

Be aware of the ethical issues that might be relevant in the measurement and application of sport confidence assessments

The next section provides an overview of confidence profiling process Hays *et al.* (2010) developed. During this section there are also a number of ethical issues which have been raised in order to develop the readers' awareness of such issues during the measurement and application of the confidence profiling technique.

Profiling confidence for sport

Following the basic method of performance profiling advocated by Butler and Hardy (1992), Hays *et al.*'s (2010) confidence profiling process adheres to three main stages:

1   introducing the idea;
2   eliciting constructs; and
3   assessment. (Please see the Appendix in this chapter for the consultancy schedule that can be used to facilitate this process.)

Before conducting any scientific support programme such as the confidence profiling technique, or carrying out research in sport psychology, it is necessary to consider the ethical implications that the work may have. For example, prior to engaging in the confidence profiling process, the athlete should be made aware that they and the practitioner can both withdraw from the consultancy relationship at any point, without any penalty. They must also understand all the associated risks of the applied work and provide written informed consent before starting the profiling technique. It is vital, if the participant is under the age of 18 years, that parental consent is obtained and that the consultancy takes place in a public setting, where both the practitioner and the athlete are in full view of a third party at all times. Furthermore, with regards to the questions asked in the confidence profiling technique, the client should be made aware that they are free to refuse to answer any of the questions put to them, and that no disadvantage would arise from a decision not to complete the consultancy.

Stage 1: introducing the idea

Introductory comments pertaining to sport confidence and the influence of sport confidence on sport performance provide the athlete with an understanding of the importance of effectively assessing their sport confidence levels.

Stage 2: eliciting constructs

The athlete's sources and types of sport confidence are elicited by adopting the questions used by Hays *et al.* (2007) to identify sources and types of sport confidence salient to world–class sport performers. Essentially, the athlete is asked, 'What are you confident about?', to elicit sport confidence types. These types are then entered on to a visual sport confidence profile. Once all types of confidence have been exhausted, the athlete is asked to identify the sources from which each type of confidence is derived. These sources of confidence are then added to their profile.

In order to help the participant construct a profile of their types and sources, they are encouraged to identify a time in their career when they had felt confident. The athlete is also asked to recall the time that they felt least confident going into an important competition and to highlight the factors responsible for debilitating their sport confidence; these factors are then also recorded. By discussing contrasting experiences the participant may provide more in-depth information. With regards to ethical considerations, being asked about a time when they were not very confident may cause some athletes to experience some discomfort. Consequently, the athletes should discuss positive experiences after this stage, in order to facilitate a more positive mind-set and offset any potential feelings of discomfort. Finally, participants should be provided with the opportunity to add any other important information that might have been overlooked during the process. Any additional sources and/or types of confidence generated from this discussion are then also entered into the athlete's sport confidence profile.

Stage 3: assessment

Each athlete is asked to rate himself or herself on each of their types of sport confidence, and these ratings are also recorded on their sport confidence profile. For each type of confidence, the athlete is asked to rate how confident he or she currently perceives him/herself to be. However, rather than the traditional Likert rating scale adopted by Butler and Hardy (1992), the questioning style commonly adopted during motivational interviewing (MI) (Miller and Rollnick, 2002) was incorporated within Hays *et al.*'s (2010) process. Specifically, the athlete is asked, 'How confident are you about your ability to remain calm under pressure (for example)?', using a scale of 1–10, with 1 being 'not at all confident' and 10 being 'extremely confident'. If the athlete indicates a low level of confidence, 4 for example, this question is followed with, 'Why do you feel that you are a 4 on that rather than a 1?'. Regardless of how low the athlete's ratings of confidence, when compared with 1, they would likely be able to identify at least one source of their identified confidence type, supplementing the in-depth exploration of their current confidence profile. Further motivational strategies are utilized along with the scaling ruler (i.e., measurement tool using the 1–10 scale) to identify reasons that confidence might be low and to help problem-solve to increase confidence (Velasquez *et al.*, 2005). For example, an athlete with a confidence rating of 4 for a particular confidence type might be asked, 'What changes do you think you would have to make in order to be a 6 or a 7?', 'How might you go about making these changes?' and 'What would be a good first step?'. Thus, the athlete is prompted to make an accurate evaluation of their current confidence levels and identify possible strategies, using a client-centred approach to change.

APPLYING THE SCIENCE 2.1

Mini case-study example to contextualize the confidence profiling process

Neil is a 22 year old semi-professional football goalkeeper. Neil has approached a sport psychologist to help him rediscover his confidence which has recently taken a hit. After an introductory session and discussing all ethical and professional issues the sport psychologist has decided to employ the confidence profiling technique to understand Neil's confidence and help him develop an awareness of his beliefs. Based upon the findings of the profile, it is noticeable that Neil's confidence is not as high as it could be, as he reported moderate levels of confidence in several physically and psychologically based types of sport confidence. He recognized that, because of mistakes he made towards the end of last season, and the added pressure of having a new goalkeeper join the squad, which provides strong competition to his place in the team, his confidence has wavered. This decreased level in confidence is further compounded by poor performances. Previously, if he had one bad game, it would not affect him, but now, because he has had several poor performances, he suffers from negative thoughts, and his concentration can also fluctuate. Potentially, negative thoughts that create a lapse in concentration could cause him to make more mistakes and then suffer from further poor performances, which would likely lead to a downwards spiral in his confidence levels. Consequently, his previous performances are important sources of sport confidence, but have also been emphasized as a confidence debilitating factor.

The implementation of scaling rulers enabled Neil to determine his current levels of sport confidence and, importantly begin to generate his own strategies to help enhance his sport confidence. For example, when Neil was asked how he could develop his confidence from a 4 to a higher score of 7 or 8 in 'catching high balls', he suggested that he could spend more time training, develop specific goals for matches and also incorporate psychological skills such as imagery to help recall previous successes. These strategies have the potential to help create a stronger foundation of sources with which to underpin his confidence belief. Interestingly, when asked how he could improve his level of confidence in his 'concentration' from a 5 to an 8, he readily explained that he would work with a sport psychologist on strategies such as imagery and self-talk.

In summary, based upon Neil's confidence profile (see Figure 2.2), it could be concluded that several of his types of sport confidence are underpinned by sources related to performance accomplishments, such as previous matches. Although performance-based sources offer evidence of success, and therefore have the potential to generate strong confidence beliefs, because he also identifies poor performance as a confidence-debilitating factor, he may need to derive confidence from additional sources (which are more controllable and not related to performance). For example, by working to improve the effectiveness of his self-talk and concentration and focusing on his training achievements he may derive confidence from sources that he has more control over and, therefore, that have the potential to create higher and more stable levels of confidence.

The confidence profiling process enables athletes to give an accurate and in-depth account of their sources and types of confidence and consider how these might influence their levels of confidence and subsequent competition performance. Enabling athletes to talk about their confidence in context (i.e. why they had felt confident on a particular day, or what had happened in the lead-up to an event that had facilitated/debilitated their confidence) ensures that they are able to identify their sources and types of sport confidence with ease. The identification of confidence debilitators is a particularly important part of the confidence profiling process, as the factors responsible for debilitating the athlete's sport confidence seemed to provide the basis from which intervention strategies might be explored.

The resulting profiles are specific to the individual athlete and also specific to the sport in which they compete. Consequently, the confidence profiling process enables individual differences in confidence to emerge. For example, one athlete might exhibit low confidence in several areas, where another might exhibit high confidence but be over-reliant on specific sources and types of confidence. Each of these examples would require a different intervention strategy. For instance, sport psychology support might be targeted towards increasing the range of sources and types of confidence utilized, or enhancing confidence in the areas already identified, depending upon the individual confidence needs of the athlete.

Athletes can enhance their feelings of confidence by using strategies to stay positive, even when they are not performing well. Let's consider the case study of Neil

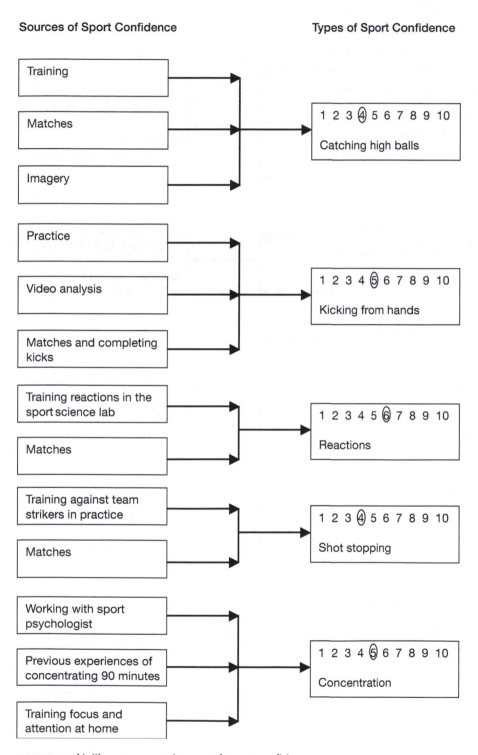

FIGURE 2.2 Neil's sources and types of sport-confidence

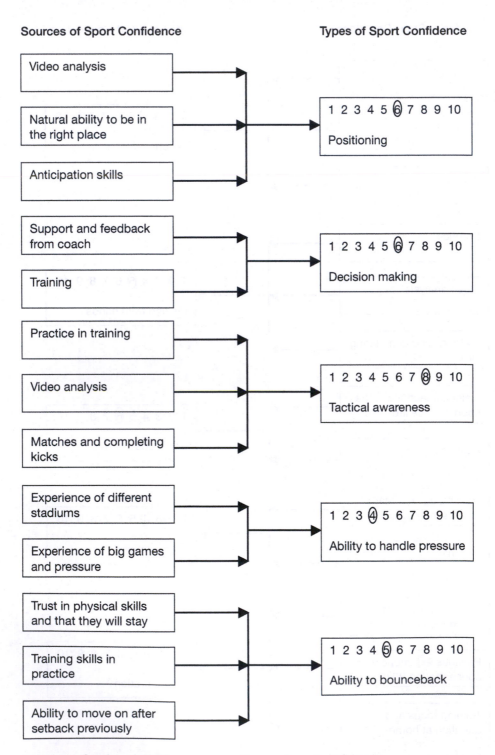

FIGURE 2.2 Continued. Neil's sources and types of sport-confidence

ACTIVITY 2.4

Confidence profiling technique

Using the confidence profiling process described above (and the method provided in the Appendix), conduct a role play consultation with a classmate to assess their confidence in sport, or a particular aspect of their sport. Reflect upon your consultancy experience and try to identify any positive and/or negative aspects of the confidence profiling process. Consider how the information obtained through this applied approach might differ from information obtained through more traditional confidence inventories. Can you think of any way in which confidence profiling might be modified or improved to best meet the needs of an athlete, sport psychologist and/or coach?

as an example. He suffered from negative self-talk and became distracted and lost concentration when he made mistakes in games. Additionally, the profiling technique highlighted that he wanted to work on his ability to control his negative thoughts in order to improve his confidence and performance. Cognitive restructuring (Davis *et al.*, 1988) is one such strategy that is used extensively in applied sport psychology consultancy and involves restructuring an athlete's negative thought patterns. The first step would be to ask Neil to review his self-talk and identify any positive thoughts and also any negative thoughts that he has had, and what impact these may have had upon his subsequent thoughts, feelings and behaviours, as well as highlighting the events and situations that are associated with his self-talk. As Neil became aware of his maladaptive thoughts, he would learn how to modify them through a process of countering. Countering is an internal dialogue that uses facts and reasons to refute the underlying beliefs and assumptions that lead to negative thinking (Zinsser *et al.*, 2001). With the help of the sport psychologist, and through a process of self-reflection, Neil would be required to identify and describe the evidence necessary to change his attitudes and beliefs, and develop a list of alternative positive self-statements to replace his negative cognitions, especially when he makes a mistake in a match. For example, instead of thinking, 'I keep fumbling the ball' or 'If I make one more mistake I am going to be substituted', Neil might think, 'I have the skills to be able to do this and I have been well prepared from lots of quality training'. Cognitive restructuring, countering and self-reflection are examples of how specific psychological skills can be employed to enhance the athlete's confidence. However, as noted previously, the model of sport confidence and the profiling technique provide a strong understanding of the athlete's types and sources of sport confidence. Therefore, the practitioner can strengthen these directly and employ strategies to support the athlete's types and sources. For example, Neil noted that he derived confidence from his training and performance accomplishments. If he were encouraged to complete a training diary, recording the number of saves or catches that he achieved in practice, then he would be able to look back on what he had mastered, which would, therefore, support these preparation- and performance-based sources and types of sport confidence.

ACTIVITY 2.5

Confidence profile technique

Repeat the role-play consultation with another classmate of a different gender and choose a different sport. Then compare the two profiles and identify the similarities and differences. What are they and how does this relate to the previous research discussed in this chapter (e.g. gender difference between Vealey *et al.*'s 1998 study and Hays *et al.*'s 2007 investigation).

CONCLUSIONS

There is a mass of research and anecdotal evidence pertaining to the important relationship between high sport confidence and successful sport performance. Recent advances in sport confidence research have provided evidence for the conceptualization of sport confidence as a multidimensional construct, derived from several sources and comprising several types of belief. These sources and types are influenced by organizational and demographic factors and, as such, are unique to each athlete. This has implications for nomothetic confidence inventories designed and developed as research tools. Consequently, confidence profiling is presented for use in an applied context, as an alternative assessment measure, and provides a basis from which interventions can be developed.

KEY CONCEPTS AND TERMS

Sport confidence
This is defined as 'the degree of certainty individuals possess about their ability to be successful in sport' (Vealey, 2001, p. 556).

Types of sport confidence
These are the types of things athletes are confident about. Hays *et al.* (2007) proposed that types of sport confidence are evidence-based belief systems grounded within sources of sport confidence.

Sources of sport confidence
This refers to the sources of information upon which individuals base their types of sport confidence belief.

Nomothetic research approaches
The vast majority of research on self-confidence in sport has used quantitative, nomothetic research approaches in which numbers are used to represent athletes'

perceived sport confidence (usually on a Likert scale). The nomothetic approach (Allport, 1937) to the study of confidence in sport assumes that all people can be characterized by the same set of descriptors or dimensions.

Idiographic research approaches
Idiographic research approaches utilize verbal descriptions as opposed to numbers and allow individual differences in confidence to emerge.

RECOMMENDED FURTHER READING

Books and book chapters

Vealey, R. S. and Chase, M. A. (2008). Self-confidence in sport: Conceptual and research advances. In Horn, T. S. (ed.) *Advances in Sport Psychology* (3rd edn), pp. 65–97. Champaign, IL: Human Kinetics.

Zinsser, N., Bunker, L. and Williams, J. M. (2001). Cognitive techniques for building confidence and enhacing performance. In Williams, J. M. (ed.) *Applied Sport Psychology: Personal growth to peak performance*, pp. 284–311. Mountain View, CA: Mayfield Publishing.

Journals

Butler, R. J. and Hardy, L. (1992). The performance profile: Theory and application. *The Sport Psychologist*, *6*, 253–64.

Hays, K., Maynard, I., Thomas, O. and Bawden, M. (2007). Sources and types of confidence identified by world class sport performers. *Journal of Applied Sport Psychology*, *19*, 434–56.

Hays, K., Thomas, O., Butt., J. and Maynard, I. (2010). The development of confidence profiling in sport. *The Sport Psychologist*, *18*, 373–92.

Hays, K., Thomas, O., Maynard, I. and Bawden, M. (2009). The role of sport-confidence. *Journal of Sport Sciences*, *27*, 1185–99.

Vealey, R. S., Hayashi, S. W., Garner-Holman, M. and Giacobbi, P. (1998). Sources of sport-confidence: Conceptualization and instrument development. *Journal of Sport & Exercise Psychology*, *21*(1), 54–80.

SAMPLE ESSAY QUESTIONS

1 With reference to relevant theory and research, critically evaluate Vealey and Chase's (2008) revised model of sport confidence.

2 Sport confidence research endorses gender difference not only in confidence levels, but also in the sources and types of confidence utilised. Describe these differences

and identify the practical implications for support staff working with male and female athletes.

3   In developing a confidence intervention for athletes, what considerations should the practitioner make with regards to confidence assessment in sport?

NOTE

1   Originally developed within the realm of clinical psychology, the central tenet of PCT is that individuals strive to make sense of themselves and their environment by devising theories about their world, testing these theories against reality and then retaining or revising their theories, depending upon their predictive accuracy (Fransella, 1981).

APPENDIX: CONFIDENCE PROFILING METHOD

Stage 1: Introducing the idea

1   Explain to the athlete the important relationship between sport confidence and performance.
2   Explain the multidimensional nature of sport confidence and the importance of assessment at the individual level.
3   Explain that the purpose of the session is to identify the athlete's types and sources of sport confidence and produce an individualized confidence profile.
4   Explain what is meant by a source and type of confidence.
5   Show the athlete the profile that will be completed during the consultancy and explain.

Stage 2: Eliciting constructs (sample questions)

1   Can you tell me what you need to be confident about to perform successfully in your sport?
2   What are you confident about?
3   Where do you think that type of confidence in yourself as an athlete comes from? Specific probe question:

    –   What makes you confident?

4   Can you think of the time that you felt most confident going into an important competition? This may not be the time when you produced your best ever performance.
5   What were you confident about as you stepped on to the track, rink, poolside, etc.? What were you confident about on that day?
6   Can you tell me about anything that happened or any factors that influenced your feelings of confidence during the lead-up to competition?
7   Can you tell me about anything that happened or any factors that influenced your levels of confidence on the day of competition?

Identifying sport confidence debilitators

8 Please could you describe to me the time when you felt least confident going into an important competition? This may not be a time when you performed unsuccessfully.

9 Can you tell me about anything that happened or any factors that affected your feelings of confidence during the lead-up to competition?

10 Can you tell me about anything that happened or any factors that affected your levels of confidence on the day of competition?

   Specific probe questions:

   – What do you think was the main factor responsible for your low levels of confidence?
   – What do you think were the most important factors affecting your confidence?

11 Are there any areas that you think we have failed to cover relating to your confidence in sport?

Stage 3: Assessment

Ask the athlete to rate themselves on each of their identified types of sport confidence.

1 On a scale of 1–10, with 1 being not confident at all and 10 being very confident, how confident are you about your . . . (type of confidence, e.g. skill execution)?

2 Why do you feel that you are a 3 (for example) on that rather than a 7 (for example)?

3 What changes do you think you would have to make in order to be a 7 (for example)?

4 How might you go about making these changes?

5 What would be a good first step?

Debrief the athlete and close the consultancy.

REFERENCES

Allport, G. W. (1937). *Personality*, pp. 173–81. New York: Holt.

Bandura, A. (1997). *Self-efficacy: The exercise of control.* New York: Freeman.

Butler, R. J. (1989). Psychological preparation of Olympic boxers [occasional paper]. In Kremer, J. and Crawford, W. (eds). *The Psychology of Sport: Theory and practice*, pp. 74–84. Belfast: BPS Northern Ireland Branch.

Butler, R. J. and Hardy, L. (1992). The performance profile: Theory and application. *The Sport Psychologist, 6,* 253–64.

Cresswell, S. and Hodge, K. (2004). Coping skills: Role of trait sport confidence and trait anxiety. *Perceptual and Motor Skills, 98,* 433–8.

Davis, M., Eschelman, E. R. and McKay, M. (1988). *The Relaxation and Stress Reduction Workbook* (3rd edn). Oakland, CA: New Harbinger.

Feltz, D. L. and Lirgg, C. D. (2001). Self-efficacy beliefs of athletes, teams and coaches. In Singer, R. N., Hausenblas, H. A. and Janelle, C. M. (eds) *Handbook of Sport Psychology*, pp. 304–61. New York: John Wiley.

Feltz, D. L. and Riessinger, C. A. (1990). Effects of *in vivo* emotive imagery and performance feedback on self-efficacy and muscular endurance. *Journal of Sport and Exercise Psychology*, *12*, 132–43.

Fransella, F. (ed.) (1981). *Personality: Theory, measurement and research* (Vol 719). London: Routledge Kegan & Paul.

Gill, D. L. (1988). Gender differences in competitive orientation and sport participation. *International Journal of Sport Psychology*, *19*, 145–59.

Hays, K., Maynard, I., Thomas, O. and Bawden, M. (2007). Sources and types of confidence identified by world class sport performers. *Journal of Applied Sport Psychology*, *19*, 434–56.

Hays, K., Thomas, O., Butt., J. and Maynard, I. (2010). The development of confidence profiling in sport. *The Sport Psychologist*, *18*, 373–92.

Hays, K., Thomas, O., Maynard, I. and Bawden, M. (2009). The role of confidence in world class sport performance. *Journal of Sport Science*, *27*(11), 1185–99.

Jones, G. and Hanton, S. (2001). Pre-competitive feeling states and directional anxiety interpretations. *Journal of Sports Sciences*, *19*, 385–95.

Jones, G., Swain, A. B. J. and Cale, A. (1991). Gender differences in precompetition temporal patterning and antecedents of anxiety and self-confidence. *Journal of Sport and Exercise Psychology*, *13*, 1–15.

Kelly, G. A. (1955). *The Psychology of Personal Constructs* (Vols I & II). New York: Norton.

Kingston, K., Lane, A. and Thomas, O. (2010). A temporal examination of elite performers' sources of sport-confidence. *The Sport Psychologist*, *18*, 313–32.

Lirgg, C. D. (1991). Gender differences in self-confidence in physical activity: A meta-analysis of recent studies. *Journal of Sport and Exercise Psychology*, *13*, 294–310.

Miller, W. R. and Rollnick, S. (2002). *Motivational Interviewing: Preparing people for change* (2nd edn). New York: Guilford Press.

Orlick, T. and Partington, J. (1988). Mental links to excellence. *The Sport Psychologist*, *2*, 105–30.

Thomas, O., Lane, A. and Kingston, K. (2011). Defining and contextualizing robust sport-confidence. *Journal of Applied Sport Psychology*, *23*, 189–208.

Vealey, R. S. (1986). Conceptualization of sport-confidence and competitive orientation: Preliminary investigation and instrument development. *Journal of Sport Psychology*, *8*, 221–46.

Vealey, R. S. (2001). Understanding and enhancing self-confidence in athletes. In Singer, R. N., Hausenblas, H. A. and Janelle, C. M. (eds) *Handbook of Sport Psychology*, pp. 550–65. New York: John Wiley.

Vealey, R. S. and Chase, M. A. (2008). Self-confidence in sport: Conceptual and research advances. In Horn, T. S. (ed.) *Advances in Sport Psychology* (3rd edn), pp. 65–97. Champaign, IL: Human Kinetics.

Vealey, R. S. and Garner-Holman, M. (1998). Measurement issues in applied sport psychology. In Duda, J. L. (ed.) *Advances in Sport and Exercise Psychology Measurement*, pp. 247–68. Morgantown, WV: Fitness Information Technology.

Vealey, R. S., Hayashi, S. W., Garner-Holman, M. and Giacobbi, P. (1998). Sources of sport-confidence: Conceptualization and instrument development. *Journal of Sport & Exercise Psychology, 21,* 54–80.

Vealey, R. S. and Knight, B. J. (2002). *Development of the Multidimensional Sport-Confidence Inventory.* Tucson, AZ: Association for the Advancement of Applied Sport Psychology.

Velasquez, M. M., Von Sternberg, K., Dodrill, C. L., Kan, L. Y. and Parsons, J. T. (2005). The transtheoretical model as a framework for developing substance abuse interventions. *Journal of Addictions Nursing, 16,* 31–40.

Zinsser, N., Bunker, L. and Williams, J. M. (2001). Cognitive techniques for building confidence and enhacing performance. In Williams, J. M. (ed.) *Applied Sport Psychology: Personal growth to peak performance,* pp. 284–311. Mountain View, CA: Mayfield Publishing.

3 Anxiety in sport

Are we any closer to untangling the knots?

Mark Uphill

CHAPTER SUMMARY

Although athletes experience a range of emotions (e.g. Hanin, 2000; Uphill and Jones, 2007a), research has predominantly focused on anxiety. This chapter explores the characteristics, antecedents, consequences and regulation of anxiety. By providing both some historical context and contemporary and contentious issues, it is intended that the reader will develop a thorough, if not exhaustive, understanding of this fascinating area of study.

LEARNING OUTCOMES

When you have studied this chapter, you should be able to:

1 Describe the main characteristics and causes of anxiety
2 Discuss the strengths and weaknesses of anxiety measures
3 Evaluate theories that address the anxiety–performance relationship
4 Describe some strategies that an applied sport psychologist might use to help athletes deal with anxiety

DEFINING ANXIETY

An enduring problem in sport psychology research has been inconsistent use of the terms 'arousal', 'stress' and 'anxiety' (cf. Woodman and Hardy, 2001). Difficulty in providing a consistent definition is an issue that is not restricted to anxiety, but applies to many constructs. The consequence of having inconsistent definitions is that the concept is assessed differently, and, as a consequence, how the concept behaves differs.

The consequence of this will be that two studies, both claiming to examine anxiety, are likely to produce different results. A working definition of anxiety is given in an attempt to provide a definition that guides the approach used in the present chapter. It is likely that, given interest in anxiety, such a definition might not be used by all, and that researchers and practitioners alike should be cognizant of how each study defines the concept.

Anxiety is proposed to refer to an unpleasant emotion and is characterized by vague but persistent feelings of apprehension and dread (Cashmore, 2002). According to Frederickson (2001), there is consensus that an emotion is a cognitively appraised response to an event, either conscious or unconscious. This is likely to 'trigger a cascade of response tendencies across loosely-coupled component systems, such as subjective experience, facial expression, cognitive processing and physiological changes' (Frederickson, 2001, p. 218).

Frederickson's (2001) definition reflects several key aspects of competition anxiety.

First, anxiety is a multifaceted response (e.g. comprising physiological, behavioural (such as fidgeting or avoidance), linguistic and cognitive elements).

Second, the notion that an emotion is a reaction to an event has often been used to differentiate emotion from the related construct of mood (see Beedie et al., 2005). Indeed, although appraisals (or evaluations of stimuli) can sometimes occur consciously and deliberately, often appraisals may occur rapidly and largely outside conscious awareness.[1] In practice, then, it may be difficult to differentiate anxiety as an emotion from the mood state of anxiety. For example, Lane and Terry (2000) contended that it may be difficult for athletes to differentiate between feelings that arise in relation to a specific stimulus and those that may already be present as part of an underlying mood state. Although the response stem 'Please rate how you are feeling in relation to the upcoming competition' may help to differentiate emotion from mood (e.g. Jones et al., 2005), difficulties nevertheless remain.

Arousal has been defined as 'the extent of release of potential energy, stored in the tissues of the organism, as this is shown in activity or response' (Duffy, 1962, p. 179). Such a response has been viewed as lying on a continuum from deep sleep to extreme excitement. This rather vague and imprecise definition of arousal has given way to increasingly sophisticated conceptualizations. For example, rather than arousal being considered a unitary response, evidence suggests that at least three different forms of arousal can be differentiated (Woodman and Hardy, 2001): electrocortical activity (electrical activity measured in the cortex via an electroencephalogram, or EEG), autonomic activity (physiological indices such as galvanic skin response, heart rate or blood pressure) or behavioural activity (overt activity).

Stress has sometimes been viewed as being synonymous with anxiety. However, stress is arguably a broader construct than anxiety (e.g. Lazarus, 1999). Jones (1990) described stress as a state in which some demand is placed on an individual, who is required to cope with the demands of the situation. Stress, then, may or may not place a 'strain' on athletes (e.g. Lazarus, 1966); it will be influenced by the appraisal (or evaluation) of one's ability to cope. Importantly, and as alluded to above, how athletes appraise particular situations is believed to impact the emotions experienced (e.g. Lazarus, 2000; Uphill and Jones, 2007a). If an athlete perceives a stressor (e.g. a footballer taking a penalty kick) as a threat and doubts their ability to succeed, then the most likely emotion elicited will be anxiety. If one accepts that anxiety is an emotion, and that some type of cognitive evaluation necessarily precedes an emotion (see Ochsner and Gross, 2007), then, to understand how anxiety arises, it is imperative to examine the cognitive precursors to anxiety.

MEASUREMENT OF ANXIETY

Since Spielberger's (1966) seminal work distinguishing between trait and state anxiety, several scales to measure these constructs have been developed. Whereas state anxiety concerns an individual's response to a specific situation, trait anxiety represents a general disposition to respond to a variety of situations with heightened levels of state anxiety (e.g. Martens *et al.*, 1990). A fifteen-item Sport Competition Anxiety Test (SCAT; Martens, 1977) has historically been used to measure a person's level of trait anxiety in sport. This *unidimensional* measure (i.e. assuming that trait anxiety has a single dimension) has, however, been superseded by the Sport Anxiety Scale (SAS; Smith *et al.*, 1990). In contrast to the SCAT, the SAS is a multidimensional instrument (anxiety is composed of several facets) comprising twenty-one items grouped into three subscales: worry, somatic anxiety (one's perception of physiological symptoms associated with the anxiety experience) and concentration disruption. Several studies have indicated that the SAS has at least three items that illustrate measurement shortcomings (e.g. Prapavessis *et al.*, 2005), particularly when administered to child athletes. Accordingly, Smith *et al.* (2006) developed a revised version of the SAS, the SAS-2. The SAS-2 has fifteen items that load on to three subscales, each comprising five items: somatic anxiety (e.g. 'My body feels tense'), worry (e.g. 'I worry that I will not play well') and concentration disruption (e.g. 'It is hard to concentrate on the game'); on initial testing, it has been demonstrated to possess adequate validity and reliability.

The Competitive State Anxiety Inventory-2 (CSAI-2; Martens *et al.*, 1990) has largely been the instrument of choice for measuring competitive *state* anxiety. The CSAI-2 comprises twenty-seven items measuring the *intensity* of cognitive anxiety (symptoms such as worry and negative expectations associated with the anxiety experience), somatic anxiety and self-confidence. Nine items are contained within each subscale, with each item rated on a four-point Likert scale ranging from 1 (not at all) to 4 (very much so). Although the CSAI-2 has been, and remains, a popular research and applied tool, it has attracted a number of criticisms.

Criticisms and limitations of the CSAI-2

First, concerns have been raised about the validity of the cognitive anxiety subscale. Although Martens *et al.* (1990) defined cognitive anxiety as reflecting negative expectations about performance, Lane *et al.* (1999) suggested that only one item ('I have self-doubts') genuinely assesses cognitive anxiety. The remaining items (e.g. 'I am concerned about this competition') may reflect, not necessarily cognitive anxiety, but rather a perception of the importance of the event. Lane *et al.* questioned whether the term 'concern' was strong enough to capture a concept Martens *et al.* defined as a 'negative expectation'.

ACTIVITY 3.1

We all know how it feels to be anxious, don't we? Think about an important competition, one in which your sport performance really mattered. Think about the days leading up to the event, the day of the competition and the minutes immediately prior to competition. How do you feel when you become anxious? What thoughts do you have? Do you notice any bodily sensations? How do you behave? Write down all the symptoms of anxiety that you can recall, whether it be single adjectives (e.g. uneasy, nervous) or complete sentences (e.g. 'I was pacing round the living room on the morning of the event' or 'I couldn't keep still'). What, if anything, changed as competition approached? How easy is it for you to recall how you felt, and how valid do you think such descriptions are?

Compare your responses with the items listed in the CSAI-2 (Martens *et al.*, 1990). Do you think this measurement instrument possesses 'face validity' (i.e. adequately captures what you perceive to be anxiety)?

Limitations have also been identified with the somatic anxiety subscale. Martens *et al.* (1990, p. 121) defined somatic anxiety as the 'physiological and affective elements of the anxiety experience that develop directly from autonomic arousal'. Kerr (1997) suggested that increases in physiological arousal may accompany other emotions (e.g. excitement). Thus, if items on the somatic anxiety scale (e.g. 'my heart is racing') are assessing perceptions of athletes' physiological state, it is conceivable that high scores on this scale may not necessarily be indicative of heightened anxiety. Although Cox *et al.* (2003) have developed a revised CSAI-2 (CSAI-2R), which addresses some of the concerns highlighted by Lane *et al.* (1999), it also arguably shares the same limitation that being concerned does not necessarily mean you are anxious.

Besides measuring the intensity of anxiety symptoms, researchers have also highlighted the necessity of measuring the frequency (Swain and Jones, 1993) and 'direction' (Jones *et al.*, 1993) of anxiety symptoms. With regards to the former, Swain and Jones (1993) appended a frequency scale to each item of the CSAI-2, asking, 'How frequently do you experience this thought or feeling?', on a scale of 1 (not at all) through to 7 (all the time). Although intensity and frequency components are related, they should nonetheless be viewed as independent dimensions that individually contribute to athletes' affective (e.g. anxiety) experience (Diener *et al.*, 1991). In sport, Mahoney and Avener (1977) first documented that anxiety could be interpreted in different ways by athletes. A measure to assess the 'direction' of anxiety – the CSAI-2(d) – was developed by Jones and Swain (1992). Similar to when assessing the frequency of anxiety symptoms, Jones and Swain attached a scale (ranging from –3, through 0, to 3) to each item of the CSAI-2, asking performers to rate the extent to which they perceive each thought or feeling to either debilitate or facilitate performance, respectively. Indeed, a model of facilitative and debilitative anxiety (Jones, 1995; Figure 3.1) presents coping and goal attainment as important mediators of anxiety interpretation.

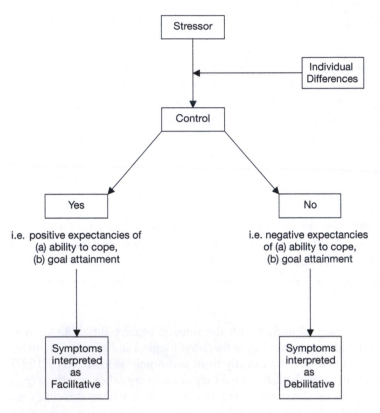

FIGURE 3.1 A model of facilitative and debilitative anxiety

Source: Jones, 1995, p. 466. Reproduced with permission of John Wiley & Sons

On the one hand, the addition of the directional dimension has arguably conferred some advantages. For instance, Jones *et al.* (1993) observed no differences between high-performance and low-performance gymnasts in cognitive anxiety intensity, somatic anxiety intensity and somatic anxiety direction. However, high-performance gymnasts reported their cognitive anxiety symptoms as more facilitative to performance than did their low-performance counterparts. The differentiation of the measurement of anxiety into separate components has also been recently supported by Hanton *et al.* (2004), who indicated that patterning of the intensity, frequency and directional interpretation of anxiety differed as competition time approached. Finally, on a practical note, it could be argued that changes in the frequency and direction of reported anxiety symptoms are useful indicators of intervention effectiveness, independent of any change in anxiety intensity (cf. Uphill and Jones, 2007b).

On the other hand, debate continues regarding the concept of 'facilitative anxiety'. Burton and Naylor (1997) suggested that 'anxiety' symptoms that are interpreted as facilitative are unlikely to be labelled as anxiety, especially if anxiety is defined as involving 'negative expectations'. Further, researchers mislabel positive emotions (e.g. excitement) as facilitative anxiety. Rephrased, if anxiety is defined and character-ized by uncertainty regarding goal attainment and perceived threat, a state in which individuals hold positive beliefs in their ability to cope with the situation and achieve their goals, by definition, cannot be anxiety (cf. Jones and Uphill, 2004)!

Given such criticisms, some caution is needed when one is interpreting data derived from the CSAI-2. Indeed, Lundqvist *et al.* (2011) illustrated a method for combining the intensity and direction scores to enhance the interpretation of 'facilitative anxiety'. In their study, Lundqvist *et al.* found that differences in 'facilitative ratings' of anxiety between elite and sub-elite athletes were observed when coupled with low anxiety intensity ratings, rather than ratings of moderate- or high-intensity anxiety.

FOCUS 3.1

Understanding the challenge of facilitative anxiety

Based on the issues reviewed, there are a number of challenges confronting researchers of anxiety in sport. Conceptually, there appears to be a consensus that an emotional state that is *felt as unpleasant* may not necessarily be associated with negative impacts on performance (e.g. Woodman and Hardy, 2001). (As an aside, positive emotional states, although felt as pleasant, need not necessarily or always be associated with adaptive response to competition either!) There is the theoretical challenge of explaining how anxiety (or any other emotional state, for that matter) may confer both advantages and disadvantages for sport performance. In addition, there is the methodological and measurement challenge of differentiating an affective state (i.e. anxiety) from *athletes' perceptions* of the impact of that affective state on performance, and from the *actual* impact on performance. With emotion being seen as a state that is influenced by athletes' appraisals, beliefs or evaluations about the impact of that state upon performance will theoretically impact the affective state itself (e.g. Lazarus, 2000; Jones and Uphill, 2004). It is disentangling this issue that has arguably generated much of the controversy surrounding 'facilitative anxiety' to date.

The CSAI-2, the CSAI-2R and the CSAI-2(d) are relatively long instruments for athletes to complete prior to, or during, competition. The Mental Readiness Form (MRF) was developed by Murphy *et al.* (1989) as a brief instrument that could potentially be used immediately prior to, or even during, competition. Krane (1994) later extended the MRF by examining three different methods of scoring the instrument (see Activity Box 3.2). Indeed, a five-item measure of anxiety is contained within the recently validated Sport Emotion Questionnaire (Jones *et al.*, 2005). Although researchers (and practitioners) are not short of instruments that purportedly assess anxiety, several of these instruments possess a number of limitations that, at the least, demand a healthy dose of scepticism when one is interpreting the results.

ACTIVITY 3.2

The three scoring systems of the MRF are provided. Based on your understanding of anxiety, decide which instrument you would be most likely to use, and justify why. Having done this, you may wish to refer to the original article by Krane (1994) and perhaps consider whether, through combination of the approaches, an MRF-4 might be viable! Use the MRF to plot your anxiety 2 weeks, 1 week, 1 day and 30 minutes prior to a forthcoming sport competition. What do you think will happen to your scores, and why?

Original MRF

My thoughts are:

Calm   Worried

_____

My body feels:

Relaxed   Tense

_____

I am feeling:

Confident   Scared

_____

(Scores are obtained by measuring in millimetres the mark on the line – which should be 10 cm long – corresponding to how you feel. Scores range from 0 to 100 for each item.)

MRF Likert

My thoughts are:

| 1 | 2 | 3 | 4 | 5 | 6 | 7 | 8 | 9 | 10 | 11 |

Calm   Worried

My body feels:

| 1 | 2 | 3 | 4 | 5 | 6 | 7 | 8 | 9 | 10 | 11 |

Relaxed   Tense

I am feeling

| 1 | 2 | 3 | 4 | 5 | 6 | 7 | 8 | 9 | 10 | 11 |

Confident   Scared

MRF-3										

My thoughts are:

1	2	3	4	5	6	7	8	9	10	11
Worried										Not worried

My body feels:

1	2	3	4	5	6	7	8	9	10	11
Tense										Not tense

I am feeling:

1	2	3	4	5	6	7	8	9	10	11
Confident										Not confident

Source: Adapted, with permission, from Krane, 1994

Sources of anxiety

According to Gould *et al.* (1984), if sport psychologists could identify the antecedents of anxiety in a competitive situation, then appropriate interventions could be designed to help athletes. Owing to the ethical challenges associated with the manipulation of variables that are hypothesized to cause anxiety, researchers have tended to examine correlations between factors that are thought to cause anxiety and the intensity of the anxiety response (cf. Woodman and Hardy, 2001). A brief selection of personal and situational antecedents of anxiety is reported below.

Ethical issues

Upholding ethical principles is a key part of research. Safeguards are put in place to ensure participants are not unduly harmed. With research that examines anxiety, ethical issues are related to increasing an unpleasant emotion: that is, making someone feel unpleasant. A great deal of research in sport has investigated anxiety in ecologically valid settings (e.g. before a race, using a self-report measure). If the researcher wishes to identify the cause of anxiety, then the research needs to be designed with control and experimental groups: that is, people in one group will do something or be asked to think in a certain way that increases the intensity of their anxiety. The challenge for the researcher is to justify whether the unpleasant feelings experienced by participants are worth the knowledge gained. It is possible to argue that if a few people become anxious, but the reasons for anxiety can be identified, then it is worth it. This might be the case, but, for an ethics committee to approve such a project, the arguments need to be persuasive. It is typical that, if a research project increases anxiety to investigate its effects, then safeguards are put in place, often involving a post-experiment debriefing. Also, ethics boards tend to approve projects that involve higher

RESEARCH METHODS 3.1

A researcher wanting to assess anxiety is faced with a difficult choice. The CSAI-2 has been the most commonly used scale, and the addition of frequency and direction scales has allowed knowledge to be generated about the frequency and perceived helpfulness of these feelings. A limitation of the cognitive anxiety scale is based on the use of 'concern' as the term to describe situations where athletes report anxiety. In addition, given that anxiety research tends to involve assessing anxiety shortly before competition, brevity is important.

With reference to arguments made in relation to measures of anxiety, what scale would you use, and why? The following task has been designed to help you make a choice. There is no one right answer to this task. You will find that researchers continue to use the CSAI-2, despite others pointing out some limitations. Researchers argue that there are strengths and limitations of each approach. And so, with that thought in mind, consider some of the questions you might consider when selecting a scale to use.

Scale	Has there been a validity study (yes or no)? Write down any issues related to its validity	Has the study been widely used (yes/no)? Has the research been supportive of the validity of the scale, and what strengths and limitations have been raised?	If you were presented with the scale 1 hour before competition, how easy would it be to complete? Are the items easy to understand, and is the scale too long/too short?
CSAI-2 (Martens *et al.*, 1990)			
Mental Readiness Scale (Krane, 1994)			
Anxiety scale (Jones *et al.*, 2005)			
On the basis of the arguments given above, I would use the . . . (insert name of scale)			

risks when the research team includes individuals with proven track records or who are registered (or accredited) psychologists. The key point is that it is possible to conduct high-risk research, but persuasive arguments needs to be presented, coupled with robust safety checks.

Trait anxiety

Athletes who exhibit high levels of trait anxiety are more likely to interpret sport situations as threatening compared with their less trait-anxious counterparts (e.g. Spielberger, 1966). 'High' and 'low' trait-anxious individuals may not represent homogeneous groups. The seminal work of Weinberger et al. (1979) indicates that some individuals exhibit physiological and behavioural reactions that are not compatible with a paper-and-pencil test of trait anxiety. Individuals who display this response are defined by (a) low scores on trait anxiety and (b) high scores on a measure of defensiveness (the Marlowe–Crowne social desirability scale). This subgroup of low trait-anxious individuals are labelled as 'repressors' in such research and are distinguished from the 'truly low anxious', who score low on both measures, of trait anxiety and defensiveness (e.g. Brosschot et al., 1999). There is a suggestion that repressors are, in fact, high trait-anxious individuals (and may not necessarily be cognizant of their symptoms) who claim not to be anxious on self-report measures. Similarly, high trait-anxious individuals may also be subdivided into groups based on their defensiveness scores. Most researchers in sport have not acknowledged this distinction.

Perfectionism

How perfectionism influences sport performance is subject to considerable debate. On the one hand, although some view perfectionism as a trait that makes Olympic champions (e.g. Gould et al., 2002), others see perfectionism as a characteristic that undermines rather than facilitates performance (Anshel and Mansouri, 2005; Flett and Hewitt, 2005). This apparent paradox has been evidenced in several studies (e.g. Stoeber et al., 2007). Stoeber et al. suggested that perfectionism is a multifaceted construct, and, although some dimensions may be harmful or maladaptive, others may be benign or adaptive. The maladaptive dimensions have the potential to adversely influence cognitive processes and, by extension, the anxiety response (Stoeber et al., 2007).

Self-handicapping

Self-handicapping is a term used to describe the process of proactively reducing effort and creating performance excuses to protect oneself from potentially negative feedback in evaluative environments such as sport (Berglas and Jones, 1978). According to Berglas and Jones (1978, p. 406), self-handicapping involves 'any action or choice of performance setting that enhances the opportunity to externalize (or excuse) failure and to internalize (reasonably accept credit for) success'. For example, a rugby player might buy a take-away meal the night before a big game, making the excuse that, in the event of a poor performance, it is attributable to poor nutrition as opposed to any deficit in personal ability. However, should a positive performance ensue, such a self-handicap affords the opportunity to enhance one's self-esteem (e.g. 'I must be a good rugby player if I can perform well after eating what I did!'). The adoption of self-handicapping strategies may serve both self-protection and self-enhancement motives then (Tice, 1991). Although self-handicapping affords athletes the opportunity to externalize a poor performance (and thereby protect self-esteem), it also increases the likelihood of failure (cf. Kuczka and Treasure, 2004). With regards to anxiety, it is proposed that self-handicapping is most likely when an individual perceives a threat to their self-esteem (Prapavessis and Grove, 1998) or feels uncertain about their ability (Berglas and Jones, 1978).

Characteristics of sport event

The type of competition (e.g. individual vs team sports or contact vs non-contact sports) has been associated with differences in state anxiety, with individual and contact-sport participants reporting higher levels of anxiety than their team and non-contact-sport counterparts (Simon and Martens, 1977). The importance of the event has also been associated with changes in anxiety: more important events are associated with a heightened anxiety response (Dowthwaite and Armstrong, 1984).

Time to competition

Studies using the 'time-to-event' paradigm (i.e. measuring competitive state anxiety in the time leading up to competition) support the multidimensional conceptualization of anxiety, in that different patterns of responding in cognitive anxiety and somatic anxiety are observed. Specifically, whereas cognitive anxiety remains high and stable in the period leading up to competition, somatic anxiety remains fairly low up until 1 or 2 days prior to competition and then increases steadily, until the point at which the competition commences (e.g. Gould et al., 1984).

Appraisal

The basic premise of appraisal theories of emotion is straightforward: emotions appear to be related to how people evaluate events in their lives (Parrott, 2001). For example, imagine that you have just lost a hockey match by a single goal, and one of your parents is criticizing you for poor positioning that allowed your opponent to score the critical goal. What emotion(s) would you experience in response to this situation? Perhaps you would respond angrily if you consider the criticism to be unjustified and you were in a poor position because a teammate had lost possession. Alternatively, if you consider that your error directly impacted upon the result, you may feel guilty or disappointed. Several appraisal theories (e.g. Smith and Ellsworth, 1985; Lazarus, 1991; Roseman, 1991), although differing slightly in their detail, attempt to understand the role of appraisal in the generation of emotion. One appraisal theory in particular, cognitive motivational relational theory (Lazarus, 1991), which has been purported to be applicable to sport (Lazarus, 2000), is increasingly being used to inform research (e.g. Skinner and Brewer, 2004) and has received support for some of its tenets (Hammermeister and Burton, 2001; Uphill and Jones, 2007a). However, in general, there is a need for more research examining the relationships between appraisal components and anxiety in athletes.

EFFECTS OF ANXIETY ON SPORT PERFORMANCE

Early approaches to the investigation of the anxiety–performance relationship, such as drive theory and the inverted-U hypothesis (see Woodman and Hardy, 2001), were based upon unidimensional conceptualizations of *physiological arousal* and are now largely ignored by anxiety researchers (see Jones, 1995; Woodman and Hardy, 2001, for the limitations of these models).

The multidimensional examination of the anxiety–performance relationship was propagated by multidimensional anxiety theory (Martens *et al.*, 1990). Martens *et al.* predicted that cognitive anxiety would exhibit a negative linear relationship with performance, because worrying depleted a limited-capacity attentional resource. A curvilinear (inverted-U) relationship was postulated between physiologically based somatic anxiety and performance.

Somewhat equivocal support has been obtained for Martens *et al.*'s predictions regarding components of anxiety and performance (Burton, 1988; Gould *et al.*, 1984). Indeed, recent meta-analyses (Craft *et al.*, 2003; Woodman and Hardy, 2003) are similarly inconclusive. Importantly, Hardy and Parfitt (1991) observe that multi-dimensional anxiety theory attempts to explain the three-dimensional relationship between cognitive anxiety, somatic anxiety and performance, in terms of a series of two-dimensional relationships.

Catastrophe models extend multidimensional anxiety theory by making predictions about the *interactive* effects of cognitive anxiety and physiological arousal on perform-ance. Two catastrophe models of the anxiety–performance relationship have been related to sport: the 'butterfly catastrophe' and, more commonly, the 'cusp catastrophe'. The cusp catastrophe model (Hardy *et al.*, 1994; see Figure 3.2) is used to describe the interactive effects of cognitive anxiety and physiological arousal on performance

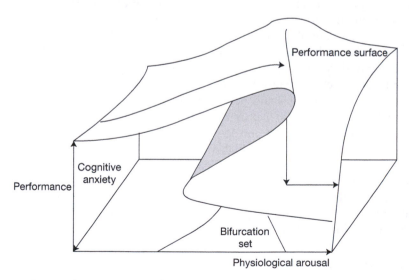

FIGURE 3.2 A cusp catastrophe model of the anxiety–performance relationship

Source: Hardy *et al.*, 1994. Reproduced by permission of Taylor & Francis

and makes several assertions with regard to the anxiety–performance relationship. Specifically, at low levels of cognitive anxiety, changes in physiological arousal should lead to small, continuous changes in performance. Second, when physiological arousal is high, a negative correlation is postulated between cognitive anxiety and performance. Finally, when cognitive anxiety is high, the effect of physiological arousal upon performance may be either positive or negative (Hardy and Parfitt, 1991). Indeed, some support for the predictions made by the cusp catastrophe model has been obtained (e.g. Hardy and Parfitt, 1991; Hardy et al., 1994).

The butterfly catastrophe model (Hardy, 1990) contains the addition of two further dimensions: a *bias* factor and a *butterfly* factor. A detailed consideration of the butterfly catastrophe model is beyond the scope of the present chapter, as it remains largely untested within sport (see Hardy, 1996, for an exception). The inclusion of a bias factor is reported to have the effect of swinging the front edge to the right or left. Although this is quite difficult to visualize, according to this contention, under high levels of cognitive anxiety, highly self-confident performers would be hypothesized to withstand a greater intensity of physiological arousal before experiencing a decrement in performance than their less confident counterparts (Hardy, 1990). Some initial support for this proposition has been obtained by Hardy and colleagues (Hardy, 1996; Hardy et al., 2004). Although catastrophe models generally seem advantageous, in that they account for some of the inconsistencies in previous research and model multiple factors in describing the impact of anxiety, they do not explain *how* anxiety impacts performance. A number of explanations about how anxiety impacts performance are described briefly below.

Processing efficiency theory

Processing efficiency theory (Eysenck and Calvo, 1992) predicts that worry (i.e. cognitive anxiety) depletes the processing and storage capacity of working memory, effectively diverting attention from task-relevant cues. Processing efficiency theory also predicts that worry may stimulate on-task effort. Specifically, to avoid aversive consequences associated with poor performance, anxious individuals may allocate additional processing resources to the task. This acts to (a) reduce processing efficiency (described as performance effectiveness divided by the processing resources required for the task) and, crucially, (b) maintain performance levels by increasing working memory capacity. Williams et al. (2002) examined participants' performance in a table-tennis accuracy task when under high and low cognitive load. Although cognitive anxiety impaired performance under both high and low cognitive load, its impact on processing efficiency was less in the low mental load condition. Processing efficiency theory as an explanation of how anxiety impacts performance, then, is beginning to receive some support within sport psychology (e.g. Murray and Janelle, 2003; Wilson et al., 2006) and may help to explain why anxiety may sometimes lead to improved performance (i.e. motivating performers to exert more effort on a task).

Attentional control theory

Attentional control theory (ACT; Eysenck et al., 2007) represents a development of processing efficiency theory and offers further hypotheses about the impact of anxiety on performance, based largely on the assumption that anxiety impairs the functioning of the central executive (cf. Eysenck and Derakshan, 2011). Briefly stated, ACT posits that anxiety impairs attentional control, whether that is the inhibition function (which prevents task-irrelevant stimuli from disrupting performance), the shifting function (which is used to allocate attention in a flexible and optimal way) or the updating function (used to monitor and update information in working memory (cf. Eysenck and Derakshan, 2011). Although space precludes a thorough exploration of this approach, it may well provide a useful account of how anxiety influences attention in sport (cf. Wilson, 2008). Indeed, some support for the predictions of ACT was found by Wilson et al. (2009) in a sample of basketball players.

Conscious processing (or reinvestment) hypothesis

The conscious processing hypothesis suggests that a reinvestment of controlled processing or a tendency to induce conscious control over a typically automated movement causes the sudden degradation of skilled performance when a performer is anxious (e.g. Baumeister, 1984; Masters, 1992). This is ostensibly an extension of the 'paralysis-by-analysis' phenomenon, whereby anxiety 'encourages' athletes to turn attention to the skill processes underlying performance and may, in extreme cases, lead to 'choking' (see also Moran, 2004). In a recent comparison of self-focus versus processing efficiency explanations of anxiety–performance associations, Wilson et al. (2007) asked participants to perform a simulated rally driving task. Conditions were manipulated to direct the focus of attention towards the explicit monitoring of driving or a secondary task, and each condition was performed under evaluative and non-evaluative conditions (designed to manipulate anxiety). Results showed little change in driving performance in the high-threat, explicit monitoring condition compared with either the low-threat or the high-threat distraction conditions. Compared with conditions of low threat, mental effort increased in both the high-threat conditions (i.e. when attention was directed towards versus away from the primary task). Performance effectiveness was maintained under threat, although this was at the expense of reduced processing efficiency, lending stronger support to the predictions of processing efficiency theory. Besides these cognitive accounts of how anxiety impacts performance, it is possible that the physiological arousal associated with anxiety could impact directly upon performance (cf. Jones and Uphill, 2004).

Physiological arousal and performance

High levels of arousal accompanying anxiety may enhance performance in simple tasks (Parfitt et al., 1995). Parfitt et al. (1995), for example, found that increased physiological arousal was positively related to height jumped in university-age basketball players. However, there are few, if any, sport tasks whereby success is determined solely by strength: even skills such as weightlifting require attention and coordination to be successful. Enhanced arousal, then, could increase muscular tension, leading to a decrement in fine motor control (Parfitt et al., 1990). Indeed, Noteboom and colleagues (2001a, 2001b) observed that performance in a submaximal isometric pinch task was characterized by a decrease in steadiness under conditions of high arousal. In sport, Collins et al. (2001) reported a change in the movement pattern of soldiers required to perform

FOCUS 3.2

Ethical issues involved in examining the emotion–performance relationship

If the 'holy grail' of anxiety research is being able to understand the processes or mechanisms by which anxiety impacts performance when it arguably matters most (i.e. at the height of competition), what ethical issues are researchers confronted with when investigating this relationship? Having identified what you perceive to be the ethical issues associated with this type of research, consider the strategies that researchers could use to circumvent these problems. How would you attempt to examine the anxiety–performance relationship, and why would you go about it in this way?

a stepping task on two parallel bars, 20 m off the ground, and weightlifters performing the snatch lift.

Theory of challenge and threat states in athletes

The theory of challenge and threat states in athletes (TCTSA; Jones *et al.*, 2009) consolidates and extends several approaches – the biopsychosocial model (Blascovich and Tomaka, 1996), adaptive approaches to competition (Skinner and Brewer, 2004) and the model of debilitative and facilitative states anxiety (Jones, 1995) – and arguably helps to provide an integrated account of the physiological effects of anxiety on perform-ance. A central premise of the model, as it applies to anxiety, is that one's motivational state (i.e. challenge or threat) influences whether anxiety is perceived as helpful or unhelpful to performance (cf. Jones *et al.*, 2009). Specifically, in a challenged state, anxiety is hypothesized to be helpful to performance, whereas, in a threatened state, anxiety is hypothesized to be unhelpful to performance. In terms of *how* anxiety may influence performance, it is proposed that a combination of the determinants of challenge and threat (self-efficacy, perceptions of control and achievement goals), together with distinctive patterns of cardiovascular and hormonal responses, may influence variables such as attention, decision-making and energy mobilization. Research examining the central tenets of the TCTSA is still in its infancy, and, although some aspects have been supported (e.g. Turner *et al.*, 2012), there may not always be consistency between cardiovascular reactivity and performance among athletes (e.g. Turner *et al.*, 2013). Moreover, the processes by which anxiety may on the one hand be helpful to performance and on the other unhelpful have yet to be fully explored.

APPLYING THE SCIENCE

Although there is often an uneasy alliance between theory and practice, literature directed towards enhancing anxiety control specifically is well established (e.g. Maynard and Cotton, 1993), and a growing body of literature on the broad regulation of emotions (e.g. Uphill et al., 2009; Lane et al., 2012) is arguably helping to build bridges across the theory–practice gap.

Uphill et al. (2009) applied Gross and Thompson's (2007) framework of emotion regulation to athletes; it suggests that there are five categories of emotion regulation strategy (situation selection, situation modification, attention deployment, cognitive change and response modulation). A number of strategies fall within each of these classes (e.g. cognitive change might involve reappraisal, imagery, self-talk), and these can be used singularly or in combination to conceivably influence athletes' experience of anxiety. Indeed, several strategies have been used or recommended to influence athletes' anxiety specifically (e.g. Hanton and Jones, 1999; Jones, 2003), and, typically, multimodal interventions (i.e. comprising a number of strategies) are used to either reduce the intensity of symptoms or encourage athletes to evaluate their symptoms more positively (e.g. Uphill and Jones, 2007b).

Importantly, these strategies may interact to influence anxiety. For instance, a strategy that may be seen primarily as 'attentional control' (i.e. 'quiet-eye' training;

APPLYING THE SCIENCE 3.1

'What if' scenarios

If anxiety is associated with uncertainty, then using a strategy to reduce athletes' uncertainty would be predicted to attenuate their anxiety. Indeed, in a qualitative study by Uphill and Jones (2004), athletes reported using 'prospective coping' or planning to minimize anxiety. One sailor remarked, 'I make sure everything that's surrounding my campaign is in decent shape . . . then I make a plan for the next day. If the race starts at 11 o'clock we'll be there at 9 o'clock to rig the boat' (Uphill and Jones, 2004, p. 85). Using 'what if' scenarios encourages athletes to (a) identify as many situations or events that might 'go wrong' prior to or during competition as possible and (b) identify solutions to these difficulties. For example, what if your contact lens falls out while you are playing rugby? What if the wicket keeper starts to 'sledge' (verbally distract) me during the innings? Think of your own 'what ifs' in relation to the sport that you participate in and try to identify solutions to the issues that you identify.

Thinking critically about simulation training

Miller (1997) described how the Australian women's hockey team practised under adverse conditions (e.g. gamesmanship, 'poor' umpiring decisions) as part of their preparation for the 1988 Olympics. Why might simulation training reduce athletes' anxiety? Using SportDiscus™ or PsycInfo™, can you locate any articles that report the use of simulation training to help athletes cope with anxiety? How confident can you be that any reduction in anxiety can be attributed to the technique of simulation training? Why do you reach this conclusion?

Vickers, 1992) may enhance athletes' perceptions of their ability to cope with the task (cf. Moore *et al.*, 2013). Practically, encouraging a golfer to extend the duration s/he fixates on the ball in some circumstances could be beneficial. Lane *et al.* (2012) suggested that strategies that encourage reappraisal might be more efficacious, compared with those strategies that suppress the emotional response. In addition to the above, and applying their conclusions to anxiety, Lane *et al.* advocated the importance of (a) understanding athletes' beliefs about the influence of anxiety on performance, (b) exploring athletes' pre-existing use of emotion regulation strategies and (c) helping athletes identify the cause of their anxiety.

Although space precludes a full consideration of strategies that athletes and practitioners may use to regulate anxiety (for reviews, see Jones, 2003; Uphill *et al.*, 2009), one common technique that may help athletes manage anxiety, used in self-paced sports, is a pre-performance routine (PPR). Moran (2004) describes a PPR as a consistent series of cognitive and behavioural actions that an individual typically uses prior to a free throw in basketball or a putt in golf, for instance. Drawing on Gross and Thompson's framework (2007), this technique could:

1 modify the situation;
2 involve an element of cognitive change (e.g. enhanced perceptions of control); and
3 facilitate an athlete's attention toward task-relevant cues (see also Mesagno and Mullane-Grant, 2010).

A sequence that involved a 'see it, feel it, breath control, do it' routine, for example, would involve a number of techniques that theoretically and empirically would be associated with a change in anxiety level. More simply, tennis players can sometimes be seen looking at some cue cards between games, which could serve to influence their anxiety. Moreover, helping players become aware of, and improve, their body positions associated with anxiety, is also implicated in an embodied view of anxiety (see below).

APPLYING THE SCIENCE 3.2

Cognitive restructuring

Because anxiety is associated with worry and appraising a situation or event in a threatening manner, restructuring such thoughts would be expected to help athletes control their anxiety. This exercise is intended to illustrate how an applied sport psychologist might help an athlete modify a threatening situation (adapted from Moran, 2004). To begin, think carefully of a situation in your sport or daily life that typically makes you feel anxious. Now describe this scenario by completing the following sentence:

   'I hate the pressure of . . .'

For example, you might write, 'I hate the pressure of trying to meet tight deadlines, when I've not done enough preparation', or 'I hate the pressure of my parents watching me perform a new gymnastics routine for the first time'. Now recall that pressure situation again. On this occasion, however, think about the situation in a different light and attempt to complete the following sentence:

'I love the challenge of . . .'

Rather than merely repeating what you wrote above, you have to focus on something else besides the fear of making a mistake in front of your parents, in the above example.

Similarly, the use of motivational self-talk could both serve as an attentional control strategy and influence athletes' confidence (cognitive change), which can impact anxiety (cf. Hatzigeorgiadis *et al.*, 2009). Some additional techniques are described briefly below. Drawing upon what media commentators might describe as 'pressure situations' and pressure responses (see also Moran, 2004), because anxiety is believed to arise as a consequence of how one appraises a situation, we might not be able to influence the situations in which we find ourselves, but we can exert some control over how we think and behave in response to them.

BEYOND THE FRONTIER

Implications and further directions

Anxiety is a multifaceted response that may help and/or hinder performance. Based on the preceding discourse, it can be suggested that researchers are faced with a number of challenges. First, differentiating the measurement of anxiety from its consequences arguably represents one important avenue where substantial progression in the field could occur. The multifaceted nature of anxiety may require a multifaceted explanation of how anxiety influences performance. Much might be gained from the thoughtful integration of existing approaches, as well as the development of new theories and models. With regard to the former, Hardy et al. (2007) have 'merged' processing efficiency theory with the cusp catastrophe model to examine the association between anxiety and performance, albeit in a non-sport-related task. With regard to the latter, developments may be made by building bridges between sport and other areas of psychology. For example, Gross and colleagues' work has indicated that how individuals regulate their emotions can have divergent physiological, cognitive and experiential consequences (e.g. Gross, 1998). Attempts to suppress emotions, for instance, have been associated with a heightened physiological response and reduced memory, compared with reappraisal.

Alternatively, a socially embedded, embodied account of anxiety (cf. Marsh *et al.*, 2009) may yield interesting hypotheses about when anxiety may likely arise and their consequences. For example, when engaging in action with another, our actions serve to both define and influence the unit of which we are a part, and, in turn, our actions are constrained and channelled by this unit (Marsh *et al.*, 2009). Consider the example of a coxless four in rowing. The anxiety of a rower could be influenced by a change in crew membership, and the extent to which s/he competes or cooperates with the new member may be influenced by whether s/he sits in their normal position or is displaced into another seat. Broadly speaking, the interpersonal effects of anxiety in sport have yet to receive much scrutiny. Cerin *et al.* (2000) highlighted that much of the research on competitive emotions has examined emotions (including anxiety) pre-competitively. Because athletes' emotional state may fluctuate during competition, assessing the impact of emotions during performance represents something of a 'holy grail' (see Focus Box 3.2). However, understanding of athletes' anxiety may benefit from a broadening of the research lens beyond 'performance'. Much research has been directed towards anxiety–performance associations, perhaps to the neglect of other important areas (cf. Uphill and Dray, 2013). For instance, athletes may exhibit anxieties about their coaches' competence, future funding or the impact of sport on romantic relationships.

Although the progression of science has been described as 'standing on the shoulders of giants', researchers not only need to follow the well-trodden paths made by these giants, but also need to be brave enough to walk in less well-charted territory. Examining *athletes'* anxiety is a well-trodden path. There remain many other populations, such as coaches, sport officials, even spectators, for whom understanding something about their anxiety might yield important advances. In coaches or spectators, for example, how might the experience of chronic anxiety relate to various health implications?

Much has been done in relation to examining athletes' emotions at different times in relation to competition (e.g. Butt *et al.*, 2003). There remains the possibility of examining, not only individuals' current experience of anxiety, but also their retrospective and prospective evaluations of their anxiety levels. Specifically, individuals may exhibit systematic biases, insofar as they are inclined to anticipate that future negative experiences will last longer and be more intense than in fact they are (e.g. Gilbert *et al.*, 2002). If such a finding were to be documented in athletes, educating athletes about such biases might be important in enhancing the efficacy of interventions, perhaps through changing participants' beliefs regarding emotion (e.g. Ochsner and Gross, 2007) or self-confidence (Mellalieu *et al.*, 2003). In summary, although sport anxiety researchers face some challenges, there are also indications that anxiety research will continue to flourish in the foreseeable future. Perhaps you are already on the way to untangling some of the anxiety-related knots.

RECOMMENDED FURTHER READING

Journals

Butt, J., Weinberg, R. and Horn, T. (2003). The intensity and directional interpretation of anxiety: Fluctuations throughout competition and relationship to performance. *The Sport Psychologist, 17,* 35–54.

Craft, L. L., Magyar, M., Becker, B. J. and Feltz, D. L. (2003). The relationship between the Competitive State Anxiety Inventory-2 and sport performance: A meta-analysis. *Journal of Sport & Exercise Psychology, 25,* 44–65.

Eysenck, M. W. and Derakshan, N. (2011). New perspectives in attentional control theory. *Personality and Individual Differences, 50,* 955–60.

Hanton, S. and Jones, G. (1999). The effects of a multimodal intervention programme on performers: II. Training the butterflies to fly in formation. *The Sport Psychologist, 13,* 22–41.

Hanton, S., Thomas, O. and Maynard, I. (2004). Competitive anxiety responses in the week leading up to competition: The role of intensity, direction and frequency dimensions. *Psychology of Sport and Exercise, 5,* 169–81.

Uphill, M. A. and Dray, K. (2013). The thrill of defeat and the agony of victory: Towards an understanding and transformation of athletes' emotional experience. *Reflective Practice, 14,* 660–71.

SAMPLE ESSAY QUESTIONS

1 With reference to theory and research, discuss the proposition that anxiety may not necessarily impair performance.

2 'Facilitative anxiety is excitement mislabelled.' Discuss this statement with reference to theory and research.

3 Describe two strategies that you would use to help an athlete cope with their anxiety. Use theory and research to explain why you believe these strategies would be effective.

NOTE

1   The role and characteristics of the appraisal process in emotion generation has attracted considerable debate. See the Special Edition of *Emotion Review* (2012) http://www.tandfonline.come/loi/uasp20?open=25&repitiion=0#vol_25 for a contemporary discussion.

REFERENCES

Anshel, M. H. and Mansouri, H. (2005). Influences of perfectionism on motor performance, affect, and causal attributions in response to critical information feedback. *Journal of Sport Behavior, 28,* 99–124.

Baumeister, R. F. (1984). Choking under pressure: Self-consciousness and paradoxical effects of incentives on skilful performance. *Journal of Personality and Social Psychology*, *46*, 610–20.

Beedie, C. J., Terry, P. C. and Lane, A. M. (2005). Distinguishing mood from emotion. *Cognition and Emotion*, *19*, 847–78.

Berglas, S. and Jones, E. E. (1978). Drug choice as a self-handicapping strategy in response to noncontigent success. *Journal of Personality and Social Psychology*, *36*, 405–17.

Blascovich, J. and Tomaka, J. (1996). The biopsychosocial model of arousal regulation. *Advances in Experimental Social Psychology*, *28*, 1–51.

Brosschot, J. F., de Ruiter, C. and Kindt, M. (1999). Processing bias in anxious subjects and repressors, measured by emotional Stroop interference and attentional allocation. *Personality and Individual Differences*, *26*, 777–93.

Burton, D. (1988). Do anxious swimmers swim slower? Reexamining the elusive anxiety–performance relationship. *Journal of Sport & Exercise Psychology*, *10*, 45–61.

Burton, D. and Naylor, S. (1997). Is anxiety really facilitative? Reaction to the myth that cognitive anxiety always impairs sport performance. *Journal of Applied Sport Psychology*, *9*, 295–302.

Butt, J., Weinberg, R. and Horn, T. (2003). The intensity and directional interpretation of anxiety: Fluctuations throughout competition and relationship to performance. *The Sport Psychologist*, *17*, 35–54.

Cashmore, E. (2002). *Sport Psychology*. London: Routledge.

Cerin, E., Szabo, A., Hunt, N. and Williams, C. (2000). Temporal patterning of competitive emotions: A critical review. *Journal of Sports Sciences*, *18*, 605–26.

Collins, D., Jones, B., Fairweather, M., Doolan, S. and Priestley, N. (2001). Examining anxiety associated changes in movement patterns. *International Journal of Sport Psychology*, *31*, 223–42.

Cox, R. H., Martens, M. P. and Russell, W. D. (2003). Measuring anxiety in athletics: The revised competitive state anxiety inventory-2. *Journal of Sport and Exercise Psychology*, *25*, 519–33.

Craft, L. L., Magyar, M., Becker, B. J. and Feltz, D. L. (2003). The relationship between the Competitive State Anxiety Inventory-2 and sport performance: A meta-analysis. *Journal of Sport & Exercise Psychology*, *25*, 44–65.

Diener, E., Sadnvik, E. and Pavot, W. G. (1991). Happiness is the frequency, not the intensity of positive vs negative affect. In Strack, F., Argyle, M. and Schwarz, N. (eds) *Subjective Well Being: An interdisciplinary perspective*, pp. 119–39. Oxford, UK: Pergamon Press.

Dowthwaite, P. K. and Armstrong, M. R. (1984). An investigation into the anxiety levels of soccer players. *International Journal of Sport Psychology*, *15*, 149–59.

Duffy, E. (1962). *Activation and Behavior*. Oxford, UK: Wiley.

Eysenck, M. W. and Calvo, M. G. (1992). Anxiety and performance: The processing efficiency theory. *Cognition and Emotion*, *6*, 409–34.

Eysenck, M. W. and Derakshan, N. (2011). New perspectives in attentional control theory. *Personality and Individual Differences*, *50*, 955–60.

Eysenck, M. W., Derakshan, N., Santos, R. and Calvo, M. G. (2007). Anxiety and cognitive performance: Attentional control theory. *Emotion*, *7*, 336–53.

Flett, G. L. and Hewitt, P. L. (2005). The perils of perfectionism in sports and exercise. *Current Directions in Psychological Science*, *14*, 14–18.

Frederickson, B. L. (2001). The role of positive emotions in positive psychology. *American Psychologist*, *56*, 218–26.

Gilbert, D. T., Driver-Linn, E. and Wilson, T. D. (2002). The trouble with Vronsky: Impact bias in the forecasting of future affective states. In Barrett, L. F. and Salovey, P. (eds) *The Wisdom in Feeling: Psychological processes in emotional intelligence*, pp. 114–43. New York: Guilford Press.

Gould, D., Dieffenbach, K. and Moffett, A. (2002). Psychological characteristics and their development in Olympic champions. *Journal of Applied Sport Psychology*, *14*, 172–204.

Gould, D., Petchlikoff, L. and Weinberg, R. S. (1984). Antecedents of temporal changes in, and relationships between CSAI-2 subcomponents. *Journal of Sport Psychology*, *6*, 289–304.

Gross, J. J. (1998). Antecedent- and response-focussed emotion regulation: Divergent consequences for experience, expression, and physiology. *Journal of Personality and Social Psychology*, *74*, 224–37.

Gross, J. J. and Thompson, R. A. (2007). Emotion regulation: Conceptual foundations. In Gross, J. J. (ed.) *Handbook of Emotion Regulation*, pp. 3–24. London: Guilford Press.

Hammermeister, J. and Burton, D. (2001). Stress, appraisal, and coping revisited: Examining the antecedents of competitive state anxiety with endurance athletes. *The Sport Psychologist*, *15*, 66–90.

Hanin, Y. L. (2000). Individual zones of optimal functioning (IZOF) model: Emotion–performance relationships in sport. In Hanin, Y. L. (ed.) *Emotions in Sport*, pp. 65–89. Champaign, IL: Human Kinetics.

Hanton, S. and Jones, G. (1999). The effects of a multimodal intervention programme on performers: II. Training the butterflies to fly in formation. *The Sport Psychologist*, *13*, 22–41.

Hanton, S., Thomas, O. and Maynard, I. W. (2004). Competitive anxiety response in the week leading up to competition: The role of intensity, direction and frequency dimensions. *Psychology of Sport and Exercise*, *5*, 169–81.

Hardy, L. (1990). A catastrophe model of performance in sport. In Jones, J. G. and Hardy, L. (eds) *Stress and Performance in Sport*, pp. 81–106. Chichester, UK: John Wiley.

Hardy, L. (1996). A test of catastrophe models of anxiety and sports performance against multidimensional theory models using the method of dynamic differences. *Anxiety, Stress and Coping: An International Journal*, *9*, 69–86.

Hardy, L. and Parfitt, G. (1991). A catastrophe model of anxiety and performance. *British Journal of Psychology*, *82*, 163–78.

Hardy, L., Beattie, S. and Woodman, T. (2007). Anxiety induced performance catastrophes: Investigating effort required as an asymmetry factor. *British Journal of Psychology*, *98*, 15–31.

Hardy, L., Parfitt, G. and Pates, J. (1994). Performance catastrophes in sport: A test of the hysteresis hypothesis. *Journal of Sports Sciences*, *12*, 327–34.

Hardy, L., Woodman, T. and Carrington, S. (2004). Is self-confidence a bias factor in higher-order catastrophe models? An exploratory analysis. *Journal of Sport & Exercise Psychology*, *26*(3), 359–68.

Hatzigeorgiadis, A., Zourbanos, N., Mpoumpaki, S. and Theodorakis, Y. (2009). Mechanisms underlying the self-talk–performance relationship: The effects of motivational self-talk on self-confidence and anxiety. *Psychology of Sport and Exercise*, *10*(1), 186–92.

Jones, G. (1990). A cognitive perspective on the processes underlying the relationship between stress and performance in sport. In Jones, J. G. and Hardy, L. (eds) *Stress and Performance in Sport*, pp. 17–42. Chichester, UK: Wiley.

Jones, J. G. (1995). More than just a game: Research developments and issues in competitive state anxiety in sport. *British Journal of Psychology*, *86*, 449–78.

Jones, J. G. and Swain, A. B. J. (1992). Intensity and direction dimensions of competitive anxiety and relationships with competitiveness. *Perceptual and Motor Skills*, *74*, 467–72.

Jones, J. G., Swain, A. and Hardy, L. (1993). Intensity and direction dimensions of competitive state anxiety and relationships with performance. *Journal of Sports Sciences*, *11*, 525–32.

Jones, M. V. (2003). Controlling emotions in sport. *The Sport Psychologist*, *14*, 471–86.

Jones, M. V. and Uphill, M. (2004). Responses to the Competitive State Anxiety Inventory–2(d) by athletes in anxious and excited scenarios. *Psychology of Sport and Exercise*, *5*, 201–12.

Jones, M. V., Lane, A. M., Bray, S. R., Uphill, M. and Catlin, J. (2005). Development and validation of the sport emotion questionnaire. *Journal of Sport and Exercise Psychology*, *27*, 407–31.

Jones, M. V., Meijen, C., McCarthy, P. J. and Sheffield, D. (2009). A theory of challenge and threat states in athletes. *International Review of Sport and Exercise Psychology*, *2*, 161–80.

Kerr, J. H. (1997). *Motivation and Emotion in Sport: Reversal theory*. Hove, UK: Psychology Press.

Kuczka, K. K. and Treasure, D. C. (2004). Self-handicapping in competitive sport: Influence of the motivational climate, self-efficacy and perceived importance. *Psychology of Sport and Exercise*, *6*, 539–50.

Krane, V. (1994). The mental readiness form as a measure of competitive state anxiety. *The Sport Psychologist*, *8*, 189–202.

Lane, A., Beedie, C., Jones, M. V., Uphill, M. and Devonport, T. (2012). The BASES expert statement on emotion regulation in sport. *Journal of Sports Sciences*, *30*, 1189–95.

Lane, A. M., Sewell, D. F., Terry, P. C., Bartram, D. and Nesti, M. S. (1999). Confirmatory factor analysis of the Competitive State Anxiety Inventory–2. *Journal of Sports Sciences*, *17*, 505–12.

Lane, A. M. and Terry, P. C. (2000). The nature of mood: Development of a conceptual model with a focus on depression. *Journal of Applied Sport Psychology*, *12*, 16–33.

Lazarus, R. S. (1966). *Psychological Stress and the Coping Process*. New York: McGraw-Hill.

Lazarus, R. S. (1991). *Emotion and Adaptation*. Oxford, UK: OUP.

Lazarus, R. S. (1999). *Stress and Emotion: A new synthesis*. London: Free Association Books.

Lazarus, R. S. (2000). Cognitive–motivational–relational theory of emotion. In Hanin, Y. L. (ed.) *Emotions in Sport*, pp. 39–63. Champaign, IL: Human Kinetics.

Lundqvist, C., Kenttä, G. and Raglin, J. S. (2011). Directional anxiety responses in elite and sub-elite young athletes: Intensity of anxiety symptoms matters. *Scandinavian Journal of Science and Medicine in Sports*, *21*, 853–61.

Mahoney, M. J. and Avener, M. (1977). Psychology of the elite athlete: An exploratory study. *Cognitive Therapy and Research, 1*, 135–41.

Marsh, K. L., Johnston, L., Richardson, M. J. and Schmidt, R. C. (2009). Toward a radically embodied, embedded social psychology. *European Journal of Social Psychology, 39*, 1217–25.

Martens, R. (1977). *Sport Competition Anxiety Test.* Champaign, IL: Human Kinetics.

Martens, R., Vealey, R. S. and Burton, D. (1990). *Competitive Anxiety in Sport.* Champaign, IL: Human Kinetics.

Masters, R. S. W. (1992). Knowledge, nerves and know-how: The role of explicit versus implicit knowledge in the breakdown of a complex motor skill under pressure. *British Journal of Psychology, 83*, 343–58.

Maynard, I. W. and Cotton, C. J. (1993). An investigation of two stress-management techniques in a field setting. *The Sport Psychologist, 7*, 375–87.

Mellalieu, S. D., Hanton, S. and Jones, G. (2003). Emotional labelling and competitive anxiety in preparation and competition. *The Sport Psychologist, 17*, 157–74.

Mesagno, C. and Mullane-Grant, T. (2010). A comparison of different pre-performance routines as possible choking interventions. *Journal of Applied Sport Psychology, 22*(3), 343–60.

Miller, B. (1997). *Gold Minds: Psychology of winning in sport.* Marlborough, UK: Crowood Press.

Moore, L. J., Vine, S. J., Freeman, P. and Wilson, M. R. (2013). Quiet eye training promotes challenge appraisals and aids performance under elevated anxiety. *International Journal of Sport and Exercise Psychology, 11*, 169–83.

Moran, A. (2004). *Sport and Exercise Psychology: A critical introduction.* London: Routledge.

Murphy, S., Greenspan, M., Jowdy, D. and Tammen, V. (1989). Development of a brief rating instrument of competitive anxiety: Comparison with the CSAI-2. Paper presented at the meeting of the Association for the Advancement of Applied Sport Psychology. Seattle, WA, October.

Murray, N. M. and Janelle, C. M. (2003). Anxiety and performance: A visual search examination of processing efficiency theory. *Journal of Sport and Exercise Psychology, 25*, 171–87.

Noteboom, J. T., Barnholt, K. R. and Enoka, R. M. (2001a). Activation of the arousal response and impairment of performance increase with anxiety and stressor intensity. *Journal of Applied Physiology, 91*, 2093–101.

Noteboom, J. T., Fleshner, M. and Enoka, R. M. (2001b). Activation of the arousal response can impair performance on a simple motor task. *Journal of Applied Physiology, 91*, 821–31.

Ochsner, K. N. and Gross, J. J. (2007). The neural architecture of emotion regulation. In Gross, J. J. (ed.) *Handbook of Emotion Regulation*, pp. 87–109. London: Guilford Press.

Prapavessis, H. and Grove, J. R. (1998). Self-handicapping and self-esteem. *Journal of Applied Sport Psychology, 10*(2), 175–84.

Parfitt, C. G., Jones, J. G. and Hardy, L. (1990). Multidimensional anxiety and performance. In Jones, J. G. and Hardy, L. (eds) *Stress and Performance in Sport*, pp. 43–80.

Parfitt, G., Hardy, L. and Pates, J. (1995). Somatic anxiety and physiological arousal: Their effects upon a high anaerobic, low memory demand task. *International Journal of Sport Psychology, 26*, 196–213.

Parrott, W. G. (2001). *Emotions in Social Psychology*. Hove, UK: Psychology Press.

Prapavessis, H., Maddison, R. and Fletcher, R. (2005). Further examination of the factor integrity of the Sport Anxiety Scale. *Journal of Sport and Exercise Psychology*, 27, 253–60.

Roseman, I. J. (1991). Appraisal determinants of discrete emotions. *Cognition and Emotion*, 5, 161–200.

Simon, J. A. and Martens, R. (1977). SCAT as a predictor of A-states in varying competitive situations. In Landers, D. M. and Christina, R. W. (eds) *Psychology of Motor Behaviour and Sport* (Vol 2), pp. 146–56. Champaign, IL: Human Kinetics.

Skinner, N. and Brewer, N. (2004). Adaptive approaches to competition: Challenge appraisals and positive emotion. *Journal of Sport and Exercise Psychology*, 26, 283–305.

Smith, C. A. and Ellsworth, P. C. (1985). Patterns of cognitive appraisal in emotion. *Journal of Personality and Social Psychology*, 48, 813–38.

Smith, R. E., Smoll, F. L., Cumming, S. P. and Grossbard, J. R. (2006). Measurement of multidimensional sport performance anxiety in children and adults: The sport anxiety scale-2. *Journal of Sport and Exercise Psychology*, 28, 479–501.

Smith, R. E., Smoll, F. L. and Schutz, R. W. (1990). Measurements and correlates of sport-specific cognitive and somatic trait anxiety. *Anxiety Research*, 2, 263–80.

Spielberger, C. D. (1966). Theory and research on anxiety. In Spielberger, C. D. (ed.) *Anxiety and Behavior*, pp. 3–20. New York: Academic Press.

Stoeber, J., Otto, K., Pescheck, E., Becker, C. and Stoll, O. (2007). Perfectionism and competitive anxiety in athletes: Differentiating striving for perfection and negative reactions to imperfection. *Personality and Individual Differences*, 42, 959–69.

Swain, A. B. J. and Jones, J. G. (1993). Intensity and frequency dimensions of competitive state anxiety. *Journal of Sports Sciences*, 11, 533–42.

Tice, D. M. (1991). Esteem protection or enhancement? Self-handicapping motives and attributions differ by trait self-esteem. *Journal of Personality and Social Psychology*, 60, 711–25.

Turner, M. J., Jones, M. V., Sheffield, D. and Cross, S. L. (2012). Cardiovascular indices of challenge and threat states predict performance under stress in cognitive and motor tasks. *International Journal of Psychophysiology*, 86, 48–57.

Turner, M. J., Jones, M. V., Sheffield, D., Slater, M. J., Barker, J. B. and Bell, J. J. (2013). Who thrives under pressure? Predicting the performance of elite academy cricketers using the cardiovascular indicators of challenge and threat states. *Journal of Sport and Exercise Psychology*, 35, 387–97.

Uphill, M. A. and Dray, K. (2013). The thrill of defeat and the agony of victory: Towards an understanding and transformation of athletes' emotional experience. *Reflective Practice*, 14, 660–71.

Uphill, M. A. and Jones, M. V. (2004). Coping with emotions in sport: A cognitive motivational relational theory perspective. In Lavallee, D., Thatcher, J. and Jones, M. V. (eds) *Coping and Emotion in Sport*, pp. 75–89. New York: Nova Science.

Uphill, M. A. and Jones, M. V. (2007a). Antecedents of emotions in elite athletes: A cognitive motivational relational perspective. *Research Quarterly for Exercise and Sport*, 78, 79–89.

Uphill, M. A. and Jones, M. V. (2007b). 'When running is something you dread': A cognitive-behavioural intervention with a club runner. In Lane, A. M. (ed.) *Mood and Human*

Performance: Conceptual, measurement and applied issues, pp. 271–95. New York: Nova Science.

Uphill, M. A., McCarthy, P. J. and Jones, M. V. (2009). Getting a grip on emotion regulation in sport: Conceptual foundations and practical applications. In Hanton, S. and Mellalieu, S. (eds) *Advances in Applied Sport Psychology*, pp. 162–94. London: Routledge.

Vickers, J. N. (1992). Gaze control in putting. *Perception, 21*, 117–32.

Weinberger, D. A., Schwarz, G. E. and Davidson, R. J. (1979). Low-anxious, high-anxious and repressive coping styles: Psychometric patterns and behavioural and physiological responses to stress. *Journal of Abnormal Psychology, 88*, 369–80.

Williams, A. M., Vickers, J. and Rodrigues, S. (2002). The effects of anxiety on visual search, movement kinematics, and performance in table tennis: A test of Eysenck and Calvo's processing efficiency theory. *Journal of Sport & Exercise Psychology, 24*, 438–55.

Wilson, M. (2008). From processing efficiency to attentional control: A mechanistic account of the anxiety–performance relationship. *International Review of Sport and Exercise Psychology, 1*, 184–201.

Wilson, M., Chattington, M., Marple-Horvat, D. E. and Smith, N. C. (2007). A comparison of self-focus versus attentional explanations of choking. *Journal of Sport and Exercise Psychology, 29*, 439–56.

Wilson, M., Smith, N. C., Chattington, M., Ford, M. and Marple-Horvat, D. E. (2006). The role of effort in moderating the anxiety–performance relationship: Testing the prediction of processing efficiency theory in simulated rally driving. *Journal of Sports Sciences, 24*, 1223–33.

Wilson, M. R., Vine, S. J. and Wood, J. (2009). The influence of anxiety on visual attentional control in basketball free-throw shooting. *Journal of Sport and Exercise Psychology, 31*, 152–68.

Woodman, T. and Hardy, L. (2001). Stress and anxiety. In Singer, R. N., Hausenblas, H. A. and Janelle, C. M. (eds) *Handbook of Sport Psychology* (2nd edn), pp. 290–318. Chichester, UK: Wiley.

Woodman, T. and Hardy, L. (2003). The relative impact of cognitive anxiety and self-confidence upon sport performance: A meta analysis. *Journal of Sports Sciences, 21*, 443–57.

4 Physical activity and self-esteem

*Michael J. Duncan and
Emma L. J. Eyre*

CHAPTER SUMMARY

The way we feel about ourselves is important in every domain of life, and we can almost certainly identify when we feel on top of the world about something. In this case, we are enjoying the benefits of high self-esteem, a concept that has been branded a 'social vaccine' that can empower individuals and make them more productive and confident in their own abilities. The self is one of the most widely examined psychological constructs in contemporary society. Historically, both the academic literature and the popular media presuppose that every person has a sense of self, and the self is a social phenomenon (Cooley, 1902; Mead, 1934; James, 1950). Who we are is directly related to our relationships with others. Our interactions with friends, family and peers provide information that guides our understanding of how and why we think, feel and behave the way we do. This is often termed global self-worth, and researchers and scientists have often conceptualized self-worth as an evaluation or collection of different but related components that reflect how we feel about particular facets of our lives, such as academic self-esteem, social self-esteem and body esteem (Sonstroem, 1998).

Indeed, self-esteem is often seen to be one of the most important indicators of psychological well-being, and, in many instances, enhanced self-esteem resulting from physical activity is one of the main benefits put forward by those individuals or agencies promoting regular exercise or within physical education in schools. Subsequently, exercise scientists have taken an interest in the role that physical activity and exercise can play in enhancing the self. Involvement in regular physical activity may improve our skills, knowledge, fitness and health and contribute to our social lives, all of which are linked to enhanced self-perception (Fox, 1997). This, in turn, may transfer to more favourable views about the self, leading to an improved sense of well-being.

Exercise psychologists should have a particular interest in the role that physical activity plays in self-esteem. This can then be transferred to practice, where the well-being of the individuals we work with can be enhanced. This topic forms the basis of this chapter. The aims of this chapter are threefold: the first is to describe the relationships between physical activity and self-esteem reported in the literature. A second aim is to evaluate the conceptual exercise–self-esteem model of Sonstroem and Morgan (1989) and evidence that has examined this model. The third aim of the chapter is to develop an understanding of the methods available to assess self-esteem in relation to physical activity.

LEARNING OUTCOMES

When you have studied this chapter, you should be able to:

1 Evaluate relationships between physical activity and self-esteem reported in the literature and be aware of methodological factors influencing this relationship
2 Evaluate the conceptual exercise–self-esteem model of Sonstroem and Morgan (1989) and evidence that has examined this model
3 Understand and evaluate the methods available to assess self-esteem in relation to physical activity
4 Consider examples of how self-esteem operates in practice across the lifespan

FOCUS 4.1

Physical activity and self-esteem: Starting point

- Self-esteem influences psychological well-being.
- Physical activity influences physical self-perceptions.
- Physical self-perceptions shape physical self-esteem.
- Physical activity can enhance self-esteem.

ACTIVITY 4.1

- Think about a physical activity, exercise or related situation that you have recently found yourself in. What made you feel that you were able to complete your chosen physical activity? Did you feel positive about what you were doing? Did you feel that you were able to complete the activity as well as anyone else could? Did you feel positive about your experience, once it had been completed?
- Write down all the factors that you think contribute to the psychological changes that are associated with regular participation in physical activity.
- Examine Fox's physical self-perception model, presented in Figure 4.1, and compare your list with this model. I suspect at least some of the factors you have noted down could fit in the subdomains within this model.
- Read Fox's (2000) description of how these subdomains contribute to the development of self-esteem through physical activity and compare this with the list of factors that made you feel that you could complete your chosen physical activity example.

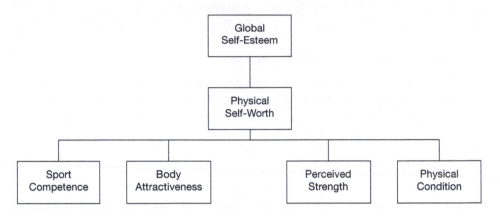

FIGURE 4.1 Physical self-perception model

Source: Fox, 2000. Reprinted with permission

LEARNING OUTCOME 1

Evaluate the relationships between physical activity and self-esteem reported in the literature and be aware of methodological factors that influence this relationship

Physical activity and self-esteem: The evidence

'Self-esteem refers to the value placed on aspects of the self, such as academic and social domains' (Biddle and Mutrie, 2007, p. 181). Although a range of studies have examined the relationship between physical activity and self-esteem, it is only recently that methodological factors in the measurement of self-esteem have been addressed. In most cases, exercise psychologists have employed a global measure of self-esteem. Global self-esteem comprises differentiations of the self, including physical, social and academic self-perceptions. In the exercise and physical-activity arena, physical self-perceptions are underpinned by subdomains best illustrated by Fox's physical self-perception model (see Figure 4.1). Fox and Corbin (1989) suggested that the subdomains of sport competence, body attractiveness, perceived strength and physical condition positively influence our feelings of physical self-worth. Physical self-worth is directly associated with global self-esteem. Therefore, if we are interested in the role that physical activity plays in shaping self-esteem, it is important to be aware of the relationship between physical activity and our physical self-perceptions, as it is these that influence our global self-esteem.

Meta-analyses

A plethora of research studies and meta-analytic studies have reported that physical activity can enhance self-esteem or physical self-worth. However, the magnitude of any enhancement in self-esteem still remains to be fully elucidated. Meta-analytical results reported by Spence *et al.* (2005) found that physical activity positively enhanced global self-esteem, although the overall effect size (0.23) showed only a small effect for physical activity in adult populations. Interestingly, the effect of exercise on self-esteem did not differ as a result of exercise programme (i.e. intensity, frequency, duration or mode). Fitness levels of participants did not influence the effect of exercise on self-esteem, but larger effect sizes were documented for lifestyle programmes that incorporated nutritional advice alongside exercise. Spence *et al.* concluded that exercise enhances self-esteem in adults, but that this effect is smaller than previously thought. However, it should be noted that Spence *et al.* included both studies that were published and unpublished studies.

The meta-analysis results of Spence *et al.* contrast to an earlier meta-analysis conducted by McDonald and Hodgdon (1991) that examined the effect of aerobic training on self-concept (this included measures of self-esteem and body image). They reported an effect size of 0.56 and concluded that fitness training is associated with improvements in ratings of the 'self'. However, the breadth of measures employed by studies included in this meta-analysis may cloud the true effect of exercise on global self-esteem. Additionally, Gruber (1986) reported an effect size of 0.41 for self-esteem, based on a meta-analysis of twenty-seven studies of play and physical-education programmes in children.

RESEARCH METHODS 4.1

Academic research published in journals is judged by a process called 'peer review'. Peer review involves other academics reviewing the work and offering critical comments. These are normally general comments, which can relate to the area of investigation and design of the research, and specific comments, which form a detailed and sometimes line-by-line commentary on issues related to the paper. A journal editor usually uses three reviewers, and each one recommends whether the work is good enough and interesting enough to be published. The review is blind, and so the reviewers do not know the authors, and the authors do not know the reviewers' names. This, of course, allows reviewers to openly criticize.

Journal editors want to publish articles that other academics will read and cite in their work. Reviewers need to be independent of the authors and so will not be colleagues. Reviews can be lengthy, with some reviews being over 1,000 words and the three reviewers writing 3,000 words, and so the review can nearly be as long as the article (around 6,000 words). An article will typically be returned to the author to make changes, and the author will address these changes and then resubmit the revised article. The revisions and comments in response to the reviewers are then examined, and a second decision is made. This process continues until the article is accepted or rejected. In short, peer review is a rigorous process, and it is difficult to publish.

Students should ask their lecturers for experiences of peer review. Most academics have had their papers criticized heavily. The review process can be fierce, and even the most extensively published researcher has been 'burned' in some way.

Randomized controlled trials

Fox (2000) reviewed thirty-six randomized control trials (RCTs) completed since 1970 that examined the efficacy of physical activity to promote self-esteem. Seventy-six per cent of all RCTs reported positive changes in physical self-perceptions or self-esteem as a result of physical activity. Fox (2000) concluded that exercise can be used to promote physical self-perceptions/self-esteem, but that the mechanisms that underpin this are not clear. Subsequently, Ekeland *et al.* (2004) asked the question: Can exercise improve self-esteem in children and young people? They completed a systematic review of twenty-three RCTs that examined the physical-activity–self-esteem relationship in children. Their review concluded that exercise has positive short-term effects on self-esteem in children, and that exercise and physical activity are important components to improve self-esteem in children. However, they stressed caution when examining this issue in younger populations, as different types of intervention have been used in studies of this nature. For example, some studies used physical activity only, some physical activity plus skills training and counselling, and some used high-intensity exercise and strength training. Furthermore, although most of the studies included in their review used valid and reliable measures of self-esteem, there was a high risk of bias in most of the studies. Further, no study had included follow-up data to demonstrate the extent to which the effects of programmes were maintained in the longer term. Despite this, because physical activity has many positive effects on physical and psychological health, it remains as an important means to promote self-esteem. Well-designed RCTs with follow-up data are, however, needed to demonstrate the extent to which the reported short-term increases in self-esteem, as a result of physical activity, are maintained over time.

Overall, the research evidence related to the relationship between physical activity and self-esteem indicates that, for both adults and children, physical activity and exercise are associated with higher self-esteem. However, the effect sizes reported in studies on this topic are generally small to moderate, owing to poor research study design or lack of consistency in the measures used to assess self-esteem across studies. Furthermore, there is still a need for research to clarify the mechanisms that facilitate the association between physical activity and self-esteem.

ACTIVITY 4.2

Randomized controlled trials

RCTs have been referred to as the 'gold standard' in scientific research (Sibbald and Roland, 1998). This is particularly the case for intervention-type research. In an RCT, participants are randomly allocated to an experimental group or a control group, after recruitment, but before any intervention or treatment is initiated. Once the whole participant group has been allocated into one of these two groups, the intervention group receives a 'treatment' of some form (e.g. a group-based exercise intervention), while the control group does not. Measures (e.g. self-esteem, weight status) are taken before and after the intervention for both groups and then compared.

- Consider this type of design and reflect to yourself why this might be effective in research examining the effect of physical activity or exercise on self-esteem.

The RCT design is robust in determining whether a given treatment (e.g. an exercise intervention) is effective, particularly in studies of drug-based treatments (Sibbald and Roland, 1998). Results from an RCT also have high internal validity: that is, we can have confidence in the causal relationship between the treatment (e.g. exercise) and the outcome (e.g. self-esteem).

Despite this, there are drawbacks to using an RCT design, as the process of randomizing a group of participants may produce systematic between-group differences in the overall sample. For example, it may be that one group (intervention or control) has higher baseline self-esteem scores than the other at the outset. This might then impact on any change in self-esteem we would be likely to see as the result of an exercise-based intervention. Also, within RCT designs, both the intervention and control groups (and, to some extent, the researcher) cannot be blinded to the intervention being delivered (or not being delivered). As a consequence, it is difficult to rule out placebo effects in human psychological research. An intervention group participant may think, 'I am part of an experimental intervention examining how exercise influences self-esteem. I'm in the exercise group so surely my self-esteem will go up'. Likewise, a control group participant may come to the conclusion that, 'I am in the control group, so there is no possibility my self-esteem will change'.

Considering the above issues is important when evaluating the impact and reach of particular scientific studies that examine the effect of exercise on psychological constructs, as evaluating human participants in an RCT is often more difficult than examining the impact of a drug treatment on a medical condition.

LEARNING OUTCOME 2

Evaluate the conceptual exercise–self-esteem model of Sonstroem and Morgan (1989) and evidence that has examined this model

Numerous researchers have examined behavioural influences on self-esteem, and physical activity has been considered to be an important component in self-evaluations (Ekeland *et al.*, 2004; McAuley *et al.*, 2005; Spence *et al.*, 2005; Moore *et al.*, 2012). Reviews of the literature have concluded that testing the relationship between physical activity and self-esteem has been hindered by two issues: (1) the measurement of self-esteem and (2) a lack of clarity regarding conceptual models of the physical activity–self-esteem relationship. The second part of this chapter will consider one conceptual model of the exercise/physical activity–self-esteem relationship, and subsequent modification of it, that has shown promise in explaining the interaction between these two variables.

Approaches to the physical activity–self-esteem relationship

Biddle and Mutrie (2007) summarized the two main approaches to examining the relationship between physical activity and self-esteem. The first approach put forward by Sonstroem (1997), termed the 'motivational approach' or 'personal development hypothesis', posits that self-esteem is a determinant of physical activity. That is, individuals high in self-esteem are more likely to engage in physical-activity behaviours as this is an area where their self-worth can be enhanced.

The second approach, the 'skill development hypothesis' (Sonstroem, 1997), suggests that self-esteem is modified through experience, and that self-esteem enhancement (or reduction) is a product of our experiences in physical activity or exercise. Biddle and Mutrie (2007) highlight that these two approaches are not mutually exclusive, and that initial participation in physical activity may be externally motivated but lead to enhanced self-esteem/self-worth, which, in turn, becomes a motivator for any subsequent physical activity.

The Sonstroem and Morgan exercise–self-esteem model

In 1989, Sonstroem and Morgan proposed a model to explain how the effects of physical activity generalize to global self-esteem. This model (See Figure 4.2) was based on the dimensions of perceived physical competence and perceived physical acceptance, as these elements were postulated to be the two foundations of global self-esteem. The base of this model consists of a self-efficacy statement specific to the physical. This

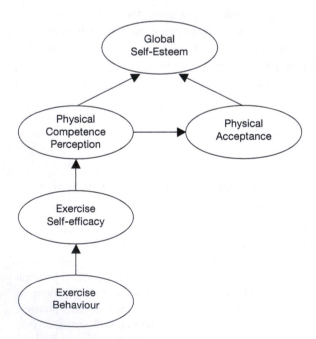

FIGURE 4.2 The exercise and self-esteem model

Source: Sonstroem and Morgan, 1989. Reprinted with permission

---

ACTIVITY 4.3

- Think about the exercise and self-esteem model of Sonstroem and Morgan (1989) and write down how you think the two elements of physical competence perception and physical acceptance influence global self-esteem.
- Read Levy and Ebbeck (2005) and compare your notes with their assertions regarding the Sonstroem and Morgan model. How do your thoughts compare with their comments regarding this self-esteem model? In particular, did your considerations of the importance of physical acceptance match theirs?

---

provides the link between the physical and how the physical is represented within the mind of an individual. Self-efficacy describes an expectation that, at a given moment, an individual can successfully perform a particular task (Bandura, 1986). In the case of the exercise–self-esteem model, self-efficacies are related to a person's perceived physical competence: that is, an individual's evaluation of their overall level of ability. The Sonstroem and Morgan (1989) model hypothesizes that increases in physical self-efficacy lead to increases in perceived physical competence, which then lead to increases in global self-esteem (Sonstroem, 1997). This model has also been termed the skill development hypothesis.

Physical activity and self-esteem: The importance of physical acceptance

Although the Sonstroem and Morgan model suggests that exercise behaviour is associated with self-esteem through perception of self-efficacy, physical competence and physical acceptance, the majority of research employing this model has primarily examined the role of physical competence perceptions in global self-esteem. Over-whelmingly, individuals who perceive that they are more competent in the physical domain report higher self-esteem (Sonstroem et al., 1992, 1993, 1994; Van de Vliet et al., 2002). However, although the role of physical competence in mediating self-esteem appears to have been well researched, the influence of physical acceptance on self-esteem has been less well examined. As physical acceptance is purported to mediate the relationship between physical competence perceptions and global self-esteem (see Figure 4.2), this may be a particularly important area for physical-activity practitioners to study, if they are to fully understand the physical activity–self-esteem relationship. Despite this, the relationship between measures of body image and body satisfaction (often used as a proxy for physical acceptance) and global self-esteem has been supported, particularly in females (Furnham et al., 2002; Mendelson et al., 2002; Stice, 2002; Palladino-Green and Pritchard, 2003). These relationships have also been noted in children. For example, Mendelson and White (1982) found body esteem to be significantly related to self-esteem in both normal and obese children. These findings have also been supported by Cohane and Pope (2001), Guinn et al. (1997) and Haugen et al. (2011). The significant relationship between self-esteem and body image may be important, as satisfaction with our body may be an important part of our global view of ourselves.

Levy and Ebbeck (2005) examined the importance of physical acceptance in mediating the physical competence perception–global self-esteem relationship in adult women who completed measures of exercise behaviour, exercise self-efficacy, perceptions of physical competence, perceptions of physical acceptance and global self-esteem. When they used multiple regression analysis, their model components explained 22 per cent of the variability in global self-esteem. More significantly, perceptions of physical acceptance made a unique contribution to the model and explained 12.6 per cent of the variability in global self-esteem. Furthermore, Levy and Ebbeck (2005) reported that, when global self-esteem was regressed on both perceptions of physical acceptance and exercise self-efficacy, the effect of self-efficacy became non-significant, suggesting perfect mediation. They concluded that, for females, physical acceptance plays a vital role in the physical self-perception and self-esteem relationship. Physical acceptance made the largest and only significant contribution to global self-esteem in their study. Haugen et al. (2011) more recently demonstrated that increased levels of physical activity enhanced adolescents' global self-worth and self-esteem by increasing their perceptions of physical competence and physical appearance. However, they also highlighted that physical appearance had a stronger effect on self-esteem in females. As physical appearance is less changeable than physical competence, exercise programmes focused on enhancing motor skills and physical competency might be better placed to enhance self-esteem in this population. Indeed, research suggests that children and adolescents suffer from considerable body dissatisfaction (and thus lower physical acceptance), and that body dissatisfaction is related to physical-activity behaviour (Duncan et al., 2006). Future research seeking to understand how physical competence, physical acceptance, physical activity and self-esteem interact in children and young people might, therefore, be useful in developing physical-activity intervention that will have a longer-lasting positive impact on self-worth.

More recently, we have examined the concept of body esteem in children (Duncan et al., 2013) in relation to weight status. Body esteem is the physical component of self-esteem and often considered synonymous with physical acceptance. In this work, we were interested in the degree to which body esteem is related to children's weight status and the extent to which this changed depending on the measure of weight status used. The most widely used measure of overweight and obesity, body mass index (BMI), has been associated with various measures of body image and self-esteem in children. However, BMI provides a measure of body mass at a given height, and, as such, when we are considering physical acceptance and body esteem, children with high BMI may have greater body fatness but also may be more muscular. In the case of fatness, literature would suggest this would be associated with lower esteem and muscularity would be associated with higher esteem.

In our work, we employed an alternative measure, named inverted body mass index (iBMI), which purports to assess muscularity rather than fatness. We also assessed body esteem in a sample of 756 children (mean age ± SD was 11.4 ± 1.64 years). Our results suggested that boys and girls differed in the associations between body esteem and iBMI, but that, in both cases, the associations were curvilinear. This is contrary to studies with BMI, which have shown a linear relationship. The peak of this association was within a weight status range considered normal for boys (i.e. highest body esteem was found in children who were normal weight). However, for girls, body esteem was highest at a weight status value associated with extreme leanness. Such data are important in developing effective interventions to enhance children's body esteem and perceptions of physical acceptance, as they suggest that different strategies may be needed for boys and girls, and that sociocultural norms related to the 'ideal' body (i.e. lean) may reflect in girls' body esteem scores. Such data are also worrying as they suggest that girls' body esteem is highest when their weight status is at a level considered a health risk owing to their being underweight.

Mediation

Let's take a moment to consider what is meant by the term mediation, which is used frequently in psychology. We will examine this through an example relevant to this chapter. When we say, 'As physical acceptance is purported to mediate the relationship between physical competence perceptions and global self-esteem', what does mediate mean?

Traditionally, psychologists have examined the effect of an independent variable (e.g. exercise) and an outcome or dependant variable (e.g. self-esteem). This enables the psychologist to determine whether exercise influences self-esteem. It doesn't help us understand how exercise influences self-esteem. In these cases, mediation may help. Mediation is defined as a relation such that an independent variable causes a mediating variable, which then causes a dependant variable (MacKinnon and Leucken, 2008). So, in the example above (Figure 4.2), physical competence (my evaluation of my physical ability) influences physical acceptance (my evaluation of how I look in relation to others), and this in turn influences global self-esteem. Put simply, if my perceptions of physical competence increase, this will lead to increases in my perception of my physical self, which will then lead to increased self-esteem. Therefore, identifying mediating variables can be extremely helpful to researchers and practitioners alike, as following the path of mediation helps identify how to raise self-esteem via exercise.

A modified exercise–self-esteem model

The development of Fox's physical self-perception model and, later, the Physical Self-Perception Profile (PSPP) by Fox and Corbin (1989), to be discussed later in this chapter, led to a reconceptualization of the original Sonstroem and Morgan (1989) exercise–self-esteem model. This revised model, or EXSEM as it is currently termed, combined the original Sonstroem and Morgan (1989) model with Fox's physical self-perception model (see Figure 4.3). Within the revised model, changes in physical activity and associated physical parameters (e.g. fitness, weight) that are brought about by exercise or physical activity are proposed to have indirect effects on changes in global self-esteem. Changes in self-efficacy as a result of changes in physical activity are proposed to influence subdomain measures of physical esteem, notably self-perceptions of physical conditioning, body attractiveness, sport competence and strength. These changes are theorized to be associated with changes in physical self-worth, which then influences global self-esteem.

The EXSEM has been supported by a number of empirical studies, although the majority of these studies have been cross-sectional in nature. The validity of this model expansion was examined by Sonstroem et al. (1994), who assessed 214 females who had enrolled on an aerobic dance programme. Participants completed the global self-worth scale (to assess self-esteem), the PSPPs (to assess the physical self-perceptions in

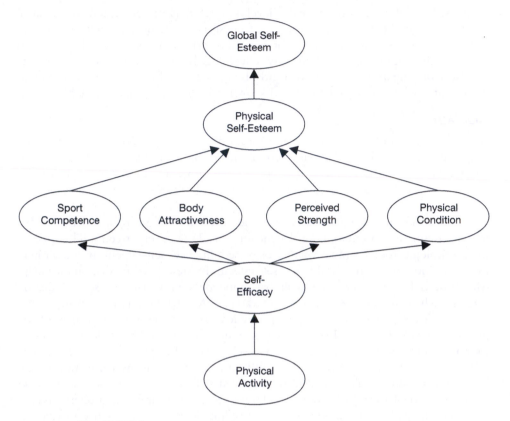

FIGURE 4.3 The EXSEM

Source: Adapted, with permission, from Sonstroem *et al.*, 1994

Fox's model) and self-efficacy measures to assess confidence to do exercises such as jogging, sit-ups and dance.

The data were analysed using regression. Standardized regression coefficients were used to explain the amount of variance within the model. The overall model was able to explain 32.8 per cent of global self-esteem variance and 88.6 per cent of the variance in physical self-worth scores. Sonstroem *et al.* (1994) therefore concluded that the EXSEM was a valid model of the association between exercise and self-esteem.

Several studies have been published that supported the utility of the EXSEM. These have supported the EXSEM in a range of populations and both cross-sectional and longitudinal study designs. For example, McAuley *et al.* (2000) reported strong support for the EXSEM over a 6-month exercise intervention in older adults. These data have also been supported by research based on a 6-month randomized control study of t'ai-chi in older adults by Li *et al.* (2002). However, these studies have also postulated that physical activity and self-efficacy both directly influence the subdomain levels of self-esteem (as opposed to physical activity indirectly influencing self-esteem through its effect on self-efficacy).

In a bid to examine this issue more closely, McAuley *et al.* (2005) reported longitudinal data from recent research on the relationships between physical activity, self-efficacy and self-esteem in older adults. They examined a group of 174 older adults (aged 60–75 years of age) at 1 and 5 years after entry into a structured physical-activity/exercise programme. Physical activity was determined using a population-specific, self-report questionnaire, global self-esteem was assessed using the Rosenberg self-esteem scale (Rosenberg, 1965), and the PSPP (Fox and Corbin, 1989) was used to assess the subdomain levels of the EXSEM (both measures will be discussed in greater depth later on in this chapter). Using covariance modelling, they found consistent relationships between the subdomain levels of self-esteem and physical activity and the subdomain levels of self-esteem and global self-esteem. These were also consistent over the 4-year period of measurement. Furthermore, those adults reporting greater reductions in physical activity also reported greater reductions in subdomain levels of self-esteem and global self-esteem. The authors also supported previous assertions that physical activity and self-efficacy both directly influenced the subdomain levels of self-esteem.

This study represents one of the more robust tests of the EXSEM in the literature. Based on its longitudinal data, 69 per cent of the variance in physical self-worth was accounted for, as was 51 per cent of the variance in global self-esteem. This is important as, if the researcher is interested in the relation between physical activity and self-esteem, the focus should be on physical self-worth (i.e. physical self-esteem), rather than global measures. Certainly, in this case, the EXSEM appears to do a good job of accounting for the variance in physical self-esteem, but also underlines how important physical activity and physical self-worth may be in contributing towards an individual's global self-esteem. Despite this, the study by McAuley et al. (2005) comprised participants from a predominantly white population, and the research design used in their study (i.e. a two-point time model) precludes any inference of causality in the physical activity–self-esteem relationship. Further research is clearly needed to address these issues.

LEARNING OUTCOME 3

Understand and evaluate the methods available to assess self-esteem in relation to physical activity

There are a variety of methods available to assess self-esteem. The aim of this section is to consider some of the issues related to the assessment of self-esteem in physical-activity research. One of the main questions the researcher or practitioner needs to begin with is whether global self-esteem is the factor that is of interest, or whether they wish to focus on the subdomains of the physical self that are predictive of global self-esteem.

Should we measure self-esteem or physical self-perceptions?

Often researchers, have employed a global measure of self-esteem such as the Rosenberg self-esteem scale (see Table 4.1). This measure has shown test–retest reliability and shows relationships with scales that assess self-perceptions that are consistent with theory, and therefore shows an adequate degree of concurrent validity (Hagborg, 1993; Robins et al., 2001). However, self-esteem, when seen as a single or

ACTIVITY 4.4

Consider how you feel generally about yourself, fill in the Rosenberg self-esteem scale presented in Table 4.1 as directed and calculate your self-esteem score. The higher the score, the higher the self-esteem. Once finished, consider the questionnaire you have just completed.

The Rosenberg self-esteem scale is a well-used measure of global self-esteem. Would you consider this to be a good measure of self-esteem that could be used in the activity domain? If not, why not?

By considering this issue you will start to learn more about the measurement of self-esteem and issues surrounding the conceptualization of self-esteem.

Table 4.1 has a list of statements dealing with your general feelings about yourself. Please read each one carefully. If you strongly agree with a statement, circle SA. If you agree with the statement, circle A. If you disagree, circle D. If you strongly disagree, circle SD.

TABLE 4.1 The Rosenberg self-esteem scale

1 On the whole, I am satisfied with myself	SA	A	D	SD
2 At times, I think I am no good at all	SA	A	D	SD
3 I feel that I have a number of good qualities	SA	A	D	SD
4 I am able to do things as well as most other people	SA	A	D	SD
5 I feel I do not have much to be proud of	SA	A	D	SD
6 I certainly feel useless at times	SA	A	D	SD
7 I feel that I'm a person of worth, at least on an equal plane with others	SA	A	D	SD
8 I wish I could have more respect for myself	SA	A	D	SD
9 All in all, I am more inclined to feel that I am a failure	SA	A	D	SD
10 I take a positive attitude towards myself	SA	A	D	SD

Scoring: SA = 3, A = 2, D = 1, SD = 0. Items 2, 5, 6, 8 and 9 are reversed scored. Sum the scores for the 10 items. The higher the score, the higher the self-esteem
Source: Rosenberg, 1989.

global construct, will influence self-perceptions from a number of domains – for example, from areas of performance such as academic self-esteem, sport self-esteem, physical self-esteem and social self-esteem. Within the area of physical activity and exercise, physical self-perceptions appear to be have a strong influence on an individual's global self-esteem. As a result, the the Rosenberg self-esteem scale is limited, because it only provides a measure of global self-esteem. It is proposed that, to truly understand the relationship between physical activity and self-esteem, it is important to examine the self-perceptions that underpin self-worth and, subsequently, self-esteem. Fox's physical self-perception model (see Figure 4.1) offers an attempt to explain how global self-esteem is influenced by the physical self and has subsequently led to the development of psychometric measures of physical self-worth and the four subdomains within this construct.

Measurement of physical self-perceptions

Considerable research has documented a number of different measures of physical self-perception and physical self-concept. These include the PSPP (Fox and Corbin, 1989) and the physical self-description questionnaire (Marsh *et al.*, 1994). Of these questionnaires, the PSPP has probably been the most widely used method to assess physical self-perceptions and self-esteem. Based on Harter's (1985) work on self-concept, the PSPP examines physical self-worth and the four subdomains of sport competence, body attractiveness, perceived strength and physical condition, which correspond to those outlined in Fox's model. Research has also demonstrated the validity and reliability of the PSPP in young people, in older adults, cross-culturally and in the context of exercise and physical-activity participation (Fox and Corbin, 1989; McAuley *et al.*, 2000, 2005; Welk and Eklund, 2005). A version of the PSPP, the children and youth physical self-perception profile (Whitehead, 1995; Eklund *et al.*, 1997) has been validated for use in 8–12-year-old children, with scores on this measure also being related to physical activity, aerobic fitness and body fatness in this group (Welk and Eklund, 2005).

The use of the PSPP allows exercise psychologists to examine how physical activity influences different aspects of our self-perceptions and, in turn, how these might influence self-esteem. For example, participation in physical activity may enhance an individual's feelings of body attractiveness and physical condition. This change may lead to enhancement of physical self-worth and increases in self-esteem. The PSPP was originally validated with American college students (Fox and Corbin, 1989), but subsequent research has demonstrated its utility and validity in older and younger people and cross-culturally (Welk and Eklund, 2005). A range of studies have measured physical self-perceptions related to sport and exercise participation (McAuley *et al.*, 2000, 2005), and the PSPP is a reliable and valid measure of the construct it purports to examine.

APPLYING THE SCIENCE 4.1

In the 1960s and 1970s, scientists and researchers such as Rosenberg understood that self-esteem was an important construct and had shown that self-esteem was associated with a variety of measures of health and well-being. However, there was subsequent recognition that self-esteem was not one-dimensional, and different facets of human behaviour impacted on self-esteem in different ways. Subsequent research by Fox and Corbin (1989) evidenced that self-esteem was a multidimensional construct, and from this developed the PSPP. The PSPP provides the most applied measure of self-esteem that can be used for both large-scale research on self-esteem and individual monitoring of self-esteem over time.

Applied case study 1: Physical self-esteem in older adults (Moore et al., 2012)

There is a great deal of evidence supporting the relationship between physical activity, self-efficacy for physical activity, physical self-perception and global self-esteem in children (Strauss *et al.*, 2001; Crews *et al.*, 2004) and adults (McAuley *et al.*, 2000, 2005; Li *et al.*, 2002). Understanding more about the beliefs individuals hold about themselves generally and physically and about their confidence to perform specific tasks is useful for the promotion and maintenance of physical activity (Fox, 2000). The EXSEM (Sonstroem and Morgan, 1989) examines the hierarchy relationship between physical activity, self-efficacy for physical activity, physical self-perceptions and global self-esteem. The modified EXSEM (Sonstroem *et al.*, 1994) provides a full, mediated model proposing that physical activity was fully mediated by self-efficacy for physical activity, and that self-efficacy for physical activity on physical self-worth is mediated by subdomains of physical self-worth. However, Moore *et al.* (2012) identified that older adults are an understudied population, and that subdomains for physical self-worth (physical condition, physical strength, attractive body and sport competence) are likely to be different from those of younger populations. For instance, in older adults, their low levels of flexibility and coordination and increased risk of chronic diseases may present a more complex association, mediation or effect than the EXSEMs suggest. For these reasons, Moore *et al.* (2012) sought to examine the modified EXSEM with a wider range of subdomains for physical self-perception, to establish if their revised model could provide a better explanation across a range of variables for physical activity, self-esteem and self-esteem for physical activity in older adults. Their findings suggest that the EXSEM does validly represent the relationship between physical activity and self-perception in older adults. However, other subdomains are important for self-esteem in older adults, such as health and attractiveness. Moore *et al.* (2012) offered a revised model that proposed that physical activity and self-efficacy to do physical activity have independent effects on subdomains of physical self-worth, and that these subdomains fully mediate the impact of physical activity and self-efficacy to do physical activity on physical self-worth and, consecutively, general self-esteem. The authors propose the revised model explains more variance than the original EXSEM (55 per cent vs 51 per cent), with the added pathways of health and attractiveness to self-esteem.

Applied case study 2: Age and gender effects on global self-esteem and physical self-perceptions in adolescents

One study that provides a good example of the utility of assessing physical self-perceptions is one conducted by Maiano *et al.* (2004). Maiano *et al.* cited a lack of data on the development of global self-esteem and physical self-perceptions in adolescents as the impetus to investigate these factors in a group of 605 French adolescents (aged 11–16 years), using an adapted language version of the PSPP. Their data reinforce the validity of Fox's hierarchical model of self-esteem in the physical domain, as physical self-worth strongly related to global self-esteem, and the four subdomains in this model showed a stronger relationship with physical self-worth than global self-esteem. They also found that self-esteem increased in both boys and girls as age

ACTIVITY 4.5

Think about the EXSEM

1 Consider the applied case study of Moore *et al.* (2012) and note down what the research paper tells the reader about the EXSEM (1994; Figure 4.3) and its ability to explain self-esteem in older adults.

2 In Moore *et al.*'s (2012) revised model, what additional physical subdomains are added to provide increased understanding about self-esteem in older adults? How much more is explained by adding these components?

3 Consider the assessment of physical activity used by Moore *et al.* (2012). Does this provide the most accurate assessment of physical activity, and, if so, why?

I suspect your notes may highlight that the work from Moore *et al.* (2012) supports the EXSEM (1994) in replicating the relationship among physical self-perceptions in older adults. Specifically, you probably noted that the paper presents a revised EXSEM in older adults, which is proposed to explain more variance in self-esteem (55 per cent) by the addition of the subdomains of health and attractiveness to self-esteem. In response to question 3, you may have acknowledged that physical and general self-esteem are not lower in older adults, despite lower scores for physical-activity subdomains when compared with adolescents.

This highlights the need for further quality methodological designs in order to generalize findings on how reduced physical ability in older adults is integrated into self-concept, to establish if self-esteem might be maintained in older populations, even though they have lower perceptions of their physical ability.

Finally, you will have highlighted how, despite a valid assessment measure of physical activity, self-report measures have inherent bias in them, and that objective measures are the most accurate assessment of physical activity in free living, providing objective information on frequency, intensity and time in most measures. When combined with diaries, these can provide fruitful information.

increased. Boys in this study reported higher scores in global self-esteem and physical self-perceptions compared with girls. Although the findings of this study are not surprising, what is of interest to practitioners, and in the context of this chapter, is the breakdown of physical self-perception scores by subdomain. This also illustrates the utility of PSPP in providing further information regarding the nature of self–esteem and physical self-perceptions. Maiano *et al.* (2004) reported that there was a general, linear increase in scores on the body attractiveness subscale of the PSPP from children aged 12–15. However, scores on the physical condition and sport competence subscales were variable. Finally, scores on the physical strength subscale were stable until the age of 14 years, when they began to rise in a linear fashion. Maiano *et al.* (2004) linked these results to physical education practice in French secondary schools.

ACTIVITY 4.6

- Think about the case study above and consider how the findings of Maiano *et al.* (2004) might be explained. Can you explain any reasons why subscale scores might differ according to age?
- Did your explanations cover areas such as puberty, primary–secondary school transition and physical-education experiences of the adolescents in this study?

Maiano *et al.* (2004) suggested that the increases in body attractiveness and physical strength subscales that occurred with age in their study may have been influenced, at least in part, by the process of puberty.

For both genders, the physical changes associated with puberty may have led to changes in their physical self-perceptions related to the attractiveness of their bodies; the increase in the physical-strength subscale may also have been linked to puberty-related physical changes, particularly in boys, and would thus explain the offset in linear age-related increase in this subscale, as boys tend to undergo puberty slightly later than females.

Finally, Maiano *et al.* (2004) suggested that the transition from primary school to secondary school and the change to more formalized physical education associated with it may have contributed to the variability in physical condition and sport competence subscales of the PSPP in their study.

Applied case study 3: Motor ability and self-perceptions and self-worth in children and adolescents

Piek *et al.* (2006) were the first to examine the influence of fine and gross motor ability on self-perceptions in both children and adolescents. To ascertain these influences, the study assessed motor ability using the McCarron assessment of neuromuscular development and self-perception profiles in 265 boys and girls. The children/adolescents were categorized into groups based on whether they had a development coordination disorder (DCD). The study findings suggest that movement ability affects perceived athletic competence and scholastic competence. Sex and age differences were found for self-perceptions and motor ability. For age, it was reported that children had increased scholastic competence and better fine motor ability than adolescents. A greater perceived athletic competence was also found in predominantly male children, and these had better gross motor skills. The study concluded that types of self-perception that influence self-worth are thus dependent on level of motor ability in young people, but that the different types of self-perception vary according to sex and age.

You should have noted that Piek *et al.* (2006) suggested that perceived scholastic competence and athletic competence were the main drivers for self-worth, but that these were dependent on motor ability, age and sex. Specifically, you probably highlighted that fine motor ability was associated only with scholastic competence, thus

ACTIVITY 4.7

1 Think about the case study of Piek *et al.* (2006) and note down what the research paper describes as the two drivers for self-worth: how do they vary based on fine and motor skill ability?

2 Considering the study mentioned above, who does Piek *et al.* (2006) suggest is at most risk of low self-worth?

3 Can you make a suggestion based on the findings as to whether it is important to assess fine and gross components of motor ability in future studies on self-perceptions and self-worth?

4 In Piek *et al.*'s (2006) paper, a variety of statistical methods are employed in order to provide the most accurate predictors of self-worth and self-perceptions. Can you describe how the utilization of these differing techniques enhanced understanding, specifically for comparisons between univariate and multivariate and regression models?

identifying that poor fine motor skills predicted low perceived scholastic ability. Adolescents and those with DCD thus had lower perceived scholastic competence. Likewise, low motor skill ability was predictive of low perceived athletic competence. This was demonstrated in adolescents and DCD subjects compared with young and controls. You should have also highlighted that perceived scholastic and athletic competence contributed to variance in self-worth differently between boys and girls.

For boys, perceived athletic competence (DCD and controls) was a determinant of self-worth but not scholastic competence. However, you should also have concluded that females are at most risk of low self-worth relating to low perceived scholastic competence and fine motor ability, regardless of whether they have DCD or not. Females with DCD also reported lower perceived athletic competence, and this was linked to gross motor ability. Therefore, psychosocial implications are more severe in girls with DCD, because self-worth is compromised, regardless of whether they have fine or gross motor ability. Based on the findings, you should have suggested that it is important to assess subcomponents of motor ability (fine and gross) when considering self-perceptions and their effects on self-worth. If the specific motor ability deficit is considered, then appropriate interventions can be designed to address motor and psychological problems in male or female children and adolescents with DCD. Finally, you should have noticed how the multivariate and regression analyses enable greater understanding of the effects of self-perceptions on self-worth, and specifically, how age, sex and motor ability predicted these. For example, univariate analysis evidenced group differences (DCD vs control) in scholastic competence, athletic competence, physical appearance and behavioural conduct. No group differences were observed for social acceptance. However, in multivariate analysis, physical appearance and behavioural conduct explained no unique variance, because they were intercorrelated with other self-perception measures and thus reflected a shared variance. Therefore, it was evident that only perceived athletic competence and scholastic competence could explain unique variances. The regression analysis was then able to predict perceived scholastic abilities and athletic competence. Low perceived scholastic ability was predicted by poor fine motor ability scores (older children). Predictors for athletic competence were age, sex and gross motor skills. Greater perceived athletic competence was predicted in children (young age group) and males with better gross motor ability.

Ethical considerations when examining the physical activity–self-esteem relationship

ACTIVITY 4.8

Consider the variety of research studies that have been outlined within this chapter. Do you think there are any ethical issues related to the examination of the impact that physical activity has on self-esteem? If so, what are they, and what should sport and exercise psychologists consider when investigating this topic?

   The consideration of ethics within the physical activity–self-esteem domain is not always explicitly considered within research studies. However, we have a duty to consider the ethical issues surrounding psychological research with any population we work with. When you considered the research presented in this chapter, did you consider that self-esteem is a dynamic construct that can change? As practitioners, we need to consider that our intervention could change the way a person feels about themselves. In some instances, we need to be prepared for a physical-activity programme that we prescribe resulting in an individual or individuals feeling worse about themselves. We also need to consider the ethical issues associated with such an occurrence and our responsibility to deal with this, should it happen to any research participant we are working with.

BEYOND THE FRONTIER

Although scrutiny of the effect of physical activity and exercise on self-esteem is not new, science has yet to fully explore this relationship. The research by Moore *et al.* (2012) underscores how little we know about the impact of physical activity on self-esteem in different populations, and future work is needed that evolves this area of research. Specifically, the scope of our knowledge needs to be extended so that we better understand how the multidimensional constructs within the EXSEM develop and change through the life course, as well as coupling this with objective measures of physical activity. This information can then be used to develop personalized applications – for example, via smartphone or tablet – to track self-esteem scores over time and create personalized, life course-specific coaching plans that can be used to promote physical activity and enhance self-esteem alongside a quantified self-perspective of health enhancement.

CONCLUSIONS

Self-esteem is often considered a central component in psychological well-being, and a range of research studies have reported that physical activity can enhance self-esteem. Meta-analytical research and studies of RCTs have concluded that physical activity can be used to promote increases in self-esteem and physical self-perceptions, although the mechanisms that underpin this change are still unclear. This chapter has also presented the conceptual physical activity–self-esteem model of Sonstroem and Morgan (1989) and its subsequent modifications to encompass Fox's physical self-perception model. At present, this latter model appears to be the most robust, and scientifically supported, model that explains the influence of physical activity and exercise on self-esteem. Despite this, the examination of the impact of physical activity on self-esteem has been clouded by use of different measures to assess self-esteem. In some cases, these measures assess different constructs within the physical activity–self-esteem model but have inferred self-esteem from them. Some research has used a general measure of global self-esteem, whereas other research has used measures of physical self-perceptions. I would argue that the use of a global measure of self-esteem in studies of the impact of physical activity on self-esteem only provides the researcher with limited information. Instead, the assessment of physical self-perceptions can provide practitioners and scientists with a more comprehensive understanding of the ways in which physical activity influences self-perceptions and, subsequently, global self-esteem. The final part of this chapter presented three case studies that illustrate the limitations of using a global measure of self-esteem and the differing contributions that the subdomains of the physical self-perception model can make if a measure such as the physical self-perception profile is used to examine the impact of physical activity on self-esteem.

KEY CONCEPTS AND TERMS

Definition of self-esteem

Biddle and Mutrie (2007, p. 181) defined self-esteem as, 'The value placed on aspects of the self, such as academic and social domains.'

Rosenberg (1965) also proposed that self-esteem was a positive or negative orientation towards oneself, or an overall evaluation of one's worth or value.

Sonstroem and Morgan conceptual model

This is a theoretical model in which exercise/physical-activity behaviour is proposed to enhance self-efficacy, which in turn influences perceptions of physical competence and physical acceptance. These perceptions then influence global self-esteem.

EXSEM

This is an amended version of the exercise–self-esteem model originally proposed by Sonstroem and Morgan (1989). In this model, physical activity influences self-efficacy, which has an impact on the four subdomains of physical condition, sport competence, body attractiveness and physical strength, any of which can influence global self-esteem.

Fox's physical self-perception model

This is a theoretical model whereby an individual's self-perceptions of physical condition, sport competence, body attractiveness and physical strength contribute to an individual's physical self-worth, which, in turn, directly influences global self-esteem.

RECOMMENDED FURTHER READING

Books and book chapters

Biddle, S. J. H. and Mutrie, N. (2007). *Psychology of Physical Activity*. London: Routledge.

Fox, K. R. (1997). The physical self and processes in self-esteem development. In Fox, K. R. (ed.) *The Physical Self*, pp. 111–40. Champaign, IL: Human Kinetics.

Rosenberg, M. (1965). *Society and the Adolescent Self-image*. Princeton, NJ: Princeton University Press.

Sonstroem, R. J. (1997). The physical self-system: A mediator of exercise and self-esteem. In Fox, K. R. (ed.) *The Physical Self*, pp. 3–26. Champaign, IL: Human Kinetics.

Journals

Crocker, P. R. E., Eklund, R. C. and Kowalski, K. C. (2000). Children's physical activity and self-perceptions. *Journal of Sports Sciences*, *18*, 383–94.

Duncan, M., Al-Nakeeb, Y., Jones, M. and Nevill, A. (2006). Body dissatisfaction, body fat and physical activity in British children. *International Journal of Pediatric Obesity*, *1*, 89–95.

Duncan, M. J., Al-Nakeeb, Y. and Nevill, A. M. (2013). Establishing the optimal body mass index–body esteem relationship in young adolescents. *BMC Public Health*, *13*, 662.

Ekeland, E., Heian, F. and Hagen, K. B. (2005). Can exercise improve self-esteem in children and young people? A systematic review of randomised control trials. *British Journal of Sports Medicine*, *39*, 792–8.

Ekeland, E., Heian, F., Hagen, K. B., Abbott, J. M. and Nordheim, L. (2004). Exercise to improve self-esteem in children and young people. *Cochrane Database of Systematic Reviews*, *1*, CD003683.

Fox, K. R. (2000). Self-esteem, self-perceptions and exercise. *International Journal of Sport Psychology*, *31*, 228–40.

Fox, K. R. and Corbin, C. B. (1989). The Physical Self-Perception Profile: Development and preliminary validation. *Journal of Sport and Exercise Psychology*, *11*, 408–30.

Hagborg, W. (1993). The Rosenberg self-esteem scale and Harter's self-perception profile for adolescents: A concurrent validity study. *Psychology and The Schools, 30*, 132–6.

Levy, S. and Ebbeck, V. (2005). The exercise and self-esteem model in adult women: The inclusion of physical acceptance. *Psychology of Sport and Exercise, 6*, 571–84.

Li, F., Harmer, P., Chaumeton, N., Duncan, T. and Duncan, S. (2002). Tai-chi as a means to enhance self-esteem: A randomised controlled trial. *The Journal of Applied Gerontology, 21*, 70–89.

McAuley, E., Blissmer, B., Katula, J., Duncan, S. C. and Mihalko, S. (2000). Physical activity, self-esteem and self-efficacy relationships in older adults: A randomised control trial. *Annals of Behavioural Medicine, 22*, 131–9.

McAuley, E., Elavsky, S., Motl, R. W., Konopack, J. F., Hu, L. and Marquez, D. X. (2005). Physical activity, self-efficacy and self-esteem: Longitudinal relationships in older adults. *Journal of Gerontology: Psychological Sciences, 60B*, 268–75.

MacKinnon, D. P. and Leucken, L. J. (2008). How and for whom? Mediation and moderation in health psychology. *Health Psychology, 27*, S99.

Maiano, C., Ninot, G. and Bilard, J. (2004). Age and gender effects on global self-esteem and physical self-perception in adolescents. *European Physical Education Review, 10*, 53–70.

Moore, J. B., Mitchell, N. G., Beets, M. W. and Bartholomew, J. B. (2012). Physical self-esteem in older adults: A test of the indirect effect of physical activity. *Sport, Exercise and Performance Psychology, 1*, 231–41.

Piek, J., Baynam, G. B. and Barrett, N. C. (2006). The relationship between fine and gross motor ability, self-perceptions and self-worth in children and adolescents. *Human Movement Science, 25*, 65–75.

Robins, R., Hendin, H. and Trezsniewski, K. (2001). Measuring global self-esteem: Construct validation of a single item measure and the Rosenberg Self-Esteem Scale. *Personality and Social Psychology Bulletin, 27*, 151–61.

Sibbald, B. and Roland, M. (1998). Understanding controlled trials: Why are randomised controlled trials important? *British Medical Journal, 316*, 201.

Sonstroem, R. J., Harlow, L. L. and Josephs, L. (1994). Exercise and self-esteem: Validity of model expansion and exercise associations. *Journal of Sport and Exercise Psychology, 16*, 29–42.

Sonstroem, R. J. and Morgan, W. P. (1989). Exercise and self-esteem: Rationale and model. *Medicine and Science in Sports and Exercise, 21*, 329–37.

Spence, J. C., McGannon, K. R. and Poon, P. (2005). The effect of exercise on global self-esteem: A quantitative review. *Journal of Sport and Exercise Psychology, 27*, 311–34.

Welk, G. J. and Eklund, B. (2005). Validation of the children and youth physical self-perceptions profile for young children. *Psychology of Sport and Exercise, 6*, 51–65.

SAMPLE ESSAY QUESTIONS

1 The conceptual model of Sonstroem and Morgan (1989) provides the most robust explanation of the physical activity–self-esteem relationship to date. With reference

to empirical evidence, discuss the validity of this model in the context of physical activity and exercise behaviour.

2 The PSPP offers the scientist with the most comprehensive tool to assess the impact of physical activity on self-esteem. Discuss this statement with reference to the measures available to assess self-esteem and the theoretical models that attempt to explain the relationship between physical activity and self-esteem.

3 Critically evaluate research evidence on the relationship between physical activity/exercise and self-esteem across the lifespan. Outline how empirical research on this topic supports the conceptual models of the physical activity–self-esteem relationship reported in the literature.

4 Body acceptance has been an overlooked component in explaining the impact of physical activity on self-esteem. Critically evaluate this statement with reference to recent empirical studies and any theoretical models of the physical activity–self-esteem relationship.

REFERENCES

Bandura, A. (1986). *Social Foundations of Thought and Action: A social cognitive theory*. Englewood Cliffs, NJ: Prentice-Hall.

Biddle, S. J. H. and Mutrie, N. (2007). *Psychology of Physical Activity*. London: Routledge.

Cohane, G. H. and Pope, H. G. (2001). Body image in boys: A review of the literature. *International Journal of Eating Disorders*, *29*, 373–9.

Cooley, C. H. (1902). *Human Nature and the Social Order*. New York: Scribner.

Crews, D. J., Lochbaum, M. R. and Landers, D. M. (2004). Aerobic physical activity effects on psychological well-being in low-income hispanic children 1, 2. *Perceptual and Motor Skills*, *98*(1), 319–24.

Duncan, M. J., Al-Nakeeb, Y. A. H. Y. A. and Nevill, A. M. (2013). Establishing the optimal body mass index–body esteem relationship in young adolescents. *BMC Public Health*, *13*, 662.

Duncan, M. J., Al-Nakeeb, Y. A. H. Y. A., Nevill, A. M. and Jones, M. V. (2006). Body dissatisfaction, body fat and physical activity in British children. *International Journal of Pediatric Obesity*, *1*(2), 89–95.

Ekeland, E., Heian, F., Hagen, K. B., Abbott, J. M. and Nordheim, L. (2004). Exercise to improve self-esteem in children and young people. *Cochrane Database of Systematic Reviews*, *1*, CD003683.

Eklund, R. C., Whitehead, J. R. and Welk, G. J. (1997). Validity of the children and youth physical self-perception profile: A confirmatory factor analysis. *Research Quarterly for Exercise and Sport*, *68*, 249–56.

Fox, K. R. (1997). The physical self and processes in self-esteem development. In Fox, K. R. (ed.) *The Physical Self*, pp. 111–40. Champaign, IL: Human Kinetics.

Fox, K. R. (2000). Self-esteem, self-perceptions and exercise. *International Journal of Sport Psychology*, *31*, 228–40.

Fox, K. R. and Corbin, C. B. (1989). The Physical Self-Perception Profile: Development and preliminary validation. *Journal of Sport and Exercise Psychology*, *11*, 408–30.

Furnham, A., Badmin, N. and Sneade, I. (2002). Body image dissatisfaction: Gender differences in eating attitudes, self esteem and reasons for exercise. *The Journal of Psychology*, *136*, 581–96.

Gruber, J. (1986). Physical activity and self-esteem development in children: A meta-analysis. In Stull, G. and Eckem, H. (eds) *Effects of Physical Activity on Children*, pp. 330–48. Champaign, IL: Human Kinetics.

Guinn, B., Semper, T. and Jorgensen, L. (1997). Mexican American female adolescent self-esteem: The effect of body image, exercise behaviour and body fatness. *Hispanic Journal of Behavioral Sciences*, *19*, 517–26.

Hagborg, W. (1993). The Rosenberg self-esteem scale and Harter's self perception profile for adolescents: A concurrent validity study. *Psychology and The Schools*, *30*, 132–6.

Haugen, T., Säfvenbom, R. and Ommundsen, Y. (2011). Physical activity and global self-worth: The role of physical self-esteem indices and gender. *Mental Health and Physical Activity*, *4*, 49–56.

Harter, S. (1985). *The Self-Perception Profile for Children: Revision of the perceived competence scale for children*. Denver, CO: University of Denver.

James, W. (1950). *The Principles of Psychology*. New York: Dover.

Levy, S. and Ebbeck, V. (2005). The exercise and self-esteem model in adult women: The inclusion of physical acceptance. *Psychology of Sport and Exercise*, *6*, 571–84.

Li, F., Harmer, P., Chaumeton, N., Duncan, T. and Duncan, S. (2002). Tai-chi as a means to enhance self-esteem: A randomised controlled trial. *The Journal of Applied Gerontology*, *21*, 70–89.

McAuley, E., Blissmer, B., Katula, J., Duncan, S. C. and Mihalko, S. (2000). Physical activity, self-esteem and self-efficacy relationships in older adults: A randomised control trial. *Annals of Behavioral Medicine*, *22*, 131–9.

McAuley, E., Elavsky, S., Motl, R. W., Konopack, J. F., Hu, L. and Marquez, D. X. (2005). Physical activity, self-efficacy and self-esteem: Longitudinal relationships in older adults. *Journal of Gerontology: Psychological Sciences*, *60B*, 268–75.

McDonald D. J. and Hodgdon, J. A. (1991). *Psychological Effects of Aerobic Fitness Training*. New York: Springer.

MacKinnon, D. P. and Leucken, L. J. (2008). How and for whom? Mediation and moderation in health psychology. *Health Psychology*, *27*, S99.

Maiano, C., Ninot, G. and Bilard, J. (2004). Age and gender effects on global self-esteem and physical self-perception in adolescents. *European Physical Education Review*, *10*, 53–70.

Marsh, H., Richards, G., Johnson, S., Roche, L. and Tremayne, P. (1994). Physical self-description questionnaires: Psychometric properties and a multi trait–multi method analysis of relations to existing instruments. *Journal of Sport and Exercise Psychology*, *16*, 270–305.

Mead, G. H. (1934). *Mind, Self and Society From the Standpoint of a Social Behaviourist*. Chicago, IL: University of Chicago Press.

Mendelson, B. K., McLaren, L., Gauvin, L. and Steiger, H. (2002). The relationship of self-esteem and body esteem in women with and without eating disorders. *International Journal of Eating Disorders*, *31*, 318–23.

Mendelson, B. K. and White, D. R. (1982). Relation between body-esteem and self-esteem of obese and normal children. *Perceptual and Motor Skills*, *54*, 899–905.

Moore, J. B., Mitchell, N. G., Beets, M. W. and Bartholomew, J. B. (2012). Physical self-esteem in older adults: A test of the indirect effect of physical activity. *Sport, Exercise and Performance Psychology*, *1*, 231–41.

Palladino-Green, S. and Pritchard, M. E. (2003). Predictors of body image dissatisfaction in adult men and women. *Social Behaviour and Personality*, *31*, 215–22.

Piek, J., Baynam, G. B. and Barrett, N. C. (2006). The relationship between fine and gross motor ability, self-perceptions and self-worth in children and adolescents. *Human Movement Science*, *25*, 65–75.

Robins, R., Hendin, H. and Trezsniewski, K. (2001). Measuring global self-esteem: Construct validation of a single item measure and the Rosenberg Self-Esteem Scale. *Personality and Social Psychology Bulletin*, *27*, 151–61.

Rosenberg, M. (1965). *Society and the Adolescent Self-Image*. Princeton, NJ: Princeton University Press.

Rosenberg, M. (1989). *Society and the Adolescent Self-Image* (revised edn). Middletown, CT: Wesleyan University Press.

Sibbald, B. and Roland, M. (1998). Understanding controlled trials: Why are randomised controlled trials important? *British Medical Journal*, *316*, 201.

Sonstroem, R. J. (1997). The Physical Self-System: A mediator of exercise and self-esteem. In Fox, K. R. (ed.) *The Physical Self*, pp. 3–26. Champaign, IL: Human Kinetics.

Sonstroem, R. J. (1998). Physical self-concept: assessment and external validity. *Exercise and Sport Science Reviews*, *26*, 133–64.

Sonstroem, R., Harlow, L., Gemma, L. and Osbourne, S. (1992). Tests of structural relationships with a proposed exercise and self-esteem model. *Journal of Personality Assessment*, *56*, 348–64.

Sonstroem, R. J., Harlow, L. L. and Josephs, L. (1994). Exercise and self-esteem: Validity of model expansion and exercise associations. *Journal of Sport and Exercise Psychology*, *16*, 29–42.

Sonstroem, R., Harlow, L. L. and Salisbury, K. (1993). Path analysis of a self-esteem model across a competitive swim season. *Research Quarterly for Exercise and Sport*, *64*, 335–42.

Sonstroem, R. J. and Morgan, W. P. (1989). Exercise and self-esteem: Rationale and model. *Medicine and Science in Sports and Exercise*, *21*, 329–37.

Spence, J. C., McGannon, K. R. and Poon, P. (2005). The effect of exercise on global self-esteem: A quantitative review. *Journal of Sport and Exercise Psychology*, *27*, 311–34.

Stice, E. (2002). Risk and maintenance factors for eating pathology: A meta-analytic review. *Psychological Bulletin*, *128*, 825–48.

Strauss, I., Rodzilsky, D., Burack, G. and Colin, M. (2001). *Psicosocial correlatos de la actividad física en niños sanos. Archivos de Medicina Pediátrica y del Adolescents*, *155*, 897–902.

Van de Vliet, P., Van Coppenolle, H. V. and Knapen, J. (2002). Physical measures, perceived physical ability and body acceptance of adult psychiatric patients. *Adapted Physical Activity Quarterly*, *16*, 113–25.

Welk, G. J. and Eklund, B. (2005). Validation of the children and youth physical self perceptions profile for young children. *Psychology of Sport and Exercise*, *6*, 51–65.

Whitehead, J. R. (1995). A study of children's physical self-perceptions using an adapted physical self-perception questionnaire. *Pediatric Exercise Science*, 7, 132–51.

How can people manage or self-regulate their own inner states?

5

Self-control in sport
Does willpower resemble a muscle?

Christopher Fullerton

CHAPTER SUMMARY

The ability, or particularly the inability, to control behaviour has major implications for sports performance. Given the unpredictable nature of sport and high-pressure environments athletes perform in, controlling behaviour becomes a challenging task. For example, regulating emotions under extreme fatigue in an ultra-endurance race poses an altogether different challenge from refraining from aggressive acts of violence towards an opponent in a team sport. In the former, regulation of emotions and internal thoughts has implications for achieving a particular goal, and so an athlete will manage his/her behaviour in accordance with their goals for the event, while managing energy expenditure. In the latter, however, failure to self-control has implications for both the individual and others, and so an athlete must be able to resist the urge to act immediately if his/her response has negative consequences for the team's performance.

In this chapter, I will introduce the concept of self-control and explain why it is important for sport. I will then discuss the benefits of being able to exert self-control, as well as some of the consequences following failure to self-control performance. A review of the current literature is provided, with an in-depth discussion of two popular theoretical models. These models consider self-control outcome from a resource perspective. In the strength model, self-control is proposed to rely on a limited resource, whereas, in the resource allocation model of self-control (RAMS), it is proposed that resources are allocated in accordance with personal priorities.

With respect to these proposals, I will review the evidence for their application within sport and discuss some of the methodological issues with studies in this area. I will then conclude with a discussion of several interventions proposed to improve self-control.

LEARNING OUTCOMES

When you have studied this chapter, you should be able to:

1   Define the concept of self-control
2   Understand the benefits of self-control for performance
3   Understand the consequences of self-control failure for performance
4   Explain the strength model of self-control
5   Explain the RAMS
6   Discuss methodological issues when investigating how self-control works and
7   Describe strategies for improving self-control

INTRODUCTION AND DEFINITION OF SELF-CONTROL

Self-control is the ability to alter one's thoughts, feelings and desires (Baumeister, 2012). People exert self-control to bring about behavioural change in the direction of some standard or idea about how something could or should be (Hoffman *et al.*, 2012). A standard or reference could be a goal, an ideal, a rule or possible state.

Self-control is often exerted when a dominant behavioural response (habit) is unhelpful or unwelcomed. When responses are perceived to be detrimental to performance, athletes will steer behaviour towards a more desired state. For example, Lane *et al.* (2011a) reported that runners use strategies to up-regulate the intensity of desired emotional states prior to and during competition. Other examples of self-regulatory behaviour within sport and exercise include delaying gratification, when exerting dietary restraint to meet long-term health and weight goals (Johnson *et al.*, 2012); controlling attention under pressure (Englert and Bertrams, 2012); and controlling thoughts, for example rethinking feelings (Jones, 2003).

Research has consistently demonstrated that there are many benefits to being able to successfully self-control, beyond those at the individual level. For example, research from team sports shows that individuals will exert restraint over selfish behaviour if it could potentially threaten group interests (Tamminen and Crocker, 2013) and regulate others' emotions as a strategy to maintain a culture-related identity (Friesen *et al.*, 2013).

BENEFITS OF SELF-CONTROL AND CONSEQUENCES OF ITS FAILURE

Within the sport and exercise domain, successful self-control has been associated with performing under pressure (Wallace *et al.*, 2005; Englert and Bertrams, 2012) and effective time management and engagement in physical activity among older adults (Umstattd *et al.*, 2008). Yet the benefits of being able to control behaviour extend beyond this arena. For example, evidence from other fields of psychology has linked successful self-control with academic achievement (Tangney *et al.*, 2004; Duckworth and Seligman, 2005), job satisfaction (Grandey *et al.*, 2005) and relationship success (Vohs *et al.*, 2011). Conversely, many personal and social problems include some degree of failure at self-control. For example, poor self-control is linked with physical inactivity (Hagger *et al.*, 2010) and poor health choices (Lappalainen *et al.*, 1997; Hankonen *et al.*, 2013; McKee *et al.*, 2013).

The benefits of self-control for performance and overall well-being are accentuated when the consequences of poor self-control are considered. Research has demonstrated that the act of self-control not only is costly in terms of behaviour, but also uses physiological substrates such as glucose. If self-control consumes glucose, then low glucose can further handicap self-control and affect performance (Gailliot *et al.*, 2007).

If one applies this logic to athletes competing, engaging in frequent acts of self-control would use physiological substrates required for physical performance. This logic appears to hold true, with evidence from endurance events indicating that regulating unpleasant emotions incurs a greater physiological cost during prolonged physical exercise. For example, Lane *et al.* (2011b) reported concurrent increases in unpleasant emotions, such as anger, depression and tension, during a 2-hour cycling time trial performed at lactate threshold. Cyclists who reported experiencing more intense unpleasant emotions were found to incur a greater physiological cost, including increased oxygen consumption and a higher ventilation rate during the middle and latter stages of the trial.

More recent work, by Beedie *et al.* (2012) lends support to the notion that emotion regulation results in a greater energy cost, including increased lactate production and heart and ventilation rates. Therefore, if self-regulation leads to drawing on more physiological resources, then it would appear that self-control is not limited by the amount of glucose within the body; rather, self-control is affected by the availability of key physiological substrates, such as glucose. The physiological resources appear to be available, if the individual is motivated to maintain performance despite experiencing unpleasant emotional states. The available findings indicate that self-control leads to both behavioural and physiological changes that, when considered together, strongly suggest that it is effortful.

How and why do athletes control behaviour?

Broadly speaking, athletes exert self-control over *emotions* and *mood*, such as managing anxiety before a competition; *performance*, such as controlling the speed and execution of a motor task requiring accuracy under pressure; *temptation*, for example, resisting the urge to retaliate to a perceived bad tackle; and *thoughts*, such as reducing self-doubt.

Emotions and mood

Emotions are a key feature of competitive sport (Jones, 2003). As such, regulating emotions prior to and during competition is of benefit for athletes wishing to compete in a desired state and attain their goals (see Beedie *et al.*, 2000, for a review). From an evolutionary perspective, emotions serve to signal a reaction to something important (Nesse and Ellsworth, 2009). In life-threatening situations, such as being attacked by a predator, emotions such as fear and anger would have triggered a physiological response in the absence of an energy supply (Nesse and Ellsworth, 2009). Although not focusing specifically on athletes, Tamir (2009) reported that individuals will tolerate or even increase unpleasant emotions, if they believe they will support goal pursuit. Examining this theory with athletes, Lane *et al.* (2011a) explored this logic among runners before competition. Of the 360 runners who took part, 15 per cent reported using strategies aimed at increasing anger and/or anxiety, whereas the remaining 85 per cent reported using strategies aimed at reducing the same emotions. The authors suggest that, if emotions associated with increased activation, such as anxiety and anger, are perceived as helpful (i.e. instrumental) for achieving success in competition, then an anxious or angry athlete might report feeling happy that he or she is in an optimal psychological state. It is, therefore, important for individuals to consider the utility of the emotion being experienced in relation to one's beliefs surrounding the emotion and its association with goal attainment. Further, Uphill and Jones (2007) reported that cognitive appraisals are associated with a range of emotions. For example, an athlete might experience anxiety if they are uncertain about the outcome of their performance or fear they might not be able to finish a race or the threat of competition.

ACTIVITY 5.1

Below are some negative self-statements. Think of the emotions most likely associated with each statement and what effect they could have upon performance.

Negative statement	Emotions
It's during a cycling race, and I'm too far off the pace; I won't be able to close the gap	*Example:* guilt – wishing he/she had not missed training; anxiety – doubt that he/she is likely to achieve his/her goal
It's the day of an important competition, and I had a poor night's sleep; I'm too tired to perform well	
My last three competitions have been poor; today feels like it is going to be the same	
I just can't seem to get my timing right; there is no rhythm to my performance	
I am being humiliated by my opposition; it's embarrassing	
That was my last chance to achieve qualification, and I failed	

Resisting temptations

Athletes are often required to forego personal interests or desires for the benefit of integrating within a team to promote cohesion and virtuous behaviour. Evolutionary psychology considers how a psychological mechanism interacts with the environment to produce behaviour, and why it gains its design (Nesse and Ellsworth, 2009). This perspective suggests self-control is situated at the individual level; unlike many living vertebrates, humans are unable to get what they need for survival directly from nature, and so they must rely on their social groups (Baumeister, 2005). According to Tamir *et al.* (2008), people improve or worsen their feelings in an appropriate manner and in the pursuit of hedonistic (personal) and instrumental goals (consequences). Conforming to what is perceived to be normal behaviour within a group or culture is often seen as a strategy for achieving individual goals and can strengthen a belief that an athlete is more likely to achieve their goal in this way.

Below is an excerpt from Paul Kimmage's autobiography *Rough Ride*. Paul Kimmage was a professional cyclist in the late 1980s, an era when doping was rife among professional riders. Paul Kimmage describes the difficulty he faced in trying to override the temptation to take performance-enhancing drugs, behaviour that went against his moral values. The conflict between personal values and beliefs and those of his teammates and, to a wider extent, the culture of cycling at the time is a classic example of when individual goals clash with team goals.

> I was the only rider in the whole peloton to be left behind when the pressure went on, twenty kilometres from the finish. The shame of it, I am totally knackered. But the real problem is tomorrow . . . One or two of the lads were preparing syringes. Cutting them down to size, preparing them for the white amphetamines they would use the next day . . . I was tempted, desperately tempted. They wanted to help me. I wanted to accept their help, but that bloody conscience of mine was stopping me. I had never smoked behind my father's back. Had always been dependable and good. I had an acute sense of right and wrong. Taking drugs was wrong. The only merit I had now was finishing this race. If I did it with the help of amphetamines I could never forgive myself. But it was so tempting. I badly wanted to be one of the boys.
>
> (Kimmage, 2007, p. 91)

Performance

Research indicates that failure to regulate one's emotions can have deleterious effects upon several psychological functions that influence performance, including attention and motor control. For example, in a study examining attentional control among soccer players, results suggested that individuals displayed attentional bias towards a threatening stimulus (the goalkeeper), rather than attending to the task-relevant stimuli (optimal target zones in between the goalposts), when experiencing high anxiety (Wood and Wilson, 2010).

In a further study, Wilson *et al.* (2009) examined the effects of attentional control among basketball free throwing. Results indicated that anxiety was shown to disrupt goal-directed behaviour. Ten male basketball players were asked to perform free throws under varying conditions of pressure. The goal was successful shooting (accuracy).

ACTIVITY 5.2

Conflicting goals: to agree or disagree?

Think of a time when you disagreed with a decision made by a team mate or coach. What did you do to resolve the conflict and ensure your position within the team was not undermined? Did you succumb to peer pressure, or were you able to override the desire to conform to the behaviour of your teammates, in the interest of staying true to your own personal beliefs? What were the consequences of your actions?

Write your thoughts here:

One group was assigned to a non-evaluative control condition (i.e. participants were simply asked to do their best), and the other group was subject to varying degrees of evaluative feedback designed to increase the intensity of anxiety experienced, including financial rewards and performance comparisons with teammates and other teams. The results showed that increased anxiety led to the speed of the free throw increasing, which impaired performance. The proposed mechanism explaining this effect was a reduction in the quiet-eye period. The quiet-eye period is the final fixation on a target, when task-relevant environmental cues are processed (e.g. targets around the basketball hoop, such as the rim or backboard) and motor plans are coordinated (i.e. throwing the ball) for the upcoming task. The natural tendency to rush a skill when under pressure provides strong evidence for self-control being compromised when concurrent self-control tasks are performed. In this case, regulating emotions compromised attentional control.

THEORIES OF SELF-CONTROL

The strength model of self-control

According to the strength model (Muraven *et al.*, 1998; Muraven and Baumeister, 2000; Baumeister *et al.*, 2007), acts of self-control consume a limited resource, with the resource becoming temporarily depleted, akin to a muscle becoming tired after exercise. This process leaves the individual in a state of *ego depletion* (Baumeister *et al.*, 1998), compromising the capacity to exert self-control in subsequent tasks. However, much like a muscle, with rest and relaxation, the resource is replenished, and the capacity for self-control is strengthened.

RESEARCH METHODS 5.1

To test this theory, researchers have typically employed the dual-task design (Baumeister *et al.*, 1998; Muraven *et al.*, 1998; Vohs *et al.*, 2008). In this experimental set-up, participants are required first to complete either a self-control task (energy depleting), such as exercising attentional control while watching a video clip (Gailliot *et al.*, 2007), or a non-self-control task (non-energy depleting). A second, unrelated, self-control task is then administered, such as the Stroop task (Gailliot *et al.*, 2007), unsolvable puzzle (Vohs *et al.*, 2008) or handgrip (Baumeister *et al.*, 1998). Depending on the availability of self-control strength at that moment, self-control in the second task – which is identical for both conditions – should differ between the two conditions, because depleted participants should perform worse than the non-depleted participants, as they do not have the same amount of self-control strength to invest in the second task (Baumeister *et al.*, 1998, 2007; Muraven *et al.*, 1998).

In a further example of a dual-task research design, Baumeister *et al.* (1998) presented both cookies and radishes to students. They asked half of the group to eat two-to-three radishes only, and the other half to eat two-to-three cookies only. Participants were then asked to complete a problem-solving task that was impossible to do. Those who resisted eating the cookies appeared to experience the consequences of exerting self-control, as they were less likely to persevere with the problem-solving task (8.35 minutes vs 18.90 minutes). Bray *et al.* (2008) measured electromyographic activation in depleted and non-depleted individuals as they isometrically squeezed a handgrip. Depleted individuals were not able to hold the handgrip as long as non-depleted individuals. Moreover, depleted individuals had greater neuromuscular activation than non-depleted individuals, despite no differences in maximum strength.

A great deal of the research conducted in this area has been outside sport and exercise science. For example, Segerstrom and Nes (2007) found that resisting eating cookies led to greater heart-rate variability than resisting eating carrots, and this heart-rate variability correlated with persistence on a subsequent anagram task. This suggests that exerting self-control requires the mobilization of effort. A recent meta-analysis (Hagger *et al.*, 2010), which is an authoritative way to review the literature, found support from eighty-three studies for the effects of ego depletion on subsequent self-control performance.

In an attempt to explain the mechanism underpinning whether the outcome of self-control is successful or not, Gailliot and colleagues (Gailliot and Baumeister, 2007; Gailliot *et al.*, 2007) proposed that glucose was an important component of self–control strength. To test this theory, Gaillot conducted a series of of experimental studies that showed that self-control lowered glucose levels, predicted poor perform-ance on a subsequent self-control task and, when replenished exogenously, eliminated

ACTIVITY 5.3

Do you struggle for energy before or during training and competition? Describe the thoughts and emotions around not wanting to expend effort. Consider the time of day when your energy is low: do you struggle to get out of bed for training in the mornings, or do you find it hard to refrain from missing training in the evenings, after a long day at university or work?

Write your thoughts here:

any performance impairments. In one of the studies, participants completed an attentional control task, which involved attending to a visual cue while watching a video, before completing a Stroop task. Although baseline glucose levels (96.07 + 22.08 mg/dl) did not predict Stroop performance, lower glucose (91.67 + 17.77 mg/dl) after watching the video was significantly associated with poorer Stroop performance.

There is certainly sufficient and consistent evidence pointing to the fact that studies have detailed lower blood glucose scores among those required to exert self-control. The notion that self-control is energy driven seems plausible, given what is already known about cerebral energy metabolism. First, blood-borne glucose is the brain's preferred fuel (Bliss and Sapolsky, 2001; van Hall et al., 2009); second, glucose is used to make neurotransmitters, which play a role in the onset of fatigue, affecting sensory and motor behaviour (Mergenthaler et al., 2013); and, finally, glucose is released from the liver into the bloodstream to fuel brain processes in response to stress (Coker and Kjaer, 2005), such as increased ketone production (Minninnen, 2004; Wang and Mariman, 2008), the metabolism of blood lactate (Oltmanns et al., 2008; Wang and Mariman, 2008), and the rapid increase of its own phosphate content (Oltmanns et al., 2008).

However, there is equivocality in support for the strength model (Job et al., 2010, 2013; Beedie and Lane, 2012; Miller et al., 2012). For instance, Job et al. (2013) reported that glucose ingestion following a self-control task did improve self-control and cognitive performance (via Stroop performance), but only when people believed willpower to be a limited resource. Conversely, when people believed willpower was not limited, glucose was not needed to sustain high levels of self-control. Similarly, Miller et al. (2012) manipulated implicit theories about willpower during a cognitive learning task and reported improved performance and sustained learning among those who believed willpower was unlimited. Together, these studies support earlier findings that individuals' coping efforts were influenced by a perception that those efforts could be minimal if they were believed to be efficacious (Aldwin and Revenson, 1987).

In a further study that investigated the mechanisms underpinning self-control, Clarkson et al. (2010) found that people's perceived levels of depletion predicted their performance on tasks that required self-control. Depleted (or not depleted) individuals were given (false) feedback about this depleting task that led them to attribute their resources to external or internal sources. For instance, participants crossed off the letter 'e' that is next to or one away from another vowel (those in the control condition simply crossed off all 'e's). Crossed with this, participants were told that the colour of the paper could either 'exhaust and deplete their ability to attend to information' or 'energize and replenish one's ability to attend to information' (p. 33). In the low-depletion condition, the replenishment feedback led to greater persistence on a subsequent task than the depletion feedback. This pattern was reversed in the high-depletion condition. In short, people's perception of their level of self-control resource was a predictor of their subsequent self-control performance, regardless of their actual level of resource.

In summary, this line of work suggests that people fail at self-control because they believe it should fail; that is, they expect to experience the effects of ego depletion. If people subscribe to the belief that self-control is a limited resource, the likelihood of subsequent self-control failure is increased. Although this perspective can explain some of the findings previously reported, it does not explain why individuals fail to perform when there is no apparent need for self-control.

Research has questioned the notion that usage of physiological substrates should lead to deterioration in self-control. Increased physiological cost associated with self-regulation could lead to deteriorated performance, but, arguably, this might not occur if an individual increased effort. Research that manipulated emotion regulation by giving false feedback during a 10-mile cycle time trial found no significant difference in performance (Beedie et al., 2012). When riders believed they were behind the pace required to attain their goals, they increased effort as evidenced via the application of greater force for short bursts, which they were unable to sustain.

Researchers have been critical of both the notion that glucose is a causal factor explaining self-control failure and the methodology employed to investigate self-control failure (Kurzban, 2010). For example, Kurzban (2010) noted that strength model studies (Gailliot et al., 2007) rely on a theory that can be likened to a drop in the charge of a battery, rather than the remaining charge in the battery. Kurzban contends that a limitation of this approach is that a battery still fulfils its function if it has charge remaining. Second, the small changes in blood glucose require a precise and accurate tool and one with minimal error. The Accu-Chek unit has been used extensively to measure blood glucose across self-control tasks. Evidence suggests that the Accu-Chek consistently fails to meet high standards of test–retest stability (Khan et al., 2006; Hoedemaekers et al., 2008). Furthermore, Vlasselaers et al. (2008) found that the bias for the Accu-Chek was 6 mg/dl, with wide limits of agreement and a variable over- and underestimation of the actual blood glucose value, depending on the level of blood glucose (hypo-, normo- or hyperglycaemia).

Consideration of the role of glucose in exercise casts further concerns about the plausibility of willpower as being limited in supply. For instance, the onset of exercise initiates elevations in both hepatic glucose production and glucose utilization

(Coker and Krajer, 2005). Glucagon and insulin are primarily responsible for glucose production during exercise. However, independent of hormonal activity, compensatory increases in hepatic glucose production occur under conditions of deficient muscle glycogenolysis; for example, the liver is capable of releasing glucose in response to decreased plasma glucose during moderate exercise.

In support of Beedie and Lane (2012), who argue that humans have developed the capacity to adapt to repeated stressors, research shows that humans are remarkably efficient when it comes to adapting to exercise. For example, exercise acutely increases muscle glucose transport, which is mediated by an increase in the glucose transporter 4 (GLUT4) in skeletal muscle membrane and t-tubules (Goodyear and Kahn, 1998). Following exercise, it is replaced by an increase in insulin sensitivity. Muscle GLUT4 content increases in humans within 7–10 days of training, although these short-term effects wear off within about 72 hours after the last exercise bout (Gulve and Spina, 1985). Exercise training has also been shown to reverse impaired insulin sensitivity, such that, for a given insulin load, there is a reduced endogenous glucose production and tighter regulation of blood glucose homeostasis. The liver also adapts to exercise-related physiological stress to enhance glucose production responsiveness.

Kratz et al. (2002) assessed a number of basic biochemical parameters in marathon runners the day before, 4 hours after, and 24 hours following, a marathon, including glucose (mg/dl), which increased before (47.4–151.4), immediately after (63–158), and 24 hours following, competition (67–167). However, Kraemer and Brown (1986) reported a significant decrease in glucose following a marathon run compared with pre-run levels: samples were collected within 1 hour 52 minutes before the run and within 5 minutes after, indicating that glucose supercompensation is not immediate. However, those with lower glycogen levels during exercise achieved greater supercompensation afterwards.

Carter, Jeukendrup and Jones (2004) examined performance improvements in high-intensity exercise associated with carbohydrate ingestion. They concluded that the mechanism responsible for improvements appeared to be driven by motivational rather than metabolic factors. They argued that ingesting glucose acts as a signal to increase the neural drive associated with motivation: that is, after drinking glucose, they felt motivated to exercise. This notion received support from the work of Chambers et al. (2009), who found that a simple mouth rinse during a 1-hour cycling time trial activated brain regions involved in reward and the mediation of emotional and behavioural responses. More recently, researchers have suggested that glucose may act as a cognition enhancer through the allocation of attentional resources, thereby linking human decision-making to metabolic cues (Scholey et al., 2009; Wang and Dvorak, 2010). Collectively, this research suggests that psychological mechanisms rather than metabolic mechanisms could offer the best explanations for variations in performance.

Resource allocation model of self-control

In their conceptual model of self-control, Beedie and Lane (2012) contend that ego depletion is not limited by a resource; rather, people allocate resources in accordance with tasks of personal importance. The authors propose a greater role for emotions as catalysts for mobilizing energy, a proposal supported by previous research. Emotions

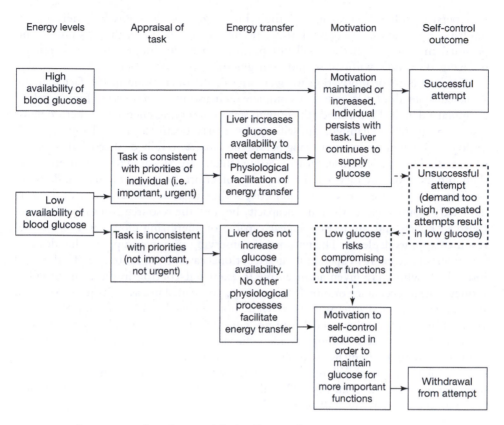

FIGURE 5.1 A resource allocation model of self-control

Source: Beedie and Lane, 2012. Reprinted by permission of Sage Publications

have action tendencies, which are automatic responses to a stimulus or stimuli, signalling a physiological urge to behave in a certain manner, representing the prospect of something important (Frijda, 2010). Beedie and Lane (2012) argued that emotions might operationalize physiological resources that counter a proposed depletion effect if there is a need to do so, thereby ensuring that glucose is able to support normal human mental functioning.

Beedie *et al.* (2012) found a similar role for emotions when providing competitive cyclists with false feedback during a 10-mile cycling time trial. Positive feedback was associated with higher glucose levels, positive emotions and a reduced metabolic cost of exercising. In contrast, negative feedback resulted in participants trying to down-regulate unpleasant emotions at the expense of effort expenditure. Given this proposition, the perceived relative importance of the task is likely to determine the effort expended to maintain self-control.

Ethical issues

Beedie and Lane (2012) propose two testable hypotheses that can account for these results: First, if a participant is presented with a task that has personal meaning, they will persist with self-control, and their blood glucose levels will either remain unchanged or increase. Second, if they are presented with a task that has little or no personal meaning, then they will not persist, and their glucose levels will remain unchanged, or they will persist, and their glucose levels will reduce.

The influence of motivation to overcome depletion may lie in the fact that the depleted state does not reflect a complete exhaustion of resources, but merely a temporary deficit. Like a tired athlete who starts conserving energy long before he or she is completely exhausted, the self-regulator may begin to cut back on effortful, biologically expensive exertions long before the capacity is fully depleted. The concept of a tired athlete is, of course, relative. Some athletes are prepared to exert more effort than others and will increase the intensity of effort to maintain the standards of performance required. Ego depletion effects thus indicate conservation of a partly depleted resource, rather than full incapacity because the resource is completely gone. Personal beliefs and motivation appear capable of energizing effort, even when the resource appears depleted. The purpose of conserving resources supports the idea that one can increase energy expenditure in exceptional cases. Even more directly, depleted individuals who were given an incentive to exert self-control, in the form of either money, social acceptance or moral expectations, performed just as well on a subsequent self-control task as participants who were not depleted (Muraven and Slessareva, 2003). For instance, when paid 1 cent per cup, individuals who had to suppress their emotional reaction to a humorous video clip drank less of a vinegar-flavoured drink compared with individuals who simply watched the video with no instructions to control their emotional reaction. On the other hand, when the incentive for drinking was high (25 cents per cup), individuals who had to suppress their emotional reaction drank just as much of the sour drink as individuals who did not suppress their reaction.

Motivation can be activated via a non-conscious process also. For instance, Alberts et al. (2007) found that depleted individuals who were given primes related to persistence (either unscrambling sentences with persistence words in them or seeing a screensaver with motivational images) performed better than depleted individuals not given these primes. The results indicate that people can overcome depletion if sufficiently motivated. Thus, a reduction in glucose levels may increase the likelihood of self-control failure, but only when the individual is poorly motivated.

Given that motivation plays a critical role in contributing to self-control failures, the question then arises why past self-control efforts matter at all. Further research, based on the idea of the conservation of limited resources, suggests they do. In particular, if self-control requires glucose or other limited resources, it makes sense to use this resource as wisely as possibly. People should be careful in how and when they exert self-control, so they can have resources for future demands or emergencies. This idea is consistent with prospect theory (Tversky and Kahneman, 1981): the less money one has, the more the remaining money should be valued.

The notion that expectations could influence self-control has also been examined. Muraven et al. (2006) tested this idea by manipulating participants' expectations for the future. If people expect to exert self-control in the future, their motivation to conserve should be increased; this should be especially likely if their ego strength is already depleted. In one experiment, participants first had to control a well-learned pattern by typing a paragraph without hitting the 'e' key (participants in the control condition just typed the paragraph as they saw it). They were then told that they would take two more tests. The first was a Stroop test, where they would have to state the font colour of words. After that, they would have to solve anagrams that were either described as requiring them to 'think hard' (low self-control) or 'override impulses' (high self-control). Participants who had to exert self-control in the first part of the experiment and who expected to exert self-control in the future exhibited poorer self-control on the Stroop task compared with those who did not exert self-control in the past or those who did not expect to exert self-control in the future.

Further evidence for conservation came from participants' actual performance on the final task, in particular, how long they persisted on difficult and frustrating anagrams before quitting. There was a negative correlation between Stroop performance and time spent on the anagrams, suggesting a trade-off in resource use. That is, worse performance on the Stroop (which would suggest conserving) was associated with greater self-control on the anagram. Janssen *et al.* (2010) found a similar effect: Depleted individuals who were warned about an upcoming persuasive attempt conserved strength and, hence, generated better counter-arguments and resisted compliance more than depleted individuals who were not forewarned.

Athletes follow different types of intervention designed to reduce perceptions of fatigue during intense exercise. These interventions could be psychological, physiological or nutritional (see Lane, 2014). Emerging research suggests that energy depletion is no more than a subjective belief that one has limited resources. In contrast, those who believe they have unlimited stores of willpower are unlikely to experience ego-depletion effects. So, to increase willpower, a viable solution may be to develop the efficacy of a particular intervention, be that a nutritional aid or a well-developed training programme. The key point is to build belief around what you are doing and a confidence that, if you follow up that belief, you will perform well. The mechanism behind the belief is a reduced perception of effort, and as several studies report, rate of perceived exertion (RPE) is in fact a very good marker of energy expenditure. Moreover, reduced RPE indicates that exercise feels easier, and so you are likely to feel relaxed. Essentially, this type of intervention is about increasing the limits of what is possible and it works very simply by reducing the perception of effort required to reach optimum performance.

Despite the equivocality for the strength model and the notion that willpower is akin to some sort of energy, the strength model does offer two testable hypotheses for those seeking to measure improvements in self-control. The first prediction is that self-control strength and performance worsen. The second is that self-control strength should become stronger with exercise. Muraven *et al.* (1999) tested these predictions in a longitudinal study, assessing first for an increase in baseline self-control (akin to a muscle increasing its power in a single, all-out effort) and, second, for its stamina (as measured by first and second efforts).

Poker face: An example of surface acting in cycling

As a bike racer, over time you develop the skill of keeping a poker face. No matter how extreme a sensation you feel – no matter how close you are to cracking – you do everything in your power to mask it. This matters in racing, when hiding your true condition from your opponents is key to success, since it discourages them from attacking. Feel paralyzing pain? Look relaxed, even bored. Can't breathe? Close your mouth. About to die? Smile.

(Hamilton and Coyle, 2012, p. 155)

The above quote comes from Tyler Hamilton, a former professional cyclist, who describes a commonly used strategy to regulate emotions in cycling. Cyclists use surface acting to consciously steer behaviour towards achieving their goals. In this example, changing how emotions are expressed is intended to deceive opponents and give them false hope of being able to increase their effort and maximize time gains over their rivals.

APPLYING THE SCIENCE 5.1

Train your willpower

In a study by Hui *et al.* (2009), participants either engaged in a strong training programme (work on the Stroop task for 5 minutes, twice a day for two weeks, and rinse with a mouthwash that produces a powerful burning sensation) or a weak training programme (no conflict between ink colour and word and diluted mouthwash). At the end of this training, participants returned to the laboratory and engaged in several tasks that required self-control. Compared with those who had no training or those who had the weak training, those who underwent the strong training held their hand in ice water significantly longer. They also performed better on a visual search task that requires regulating attention and concentration, had better dental care (based on amount of dental floss and toothpaste used) and reported better health-related behaviours.

Recent research by Muraven (2010) has further extended these findings to make it clear that the effects of practising self-control are above and beyond any effects expected from expectation or self-efficacy. Smokers who were interested in quitting were assigned one of four tasks to practise for 2 weeks before beginning a cessation attempt. Two of these conditions required self-control (avoid eating sweets and squeeze a handgrip for as long as possible, twice a day), and two did not (maintain a diary of any time they exerted self-control and work on difficult maths problems). Consistent with previous research, smokers who practised tasks that required self-control remained abstinent longer than smokers who practised tasks that did not require self-control. Moreover, the control tasks evoked awareness of self-control, increased self-monitoring and increased self-efficacy, and participants expected these tasks to be helpful in their cessation attempt. This means that the effects of practising self-control on subsequent improvements in self-control are above and separate from the smokers' expectation that it should help them quit smoking, improvements in self-efficacy or greater self-monitoring. Put another way, practising self-control has a direct effect on subsequent self-control performance.

Implementation intentions

One way in which a person may exert self-control and support goal-directed behaviour is to form an implementation intention, or an 'if–then' plan (Gollwitzer, 1996). An if–then plan has the structure of, 'If situation X arises, then I will perform the goal-directed response Y!' Webb and Sheeran (2003) found support for the use of if–then plans to overcome the effects of ego depletion.

ACTIVITY 5.4

Think of a barrier to achieving your goal for your next competition. Then think of a solution to overcoming this barrier – one that, if you commit to it, will see you achieve your goal. Now write your own if–then plan:

Example	Your own if–then plan
A goal intention for a runner might be: 'I want to achieve Z time for XX distance!' An example of an if–then plan designed to help the runner attain their goal might be: '*If* I notice my pace is too quick and I find myself drifting to the back of the group and I feel I sense a fear of being humiliated, *then* I will remember my target pace and say to myself, "If I run that pace, the race will be a success!"'	

BEYOND THE FRONTIER

As Beedie and Lane (2012) suggested, whatever the task or population chosen for a study, identifying the priorities of participants, or recruiting participants to whom the task is meaningful, should form part of the research process. Even so, the degree to which any selected task is meaningful to any one individual will vary substantially, even within apparently homogeneous groups. On this basis, over and above the strategic selection of hypothetically matched tasks and participants described above, post hoc quantitative and qualitative assessment of the degree to which participants perceived the task as meaningful should be conducted. The mechanisms of self-control are more likely to be elucidated if researchers have data indicating the perceived meaningfulness of a task, and if they are able to ascertain from participants, in those participants' own words, why they believe they did or did not achieve self-control in relation to the task(s) performed. Including this should be an important part of future research.

The challenge for researchers is to select meaningful tasks in experimental research designs. For example, athletes need to exert self-control over their emotions before a competition. Arriving late at a competition and not being able to warm up properly can be a stressful experience. And so researchers could ask athletes to prepare for a simulated competition at a pre-agreed set time, but bring forward or delay the test to disrupt the athlete's pre-race routine. Although selecting a meaningful independent task for a population may appear straightforward and offers researchers the chance to be creative, identifying an unrelated self-control task for the dependent task is more problematic. To date, researchers have struggled to use a suitable task with high external validity to measure baseline self-control. Assessing self-control via a handgrip dynamometer or Stroop task has little real-world application for athletes and exercisers. Pre-existing differences may already exist in self-control tasks requiring both physical and mental effort. Research should, therefore, look to use existing data and make use of technology to track self-control behaviour in real-world settings.

CONCLUSIONS

Self-control is a key factor explaining individual and cultural success. Self-control has been proposed to operate like a muscle. According to the strength model, acts of self-control rely on a single resource, limited in its supply – blood glucose is thought to be a key component of this resource. Like using a muscle, exerting self-control is tiring, but with rest and recovery it becomes stronger. However, alternative theories have begun to challenge the notion that the resource is limited. Despite these challenges, the basic premise that willpower is like a muscle (i.e. is effortful and becomes tiring, and with rest becomes stronger) does provide a model for practitioners to explore interventions to overcome the effects of ego depletion. A range of strategies designed to help people preserve or restore this resource have been used to demonstrate that performance can be influenced by manipulating both physiological and psychological mechanisms. For example, cyclists who received negative feedback were motivated to use glucose (Beedie *et al.*, 2012), and students who believed willpower was unlimited appeared to experience fewer ego–depletion effects (Miller *et al.*, 2012).

KEY CONCEPTS AND TERMS

Self-control
The deliberate effort to alter the way one thinks, feels or behaves, so as to inhibit dominant responses.

Ego depletion
A temporary state of diminished resources following an acute bout of self-control.

RECOMMENDED FURTHER READING

Baumeister, R. F., Vohs, K. D. and Tice, D. M. (2007). The strength model of self-control. *Current Directions in Psychological Science, 16*, 351–5.

Beedie, C. J. and Lane, A. M. (2012). The role of glucose in self-control: Another look at the evidence and an alternative conceptualization. *Personality and Social Psychology Review, 16*, 143–53.

Beedie, C. J., Lane, A. M. and Wilson, M. G. (2012). A possible role for emotion and emotion regulation in physiological responses to false performance feedback in 10 mile laboratory cycling. *Applied Psychophysiology and Biofeedback, 37*(4), 269–77.

Hagger, M. S., Wood, C., Stiff, C. and Chatzisarantis, N. L. D. (2010). Ego depletion and the strength model of self-control: A meta-analysis. *Psychological Bulletin, 136*, 495–525.

Kurzban, R. (2010). Does the brain consume additional glucose during self-control tasks? *Evolutionary Psychology, 8*, 244–59.

SAMPLE ESSAY QUESTIONS

1 With reference to theory and research, discuss the assumption that exerting self-control depletes a limited resource.

2 Describe a hypothetical dual-task experiment and highlight why it is necessary to provide a true baseline for performance. Provide a detailed example of how the dual-task design could be used in a study of a sport psychology intervention.

3 Many ego-depletion studies have used tasks that vary in relevance and meaning to participants and, therefore, are likely to vary in the extent to which they require self-control resources. Discuss the contention that the degree to which one must exert self-control moderates the ego-depletion effect.

4 Although the short-term effects of exerting self-control may be diminished resources, the long-term effect may be the opposite. Discuss the idea that self-control operates like a muscle or strength.

REFERENCES

Alberts, H. J. E. M., Martijn, C., Greb, J., Merckelbach, H. and de Vries, N. K. (2007). Carrying on or giving in: The role of automatic processes in overcoming ego depletion. *British Journal of Social Psychology, 46*, 383–99.

Aldwin, C. M. and Revenson, T. A. (1987). Does coping help? A re-examination of the relation between coping and mental health. *Journal of Personality and Social Psychology, 53*(2), 337–48.

Baumeister, R. F. (2005). *The Cultural Animal: Human nature, meaning, and social life.* New York: Oxford University Press.

Baumeister, R. F. (2012). Self-control – the moral muscle. *The Psychologist, 25*(2), 112–15.

Baumeister, R. F., Vohs, K. D. and Tice, D. M. (2007). The strength model of self-control. *Current Directions in Psychological Science, 16*, 351–5.

Baumeister, R. F., Bratslavsky, E., Muraven, M. and Tice, D. M. (1998). Ego depletion: Is the active self a limited resource? *Journal of Personality and Social Psychology, 74*(5), 1252–65.

Beedie, C. J. and Lane, A. M. (2012). The role of glucose in self-control: Another look at the evidence and an alternative conceptualization. *Personality and Social Psychology Review, 16*, 143–53.

Beedie, C. J., Lane, A. M. and Wilson, M. G. (2012). A possible role for emotion and emotion regulation in physiological responses to false performance feedback in 10 mile laboratory cycling. *Applied Psychophysiology and Biofeedback, 37*(4), 269–77.

Beedie, C. J., Terry, P. C. and Lane, A. M. (2000). The profile of mood states and athletic performance: Two meta-analyses. *Journal of Applied Sport Psychology, 12*(1), 49–68.

Bliss, T. M. and Sapolsky, R. M. (2001). Interactions among glucose, lactate and adenosine regulate energy substrate utilization in hippocampal cultures. *Brain Research, 899*(1–2), 134–41.

Bray, S. R., Martin Ginis, K. A., Hicks, A. L. and Woodgate, J. (2008). Effects of self-regulatory strength depletion on muscular performance and EMG activation. *Psychophysiology, 45*(2), 337–43.

Carter, J. M., Jeukendrup, A. E., & Jones, D. A. (2004). The effect of carbohydrate mouth rinse on 1-h cycle time trial performance. *Medicine and Science in Sports and Exercise*, 36(12), 2107–2111.

Carver, C. S. and Scheier, M. F. (2004). Self-regulation of action and affect. In Vohs, K. D. and Baumeister, R. F. (eds) *Handbook of Self-regulation: Research, theory, and applications*, 13–39. New York: Guilford Press.

Chambers, E. S., Bridge, M. W. and Jones, D. A. (2009). Carbohydrate sensing in the human mouth: Effects on exercise performance and brain activity. *The Journal of Physiology, 587*(8), 1779–94.

Clarkson, J. J., Hirt, E. R., Jia, L. and Alexander, M. B. (2010). When perception is more than reality: The effect of perceived versus actual resource depletion on self-regulatory behavior. *Journal of Personality and Social Psychology, 98*, 29–46.

Coker, R. H. and Kjaer, M. (2005). Glucoregulation during exercise: The role of the neuroendocrine system. *Sports Medicine, 35*(7), 575–83.

Duckworth, A. L. and Seligman, M. E. P. (2005). Self-discipline outdoes IQ in predicting academic performance of adolescents. *Psychological Science, 6*(12), 939–44.

Englert, C. and Bertrams, A. (2012). Anxiety, ego depletion, and sports performance. *Journal of Sport & Exercise Psychology, 34*, 580–99.

Friesen, A., Devonport, T. J., Sellars, C. N. and Lane, A. M. (2013). A narrative account of decision-making and interpersonal emotion regulation using a social–functional approach to emotions. *International Journal of Sport and Exercise Psychology, 11*(2), 203–14.

Frijda, N. H. (2010). Impulsive action and motivation. *Biological psychology, 84*(3), 570–9.

Gailliot, M. T. and Baumeister, R. F. (2007). The physiology of willpower: Linking blood glucose to self-control. *Journal of Personality and Social Psychology, 11*, 303–27.

Gailliot, M. T., Baumeister, R. F., DeWall, C. N., Maner, J. K., Ashby Plant, E., Tice, D. M., Brewer, L. E. and Schmeichel, B. J. (2007). Self-control relies on glucose as a limited energy sources: Willpower is more than a metaphor. *Journal of Personality and Social Psychology*, *92*, 325–36.

Gollwitzer, P. M. (1996). The volitional benefits of planning. In Gollwitzer, P. M. and Bargh, J. A. (eds) *The Psychology of Action: Linking cognition and motivation to behavior*, pp. 287–312. New York: Guilford Press.

Goodyear, PhD, L. J., & Kahn, MD, B. B. (1998). Exercise, glucose transport, and insulin sensitivity. *Annual Review of Medicine*, *49*(1), 235–261.

Grandey, A. A., Fisk, G. M. and Steiner, D. D. (2005). Must 'service with a smile' be stressful? The moderating role of personal control for American and French employees. *Journal of Applied Psychology*, *90*(5), 893–904.

Gulve, E. A., & Spina, R. J. (1995). Effect of 7–10 days of cycle ergometer exercise on skeletal muscles. GLUT-4 protein content. *Journal of Applied Physiology*, *79*(5), 1562–1566.

Hagger, M. S., Wood, C., Stiff, C. and Chatzisarantis, N. L. D. (2010). Ego depletion and the strength model of self-control: A meta-analysis. *Psychological Bulletin*, *136*, 495–525.

Hamilton, T. and Coyle, D. (2012) *The Secret Race: Inside the hidden world of the Tour de France: doping, cover-ups, and winning at all costs*. London: Bantam Press.

Hankonen, N., Absetz, P., Kinnunen, M., Haukkala, A. and Jallinoja, P. (2013). Toward identifying a broader range of social cognitive determinants of dietary intentions and behaviours. *Applied Psychology: Health and Well-being*, *5*(1), 118–35.

Hoedemaekers, C. W. E., Klein Gunnewiek, J. M. T., Prinsen, M. A., Willems, J. L. and Van der Hoeven, J. G. (2008). Accuracy of bedside glucose measurement from three glucometers in critically ill patients. *Critical Care Medicine*, *36*, 3062–6.

Hoffman, W., Baumeister, R. F., Förster, G. and Vohs, K. D. (2012). Everyday temptations: An experience sampling study of desire, conflict, and self-control. *Journal of Personality and Social Psychology*, *102*(6), 1318–35.

Hui, S.-K. A., Wright, R. A., Stewart, C. C., Simmons, A., Eaton, B. and Nolte, R. N. (2009). Performance, cardiovascular, and health behavior effects of an inhibitory strength training intervention. *Motivation and Emotion*, *33*, 419–34.

Janssen, L., Fennis, B. M. and Pruyn, A. T. H. (2010). Forewarned is forearmed: Conserving self-control strength to resist social influence. *Journal of Experimental Social Psychology*, *46*(6), 911–21.

Job, V., Dweck, C. S. and Walton, G. W. (2010). Ego depletion – Is it all in your head? Implicit theories about willpower affect self-regulation. *Psychological Science*, *21*, 1686–93.

Job, V., Walton, G. M., Bernecker, K. and Dweck, C. S. (2013). Beliefs about willpower determine the impact of glucose on self-control. *Proceedings of the National Academy of Sciences*, *110*(37), 14837–42.

Johnson, F., Pratt, M. and Wardle, J. (2012). Dietary restraint and self-regulation in eating behaviour. *International Journal of Obesity*, *36*, 665–74.

Jones, M. (2003). Controlling emotions in sport. *The Sport Psychologist*, *17*, 471–86.

Khan, A. I., Vasquez, Y., Gray, J., Wians, F. H., Jr. and Kroll, M. H. (2006). The variability of results between point-of-care testing glucose meters and the central laboratory analyzer. *Archives of Pathology & Laboratory Medicine*, *130*, 1527–32.

Kimmage, P. (2007). *Rough Ride*. London: Yellow Jersey Press.

Kraemer, R. R. and Brown, B. S. (1986). Alterations in plasma-volume-corrected blood components of marathon runners and concomitant relationship to performance. *European Journal of Applied Physiology and Occupational Physiology*, *55*(6), 579–84.

Kratz, A., Lewandrowski, K. B., Siegel, A. J., Chun, K. Y., Flood, J. G., Van Cott, E. M. and Lee-Lewandrowski, E. (2002). Effect of marathon running on hematologic and biochemical laboratory parameters, including cardiac markers. *American Journal of Clinical Pathology*, *118*(6), 856–63.

Kurzban, R. (2010). Does the brain consume additional glucose during self-control tasks? *Evolutionary Psychology*, *8*, 244–59.

Lane, A. (2014). Using self-help interventions. *Peak Performance*, *322*, 5–7.

Lane, A. M., Beedie, C. J., Devonport, T. J. and Stanley, D. M. (2011a). Instrumental emotion regulation in sport: Relationships between beliefs about emotion and emotion regulation strategies used by athletes. *Scandinavian Journal of Medicine and Science in Sports*, *21*(6), 445–51.

Lane, A. M., Wilson, M. G., Whyte, G. P. and Shave, R. (2011b). Physiological correlates of emotion-regulation during prolonged cycling performance. *Applied Psychophysiology and Biofeedback*, *36*(3), 181–4.

Lappalainen, R., Saba, A., Holm, L., Mykkanen, H., Gibney, M. J. and Moles, A. (1997). Difficulties in trying to eat healthier: Descriptive analysis of perceived barriers for healthy eating. *European Journal of Clinical Nutrition*, *51*(9), 641.

McKee, H., Ntoumanis, N. and Smith, B. (2013). Weight maintenance: Self-regulatory factors underpinning success and failure. *Psychology and Health*, *28*(10), 1207–23.

Mergenthaler, P., Lindauer, U., Dienel, G. A. and Meise, A. (2013). Sugar for the brain: The role of glucose in physiological and pathological brain function. *Trends in Neurosciences*, *36*(10), 587–97.

Miller, E. M., Walton, G. M., Dweck, C. S., Job, V., Trzesniewski, K. H. and McClure, S. M. (2012). Theories of willpower affect sustained learning. *PLoS ONE*, *7*(6), e38680.

Minninnen, A. H. (2004). Metabolic effects of the very-lowcarbohydrate diets: Misunderstood 'villains' of human metabolism. *Journal of the International Society of Sports Nutrition*, *1*, 7–11.

Muraven, M. (2010). Building self-control strength: Practicing self-control leads to improved self-control performance. *Journal of Experimental Social Psychology*, *46*(2), 465–8.

Muraven, M. and Baumeister, R. F. (2000). Self-regulation and depletion of limited resources: Does self-control resemble a muscle? *Psychological Bulletin*, *126*, 247–59.

Muraven, M., Baumeister, R. F. and Tice, D. M. (1999). Longitudinal improvement of self-regulation through practice: Building self-control strength through repeated exercise. *The Journal of Social Psychology*, *139*, 446–57.

Muraven, M., Shmueli, D. and Burkley, E. (2006). Conserving self-control strength. *Journal of Personality and Social Psychology*, *91*(3), 524–37.

Muraven, M. and Slessareva, E. (2003). Mechanisms of self-control failure: Motivation and limited resources, *29*(7), 894–906.

Muraven, M., Tice, D. M. and Baumeister, R. F. (1998). Self-control as a limited resource: Regulatory depletion patterns. *Journal of Personality and Social Psychology*, *74*, 774–89.

Nesse, R. M. and Ellsworth, P. C. (2009). Evolution, emotions, and emotional disorders. *American Psychologist, 64*(2), 129–39.

Oltmanns, K. M., Melchert, U. H., Scholand-Engler, U. G., Howitz, M. C., Schultes, B., Schweiger, U. and Pellerin. L. (2008). Differential energetic response of brain vs. skeletal muscle upon glycemic variations in healthy humans. *American Journal of Physiology: Regulatory, Integrative, Comparative Physiology, 294*, R12–R16.

Scholey, A. B., Sünram-Lea, S., Greer, J., Elliot, J. M. and Kennedy, D. O. (2009). Glucose administration prior to a divided attention task improves tracking performance but not word recognition: Evidence against differential memory enhancement? *Psychopharmacology, 202*, 549–88.

Segerstrom, S. C. and Nes, L. S. (2007). Heart rate variability reflects self-regulatory strength, effort, and fatigue. *Psychological Science, 18*, 275–81.

Tamir, M. (2009). What do people want to feel and why? Pleasure and utility in emotion regulation. *Current Directions in Psychological Science, 18*, 101–5.

Tamir, M., Mitchell, C. and Gross, J. J. (2008). Hedonic and instrumental motives in anger regulation. *Psychological Science, 19*, 324–8.

Tamminen, K. A. and Crocker, P. R. E (2013). 'I control my own emotions for the sake of the team': Emotional self-regulation and interpersonal emotion regulation among female high-performance curlers. *Psychology of Sport and Exercise, 14*(5), 737–47.

Tangney, J. P., Baumeister, R. F. and Boone, A. L. (2004). High self-control predicts good adjustment, less pathology, better grades, and interpersonal success. *Journal of Personality, 72*(2), 271–324.

Tversky, A. and Kahneman, D. (1981). The framing of decisions and the psychology of choice. *Science, 211*(4481), 453–8.

Umstattd, M. R., Wilcox, S., Saunders, R., Watkins, K. and Dowda, M. (2008). Self-regulation and physical activity: The relationship in older adults. *American Journal of Health Behavior, 32*(2), 115–24.

Uphill, M. A. and Jones, M. V. (2007). Antecedents of emotions in elite athletes: A cognitive motivational relational theory perspective. *Research Quarterly for Exercise and Sport, 78*(1), 79–89.

van Hall, G., Stromstad, M., Rasmussen, P., Jans, O., Zaar, M., Gam, C., Quistorff, B., Secher, N. H. and Nielsen, H. B. (2009). Blood lactate is an important energy source for the human brain. *Journal of Cerebral Blood Flow and Metabolism, 29*(6), 1121–9.

Vlasselaers, D., Van Herpe, T., Milants, I., Eerdekens, M., Wouters, P. J., De Moor, B. and Van den Berghe, G. (2008). Blood glucose measurements in arterial blood of intensive care unit patients submitted to tight glycemic control: Agreement between bedside tests. *Journal of Diabetes Science and Technology, 2*, 932–8.

Vohs, K. D., Baumeister, R. F., Schmeichel, B. J., Twenge, J. M., Nelson, N. M. and Tice, D. M. (2008). Making choices impairs subsequent self-control: A limited resource account of decision making, self-regulation, and active initiative. *Journal of Personality and Social Psychology, 94*, 883–98.

Vohs, K. D., Finkenauer, C. and Baumeister, R. F. (2011). The sum of friends' and lovers' self-control scores predicts relationship quality. *Social Psychological and Personality Science, 2*(2), 138–45.

Wallace, H. M., Baumeister, R. F. and Vohs, K. D. (2005). Audience support and choking under pressure: A home disadvantage? *Journal of Sports Sciences*, *23*(4), 429–38.

Wang, X. T. and Dvorak, R. D. (2010). Sweet future: Fluctuating blood glucose levels affect future discounting. *Psychological Science*, *21*(2), 183–8.

Wang, P. and Mariman, E. C. (2008). Insulin resistance in an energy-centered perspective. *Physiology and Behavior*, *94*, 198–205.

Webb, T. L. and Sheeran, P. (2003). Can implementation intentions help to overcome ego-depletion? *Journal of Experimental Social Psychology*, *39*, 279–86.

Wilson, M. R., Wood, G. and Vine, S. J. (2009). The influence of anxiety on visual attentional control in basketball free throw shooting. *Journal of Sport & Exercise Psychology*, *31*(2), 152–68.

Wood, G. and Wilson, M. R. (2010). A moving goalkeeper distracts penalty takers and impairs shooting accuracy. *Journal of Sports Sciences*, *28*(9), 937–46.

6 Understanding stress and coping among competitive athletes in sport

Applying psychological theory and research

Tracey Devonport

CHAPTER SUMMARY

It is commonly accepted that the competitive sports environment is characterized by situations of intense pressure presenting a potentially stressful environment (Hanton et al., 2005; Rumbold et al., 2012). Sport performers must manage a range of pressures and psychological responses if they are to fulfil their potential. Consider the case of Rebecca Adlington: during the Beijing Olympic Games (2008) she became the first British woman to win two Olympic swimming gold medals. Four years later, at the London 2012 Olympic Games, Rebecca talked about the pressures of trying to emulate her 2008 success while competing at a home games:

> *The most I've ever competed in front of at home is 2,500. I'm not used to that crowd reaction coming out . . . maybe it's a little bit overwhelming for us all . . . I think the pressure, the expectation and everything going into this meet has been a little bit of a battle.[1]*

Being able to successfully help individuals fulfil their potential presents an ambitious objective for someone in any profession. In sport, as illustrated above, there may be occasions where an athlete's mind is invaded by unpleasant thoughts and emotions that are associated with perceiving competition as a huge pressure.

High-profile examples such as Rebecca's could represent the tip of a metaphoric iceberg whereby the pressures of achieving and maintaining sporting excellence may lead to unhappiness and underperformance. Where individuals are unable to effectively cope with such pressures, they are likely to experience poor performance, feel dissatisfied with their experiences and possibly drop out of sport (Sagar et al., 2009; Voight, 2009). Research indicates that, as well as experiencing stressors resulting directly from the sport organization (selection pressures, personal performance), athletes may at the same time be experiencing academic, employment, developmental and social stressors (Devonport and Lane, 2009; Devonport et al., 2013; Smetana et al., 2006; Sullivan and Nashman, 1998). Sport stressors (such as selection issues or training demands) and non-sport stressors (such as relationship issues or exam pressures) may occur independently of each other, or may co-occur and/or interact. Any one stressor or combination of stressors has the potential to challenge an athlete's ability to cope and, ultimately, may influence their ability to train and compete optimally. Rebecca Adlington illustrated the challenges of managing combined stressors during a television interview recorded in December 2009 with the BBC.[2] Within this interview, she comments:

> *It's been hard for me to deal with everything after Beijing, like being recognised, and there are other things like moving house and personal situations, your swimming gets affected by that . . . Growing up, it's hard enough to deal with change anyway, with your body shape, and changing as a woman.*

A responsibility for researchers and applied practitioners alike is to seek to understand the environments in which athletes operate, and identify and develop strategies to manage stressors. Enhancing coping skills that could be used to manage stress in different domains of an athlete's life is a strategy that is worth pursuing. The development of generic coping-skill interventions may help attenuate stressors and facilitate the achievement of personal goals across domains (Smith, 1999).

LEARNING OUTCOMES

When you have studied this chapter, you should be able to:

1 Identify stressors and consequences of stress among athletes
2 Describe key features of Lazarus's TMSC (Lazarus and Folkman, 1984) and CMRT of emotions (Lazarus, 1991)
3 Describe common coping classifications and the characteristics of effective coping
4 Detail typical features of coping interventions and considerations of application

THE IMPORTANCE OF APPLYING THEORY IN PRACTICE

A criticism of sport and exercise psychology research generally, and coping research specifically, has been the lack of applied research that strives to bridge the gap between theory and practice (Lane and Terry, 2000; Lazarus, 2001). Folkman (2009, p. 76) notes that, in most coping research, 'what may ultimately be the most important translation – the translation to practice – is barely touched upon. Often those who do theory development or research consider the translation from theory and research to practice to be another person's job'. The application of coping theory in applied practice is important for three reasons:

1   Theory can focus attention on key determinants of stressors and coping behaviours, thereby improving intervention design and efficacy (Michie *et al.*, 2008; Crosby *et al.*, 2009).
2   Theory can help identify indicators that enable the evaluation of an intervention.
3   Utilizing theory to inform practice enables its practical utility to be evaluated and subsequently corroborated or modified (Michie *et al.*, 2008).

This chapter will explore literature pertaining to stress and coping in sport. It begins by exploring the sources of sports stressors encountered by competitive athletes and continues by exploring the potential consequences of stress. The chapter will then review the work of Lazarus, which is commonly utilized in the sport coping literature; this includes the transactional model of stress and coping (TMSC) (Lazarus and Folkman, 1984) and the cognitive–motivational–relational theory (CMRT) of emotions (Lazarus, 1991, 1999, 2000). As we unpack this body of work, a range of coping typologies that may be utilized when anticipating, or in response to, stress will be explored. Finally, the chapter will examine research that has sought to apply coping interventions; this will include issues relating to their implementation and evaluation. Throughout this chapter, readers will be encouraged to consider the practical application of materials presented.

LEARNING OUTCOME 1

Identify stressors and consequences of stress among athletes

Stress is a common experience in sport

Andrew Murray (18 years old) made the biggest jump of any player in 2005 as he surged from 514 in the world rankings to number 65 by the end of the year. As a result, Murray was then touted as a future champion. Having lost in straight sets to Juan Ignacio Chela in the first round of the 2006 Australian Open (Tennis), he gave an insight into the stressors he faced: 'It's difficult for me to go out there and try and perform to the best that I can when I'm expected to win all these matches.' After it was then suggested in the media conference that he had received nothing but good press since he arrived on the circuit, Murray answered, 'You don't think there's any pressure on me? . . . If you guys [the media] don't think you're putting pressure on me, then that's fine. I'll forget about it.'[3]

Athletes can learn to manage stressors

In June 2013, having won a gold medal at the London 2012 Olympic Games, followed by the US Open title, Murray reflected, 'Because of what's happened since [Wimbledon 2012], if I can manage to get myself into the latter stages of the tournament I'd be better equipped to deal with the pressures that go with that.'[4] Murray went on to win Wimbledon in 2013, the first British male winner since 1936.

It is important to identify stressors experienced by athletes so that they can be offered assistance and guidance in developing adaptive coping. This is not to suggest that all athletes require coping assistance, but, by monitoring coping, it is possible to help ensure that an athlete is fulfilling or continues to fulfil their potential. Stressors identified to date include coach/teammate relationships (Gould *et al.*, 1993); critical comments (Anshel and Delany, 2001); competition preparation issues (McKay *et al.*, 2008; Devonport *et al.*, 2013); excessive pressure (Smoll and Smith, 1996); lack of role clarity or role structure (Woodman and Hardy, 2001); not performing to required standard (Reeves *et al.*, 2009); observing an opponent playing well or cheating (Nicholls *et al.*, 2006); opponents (Anshel and Delany, 2001; Nicholls *et al.*, 2005); overemphasis on winning (Nicholls *et al.*, 2005); personal goals and expectations (Hatzigeorgiadis, 2006; Thelwell *et al.*, 2007); physical and mental errors (Gould *et al.*, 1993; Holt, 2003); receiving a wrong call from officials (Reeves *et al.*, 2009); selection issues (Woodman and Hardy, 2001); spectators/selectors (Nicholls *et al.*, 2005; Devonport *et al.*, 2013); self-doubts about talent (Holt and Dunn, 2004); self-presentational concerns (McKay *et al.*, 2008); suffering pain or injury (Smith *et al.*, 1990; Nicholls *et al.*, 2006); and training environment (Woodman and Hardy, 2001).

A good way of exploring stressors in sport is through introspection: see Activity Box 6.1.

Identifying the possible consequences of stress

Anshel and Delany (2001) suggest stress appraisals can cause significant psychological, physiological, emotional and behavioural responses (see Table 6.1). Experiencing the debilitating effects of stress can affect mood (see Lane, this issue), cause anxiety (see Uphill, this issue) and reduce confidence (see Hays *et al.*, this issue). By contrast, some individuals appear to thrive on stress, and, although such individuals sometimes experience unpleasant mood and emotional responses (see Lane, this issue; Uphill, this issue), these tend not to debilitate performance.

In order to better understand how to anticipate and manage stress appraisals and their consequences, it is necessary to consider and apply theory.

ACTIVITY 6.1

Reflect back over your personal experiences and identify the extent to which you agree with the stressors identified, offering a justification for your decision.

Stressor	Agree	Disagree	Justification
Coach/teammate relations	Yes		A teammate always tries to build me up, 'you are looking good' and that sort of thing. It does the opposite though, as I start feeling nervous. I don't know if he knows it has this effect on me; I think he does it so I say something positive about him – stresses me out'
Critical comments			
Competition preparation issues			
Excessive pressure			
Lack of role clarity or role structure			
Not performing to required standard			
Observing an opponent playing well or cheat			
Opponents			
Overemphasis on winning			
Personal goals and expectations			
Physical and mental errors			
Receiving a wrong call from officials			
Selection issues			
Spectators/ selectors			
Self-doubts about talent			
Self-presentational concerns			
Suffering pain or injury			
Training environment			

TABLE 6.1 Symptoms of stress

Psychological symptoms	Emotional symptoms
Memory problems	Moody and hypersensitive
Difficulty making decisions	Restlessness and anxiety
Inability to concentrate	Depression
Confusion	Anger and resentment
Catastrophizing/generalizing	Easily irritated
Repetitive or racing thoughts	Sense of being overwhelmed
Poor judgement	Lack of confidence
Loss of objectivity	Apathy
Physical symptoms	**Behavioural symptoms**
Headaches	Eating more or less
Digestive problems	Too much or too little sleep
Muscle tension and pain	Self-imposed isolation
Sleep disturbances	Neglecting responsibilities
Fatigue	Increased substance use
Chest pain, irregular heartbeat	Nervous habits (e.g. nail-biting, pacing)
High blood pressure	Teeth-grinding or jaw-clenching
Weight gain or loss	Overreacting to unexpected problems
Skin problems	
Decreased sex drive	

LEARNING OUTCOME 2

Describe key features of Lazarus's (Lazarus and Folkman, 1984)
TMSC and CMRT of emotions (Lazarus, 1991)

It has been suggested that the theoretical frameworks of stress and coping offered by Lazarus (TMSC; Lazarus and Folkman, 1984; CMRT, Lazarus, 1991) are the most widely accepted (Aldwin, 1994; Frydenberg and Lewis, 2004). In this section, we will consider, first, the main ideas presented by the TMSC, and then conceptual developments outlined in the CMRT.

The TMSC (Lazarus and Folkman, 1984) suggests that, when an individual is faced with something that is potentially stressful, personal and situational factors interact and ultimately influence the appraisal process (see Figure 6.1). The appraisal process consists of primary and secondary appraisals. During primary appraisal, the individual essentially asks themselves:

- What are the implications of this for me?
- Does it have potential to harm, hinder or benefit?

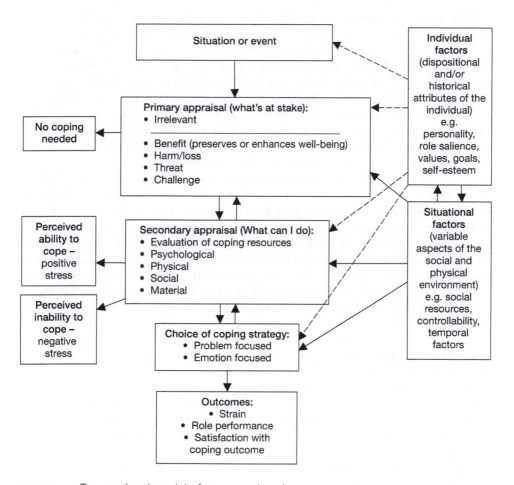

FIGURE 6.1 Transactional model of stress and coping

Source: Lazarus and Folkman, 1984

Primary appraisal results in an event being interpreted in one of three ways:

1   as irrelevant, where there are no implications for well-being;
2   as beneficial, where the event is perceived to preserve or enhance well-being; and
3   as stressful, where there is a perceived harm/loss, threat and/or challenge to well-being.

Appraisals of harm/loss are characterized by perceptions that damage has already been sustained. A threat appraisal occurs when harm or loss are possible. A challenge appraisal reflects a perception that there may be an opportunity for mastery and gain (Lazarus and Folkman, 1984). The primary appraisals of harm/loss, threat or challenge are not mutually exclusive, and thus it is possible for an individual to appraise an event in more than one way at the same time.

If the situation is appraised as stressful, the individual then engages secondary appraisal and considers what they can do to prevent or minimize stress. Secondary appraisal focuses on minimizing harm or maximizing gains through coping responses (Lazarus and Folkman, 1984). There is an evaluation of coping options and available resources that may include social, physical, psychological and material assets (Lazarus and Folkman, 1984). Primary and secondary appraisals occur at virtually the same time and interact to determine the significance and meaning of events with regards to well-being. Depending on how a stressor is perceived, it will have different emotional and behavioural responses. An individual may feel fearful and try to avoid the situation, or may feel challenged and take action to try to remedy the situation.

Lazarus presented conceptual developments from the early TMSC in the CMRT of emotions (Lazarus, 1991; Lazarus and Lazarus, 1994). Whereas the TMSC is centred on psychological states experienced during transactions between the person and the environment in situations appraised as taxing, exceeding resources and/or endangering well-being (Lazarus and Folkman, 1984), the CMRT is focused on emotion. The CMRT suggests that emotions arise from the relational meaning of an encounter between a person and the environment. Relational meaning refers to the meaning a person construes from their relationship with the environment (Lazarus, 1998). An emotion is elicited by primary and secondary appraisals of considerations such as environmental demands, constraints and resources, and also by their juxtaposition with a person's motives and beliefs. Each emotion involves a different core relational theme (Lazarus, 1991), as each emotion is brought about by appraisal of the personal significance of an encounter.

With reference to the core relational themes, the CMRT suggests that, 'for each emotion, there are at most six appraisal-related decisions to make, sometimes less, creating a rich and diverse cognitive pattern with which to describe the relational meanings which distinguish any emotion from each of the others' (Lazarus, 1991, p. 216).

Three are primary appraisal components, including: goal relevance (the extent to which an encounter relates to personal goals); goal congruence or incongruence (the extent to which a transaction is consistent or inconsistent with what the person wants); and type of ego involvement (consideration of diverse aspects of ego–identity or personal commitments). The remaining three are secondary appraisal components, including: an evaluation of blame or credit (establishing where possible who or what is accountable or responsible); coping potential (if and how the demands can be managed by the individual); and future expectations (whether, for any reason, things are likely to change, becoming more or less goal congruent). The specific combination of primary and secondary appraisals is proposed to influence the intensity and type of emotion elicited. In addition to appraisals, how the individual copes with situations or events will also mediate the types and intensity of emotion they experience (Lazarus, 1991).

The TMSC and CMRT are both structured around transactions between:

1   antecedent variables (environmental variables, such as demands, resources and constraints, and personality variables, such as motives and beliefs about the self and the world);

2   mediating processes (appraisal, core relational themes, and coping processes); and

3   outcomes (acute outcomes, such as immediate emotions, and long-term outcomes, such as chronic emotional patterns, well-being and physical health).

Both the TMSC and CMRT acknowledge that there are many factors that may increase the probability of stress perceptions. For illustrative purposes, the role of personal goals on stress appraisal, and subsequent coping processes will be examined. A goal is a mental representation of a desired future state that can influence evaluations, emotions and behaviours (Aarts et al., 2004). Lazarus (1999) suggested that goal commitment is an important appraisal variable because, without this, an individual has nothing at stake. Lazarus described how primary appraisal is heavily focused on personal goals, including considerations such as goal relevance and goal congruence or incongruence (Lazarus and Folkman, 1984; Lazarus, 1991). Individuals can intensively strive to achieve two competing goals simultaneously. This phenomenon is known as goal conflict and can be associated with psychological distress (Kelly et al., 2013). In competitive sport, goal conflict commonly arises when an individual is looking to manage competing sport and family goals. Former England rugby union international Lawrence Dallaglio felt that, 'there has to be a selfishness in sport if you want to be at the top'.[5] Lawrence featured in the interview show *Piers Morgan's Life Stories* and noted that, since retiring from international sport, he felt he had become a better person. He explained that, as an athlete, his needs came first; others, including family, came second. The need to make personal sacrifices was echoed by Mo Farah upon becoming double world champion in the 5,000 and 10,000 m. Mo revealed, 'I've been away for four months and my twin girls don't recognise me. That's hard. Rihanna understands what daddy needs to do, but the kids grow so fast and that's what I was thinking about there'.[6] Athletes must learn to prioritize goals and reconcile these priorities, if they are to avoid or delimit the potentially stressful consequences of goal conflict. Furthermore, they must find ways of fulfilling the emotional and practical needs of significant others, if they are to maintain these relationships (e.g. with family, friends, partner, coach). I (Devonport) am not a high-performing athlete, nor do I compete any longer, but, having recently completed a marathon, I experienced frequent conflict of training (completing long runs) and family (I have a 1-year-old and 3-year-old) goals. I had to manage this conflict carefully in order to ensure I completed the necessary marathon training while blocking out time for family.

In looking to explain the relationships between goals and behaviour, Carver and Scheier (1998) proposed the control process model of behaviour. This proposes that, during the execution of a task, individuals constantly monitor their performance in relation to their goal(s). When discrepancies between a goal and performance are detected (attainment of goal or rate of progress towards goal), the individual experiences worry. Any threat to goal achievement may motivate an individual towards a course of action that can reduce the threat and sustain coping efforts. When individuals perceive they can attain a goal, approach-focused coping strategies are adopted (planning, effort increase), whereas, when the perception is that they will not attain a goal, avoidance coping strategies (behavioural and mental disengagement) are utilized (Hatzigeorgiadis, 2006). Where goals are no longer attainable or are even counter-productive, individuals who fail to adapt or relinquish such goals are likely to experience distress and reduced well-being, as they experience repeated failure (Carver and Scheier, 1990; Kelly et al., 2013; Wrosch et al., 2003).

FIGURE 6.2 Completing the Abingdon marathon for the challenge, for fitness and for charity

ACTIVITY 6.2

You can probably recall occasions when you have experienced stress yourself. Such self-reflection is usually quite revealing in determining the underlying causes of these feelings. Reflecting on your own experiences, what personal and situational factors do you believe have influenced your own appraisal of a stressor and subsequent coping?

LEARNING OUTCOME 3

Describe common coping classifications and the characteristics of effective coping

Coping can be construed as a continuum that extends from the management of stress and adaptation to achieving success and flourishing in the pursuit of goals (Frydenberg, 2002). Coping is typically associated with threats and stress; however, performance success and/or an increased record of success can potentially tax or exceed the resources of the person (Lazarus and Folkman, 1984). As illustrated in the Rebecca Adlington example provided earlier, achieving success in sport attracts the attention of opponents and audiences and can raise expectations for future performance achievements. For some performers, as with Rebecca, these expectations may constitute a fundamental challenge (Lazarus, 2000).

Coping involves cognitive, affective and behavioural efforts to manage a stressor (Lazarus, 1999). The specific skills and strategies used to cope with stressors are typically classified into broad categories that identify the intended purpose of the coping response (Poczwardowski and Conroy, 2002). Some researchers (Gould *et al.*, 1997) suggest that such patterns of coping might not exist, and classifying coping may oversimplify the coping process (e.g. problem- and emotion-focused coping). For example, Poczwardowski and Conroy (2002) noted that certain coping strategies did not fit neatly into a single category. They felt that the coping strategy 'putting things in perspective' could equally be categorized as both emotion-focused and appraisal-focused. This finding is increasingly noted among coping researchers in sport (Nicholls *et al.*, 2005) and is consistent with the transactional model (Lazarus and Folkman, 1984). Lazarus (2000) explains that coping functions are determined by the individual's appraisal of the stress, which in turn is influenced by meaning structures developed from personal experiences (Eklund *et al.*, 1993). As such, Lazarus (1999) noted that a single coping strategy may serve multiple functions. However, an understanding of coping functions is useful when one considers the development of coping interventions. Table 6.2 presents those coping classifications that have been identified within the literature to date.

There are conditions emerging that are seemingly influential on the outcome of coping efforts. It is important to be aware of these conditions when advising and helping individuals cope with a stressful event.

TABLE 6.2 Classifications of coping

Coping classification	Description
Problem-focused coping	Intended to alter the circumstances causing distress using strategies directed towards the environment and the self
Emotion-focused coping	Involves the regulation of dysfunctional emotions
Active coping	Taking measures to alleviate the effects of a stressor, including strategies characterized by an orientation towards the threatening aspects of a situation
Avoidance-focused coping	Actions intended to disengage from the stressor and focus attention on alternative tasks
Appraisal-focused coping	Appraising or reappraising stressful situations
Reactive coping	Efforts to deal with a stressful encounter that has already happened, or is happening at the present time
Anticipatory coping	Coping behaviours intended to deal with a critical event that is certain or fairly certain to occur in the near future
Preventative coping	Concerned with preparation for uncertain events in the more distant future
Proactive coping	Proactive coping is distinguished by three main features: 1 It integrates planning and prevention strategies with proactive self-regulatory goal attainment 2 It integrates proactive goal attainment with identification and utilization of social resources 3 It utilizes proactive emotional coping for self-regulatory goal attainment

These are as follows:

- Problem–focused coping attempts to directly manage the problem or stressor and is more suitable in situations that are seen as controllable. Emotion-focused and/or avoidance-focused coping, which tries to deal with the emotions resulting from a stressor, may be most suitable in response to stressors or problems that are uncontrollable (Lazarus and Folkman, 1984).
- Those coping strategies used with acute (short–term) stressors may become less effective if the stressor becomes chronic stress (long term) (Wethington and Kessler, 1991). For example, avoidance strategies may be effective for short-term stressors, but non–avoidant strategies may be effective for long-term stressors.
- Individuals typically use more than one coping strategy at any point in time (Gould *et al.*, 1993; Tamminen and Holt, 2010). Research indicates that those individuals who possess a wider range of coping responses adapt more effectively to stress than those with fewer coping options (Gould *et al.*, 1993). However, it should not be assumed that using lots of coping strategies within a short time frame is adaptive. It may be because the coping strategies the individual tries are not effective, and so they try many different coping strategies (Carver *et al.*, 1993; Devonport and Lane, 2014).

- In order to cope effectively, an individual must deal with any emotions resulting from a stressful encounter. Strong emotions may lead to poor performance (see Lane, this issue) and inappropriate behaviours, such as aggression resulting from anger (Lazarus, 1999).

LEARNING OUTCOME 4

Detail typical features of coping interventions and considerations of application

Review of coping interventions: Implications for application

Research indicates that individuals can be assisted in the development of their coping skills (Frydenberg and Lewis, 2002; Rumbold *et al.*, 2012). A review of sport coping interventions revealed that they typically focused on different aspects of the transactional stress process – for example, interventions intended to (a) reduce stressors, (b) modify cognitive appraisals, (c) reduce negative affect and increase positive affect, or (d) facilitate effective coping behaviours (Rumbold *et al.*, 2012). Coping assistance can be provided formally through coping programmes and/or informally using those individuals with whom the individual has frequent contact (Frydenberg and Lewis, 2002).

However, the benefit of coping-skills programmes that are fully scripted to facilitate implementation is becoming increasingly recognized. An example of such a programme was the Best of Coping, developed by Frydenberg and Brandon (2002). This was designed to help adolescents cope with daily stressors. This programme comprised ten sessions, including the exploration of coping strategies such as thinking optimistically, effective communication skills, steps to effective problem-solving, decision-making, goal setting and time management. The programme also included a session facilitating the practical use of those coping skills learned during the programme. When the Best of Coping programme was reviewed, the self-efficacy of participants dealing with stress increased significantly more than that of non-participants.

Implication: Scripted, or partially scripted, coping interventions facilitate the success of an intervention

Previous research indicates that the provision of a supportive environment during coping-skills training develops an individual's self-efficacy (Bandura, 1997) perceptions regarding their ability to deal with stress (Zeidner, 1990; Schwarzer and Knoll, 2007). This is important, because individuals with high coping efficacy are more likely to approach problems with the aim of solving them, rather than avoiding them (Frydenberg and Lewis, 2002). Some researchers believe that social support is particularly important for athletes whose coping skills are underdeveloped, because it may provide a more positive interpersonal environment for the development of coping by providing esteem support (Freeman and Rees, 2009) and could act as a buffer against stress (Piko, 2001; Schulz and Schwarzer, 2004).

Implication: It is important to provide a supportive environment for the development of coping skills

Smith (1999) suggests that the generalization of coping-skills training should become a focal rather than incidental consideration. A number of factors are believed to enhance the generalizability of coping:

* the extent to which a person believes that a new coping situation calls for the same coping behaviours learned in training, promoting the use of the learned coping behaviours in the new situation;
* the extent to which newly acquired coping skills can be successfully applied across a wide range of situations;
* the perceived control of the competencies and relationship with an individual's values and motives;
* the development of global self-regulatory skills.

Implication: It is important that coping interventions work towards the generalization of coping skills

Types of coping intervention

Although there are varied approaches to helping individuals cope with negative events (Sandler *et al.*, 1997; Ntoumanis and Biddle, 1998), a common format does appear to exist. This consists of:

* providing recipients with a rationale for the programme;
* modelling or demonstrating the procedure;
* having the participants rehearse or practise the skills;
* motivating the participants to transfer the learning via self-directed activities (Baker, 2001).

Appraisal is an important first step in the coping process (Lazarus and Folkman, 1984; Lazarus, 2000). As such, any programme that attempts to develop coping skills also needs to teach skills of positive cognitive appraisal. Most recent programmes intended to facilitate the development of coping skills are based upon Lazarus's transaction model of stress (Lazarus and Folkman, 1984), in that the intention is to change an individual's cognition about the nature of stress and their ability to cope with stress (Isrealasvili, 2002). Consequently, all coping interventions carry a cognitive component. These include cognitive–behavioural methods, emotional–cognitive methods and action theory approaches (Sandler *et al.*, 1997; Isrealasvili, 2002). Each is considered in turn.

Cognitive–behavioural approaches

A cognitive–behavioural approach to coping-skills training is based on the principle that maladaptive emotions and behaviours are influenced by an individual's beliefs, attitudes and perceptions (Cormier and Cormier, 1998). As such, the focus of cognitive–behavioural interventions is learning to recognize, interrupt and replace maladaptive cognitions with adaptive ones. For example, Baker (2001) implemented a cognitive–behavioural programme that consisted of four 45-minute sessions aimed at identifying self-defeating thoughts and replacing these with self-improving thoughts. Participants were asked to monitor the circumstances surrounding self-defeating thoughts, the level of emotion resulting from this, the self-improving thought used to replace self-defeating thoughts and the level of emotion they felt having made this cognitive change. A ten-page training booklet was also provided to all participants to facilitate self-instruction. A review of the programme revealed improved cognitive self-instruction and decreased state anxiety.

Implication: Teach individuals to recognize, interrupt and replace maladaptive cognitions with adaptive ones

Emotional–cognitive approaches

Studies have found that encouraging positive appraisals leads to improved affect, especially when the participants can choose the exact appraisal to adopt (Wenzlaff and LePage, 2000). Within sport psychology, studies have found that helping athletes think more positively led to reduced performance anxiety during competition (Hanton and Jones, 1999; Arathoon and Malouff, 2004). For example, Arathoon and Malouff (2004) encouraged field hockey players (aged 19–47) to select one of five positive thoughts (e.g. 'something you did well in a game') and one of six coping thoughts (e.g. 'we didn't win but we played well') following loss. This intervention reduced the decrease in positive affect significantly when compared with a control group, supporting the contention that inducing realistic positive cognitions is an effective way to improve affect.

Implication: Encourage positive appraisals, so that individuals may be more predisposed to enjoy a challenging situation

Action theory approach

Action theory addresses, not only the cognitive and emotional aspects of stress encounter, but also the motivational, behavioural and contextual aspects (Young and Valach, 2000; Isrealasvili, 2002). Isrealasvili (2002) contends that this offers a more comprehensive strategy to foster a person's ability to confront a stressful episode in life. It does so by addressing three aspects of action: the manifest behaviour of the individual, the conscious recognition that accompanies this manifest behaviour, and the social meaning in which the action is embedded (Young and Valach, 2000). Within action theory, intervention counsellors have the task of helping individuals make sense of their actions. They encourage individuals to evaluate stressful stimuli differently and equip them with a wider range of coping skills.

Isrealasvili (2002) explored the use of this approach with Israeli adolescents facing a school-to-army transition. The programme was implemented by school counsellors, with the support of teachers, parents, school graduates and army representatives. The programme addressed anticipated sources of stress in the transition from civilian to basic training, and the acquisition of coping skills through group discussion. The intervention also addressed a person's awareness of their goals and of the relationship between these goals and possible ways of coping. The intervention was found to increase enlistees' self-efficacy to adjust to military life. It was concluded that coping is effective only if it adequately relates to the person's goals.

Implication: It is important that coping-skills training considers an individual's personal goals to optimize the effectiveness of coping

In conclusion, a range of coping interventions have been developed and applied in both sport and general psychology. When these interventions are presented and reviewed, there are key implications for application that emerge. These are as follows:

* Scripted, or partially scripted, coping interventions facilitate the success of an intervention.
* It is important to provide a supportive environment for the development of coping skills.
* Coping interventions should work towards the generalization of coping skills.
* Coping interventions should encourage positive appraisals.
* Coping interventions should teach individuals to recognize, interrupt and replace maladaptive cognitions with adaptive ones.
* Coping-skills training should consider an individual's personal goals to optimize the effectiveness of coping.

With these implications in mind, Devonport and Lane (2009, 2014) developed a 12-month coping intervention for use with nine junior national netball players (aged 15–19), titled the Mentor Programme. In an attempt to provide a supportive environment for coping-skills development, a mentor was identified for participants. Mentoring offers a one-to-one developmental relationship, where the mentor and mentee work together to establish goals, driven by the needs of the mentee (Linney, 1999). The role of each mentor was to guide players through activities presented in a series of coping packs. These scripted packs were designed to develop five key coping skills, including planning and organizational ability, goal setting, emotional intelligence, problem-solving and communication skills. The planning pack was intended to facilitate preventative and proactive coping by determining an athlete's forthcoming commitments and helping them work towards the attainment of a balanced lifestyle. Goal setting was incorporated into the Mentor Programme in order to increase an athlete's repertoire of problem-focused coping strategies and facilitate proactive coping. Emotional intelligence was included because of the influence it has on adaptive and emotion-focused coping (Zeidner et al., 2004). The problem-solving pack was designed to develop an athlete's ability to adopt a careful, analytical, planned and systematic approach to the solution process, thus facilitating problem-focused coping. Finally, the communication pack was designed to enhance the ability of athletes to communicate effectively and covered skills such as verbalizing ideas and listening effectively to others (Anderson, 1993; Rivers, 2005). This was intended to accrue benefits such as enhancing an athlete's ability to utilize social support.

Within the activities designed for completion in the Mentor Programme, mentors and athletes were encouraged to apply the coping skills addressed across sporting, academic, work and social domains. Smith (1999) suggests that, when coping-skills interventions are developed, the generalization of coping-skills training should become a focal, rather than incidental, consideration. Applying coping skills in this way may improve coping efficiency and effectiveness, thus encouraging subsequent use. For example, goal setting can be a time-intensive activity, but, with practice, an individual is able to set, monitor and adjust goals more efficiently. Furthermore, generalizing the use of goal setting can help establish a more balanced lifestyle, as the individual strives to achieve goals across domains.

It was considered important to address ethical considerations when completing this longitudinal research. It was important to ensure that all individuals working with adolescents had completed a criminal records check and received certification of approval to work with children. In compliance with recommendations from the British Psychological Society, consent for continued involvement in the longitudinal research was secured from mentors and athletes every 3 months. Finally, as the topic of investigation was stress and coping, it was necessary to ensure that appropriate support mechanisms were in place for individuals evidencing debilitating levels of stress or demonstrating clinical disorders during the research (e.g. depression, body image dysmorphia). Mentors were asked to refer any emergent issues on to the lead researcher, who then had access to clinical and counselling support as necessary.

An important part of intervention development and redevelopment is to review intervention effectiveness. Effectiveness refers to 'the applicability, feasibility, and usefulness of the intervention in the local or specific setting where it is to be offered' (American Psychological Association, 2002, p. 1053). In reviewing intervention effectiveness, Devonport and Lane (2009, 2014) completed both quantitative and qualitative analysis of participants' experiences. The Brief COPE (Carver, 1997) was used to monitor frequency in the use of coping strategies. This measure of dispositional coping enabled the monitoring of potentially maladaptive strategies (e.g. substance use) over time, as well as recording any changes in coping. Should frequency of coping increase, it is not a certainty that this reflects enhanced coping. Devonport and Lane (2014) note that it is plausible that an increased use of coping strategies may represent ineffective coping. For example, if the coping-strategy planning does not work, an individual may try social support and, if this does not work, they may utilize venting or behavioural disengagement. Such coping behaviours may be reflected on the Brief COPE as an increase in coping behaviour. So, it follows that, when interpreting frequency of coping use scores, caution must be exercised.

On completion of the 12-month Mentor Programme, statistical analysis revealed small-to-moderate effect size for changes in coping over time. Athletes completing the Mentor Programme showed, on average, a slight increase in the use of coping, particularly the use of future-oriented strategies, such as planning and active coping. Qualitative data indicated that athletes perceived coping and coping-associated benefits resulting from participation in the Mentor Programme. Although athletes did not necessarily feel that they used the future-oriented coping strategies more often, they felt better able to identify appropriate opportunities for use. As a result, athletes gained coping efficacy based upon their enhanced ability to know when to plan ahead, organize time and establish appropriate short-to-long-term goals.

In order to illustrate an athlete's experience with the coping intervention, extracts will be presented from qualitative data provided by Ellis. When choosing to participate in the Mentor Programme, Ellis set a goal to improve her communication on court. She also set goals to improve her emotional awareness of self and others and her ability to regulate emotions. These goals were agreed by her mentor, who then sought to support the attainment of them during the Mentor Programme. Both Ellis and her mentor commented that the resultant improvements had accrued positive effects for her on–court performances.

Regarding the planning and time-management pack, Ellis said:

> The wall planner was good . . . Jasmine (mentor) set out agendas for me, like we'd do titles of what I wanted to achieve, when by, what I had on that month and how I could sort out what I wanted to achieve and things like that.

APPLYING THE SCIENCE 6.1

Kirsty Devonport is a 31-year-old female who sought support to help her prepare for the North Pole marathon. Kirsty was concerned because, having never completed a marathon in extreme cold, she was unable to anticipate the conditions and challenges she might face. Over two consecutive weekends, Kirsty spent 100–120 minutes completing coping-focused activities in an environmental chamber designed to recreate the conditions of the North Pole (temperatures between –20 and –25°C and large fans creating wind chill). Kirsty was asked to complete a Brief COPE (Carver, 1997) to assess the usage of fourteen coping strategies, including planning, positive thinking and using emotional support. She completed this measure before entering the environmental chamber and 90 minutes into testing, to identify the coping strategies she was utilizing at that point in time. The data were used to provide guidance on the ways in which Kirsty could manage any stressors, emotions and thoughts in response to actual or anticipated exposure to extreme cold.

During her first session in the environmental chamber, Kirsty was encouraged to use strategies such as mentally picturing herself completing the North Pole marathon and successfully managing physical, emotional and cognitive responses to the conditions. Having completed this session, Kirsty concluded: 'I'm definitely a lot more confident about it because I didn't really know how much to trust my kit and I'm a lot more confident now I know it's completely comfortable and warm'. During her second training session in the chamber, her use of coping strategies that focused on managing the situation remained consistent with those used in the previous week. However, her use of strategies focused on *managing emotion* reduced. For example, in comparison with the first session, her use of humour reduced (from a lot to a little), acceptance reduced (from a lot to not at all) and positive reframing reduced (from a medium amount to not at all). These changes indicate that there were fewer emotional consequences resulting from cold exposure requiring management, which indicated more perceived confidence in the situation. The conclusion that Kirsty derived from the lab-based work was a belief that she could cope with the cold, even if this involved being unable to maintain warmth through running.

BEYOND THE FRONTIER

In order to gain a greater insight into the coping process, a more holistic approach towards research is warranted to better understand the *unique* and *contextually situated* demands that unique populations face (Lazarus, 1999, 2000). Reviewing the sport coping literature, it is notable that few researchers acknowledge stressors beyond the sporting domain (McKenna and Dunstan-Lewis, 2004; MacNamara and Collins, 2010). The majority of athletes partaking in sport, from entry level to high performance, do so while completing their education or maintaining part- or full-time employment. A holistic approach acknowledges that sport considerations (such as selection issues or training demands) and non-sport considerations (such as relationship issues or exam pressures) all influence an athlete's ability to cope and ultimately influence their ability to train and compete optimally. As such, it could be argued that an exclusive focus on sports stressors offers an incomplete account of the individual's stress and coping experiences. Devonport and Lane (2009, p. 170) reported the difficulties encountered by young student–athletes when striving to attain personally meaningful goals in sporting, social, academic and sometimes work domains. They noted that, 'more than one young athlete described the efforts required in pursuing multiple goals as a "superhuman" endeavour, thereby using terms to indicate the complexity and difficulty of achieving such goals'.

An area as yet unexplored in the sport coping literature is dyadic coping and its contribution towards the management of stressors. Given the notion evidenced earlier that sporting commitments may produce stressors that affect both the athlete and their family, dyadic coping offers a potentially fruitful line of enquiry when developing coping interventions. Dyadic coping can be conceptualized as couples interacting to deal with a significant life stressor (Revenson, 2003; Berg and Upchurch, 2007). It is a transactional, interpersonal process, wherein one partner attempts to help manage a stressor perceived by his/her partner (Bodenmann *et al.*, 2006; Berg and Upchurch, 2007). Successful coping involves management of the circumstances causing stress and/or any negative emotions generated by stress. From a dyadic perspective, successful coping also involves maintaining relationships during stressful periods, particularly when stressors impact upon the couple (Herzberg, 2013). Herzberg (2013) identified a need to better understand the interaction of stressors and individual and dyadic coping. High-performance sport presents a meaningful context within which to address this need, owing to the longitudinal investments and associated sacrifices required of both the athlete and their family.

When reflecting on the problem-solving pack, Ellis felt this pack structured thinking and increased options: 'she just used to branch off with all these different options and it made me kind of understand like a wider picture'. Jasmine (Ellis's mentor) described how Ellis had become better able to deal with others, including confrontational situations: 'Ellis [player] was always very concerned about how other people saw her, so I think that was quite useful just reading that pack [emotional intelligence] through you know, how to cope with people's reactions and confrontations'. Finally, regarding the communication pack, Ellis and her mentor would use it to work through 'different scenarios, and also outside of netball things, like how will it affect me? what will I do? . . . That was quite good it made me put things more in perspective'. Ellis concluded that the Mentor Programme had been beneficial for her because, 'I think I'm a lot more organised . . . and again that's 'cause of mentoring where I just had to organise myself and think what am I going to achieve and things like that'.

The partially scripted coping intervention devised and applied by Devonport and Lane (2009) provided a longitudinally supportive environment for the development of coping skills. A key focus, and consequently benefit, of the coping intervention was the generalization of coping skills. In working towards the development of coping competencies, personal goals and the appraisal process were central to intervention activities. This enabled an individualized coping programme to be developed and maintained. The consideration and implementation of these factors were partly attributed to the success of the programme. As such, future coping interventions should strive to devise longitudinal coping interventions, taking into consideration the personal idiosyncrasies.

CONCLUSIONS

There is a wealth of anecdotal and empirical evidence to suggest that athletes commonly experience the debilitating effects of stress on performance (Hoar *et al.*, 2006; Jones and Tenenbaum, 2009). Research has sought to identify the sources of stress typically encountered by athletes and explore those coping strategies that appear to be effective in the management of such stressors. This chapter has sought to summarize the stress and coping literature and explore coping interventions that have resulted from such research. The main implications for the construction and implementation of coping interventions have been highlighted as the chapter has drawn to a conclusion. The tasks that have been set are designed around the main contentions of Lazarus's theories of stress and coping. It is hoped that this will facilitate understanding and subsequent application of theory.

KEY CONCEPTS AND TERMS

Commonly used definitions of stress, cognitive appraisal and coping used in the coping literature are as follows:

Definition of stress

'An imbalance between environmental demands and response capability, under conditions where failure to meet demand is perceived as having important consequences, it is responded to with increased levels of A-state (state anxiety)' (Martens, 1977, p. 9).

Definition of cognitive appraisal

Cognitive appraisal has been defined as 'a process through which the person evaluates whether a particular encounter with the environment is relevant to his or her well-being, and if so, in what ways' (Folkman *et al.*, 1986, p. 992).

Definition of coping

Coping refers to 'constantly changing cognitive and behavioural efforts to manage specific external and/or internal demands that are appraised as taxing or exceeding the resources of the person' (Lazarus and Folkman, 1984, p. 141).

RECOMMENDED FURTHER READING

Books and book chapters

Devonport, T. J. (2012). *Stress and Coping: From theory to practice*. Hauppage, NY: Nova.

Frydenberg, E. (2002). *Beyond Coping: Meeting goals, visions, and challenges*. Oxford, UK: Oxford University Press.

Hoar, S. D., Kowalski, K. C., Gadreau, P. and Crocker, P. R. E. (2006). A review of coping in sport. In Hanton, S. and Mellalieu, S. (eds) *Literature Reviews in Sport Psychology*, pp. 53–103. Hauppauge, NY: Nova Science.

Lazarus, R. S. (1999). *Stress and Emotion: A new synthesis*. New York: Springer.

Journals

Devonport, T. J. and Lane, A. M. (2014). Evaluation of a twelve-month coping intervention intended to enhance future-oriented coping in goal oriented domains. *Journal of Clinical Sport Psychology*, *8*, 38–56.

Devonport, T. J., Lane, A. M. and Biscomb, K. (2013). Exploring coping strategies used by national adolescent netball players across domains. *Journal of Clinical Sport Psychology*, 7, 161–77.

Rees, T. and Hardy, L. (2004). Matching social support with stressors: Effects on factors underlying performance in tennis. *Psychology of Sport and Exercise, 5*, 319–37.

Rumbold, J., Fletcher, D. and Daniels, K. (2012). A systematic review of stress management interventions with sport performers. *Sport, Exercise, and Performance Psychology, 1*, 173–93.

Skinner, E. A., Edge, K., Altman, J. and Sherwood, H. (2003). Searching for the structure of coping: A review and critique of category systems for classifying ways of coping. *Psychological Bulletin, 129*, 216–69.

SAMPLE ESSAY QUESTIONS

1   To what extent can the transactional model of stress and coping and/or the cognitive–motivational–relational theory of emotions predict coping behaviours in sport? Discuss with reference to relevant literature.

2   Discuss, with reference to relevant literature, those factors that determine the effectiveness of coping.

3   In developing a coping intervention for athletes, what considerations should the practitioner make? Explore each consideration with reference to relevant literature.

4   With the use of relevant literature, identify the influence that personal and situational factors may have on the appraisal of stress.

NOTES

1   Cited in *The Telegraph*; available online at: www.telegraph.co.uk/sport/olympics/swimming/9451060/Rebecca-Adlington-admits-pressure-and-expectation-got-to-her-in-800m-freestyle-final-at-London-2012-Olympics.html (accessed 19 November 2013).

2   Available online at: www.bbc.co.uk/blogs/olliewilliams/2009/12/adlingtons_phelps_awe_high ligh.shtml (accessed 19 November 2013).

3   Available online at: http://news.bbc.co.uk/sport1/hi/tennis/4620592.stm (accessed 19 November 2013).

4   Available online at: http://m.atpworldtour.com/News/Tennis/2013/06/25/Wimbledon-Murray-Preview.aspx (accessed 19 November 2013).

5   Available online at: www.independent.co.uk/sport/rugby/rugby-union/international/lawrence-dallaglio-england-have-had-no-strategy-since-we-won-the-world-cup-1815575.html (accessed 26 March 2015).

6   Available online at: www.telegraph.co.uk/sport/othersports/athletics/10248915/Mo-Farah-says-5000m-victory-at-World-Athletics-Championships-was-definitely-the-sweetest-by-far.html (accessed 6 December 2013).

REFERENCES

Aarts, H., Gollwitzer, P. M. and Hassin, R. R. (2004). Goal contagion: Perceiving is for pursuing. *Journal of Personality and Social Psychology, 87*, 23.

Aldwin, C. M. (1994). *Stress, Coping, and Development: An integrative perspective.* New York: Guilford Press.

American Psychological Association (2002). Criteria for evaluating treatment guidelines. *American Psychologist, 57,* 1052–9.

Anderson, K. (1993). *Getting What You Want: How to reach agreement and resolve conflict every time.* New York: Penguin-Puttnam/Dutton.

Anshel, M. H. and Delany, J. (2001). Sources of acute stress, cognitive appraisals, and coping strategies of male and female child athletes. *Journal of Sport Behavior, 24,* 329–53.

Arathoon, S. M. and Malouff, J. M. (2004). The effectiveness of a brief cognitive intervention to help athletes cope with competitive loss. *Journal of Sport Behavior, 27,* 213–29.

Baker, S. B. (2001). Coping-skills training for adolescents: Applying cognitive behavioural principles to psychoeducational groups. *Journal for Specialists in Group Work, 26,* 219–27.

Bandura, A. (1997). *Self-efficacy: The exercise of control.* New York: W.H. Freeman.

Berg, C. A. and Upchurch, R. (2007). A developmental–contextual model of couples coping with chronic illness across the adult life span. *Psychological Bulletin, 133,* 920–54.

Bodenmann, G., Pihet, S. and Kayser, K. (2006). The relationship between dyadic coping and marital quality: A 2-year longitudinal study. *Journal of Family Psychology, 20,* 485.

Carver, C. S. (1997). You want to measure coping but your protocol's too long: Consider the Brief COPE. *International Journal of Behavioral Medicine, 4,* 92–100.

Carver, C. S. and Scheier, M. F. (1990). Origins and functions of positive and negative affect: A control-process view. *Psychological Review, 97,* 19–35.

Carver, C. S. and Scheier, M. F. (1998). *On the Self-regulation of Behavior.* New York: Cambridge University Press.

Carver, C. S., Pozo, C., Harris, S. D., Noriega, V., Scheier, M. F., Robinson, D. S., Ketcham, A. S., Moffat, F. L. and Clark, K. C. (1993). How coping mediates the effect of optimism on distress: A study of women with early stage breast cancer. *Journal of Personality and Social Psychology, 65,* 375–90.

Cormier, S. and Cormier, B. (1998). *Interviewing Strategies for Helpers: Fundamental skills and cognitive-behavioural interventions* (4th edn). Pacific Grove, CA: Brooks/Cole.

Crosby, R. A., Kegler, M. C. and DiClemente, R. J. (2009). Theory in health promotion practice and research. In DiClemente, R. J., Crosby, R. A. and Kegler, M. C. (eds) *Emerging Theories in Health Promotion Practice and Research* (2nd edn), pp. 4–17. San Francisco, CA: Jossey Bass.

Devonport, T. J. and Lane, A. M. (2009). Utilizing mentors to facilitate the delivery of a longitudinal coping intervention amongst national junior netball players. *International Journal of Evidence Based Coaching and Mentoring, 7*(2), 50–63.

Devonport, T. J. and Lane, A. M. (2014). Evaluation of a twelve-month coping intervention intended to enhance future-oriented coping in goal oriented domains. *Journal of Clinical Sport Psychology, 8,* 38–56.

Devonport, T. J., Lane, A. M. and Biscomb, K. (2013). Exploring coping strategies used by national adolescent netball players across domains. *Journal of Clinical Sport Psychology, 7,* 161–77.

Eklund, R., Gould, D. and Jackson S. (1993). Psychological foundations of Olympic wrestling excellence: Reconciling individual differences and nomothetic characterization. *Journal of Applied Sport Psychology, 5*, 35–47.

Folkman, S. (2009). Commentary on the special section 'Theory-based approaches to stress and coping': Questions, answers, issues, and next steps in stress and coping research. *European Psychologist, 14*, 72–7.

Folkman, S., Lazarus, R. S., Dunkel-Schetter, C., De Longis, A. and Gruen, R. J. (1986). The dynamics of a stressful encounter: Cognitive appraisal, coping, and encounter outcomes. *Journal of Personality and Social Psychology, 50*, 992–1003.

Freeman, P. and Rees, T. (2009). How does perceived support lead to better performance? An examination of potential mechanisms. *Journal of Applied Sport Psychology, 21*, 429–41.

Frydenberg, E. (2002). *Beyond Coping: Meeting goals, visions, and challenges.* Oxford, UK: Oxford University Press.

Frydenberg, E. and Brandon, C. (2002). *The Best of Coping: Developing coping skills.* Melbourne, Australia: OzChild.

Frydenberg, E. and Lewis, R. (2002). Adolescent well-being: Building young people's resources. In Frydenberg, E. (ed.) *Beyond Coping: Meeting goals, vision and challenges,* pp. 175–94. Oxford, UK: Oxford University Press.

Frydenberg, E. and Lewis, R. (2004). Adolescents least able to cope: How do they respond to their stresses? *British Journal of Guidance and Counselling, 32*, 25–37.

Gould, D., Eklund, R. C. and Jackson, S. A. (1993). Coping strategies used by more or less successful U.S. Olympic wrestlers. *Research Quarterly for Exercise and Sport, 64*, 83–93.

Gould, D., Udry, E., Bridges, D. and Beck, L. (1997). Coping with season ending injuries. *The Sport Psychologist, 11*, 379–99.

Hanton, S., Fletcher, D. and Coughlan, G. (2005). Stress in elite sport performers: A comparative study of competitive and organizational stressors. *Journal of Sports Sciences, 23*, 1129–141.

Hanton, S. and Jones, G. (1999). The effects of a multimodal intervention program on performers: II. Training the butterflies to fly in formation. *The Sport Psychologist, 13*, 22–41.

Hatzigeorgiadis, A. (2006). Approach and avoidance coping during task performance in young men: The role of goal attainment expectancies. *Journal of Sport Sciences, 24*, 299–307.

Herzberg, P. Y. (2013). Coping in relationships: The interplay between individual and dyadic coping and their effects on relationship satisfaction. *Anxiety, Stress & Coping: An International Journal, 26*, 136–53.

Hoar, S. D., Kowalski, K. C., Gadreau, P. and Crocker, P. R. E. (2006). A review of coping in sport. In Hanton, S. and Mallalieu, S. (eds) *Literature Reviews in Sport Psychology,* pp. 53–103. Hauppauge, NY: Nova Science.

Holt, N. L. (2003). Coping in professional sport: A case study of an experienced cricket player. *Athletic Insight, 5*(1). Available online at: www.athleticinsight.com/Vol5Iss1/CricketPlayer Coping.htm (accessed 26 March 2015).

Holt, N. L. and Dunn, J. G. H. (2004). Longitudinal idiographic analysis of appraisal and coping responses in sport. *Psychology of Sport and Exercise, 5*, 213–22.

Isrealasvili, M. (2002). Fostering adolescents' coping skills: An action approach. *Canadian Journal of Counselling, 36*, 211–20.

Jones, C. M. and Tenenbaum, G. (2009). Adjustment disorder: A new way of conceptualizing the overtraining syndrome. *International Review of Sport and Exercise Psychology, 2,* 181–97.

Kelly, R. E., Wood, A. M. and Mansell, W. (2013). Flexible and tenacious goal pursuit lead to improving well-being in an aging population: A ten-year cohort study. *International Psychogeriatrics, 25,* 16–24.

Lane, A. M. and Terry, P. C. (2000). The nature of mood: Development of a conceptual model with a focus on depression. *Journal of Applied Sport Psychology, 12,* 16–33.

Lazarus, R. S. (1991). *Emotion and Adaptation.* New York: Oxford University Press.

Lazarus, R. S. (1998). *Fifty Years of the Research and Theory of R. S. Lazarus: An analysis of historical and perennial issues.* Mahwah, NJ: Lawrence Erlbaum.

Lazarus, R. S. (1999). *Stress and Emotion: A new synthesis.* New York: Springer.

Lazarus, R. S. (2000). How emotions influence performance in competitive sports. *The Sport Psychologist, 14,* 229–52.

Lazarus, R. S. (2001). Stress and emotion: A new synthesis. *Human Relations, 54,* 792–803.

Lazarus, R. S. and Folkman, S. (1984). *Stress Appraisal and Coping.* New York: Springer.

Lazarus, R. and Lazarus, B. (1994). *Passion and Reason.* New York. Oxford University Press.

Linney, B. J. (1999). Characteristics of good mentors. *Physician Executive, 25,* 70–82.

McKay, J., Niven, A. G., Lavallee, D. and White, A. (2008). Sources of strain among elite UK track athletes. *The Sport Psychologist, 22,* 143–63.

McKenna, J. and Dunstan-Lewis, N. (2004). An action research approach to supporting elite student–athletes in higher education. *European Physical Education Review, 19,* 179–98.

MacNamara, A. and Collins, D. (2010). The role of psychological characteristics in managing the transition to university. *Psychology of Sport and Exercise, 11,* 353–62.

Martens, R. (1977). *Sport Competition Anxiety Test.* Champaign, IL: Human Kinetics.

Michie, S., Johnston, M., Francis, J., Hardeman, W. and Eccles, M. (2008). From theory to intervention: Mapping theoretically derived behavioural determinants to behaviour change techniques. *Applied Psychology, 57,* 660–80.

Nicholls, A. R., Holt, N. L. and Polman, R. C. J. (2005). A phenomenological analysis of coping effectiveness in golf. *The Sport Psychologist, 19,* 111–30.

Nicholls, A. R., Holt, N. L., Polman, R. C. J. and Bloomfield, J. (2006). Longitudinal analyses of stress and coping among professional rugby players. *The Sport Psychologist, 20,* 314–29.

Ntoumanis, N. and Biddle, S. J. H. (1998). The relationship of coping and its perceived effectiveness to positive and negative affect in sport. *Personality and Individual Differences, 24,* 773–8.

Piko, B. (2001). Gender differences and similarities in adolescents' ways of coping. *The Psychological Record, 51,* 223–35.

Poczwardowski, A. and Conroy, D. E. (2002). Coping responses to failure and success among elite athletes and performing artists. *Journal of Applied Sport Psychology, 14,* 313–29.

Reeves, C., Nicholls, A. R. and Mckenna, J. (2009). Stress and coping among academy footballers: Age-related differences. *Journal of Applied Sport Psychology, 21,* 31–48.

Revenson, T. A. (2003). Scenes from a marriage: Examining support, coping, and gender within the context of chronic illness. In Suls, J. and Wallston, K. (eds) *Social Psychological Foundations of Health and Illness*, pp. 530–59. Oxford, UK: Blackwell.

Rivers, D. (2005). *The Seven Challenges Workbook* (web edn). Available online at: http://new conversations.net/communication_skills_worksbook_summary_and_toc.htm (accessed 11 July 2006).

Rumbold, J., Fletcher, D. and Daniels, K. (2012). A systematic review of stress management interventions with sport performers. *Sport, Exercise, and Performance Psychology, 1*, 173–93.

Sagar, S. S., Lavallee, D. and Spray, C. M. (2009). Coping with the effects of fear of failure: A preliminary investigation of young elite athletes. *Journal of Clinical Sport Psychology, 3*, 73–98.

Sandler, I. N., Wolchick, S. A., MacKinnon, D., Ayers, T. S. and Roosa, M. W. (1997). Developing linkages between theory and intervention in stress and coping processes. In Wolchick, S. A. and Sandler, I. N. (eds) *Principles and Practice of Stress Management*, pp. 373–406. New York: Guilford Press.

Schulz, U. and Schwarzer, R. (2004). Long-term effects of spousal support on coping with cancer after surgery. *Journal of Social and Clinical Psychology, 23*, 716–32.

Schwarzer, R. and Knoll, N. (2007). Functional roles of social support within the stress and coping process: A theoretical and empirical overview. *International Journal of Psychology, 42*, 243–52.

Smetana, J. G., Campione-Barr, N. and Metzger, A. (2006). Adolescent development in interpersonal and societal contexts. *Annual Review of Psychoogy, 57*, 255–84.

Smith, R. E. (1999). Generalization effects in coping skills training. *Journal of Sport and Exercise Psychology, 21*, 189–204.

Smith, R. E., Smoll, F. L. and Ptacek, J. T. (1990). Conjunctive moderator variables in vulnerability and resilience research: Life stress, social support, and coping skills, and adolescent sport injuries. *Journal of Personality and Social Psychology, 58*, 360–70.

Smoll, F. L. and Smith, R. E. (eds) (1996). *Children and Youth in Sport: A biopsychosocial perspective*. Dubuque, IA: Brown & Benchmark.

Sullivan, P. A. and Nashman, H. W. (1998). Self-perceptions of the role of USOC sport psychologists in working with Olympic athletes. *The Sport Psychologist, 12*, 95–103.

Tamminen, K. A. and Holt, N. L. (2010). Female adolescent athletes' coping: A season-long investigation. *Journal of Sports Sciences, 28*, 101–14.

Thelwell, R. C., Weston, N. J. V. and Greenlees, I. A. (2007). Batting on a sticky wicket: Identifying sources of stress and associated coping responses for professional cricket batsmen. *Psychology of Sport and Exercise, 8*, 219–32.

Voight, M. (2009). Sources of stress and coping strategies of US soccer officials. *Stress and Health, 25*, 91–101.

Wenzlaff, R. M. and LePage, J. P. (2000). The emotional impact of chosen and imposed thoughts. *Personality and Social Psychology Bulletin, 26*, 1502–14.

Wethington, E. and Kessler, R. C. (1991). Situations and processes of coping. In Eckenrode, J. (ed.) *The Social Context of Coping*, pp. 13–29. New York: Plenum Press.

Woodman, T. and Hardy, L. (2001). A case study of organisational stress in elite sport. *Journal of Applied Sport Psychology*, *13*, 207–38.

Wrosch, C., Scheier, M. F., Miller, G. E., Schulz, R. and Carver, C. S. (2003). Adaptive self-regulation of unattainable goals: Goal disengagement, goal reengagement, and subjective well-being. *Personality and Social Psychology Bulletin*, *29*, 1494–508.

Young, R. A. and Valach, L. (2000). Reconceptualising career theory and research: An action-theoretical perspective. In Collin, A. and Young, R. A. (eds) *The Future of Career*, pp. 181–96. Cambridge, UK: Cambridge University Press.

Zeidner, M. (1990). Life events and coping resources as predictors of stress symptoms of adolescents. *Personality and Individual Differences*, *11*, 693–703.

Zeidner, M., Matthews, G. and Roberts, R. D. (2004). Emotional intelligence in the workplace: A critical review. *Applied Psychology: An International Review*, *53*, 371–99.

7 Managing own and others' emotions in sport

Applied and research considerations

Andrew Friesen

CHAPTER SUMMARY

Emotions are pervasive within sports. Managing emotions effectively is arguably one of the most essential skills that athletes can develop to aid their quests for excellence and victory. In individual sports, athletes might seek out help from their coaches, sports science staff, managers, friends and family to help them reach helpful or preferred emotion states. In team sports, teammates need to regulate each other's emotions to help ensure teammates are in an emotional state that maximizes their ability to coordinate tactics.

LEARNING OUTCOMES

When you have studied this chapter, you should be able to:

1 Define what is an emotion
2 Discuss the theory behind a social–functional approach to emotions and how it might be applied to sport settings
3 Discuss why and how we might try to regulate our own emotions in sport
4 Offer different examples of how to classify emotion regulation strategies
5 Discuss why and how we might try to regulate others' emotions

LEARNING OUTCOME 1

Define emotions

Before we can begin to manage our emotions, it is important to first define what emotions are. This might seem redundant, because everyone seems to know intuitively what emotions are – right? Beverly Fehr and James Russell once noted that, 'Everyone knows what an emotion is until asked to give a definition. Then, it seems no one knows' (1984, p. 464). This has almost become a mantra for emotion researchers. Emotions are difficult to define, because they are somewhat intangible. This highlights a common difficulty for sport psychology practitioners. The concepts that sport psychologists have to work with are far more intangible than their sport science counterparts in physiology, biomechanics, nutrition, and strength and conditioning. For example, a physiologist can accurately measure an athlete's VO_2 max with proper equipment and procedures, prescribe an exercise designed to increase VO_2 over time, and then perform another measurement to determine the success of the intervention. However, emotions are more difficult to reliably isolate, record and measure.

Despite decades of research interest, there remains a lack of consensus for the definition of 'emotion' (Izard, 2010). The definition of emotion is a continually evolving endeavour that makes emotion research an ongoing challenge for researchers: that is, when conducting emotion research, not only do researchers have their methods scrutinized but their conceptualization and theorization of what emotions actually are, are also questioned. Textbooks commonly define emotion as a mixture of feelings, physiology, behaviours, expressions and cognitions (Campos *et al.*, 2011). In order to obtain a universal understanding of what emotions are, Izard questioned thirty-five distinguished emotion researchers and scientists to outline their understandings of the important aspects that define emotions.

After surveying his participants, Izard offered the following description of the more commonly shared structures and functions of *emotions*:

> Emotion consists of neural circuits (that are at least partially dedicated), response systems, and a feeling state/process that motivates and organizes cognition and action. Emotion also provides information to the person experiencing it, and may include antecedent cognitive appraisals and ongoing cognition including an interpretation of its feeling state, expressions or social–communicative signals, and may motivate approach or avoidant behaviour, exercise control/regulation of response, and be social or relational in nature.
>
> (2010, p. 367)

ACTIVITY 7.1

Before reading on about what Izard's participants reported as defining what emotions are, take a moment to discuss with a partner what your answer might be if you were asked, 'What is an emotion?' Compare your answers: are there points of agreement and disagreement?

Each characteristic of emotion presented in the above definition could potentially initiate considerable research programmes in every subdiscipline of psychology, and you might see these characteristics of emotions highlighted in other chapters of this textbook (for example, see chapters on anxiety, confidence, mood and performance, placebo effect). For our purposes here, we will be focusing on only two key aspects of emotions: (a) emotions organize behaviour, and (b) emotions are social or relational in nature. These two aspects of emotion feature prominently in a social–functional approach to emotions.

LEARNING OUTCOME 2

Introduction to social–functional approaches to emotion

Appreciating the instrumental and social characteristics of emotions represents a *social–functional approach to emotions* (Manstead, 1991; Parkinson, 1996, 2011; Fischer and Van Kleef, 2010; Campos *et al.*, 2011; Van Kleef *et al.*, 2011). A social–functional approach to emotions presents emotions as coordinating the behaviour of individuals to meet the shared challenges in the environment: that is, emotions communicate particular information about an individual's attitudes, goals and intentions to others (Frijda and Mesquita, 1994; Keltner and Haidt, 1999; Fischer and Manstead, 2008; Van Kleef, 2009; Côté and Hideg, 2011). An example of a social–functional approach in sport might be when two tennis partners rely on each other's cues as to the other's emotional state, to gauge whether they are on track to win or lose the match. If Player A sees Player B cursing, pouting or taking frustrations out on the racquet, Player B would consider the match is going poorly for the pairing. Another example might be between a synchronized-swimming pair. If one swimmer is energetic and confident about an upcoming competition – demonstrated by their being animated before their performance, smiling, being focused in the moment, the second swimmer might infer that the duo is well prepared to perform at a level that helps achieve their goal.

Each emotion theoretically will have a unique social function. These social functions have been debated and researched. Although conclusive evidence is hard to provide, there have been some shared conclusions. Table 7.1 displays hypothesized social functions of common emotions, as adapted from Shariff and Tracy (2011).

A social–functional approach to emotions combines theory from both evolutionary psychology and social constructionism (Keltner and Gross, 1999). Balish *et al.* (2013) suggested that evolutionary psychology offers the opportunity to explain *how* emotions interact with the environment to produce behaviour by explaining *why* emotions evolved to a particular design. Evolutionary psychology theorizes that emotions evolved to help individuals respond effectively to the environment around them (Keltner *et al.*, 2006). For example, the reason we feel anxious about an upcoming event is so that we will be motivated to prepare properly for the event. When we feel anxious about achieving our goals, we (ideally) respond by spending extra time preparing for the event. If emotions did not have functional value for humanity, they likely would have been phased out of humanity's evolution (Baumeister *et al.*, 2007): that is, emotions must have served a purpose that helped human survival; if this was not the case, then the argument is that they would have been phased out.

TABLE 7.1 Social functions of emotions in sport, as adapted from Shariff and Tracy (2011)

Emotion	Hypothesized social function	Potential application to sport teammates
Happiness	Communicates a lack of threat	Signals that performance has been satisfactory and goal achievement is likely
Sadness	Tears handicap vision, to signal appeasement and elicit sympathy	Signals that goals have not been achieved and rallies teammates to devote more resources for future competition or training
Anger	Alerts to impending threat; communicates dominance	Signals that goal achievement is threatened and aggressive tactics are needed to achieve goal
Fear	Alerts to possible threat; appeases potential aggressors	Signals that goal achievement is becoming less likely; motivates additional preparation
Surprise	Alerts to unexpected circumstances*	Signals that tactics and efforts need to change to accommodate change in circumstances
Disgust	Warns about distasteful ideas and behaviours	Signals that social norms have been violated
Pride	Communicates heightened status	Signals past history of goal achievement
Shame/ embarrassment	Communicates lessened social status and desire to appease	Acknowledges that social norms have been violated and goals have subsequently been jeopardized

* Shariff and Tracy, 2011, did not offer a hypothesized function of surprise

Therefore, from an evolutionary psychology perspective, emotions function to coordinate physiological, cognitive, motivational, behavioural and subjective responses in patterns that increase the ability to meet the adaptive challenges of situations that have recurred over evolutionary time (Nesse and Ellsworth, 2009). Similar to feeling pain or perspiring, emotions remain dormant until we detect cues within our environment that suggest an emotional response might be beneficial. Evolutionary psychologists try to emphasize that emotions are functional in nature. Therefore, describing emotions using terms such as 'positive', 'negative', 'pleasant', 'unpleasant', 'helpful', 'unhelpful' is deemed inappropriate (Nesse and Ellsworth, 2009). Consider the emotion anxiety: it is commonly associated with unpleasant feelings and is, therefore, often regarded as 'negative' or 'unhelpful'. However, each emotion might provide valuable information to the individual. Consider perspiration – it is a functional physiological response that prevents us from fatally overheating. Perspiring is seen as undesirable in social situations, and yet sweating itself is not necessarily a 'negative' bodily response. Similarly, emotions are adaptations that are useful only in certain situations. For example, anxiety might be hedonically unpleasant but serves an important function to inform the individual of the meaningfulness of the activity (among other functions).

Tamir and colleagues (e.g. Tamir *et al.*, 2007, 2008; Tamir, 2008) have researched how we regulate our emotions in order to achieve goals. It is worth noting that Tamir's research has not focused specifically on athletic samples. However, the work is robust, meaning that the hypotheses are tested under strict conditions, and the implications of this theory for sport and exercise are clear. Their studies have shown that individuals will increase the intensity or duration of unpleasant emotions, such as anger and fear, in order to accomplish meaningful goals (Tamir, 2011). People might also deny the opportunity to increase hedonically pleasant emotions, such as happiness. For example, Tamir *et al.* (2008) studied eighty-two undergraduate students as they prepared to play either confrontational or non-confrontational video games. Tamir and colleagues found that, when participants prepared to play confrontational video games, they preferred to increase their anger levels (e.g. by listening to anger-inducing music and recalling past anger-evoking events) in order to feel an emotion perceived to be most beneficial to their goal. This supports the notion that emotions are regulated for functional purposes. In a similar study, Tamir and Ford (2009) also reported that participants chose to engage in activities that increased fear (i.e. another hedonically unpleasant emotion) if they believed it would help them achieve their goals.

Athletes often place themselves intentionally in hedonically unpleasant emotional states, if they perceive these states will bring about ideal cognitive, physiological or behavioural consequences (e.g. Robazza *et al.*, 2004). This suggests that athletes have *meta-emotional beliefs* about how their emotions influence their performance. Meta-emotional beliefs are attitudes about how emotions influence performance. For example, one wrestler might believe he performs best when angry, whereas another wrestler believes she performs best when calm. Meta-emotional beliefs have been a feature of the research of Hanin and colleagues (e.g. Robazza *et al.*, 2004, 2006) and the individualized zone of optimal functioning (IZOF) model (Hanin, 2000). Research using the IZOF approach has suggested a multifaceted, highly personalized nature for the relationship between emotions and sport performance.

However, much of humanity does not face the same challenges as our ancestors, and so the functions of emotions have perhaps changed. This is where evolutionary psychology can benefit by adopting social constructionist perspectives, which focus on how emotions are constructed according to social, structural and moral–ideological forces that define culture and social context (Keltner and Gross, 1999). We experience emotions, not exclusively in relation to survival and reproductive fitness, but also in relation to cultural institutions that are strongly meaningful to us – for example, sport.

So, what might a social–functional approach to emotions look like in sport? In one of our studies (Friesen *et al.*, 2013a), we conducted a narrative analysis on two ice hockey captains' experiences regulating their teammates' emotions. What became

ACTIVITY 7.2

Recall some of the emotions that you have felt during competition or training. What might have been the function of these emotions? Did you perceive them as helpful or hurtful to your performance?

apparent from the stories the captains shared was that social functions of emotion changed depending upon whether the target of emotion regulation was the self, someone else, the team or the team in relation to the broader culture of ice hockey players. At an individual level, the captains described how emotions informed them of important circumstances in their environment that required attention and helped them prepare for such challenges. For example, when one captain became embarrassed at the weak effort being exerted by her teammates, she responded by trying to 'guilt' her teammates into playing better. At a dyadic level, emotions helped participants gauge the emotional states and intentions of their teammates, contributing towards an assessment of the extent to which they were prepared to face their challenges. For example, seeing a teammate feeling disheartened would inform the captain that the teammates needed some emotion regulation, because rarely do players perform at their best when feeling sad. At a group level, emotions helped participants lead their teammates in meeting shared goals. For example, captains often try to manage the emotional atmosphere in a dressing room such that the emotional mood that is believed most likely to yield ideal performance benefits is regulated to reach an ideal state. Finally, at a cultural level, emotions helped participants maintain culture-related identities. Ice

ACTIVITY 7.3

Reflect on your most recent performance. List the emotions that your teammates experienced, what triggered them, and how they might have influenced their performance.

Emotion	Cause	Performance impact

hockey (like all sports) is associated with subcultural norms. Whenever these norms are violated, it can signal that emotions need to be regulated such that a more facilitative behaviour is evoked.

Emotions have been suggested to serve numerous useful performance functions. These include improving maximal strength (Perkins *et al.*, 2001), influencing weight loss processes (Hall and Lane, 2001), reducing the risk of losing self-control (Hagger *et al.*, 2010; Beedie and Lane, 2012) and reducing the risk of injury (Devonport *et al.*, 2005). Emotional responses might also improve relationships between key individuals in the sporting environment, such as coaches, athletes, teammates and officials (e.g. Jowett, 2003; Wickwire *et al.*, 2004; Sève *et al.*, 2007). Jones (2003) also highlighted that emotions might influence the motivation for action responses, physical functioning through heightened arousal, and cognitive functioning through working memory, long-term recall, perceptual-motor speed, attentional focus and reduction of cognitive resources.

LEARNING OUTCOME 3

Discuss why and how we might try to regulate our own emotions in sport

Because intense emotions are often evoked in sport, and because they are perceived to help performance, skills and strategies to manage emotions have become fundamental components of applied sport psychology interventions (e.g. Botterill and Brown, 2002; Woodcock *et al.*, 2012). Eisenberg *et al.* (2000) defined *emotion regulation* as, 'the process of initiating, maintaining, modulating, or changing the occurrence, intensity, or duration of internal feeling states and emotion-related physiological processes, often in the service of accomplishing one's goals' (p. 137). Consider the swimmer who wants to remain calm, even when feeling anxious at the beginning of an Olympic race; or a skier who is about to race down the same slope where she sustained an injury the year before; or a tae kwon do fighter who has just taken the lead in the closing stages of a match, but needs to delay celebration until the final round is over. All these athletes might be experiencing emotions that are not necessarily functional in achieving their goals and are, therefore, in need of some method or strategy to help manage their current emotional state.

How athletes and coaches regulate their emotions in sport has received considerable research attention. Many skills and strategies used to change the intensity or duration of an emotion, or even the emotion itself, have been empirically investigated (e.g. Hanton and Jones, 1999; Thelwell and Greenlees, 2003; Robazza *et al.*, 2004; Cohen *et al.*, 2006; Thelwell *et al.*, 2006). For example, in a study that examined how athletes regulate their own mood, Stevens and Lane (2001) found that listening to music, seeking social support and reappraising the situation were popular strategies during competition. It should be noted that training also provides an opportunity to practise emotion regulation strategies (Thomas *et al.*, 1999). Along similar lines, Stanley *et al.* (2012) surveyed runners, 1 hour before their competition. Their results revealed twenty-eight different kinds of emotion regulation strategy. Generally, these were grouped into five dimensions: task preparation, avoidance, positive and negative thinking, and using others to regulate their emotions.

LEARNING OUTCOME 4

Classify emotion regulation strategies

> **ACTIVITY 7.4**
>
> With a partner, come up with as many emotion regulation strategies as you can in a span of 3 minutes. Afterwards, discuss how you might organize these strategies. Consider a classification scheme that might be most appropriate for your sport.

As you found from Activity Box 7.4, there are a considerable number of potential strategies athletes might use to manage emotions. Parkinson and Totterdell (1999) offered that there are in excess of 150 distinct strategies that individuals might use.

It is important to note that we are often unaware of the strategies that we use to regulate our emotions. Because emotion regulation is a process so inherent in human functioning, we engage in many instances of automatic emotion regulation where we are not even aware we are regulating our emotions. For example, a footballer might be subconsciously aware that a certain teammate causes them to feel anxious before a match. Without deliberately doing so, the footballer then might distance themselves from that teammate before or during the match, in order to manage their own anxiety levels. Therefore, although the footballer is actively managing their anxiety by avoiding their teammate, they might not be consciously aware that they are doing so. Automatic emotion regulation is difficult to research, in part because asking people what strategies they use implies that they are consciously aware of these strategies. Alternatively, a researcher might observe an athlete's behaviour and infer instances of emotion regulation, but researchers are left without confirmation that the observed actions are emotion regulation rather than simply innocuous behaviours. For example, a tennis player might take a deep breath to calm herself after losing a close rally, or that deep breath might just be an attempt to catch her breath after being physically taxed from the rally.

TABLE 7.2 Parkinson and Totterdell's (1999) categories of emotion regulation strategy

	Cognitive	*Behavioural*
Approach	A mixed-martial artist and coach will discuss tactics and strategy to combat feelings of anxiety before a fight	An Olympian might scout out the Olympic venue months before the Olympics, to keep from feeling overwhelmed by the Olympic experience
Avoid	A playoff-bound team might actively resolve to focus on small, immediate goals, to keep them from thinking about the playoffs	A team on the cusp of making the playoffs might avoid 'scoreboard gazing' on opposing-team results, to keep from potential feelings of sadness or anger

Numerous attempts have been made in psychology to classify emotion regulation strategies. Koole (2009) suggested that finding an underlying order by which to classify such strategies becomes a formidable scientific challenge, given the substantial number of reported emotion regulation strategies. Parkinson and Totterdell (1999) offered a classification placing each emotion regulation strategy into one of four categories,

TABLE 7.3 Gross's (1998) categories of emotion regulation strategy

	Situation selection	Situation modification	Attentional deployment	Cognitive change	Response modulation
Example	A sprinter might avoid an aggressive opponent right before a competition, to keep from feeling angry	A golfer might play a safe shot from the tee instead of a risky shot, to avoid the potential anxiety that might arise from a missed risky shot	A basketball player will actively focus on his defensive duties instead of focusing on the clock	A young tennis player who lost the championship might choose to be thankful and inspired by the opportunity, rather than saddened by the loss	A wrestler who believes he has already won a match on points might suppress his happiness to ensure he remains focused, so as to not allow himself to be pinned in the final seconds

TABLE 7.4 Koole's (2009) categories and examples of emotion regulation strategies

		Psychological function		
		Need oriented	Goal oriented	Person oriented
Emotion generating system	Attentional response systems	An anxious luger might choose to focus on how happy he will feel after competing	A footballer might suppress her joy in the remaining seconds of a match so as not to allow a goal	A fencer might practise meditation to be able to compete in a calmer manner
	Knowledge response systems	A triathlete, after having a fight with her coach, might confront the coach to find some resolution	Hockey players might adopt a 'What have we got to lose?' mentality to energize them	A netballer might engage in keeping a journal and expressive writing to help reflect on effective emotion regulation practices
	Bodily response systems	A bodybuilder might build confidence in knowing he has followed a strict diet leading up to a competition	A head coach might vent to an assistant in order to process his emotions	A diver might consciously control her breathing to reduce pre-dive anxiety

depending on whether they are cognitive or behavioural, and whether they encourage the individual to approach or avoid the cause of the emotion. The multitude of emotion regulation strategy classifications highlights the complexity of researching emotions and the opportunity to approach emotion regulation from many different perspectives.

Gross (1998) developed a process model that classifies emotion regulation strategies into five categories, based on the moment at which they impact the emotion generation phase: situation selection, situation modification, attentional deployment, cognitive change and response modulation; see Table 7.3.

Koole (2009) categorized emotion regulation strategies based on which emotion response system they target, namely: attentional, knowledge and bodily response systems. Emotion regulation strategies that target attentional systems include strategies. Koole then further distinguished between strategies that are needs oriented, goal oriented or person oriented.

LEARNING OUTCOME 5

Discuss why and how we might try to regulate others' emotions

As sports are played in a social setting, athletes' emotions could emanate from teammates, coaches, opponents, officials, sport science staff or fans. For example, Totterdell (2000) showed how the mood states of cricketers might be collectively linked: that is, one cricketer's mood was significantly associated with his teammates' average moods. This link was further associated with subjective perceptions of performance. Additionally, in a study by Mankad *et al.* (2009), athletes undergoing long-term injury rehabilitation explained how they tried to maintain a hedonically pleasant emotional climate for the benefit of the team. They did this through surface acting or carefully managing their emotional expressions, in particular suppressing their own unpleasant emotions. Results from Moll *et al.* (2010) suggested that players' celebratory emotional expressions during penalty goals were associated with, not only beneficial performance in teammates, but also reciprocal counter-performance in opposing players.

Researchers in psychology (in many different disciplines in psychology, including sport business, social, work, etc.) are increasingly recognizing that the emotion process is inherently social and interpersonal (e.g. Niven *et al.*, 2009; Van Kleef, 2009; Campos *et al.*, 2011). Consequently, increased attention is being given to *interpersonal emotion regulation*, defined as deliberate attempts by one social entity, known as the 'agent', to change the emotions or moods of another social entity, known as the 'target' (Gross and Thompson, 2007). Van Kleef (2009) presented the 'emotions as social information' (EASI) model to explain how emotional expressions from one individual can influence others' emotions (see Figure 7.1). According to the EASI model, interpersonal emotion regulation occurs through affective reactions (such as emotion contagion and interpersonal liking) and inferential processing (whereby the appraisals of the situation are communicated to targets, who subsequently align their own emotional responses with the agent). For example, consider an alpine skier who is late arriving for training, which naturally upsets her coach, who verbally expresses her disappointment and anger (expression). The skier might infer that her tardiness is a violation of the ski team's

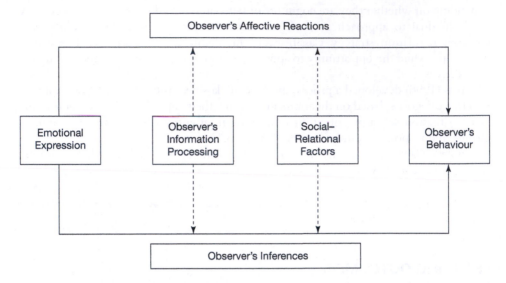

FIGURE 7.1 Van Kleef's EASI model

Source: © Van Kleef, 2009. Reprinted by permission of Sage Publications

code of conduct and is inappropriate, considering everyone else makes the effort to arrive on time (a series of inferences), which might in turn lead her to ensure she is punctual for the next practice (behaviour). Conversely, the coach's anger might offend the skier, leading her to dislike the coach (affective reactions), which might possibly cause her to seek out a new coach (behaviour). The extent to which either process occurs is moderated by such variables as the other's information processing motivation or abilities and by social–relational factors. To continue the above example, if the skier has lost her passion for skiing (signifying a low information processing motivation), or if their relationship is already strained (signifying social–relational factors), these might also influence the subsequent behaviours.

In a review of theory and research, Friesen *et al.* (2013b) proposed that the EASI model could have utility for studying interpersonal emotion regulation in sport. Therefore, studies that seek to investigate this model should be encouraged (Friesen *et al.*, 2013b).

In examining interpersonal regulation strategies Niven *et al.* (2009) presented a classification scheme categorizing nearly 400 distinct strategies. Their final classification of interpersonal affect regulation strategies distinguished between strategies intended to improve or worsen another's affect, as well as strategies intended to engage the other in their task or situation and strategies intended to focus on the nature of the relationship between target and agent. A limitation recognized by Niven *et al.* (2009) was that the context in which regulation strategies were situated spanned nearly every conceivable social setting. Niven and colleagues suggested that, within a specific context, other classifications might prove more relevant, particularly when seeking to transfer research to practice. Given that sport (Dosil, 2006) features unique subcultures, research documenting how subcultural nuances are manifested in emotion regulation becomes an important line of enquiry for the sporting community.

ACTIVITY 7.5

Think about and write out all the different ways you could change someone's emotions in your sport. Once you have done that, read over your list. Are there any commonalities between the strategies – characteristics that distinguish some strategies more prominently than others? Start grouping your strategies, based on these commonalities. You might want to consider the following situational circumstances: (a) the target emotion and response (physiology, subjective feeling, actions), (b) the target individual (e.g. teammate, coach, opponent, referee) and (c) setting (training vs performance). When you have a list of the commoner interpersonal emotion regulation strategies, you can begin to look at when and how you might try to effectively implement these to increase performance in your sport.

ACTIVITY 7.6

Read the following story about interpersonal emotion regulation in ice hockey. Identify (a) possible emotion-eliciting events or circumstances, (b) the generated emotion, (c) emotion regulation strategies and (d) indication of their effectiveness.

A teammate of mine had just moved up from the juniors where he scored tons of points and he stepped up to the senior league thinking that he'd just do exactly the same and he'd be fine. So he would try to pull the same moves over and over and over again on senior players and it wouldn't work. And he got really really emotional – he worked himself up so much and things weren't coming, he resorted to tears on the bench and in the dressing room. And nobody – not the coach or the manager really said anything to him. I wasn't one of the senior players at the time, but I thought, 'Well if nobody else is going to speak to him, somebody has to.' So I went up to him and asked him what the matter was? He replied, 'I can't do this, I can't do anything right in senior hockey.' I said, 'It's been three or four games, you've moved up from junior, it's a whole different kettle of fish – the game, the speed, the skill level, the physical contact, everything is totally different. Why don't you try doing a different play or different move?' 'But that's not my game.' I said, 'Well, we've all got to adapt to the game, change the way we play for the better of the team, not for yourself.' And it was like the quiet word in his ear that really helped. Then he could really change his focus and change his way of playing. And now he's a fantastic player.

Not only is the research into interpersonal emotion regulation strategies an important line of enquiry, but the factors that potentially influence their effectiveness might also be a worthwhile research endeavour. According to the EASI model, the inferential processing and affective reactions pathways can bring about comparable or opposing effects (Van Kleef, 2010). Van Kleef *et al.* (2011) explained how interpersonal emotion regulation can be moderated by the inferential motivations and abilities of the target and social–relational factors. These moderators further exemplify the complexity of interpersonal emotion regulation, as one regulation strategy might bring about intended effects in one person and opposite effects in another person. For example, a coach might chastise a pair of teammates for missing a defence assignment. One player might respond by resolving to be more attentive to her defence duties. Conversely, the second player might take offence at the chastisement and lose motivation to attend to her defence duties. In a meta-analysis designed to examine the effectiveness of using emotion regulation strategies, Augustine and Hemenover (2009) postulated that gender, the length of the regulation attempt and the intensity and valence of the emotion might all influence strategy effectiveness.

CONCLUSIONS

Emotions play a prominent role in all meaningful sport and performances. Depending on meta–emotion beliefs, these emotions can help or hinder an athlete's performance. When an athlete's emotions hinder performance (either their own or their teammates' performance), the athlete can engage in a wide variety of emotion regulation strategies. This chapter has presented some of these strategies and proposed the EASI model as a potentially viable theory to explain interpersonal emotion regulation attempts in sport.

CASE STUDY 7.1

Consider the following fictitious example from an ice hockey game featuring the Steinbach Kings and Kleefeld Stingers. The Kings held a 1–0 lead heading into the final minutes of the third and final period. With a little over 1 minute left in the game, Albert Dueck of the Stingers appeared to score a game-tying goal on the Kings' goaltender. However, moments before the puck had entered the net, the goaltender and another Stingers forward appeared to have entangled their equipment, preventing the goaltender from properly defending the shot from Dueck. The referees asked for a video review to determine the legitimacy of the goal.

- If you were a referee, what emotions might you and your crew be experiencing? How might these influence your actions?

The review showed that Kings' defenceman had pushed the Stingers' forward into the Kings' goaltender, who had then intentionally prolonged the struggle with the Stingers' forward, who was trying to exit the crease area. Nevertheless, the referees ruled that the goal would be disallowed. The crowd protested the call by littering the ice with refuse.

- If you were captain of the Stingers, would you try to manage your teammates' emotions? If so, how would you do so?

In a post-game interview, Dueck shared his feelings and how the team reacted to the disallowed goal: 'It's obviously a tough feeling to be the one responsible for [the disallowed goal] but the guys rallied and gave me a tap on the pads and that helps to put it behind you.'

As play began again, the action led once more into Steinbach's end of the ice. The Stingers held puck possession, and, with 4.7 seconds remaining, rookie Adam Klassen scored the game-tying goal. The arena erupted with elation, and Klassen, rather than celebrate with his linemates with typical stoicism, streaked to centre ice in jubilation and celebration.

- If you were coach of the Kings, would you try to manage your players' emotions? If so, how would you do so?

The excitement of Klassen's celebration transferred to his teammates. Dueck explained after the game, 'The passion and excitement he plays with is unbelievable . . . It gets his teammates and the fans going. I think it's great.' Regulation time ended, and, with an extra point in the standings awarded to the victorious team, the Stingers had to down-regulate their excitement and refocus on scoring a game-winning goal in overtime. Stingers' captain Jareth Duncan, in a post-game interview, commented, 'After all that excitement, we had to tell each other that we hadn't won anything yet, calm down, and get the job done.'

- As a member of either team, how might you try to manage your linemates' emotions at this point in the game?

During overtime, the Kings took an undisciplined penalty for having too many men on the ice. With the man advantage, the Stingers executed their tactics and were once again in possession of the puck in the Kings' zone. With just under 2 minutes remaining in overtime, Dueck, who had been the cause of the disallowed goal, shot the puck past the Kings' goaltender, securing victory for the Stingers. The crowd once again erupted with joy, and the Stingers celebrated an emotional victory. Their coach commented, 'The persistence at the end of the game showed truly the character of this group. To finish it off in overtime was a very mature step in a very difficult situation emotionally.'

APPLYING THE SCIENCE 7.1

Choosing the team captain

Choosing a captain is something that almost every team has to do. Sometimes, captains are nominated by themselves or from their fellow teammates; at other times, the coaching staff will choose the captain(s). Because of the captain's leadership role, a captain who is capable of effectively managing the team's collective mood and an individual player's emotions would be desirable. But what qualities or characteristics might suggest your nominated captain is capable of that task?

According to Van Kleef's EASI model, an athlete will influence the emotions and performance of his or her teammates through (a) affective reactions and (b) inferential processing. One type of affective reaction is known as emotion contagion. With emotion contagion, a captain will try to express or emulate a certain emotion or mood, hoping that teammates will 'catch' those feelings. This is the kind of captain who will 'lead by example'. A captain who uses emotion contagion would likely need to be able to manage their own emotions extremely well if they intend to be able to manage their teammates' emotions, because any attempt to manage a teammate's emotions will be influenced by whatever emotional state the captain is experiencing. Therefore, one quality you might look for in a potential captain is the extent to which they are able to self-regulate their emotions.

Another affective reaction comes through interpersonal liking. That is, we tend to adopt the emotions of people we have an affinity for and express opposing emotions to those of people we dislike. Theoretically then, an individual who has an attractive personality will be able to influence teammates more effectively than someone whose personality alienates teammates and builds walls in the clubhouse. Many coaches who insist on choosing captains themselves have commented that they do so because, otherwise, teammates simply select the most popular person on the team to be captain, regardless of whether or not they have the qualities that captains should possess. However, according to social psychology theory, being popular can be very advantageous when it comes to having the capacity to manage the emotions of the people around you. When someone is trying to manage how you are feeling, it is more likely to work when you have an affinity with that person. Therefore, another quality that you might hope your captain possesses is a high level of agreeableness or sociability.

Alternatively, a captain who is more vocal might rely more on interpersonal emotion regulation through inferential processing. Through this channel, a captain will try to regulate a teammate's emotion by trying to change their thoughts, perspectives or appraisals of a situation. For example, when trailing another team in the late stages of a game, a football team captain might remind teammates about previous matches where the team was in a similar situation and rallied to win the game. In this manner, the captain is trying to increase feelings of hope in the teammates, with the expectation that hopeful teammates will perform better than downhearted teammates. Therefore, being able to see situations from different perspectives and having the capacity to articulate these alternative perspectives to teammates become valuable characteristics for a team captain.

Van Kleef's EASI model also offers a number of moderating factors that influence the extent to which a captain might be successful in regulating a teammate's emotions. The first takes into account the teammate's capacity and current emotional state. If your captain is trying to manage a teammate's mood, the teammate must be relatively open or motivated to let that change occur. There are a number of factors that will influence that motivation to change. For example, perceived status of the captain is a potential moderator that might influence the extent to which the teammate is receptive to interpersonal emotion regulation. Similar to the situation regarding interpersonal liking, someone who is highly respected and who is perceived to have an impressive knowledge of the game will be able to command more influence in the team dressing room or clubhouse than someone who might be new to the game and who has not established a renowned reputation. Therefore, it might be more beneficial to have a seasoned captain who has been 'battle-tested' than having a younger or even a rookie captain, who might display more energy and enthusiasm, but has yet to establish a respected career.

Social–relational factors will also influence the interpersonal emotion regulation process. This might be manifested in whether or not the teammate believes the emotion the captain is targeting is helpful or hurtful to performance. For example, if an ice hockey captain believes that a teammate plays best when angry, but the teammate believes he plays best when calm, then the captain will likely not be too effective in regulating the teammate's emotions. Therefore, being attentive to the emotion–performance relationships (or meta-emotion beliefs) would be an important quality for the captain to possess.

In conclusion, when choosing your captain (either as a teammate or a coach), consider whether the captain portrays the qualities that have been discussed. Particularly, does this person have the ability to manage his or her own emotions well? Is this person relatively agreeable and popular on the team? Are they perceptive, and can they see opportunities from different perspectives? Have they accumulated a career that commands respect and admiration? Are they attentive to their teammates' emotional states and able to discern whether or not these emotional states bring out the best performances? If you've found someone on your team who demonstrates these qualities, it is very likely they would be effective in managing the collective emotions on the team, as well as the individual emotional states of teammates.

BEYOND THE FRONTIER

Although the study of intrapersonal emotion regulation processes and strategies has received considerable attention in the research literature, there are still many valuable questions to explore empirically pertaining to interpersonal emotion regulation. These include research meta-emotion beliefs, interventions to improve interpersonal emotion regulation, emotion regulation within officials, and emotion regulation in relation to popular emotion regulation personality traits.

Van Kleef's EASI model explaining interpersonal emotion regulation was formulated within the sub-psychology discipline of negotiation and conflict resolution. Only recently (e.g. Friesen *et al.*, 2013a) has the EASI model been applied to sport psychology. However, there is potential for the EASI model in sport, because negotiation and conflict resolution, like sport, posits participants regulating their emotions to achieve instrumental goals. That is, in both settings, people do not regulate their emotions purely for hedonic purposes or to feel good and avoid feeling bad. Rather, negotiators and sport participants both regulate their emotions because they believe certain emotions will help them achieve their goals. For example, whereas the general population would typically prefer to avoid feeling anxious, because anxiety is an unpleasant emotion to experience, high-performance athletes find the benefit in feeling anxiety. That is, anxiety might motivate athletes to devote extra time to training and preparation for an upcoming event. Anxiety can also increase arousal levels, which can also be advantageous, depending on the sport. Therefore, the study of these meta-emotion beliefs is an important line of enquiry (Lane *et al.*, 2011). Within the context of interpersonal settings, however, the opportunity exists for teammates to have conflicting meta-emotion beliefs. The questions then become:

- How do these teammates reconcile conflicting meta-emotion beliefs to help coordinate their performance?
- What moderates the effectiveness of this process?
- Can interventions be developed to help facilitate this process?

Moving beyond coaches and athletes as research participants, officials, referees and umpires represent a population in sports settings where additional research efforts could be focused. Referees and their compatriots are unique in their roles, because they hold an authority over athletes and coaches. They have the power and opportunity to penalize players and subsequently affect the outcome of any game. According to the EASI model, authority would represent a potential social–relational moderator that could influence the method and effectiveness of interpersonal emotion regulation tactics.

Some potential future research questions might include:

- How do referees attempt to manage the emotions of athletes and coaches throughout the course of a game or multiple gamed events?
- How do athletes and coaches attempt to manage the emotions of referees?
- How do referees attempt to manage their own emotions, and what effect does this have on their capacity or ability to manage others' emotions?
- Does the type and culture of sport influence the appropriateness or style of the interpersonal emotion regulation strategies that referees use with coaches and athletes?

The sport psychology literature is also highly devoted to applying theory to interventions and practices that potentially influence the performance of athletes. Because the EASI model stipulates that emotions are regulated in order to accomplish specific behavioural and performance outcomes, it represents a viable theory with which to study applied interventions in sport. The EASI model provides numerous potential points of intervention by which to manipulate for the purposes of improving interpersonal emotion regulation and thereby improving performance. These points of intervention can therefore become opportunities for intervention research in sport psychology:

- How can interpersonal emotion regulation through either affective reactions or inferential processing be improved?
- Can the potential moderators be adequately controlled outside the laboratory, in real-world settings?
- Does the regulation of teammates' emotions actually result in improved performance?
- How might interpersonal emotion regulation be measured?

The EASI model theorizes that certain personality characteristics can influence the regulation of others' emotions. Therefore, it would be appropriate to see test relationships between certain personality characteristics and interpersonal emotion regulation. Moving beyond the big five personality traits (openness, conscientiousness, extraversion, agreeableness and neuroticism), there is opportunity to examine interpersonal emotion regulation in relation to some of the emotion-laden personality characteristics popular in the sport psychology literature. For example:

- trait anxiety and anger;
- perfectionism;
- motivation;
- emotional intelligence.

KEY CONCEPTS AND TERMS

Emotions

Emotion consists of neural circuits (that are at least partially dedicated), response systems and a feeling state/process that motivates and organizes cognition and action. Emotion also provides information to the person experiencing it and may include antecedent cognitive appraisals and ongoing cognition, including an interpretation of its feeling state, expressions or social–communicative signals, and it may motivate approach or avoidant behaviour, exercise control/regulation of response, and be social or relational in nature (Izard, 2010, p. 367).

Social–functional approach to emotions

This is a theory that presents emotions as coordinating the behaviour of individuals to meet the shared challenges in the environment.

Meta-emotional beliefs

These are ideas, philosophies or attitudes about how emotions influence performance.

Emotion regulation

This is the process of initiating, maintaining, modulating or changing the occurrence, intensity or duration of internal feeling states and emotion-related physiological processes, often in the service of accomplishing one's goals (Eisenberg et al., 2000, p. 137).

Interpersonal emotion regulation

This relates to deliberate attempts by one social entity, known as the 'agent', to change the emotions or moods of another social entity, known as the 'target' (Gross and Thompson, 2007).

RECOMMENDED FURTHER READING

Books and book chapters

Botterill, C. and Patrick, T. (2003). Understanding and managing emotions in team sports. In Lidor, R. and Henschen, K. P. (eds) *The Psychology of Team Sports*, pp. 115–30. Ann Arbor, MI: Fitness Information Technology.

Hanin, Y. L. (2007). Emotions in sport: Current issues and perspectives. In Tenenbaum, G. and Eklund, R. C. (eds) *Handbook of Sport Psychology* (3rd edn), pp. 33–58. Hoboken, NJ: John Wiley.

Totterdell, P. and Niven, K. (2012). *Should I Strap a Battery to My Head? (And other questions about emotion)*. Charleston, SC: Createspace.

Journals

Augustine, A. A. and Hemenover, S. H. (2009). On the relative effectiveness of affect regulation strategies: A meta-analysis. *Cognition and Emotion*, *23*, 1181–220.

Campo, M., Mellalieu, S., Ferrand, C., Martinent, G. and Rosnet, E. (2012). Emotions in team contact sports: A systematic review. *The Sport Psychologist*, *26*, 62–97.

Friesen, A. P., Lane, A. M., Devonport, T. J., Sellars, C. N., Stanley, D. N. and Beedie, C. J. (2013). Emotion in sport: Considering interpersonal regulation strategies. *International Review of Sport and Exercise Psychology*, *6*(1), 139–54.

Lane, A. M., Beedie, C. J., Jones, M. V., Uphill, M. and Devonport, T. J. (2012). The BASES Expert Statement on emotion regulation in sport. *Journal of Sports Sciences*, *30*, 1189–95.

Lane, A. M., Beedie, C. J., Devonport, T. J. and Stanley, D. M. (2011). Instrumental emotion regulation in sport: Relationships between beliefs about emotion and emotion regulation strategies used by athletes. *Scandinavian Journal of Medicine & Science in Sports*, *21*(6), e445–e451.

SAMPLE ESSAY QUESTIONS

1 Discuss a social–functional approach to emotions in sport, drawing on specific emotion–performance relationships.

2 Discuss the role that meta-emotional beliefs play in emotion regulation.

3 Compare and contrast the emotion regulation strategy classifications as presented by Parkinson and Totterdell (1999), Gross (1998) and Koole (2009).

4 Explain interpersonal emotion regulation in sport using Van Kleef's (2009) EASI model.

REFERENCES

Augustine, A. A. and Hemenover, S. H. (2009). On the relative effectiveness of affect regulation strategies: A meta-analysis. *Cognition and Emotion*, *23*, 1181–20.

Balish, S. M., Eys, M. A. and Schulte-Hostedde, A. I. (2013). Evolutionary sport and exercise psychology: Integrating proximate and ultimate explanations. *Psychology of Sport and Exercise*, *14*, 413–22.

Baumeister, R. F., Vohs, K. D., DeWall, C. N. and Zhang, L. (2007). How emotion shapes behaviour: Feedback, anticipation, and reflection, rather than direct causation. *Personality and Social Psychology Review*, *11*, 167–203.

Beedie, C. J. and Lane, A. M. (2012). The role of glucose in self-control: Another look at the evidence and an alternative conceptualization. *Personality and Social Psychology Review*, *16*, 143–53.

Botterill, C. and Brown, M. (2002). Emotion and perspective in sport. *International Journal of Sport Psychology, 33*, 38–60.

Campos, J. J., Walle, E. A., Dahl, A. and Main, A. (2011). Reconceptualizing emotion regulation. *Emotion Review, 3*, 26–35.

Cohen, A. B., Tenenbaum, G. and English, R. W. (2006). Emotions and golf performance: An IZOF-based applied sport psychology case study. *Behaviour Modification, 30*, 259–80.

Côté, S. and Hideg, I. (2011). The ability to influence others via emotion displays: A new dimension of emotional intelligence. *Organizational Psychology Review, 1*, 53–71.

Devonport, T. J., Lane, A. M. and Hanin, Y. (2005). Emotional states of athletes prior to performance-induced injury. *Journal of Sports Science and Medicine, 4*, 382–94. Available online at: www.tandfonline.com/loi/rjsp20 (accessed 27 March 2015).

Dosil, J. (2006). *The Sport Psychologist's Handbook: A guide for sport-specific performance enhancement.* Chichester, UK: John Wiley.

Eisenberg, N., Fabes, R. A., Guthrie, I. K. and Reiser, M. (2000). Dispositional emotionality and regulation: Their role in predicting quality of social functioning. *Journal of Personality and Social Psychology, 78*, 136–57.

Fehr, B. and Russell, J. A. (1984). Concept of emotion viewed from a prototype perspective. *Journal of Experimental Psychology: General, 113*, 464–86.

Fischer, A. H. and Manstead, A. S. R. (2008). Social functions of emotion. In Lewis, M., Haviland, J. and Feldman Barrett, L. (eds) *Handbook of Emotion* (3rd edn), pp. 456–70. New York: Guilford Press.

Fischer, A. H. and Van Kleef, G. A. (2010). Where have all the people gone? A plea for including social interaction in emotion research. *Emotion Review, 2*, 208–11.

Friesen, A., Devonport, T. J., Sellars, C. N. and Lane, A. M. (2013a). A narrative account of decision-making and interpersonal emotion regulation using a social–functional approach to emotions. *International Journal of Sport & Exercise Psychology.* DOI:10.1080/1612197X. 2013.773664

Friesen, A., Lane, A., Devonport, T., Sellars, C., Stanley, D. and Beedie, C. (2013b). Emotion in sport: Considering interpersonal emotion regulation strategies. *International Review of Sport and Exercise Psychology, 6*, 139–54.

Frijda, N. H. and Mesquita, B. (1994). The social roles and functions of emotions. In Kitayama, S. and Markus, H. S. (eds) *Emotion and Culture: Empirical studies of mutual influence*, pp. 1–87. Washington, DC: American Psychological Association.

Gross, J. J. (1998). The emerging field of emotion regulation: An integrative review. *Review of General Psychology, 2*, 271–99.

Gross, J. J. and Thompson, R. A. (2007). Conceptual foundations. In Gross, J. J. (ed.) *Handbook of Emotion Regulation*, pp. 3–26. New York: Guilford Press.

Hagger, M. S., Wood, C. W., Stiff, C. and Chatzisarantis, N. L. (2010). Self-regulation and self-control in exercise: The strength–energy model. *International Review of Sport and Exercise Psychology, 3*, 62–86.

Hall, C. J. and Lane, A. M. (2001). Effects of rapid weight loss on mood and performance among amateur boxers. *British Journal of Sports Medicine, 35*, 390–95.

Hanin, Y. L. (2000). *Emotions in Sport.* Champaign, IL: Human Kinetics.

Hanton, S. and Jones, G. (1999). The effects of a multimodal intervention program on performers: II. Training the butterflies to fly in formation. *The Sport Psychologist, 13*, 22–41. Available online at: http://journals.humankinetics.com/tsp (accessed 27 March 2015).

Izard, C. E. (2010). The many meanings/aspects of emotion: Definitions, functions, activation, and regulation. *Emotion Review, 2*, 363–70.

Jones, M. V. (2003). Controlling emotions in sport. *The Sport Psychologist, 17*, 471–86. Available online at: http://journals.humankinetics.com/tsp (accessed 27 March 2015).

Jowett, S. (2003). When the 'honeymoon' is over: A case study of a coach–athlete dyad in crisis. *The Sport Psychologist, 17*, 444–60. Available online at: http://journals.humankinetics.com/tsp (accessed 27 March 2015).

Keltner, D. and Gross, J. J. (1999). Functional accounts of emotions. *Cognition & Emotion, 13*, 467–80.

Keltner, D. and Haidt, J. (1999). Social functions of emotions at four levels of analysis. *Cognition & Emotion, 13*, 505–21.

Keltner, D., Haidt, J. and Shiota, M. N. (2006). Social-functionalism and the evolution of emotions. In Schaller, M., Simpson, J. A. and Kenrick, D. T. (eds) *Evolution and Social Psychology*, pp. 115–42. Madison, CT: Psychosocial Press.

Koole, S. L. (2009). The psychology of emotion regulation: An integrative review. *Cognition & Emotion, 23*, 4–41.

Lane, A. M., Beedie, C. J., Devonport, T. J. and Stanley, D. M. (2011). Instrumental emotion regulation in sport: Relationships between beliefs about emotion and emotion regulation strategies used by athletes. *Scandinavian Journal of Medicine & Science in Sports, 21*(6), e445–e451.

Mankad, A., Gordon, S. and Wallman, K. (2009). Psycho-immunological effects of written emotional disclosure during long-term injury rehabilitation. *Journal of Clinical Sport Psychology, 3*, 205–17. Available online at: http://journals.humankinetics.com/tsp (accessed 27 March 2015).

Manstead, A. S. (1991). Emotion in social life. *Cognition & Emotion, 5*, 353–62.

Moll, T., Jordet, G. and Pepping, G. J. (2010). Emotional contagion in soccer penalty shootouts: Celebration of individual success is associated with ultimate team success. *Journal of Sports Sciences, 28*, 983–92.

Nesse, R. M. and Ellsworth, P. C. (2009). Evolution, emotions, and emotional disorders. *American Psychologist, 64*, 129–39.

Niven, K., Totterdell, P. and Holman, D. (2009). A classification of controlled interpersonal affect regulation strategies. *Emotion, 9*, 498–509.

Parkinson, B. (1996). Emotions are social. *British Journal of Psychology, 87*, 663–83.

Parkinson, B. (2011). How social is the social psychology of emotion? *British Journal of Social Psychology, 50*, 405–13.

Parkinson, B. and Totterdell, P. (1999). Classifying affect-regulation strategies. *Cognition and Emotion, 13*, 277–303.

Perkins, D., Wilson, G. V. and Kerr, J. H. (2001). The effects of elevated arousal and mood on maximal strength performance in athletes. *Journal of Applied Sport Psychology, 13*, 239–59.

Robazza, C., Bortoli, L. and Hanin, Y. (2006). Perceived effects of emotion intensity on athletic performance: A contingency-based individualized approach. *Research Quarterly for Exercise & Sport*, 77, 372–85.

Robazza, C., Pellizzari, M. and Hanin, Y. (2004). Emotion self-regulation and athletic performance: An application of the IZOF model. *Psychology of Sport and Exercise*, 5, 379–404.

Sève, C., Ria, L., Poizat, G., Saury, J. and Durand, M. (2007). Performance-induced emotions experienced during high-stakes table tennis matches. *Psychology of Sport and Exercise*, 8(1), 25–46.

Shariff, A. F. and Tracy, J. L. (2011). What are emotion expressions for? *Current Directions in Psychological Science*, 20, 395–9.

Stanley, D. M., Lane, A. M., Beedie, C. J., Friesen, A. P. and Devonport, T. J. (2012). Emotion regulation strategies used in the hour before running. *International Journal of Sport and Exercise Psychology*, 10(3), 159–71.

Stevens, M. J. and Lane, A. M. (2001). Mood-regulating strategies used by athletes. *Athletic Insight*, 3(3). Available online at: www.athleticinsight.com (accessed 27 March 2015).

Tamir, M. (2008). What do people want to feel and why? Pleasure and utility in emotion regulation. *Current Directions in Psychological Science*, 18, 101–5.

Tamir, M. (2011). The maturing field of emotion regulation. *Emotion Review*, 3, 3–7.

Tamir, M., Chiu, C. Y. and Gross, J. J. (2007). Business or pleasure? Utilitarian versus hedonic considerations in emotion regulation. *Emotion*, 7, 546–54.

Tamir, M. and Ford, B. Q. (2009). Choosing to be afraid: Preferences for fear as a function of goal pursuit. *Emotion*, 9, 488–97.

Tamir, M., Mitchell, C. and Gross, J. J. (2008). Hedonic and instrumental motives in anger regulation. *Psychological Science*, 19, 324–8.

Thelwell, R. C. and Greenlees, I. A. (2003). Developing competitive endurance performance using mental skills training. *The Sport Psychologist*, 17, 318–37. Available online at: http://journals.humankinetics.com/tsp (accessed 27 March 2015).

Thelwell, R. C., Greenlees, I. A. and Weston, N. (2006). Using psychological skills training to develop soccer performance. *Journal of Applied Sport Psychology*, 18, 254–70.

Thomas, P. R., Murphy, S. and Hardy, L. (1999). Test of performance strategies: Development and preliminary validation of a comprehensive measure of athletes' psychological skills. *Journal of Sports Sciences*, 17, 697–711.

Totterdell, P. (2000). Catching moods and hitting runs: Mood linkage and subjective performance in professional sport teams. *Journal of Applied Psychology*, 85, 848–59.

Van Kleef, G. A. (2009). How emotions regulate social life. *Current Directions in Psychological Science*, 18, 184–8.

Van Kleef, G. A. (2010). The emerging view of emotion as social information. *Social and Personality Psychology Compass*, 4, 331–43.

Van Kleef, G. A., Van Doorn, E. A., Heerdink, M. W. and Koning, L. F. (2011). Emotion is for influence. *European Review of Social Psychology*, 22, 114–63.

Wickwire, T. L., Bloom, G. A. and Loughead, T. M. (2004). The environment, structure, and interaction process of elite same-sex dyadic sport teams. *The Sport Psychologist*, *18*, 381–96. Available online at: http://journals.humankinetics.com/tsp (accessed 27 March 2015).

Woodcock, C., Cumming, J., Duda, J. L. and Sharp, L. A. (2012). Working within an Individual Zone of Optimal Functioning (IZOF) framework: Consultant practice and athlete reflections on refining emotion regulation skills. *Psychology of Sport and Exercise*, *13*, 291–302.

8 Exercise addiction

Attila Szabo and Alexei Y. Egorov

CHAPTER SUMMARY

This chapter presents a dark side of exercise behaviour known as exercise addiction or exercise dependence. This morbidity is a unique form of addictive behaviour because, in contrast to other addictions, it involves major physical effort and high energy expenditure. The bulk of the theoretical knowledge is summarized on the basis of an up-to-date literature review. The possible mechanisms of exercise addiction are examined from a behaviouristic perspective. Additionally, older and recent models for the aetiology of exercise addiction are presented. Six common symptoms of exercise addiction, on the bases of which a popular screening scale was developed, are illustrated with examples. It is strongly stressed that a questionnaire-based evaluation of exercise addiction may be misleading, because it reflects only the proneness to the disorder, rather than providing a diagnosis. The chapter concludes with a brief discussion of the possible actions to be taken by addicted exercisers, health professionals and researchers.

LEARNING OUTCOMES

When you have studied this chapter, you should be able to:

1 Understand and define the concept of exercise addiction
2 Differentiate between commitment and addiction to exercise
3 Understand the key motivational incentives in exercise addiction
4 Be familiar with the various theoretical models of exercise addiction
5 Recognize and know how to assess the symptoms of exercise addiction

INTRODUCTION AND DEFINITION OF EXERCISE ADDICTION

In sport and leisure physical activity, the frequency, duration and effort of the activity altogether represent the *volume of exercise*. Adequate exercise volume – in harmony with one's physical condition – in sport and physical activity is important to prevent overtraining, which could result in physical and psychological damage. Even when training for world-class competitions, athletes and, in particular, their coaches must plan the training sessions carefully to avoid injury and *staleness* before the crucial event. Nevertheless, innocent or careless miscalculations occur, and athletes pay the price in such circumstances. Overtraining in sports is a serious issue, but the scope of this chapter is to present, discuss and evaluate exercise addiction, a condition in which the volume of exercise is *self-selected* or self-imposed by the exerciser. Those who wish to learn more about overtraining in competitive sports should refer to Richardson *et al.* (2008 – see the recommended reading list at the end of the chapter).

Overdoing an adopted recreational physical activity may lead to severe physical injuries, as well as to the neglect of other personal responsibilities. Indeed, in some rare cases, exercisers may lose control over their exercise and walk on a path of self-destruction (Morgan, 1979). The psychological condition linked to over-exercising is known as *exercise addiction* (Szabo, 2010). Another term frequently used is *exercise dependence* (Hausenblas and Symons Downs, 2002), and some scholars have called it *obligatory exercise* (Pasman and Thompson, 1988). In the public media, the condition has been described as *compulsive exercise* (Eberle, 2004) or *exercise abuse* (Davis, 2000). Although all these synonyms could be describing the same psychological condition, in light of some arguments, as elaborated below, alternating the terminology may be misleading.

Although the term 'dependence' is used as a synonym for addiction, the latter includes the former and also includes 'compulsion' (Goodman, 1990). Accordingly, a formula for addiction may be: *addiction = dependence + compulsion*. Goodman specifies that not all dependencies and compulsions may be classified as addiction. Therefore, in this chapter, the term *addiction* is considered to be the most appropriate, because it encompasses both dependence and compulsion. Further, addiction is defined as the behavioural process that could lead to either pleasure and/or relief from internal discomfort (stress, anxiety, etc.). Addiction is characterized by repeated failure to control the behavioural process (powerlessness) and a reliance on repeating the behaviour, in spite of negative consequences (Goodman, 1990). This definition is complemented by six symptoms of addiction (discussed in detail herein) as criteria for identifying the condition: salience, mood modification, tolerance, withdrawal symptoms, personal conflict and relapse (Brown, 1993; Griffiths, 1997).

Exercise addiction has been classified as *primary exercise addiction* when it manifests itself as a behavioural addiction and as *secondary exercise addiction* when it is present as a co-symptom to eating disorders (De Coverley Veale, 1987). In the former, the motive for exercise abuse is often unknown, even to the affected person. In the latter, however, exercise is used as a means of weight loss, in addition to strict dieting. Therefore, secondary exercise addiction has a different mechanism from primary exercise addiction. However, many symptoms are common to both primary and secondary exercise addictions. The distinguishing difference between the two is that, in primary exercise addiction, *exercise is the objective*, whereas, in secondary exercise addiction, *the objective is weight loss*. This chapter focuses on primary exercise addiction.

FOCUS 8.1

It is unproductive and misleading to use various connotations for exercise addiction. The term 'addiction' is the most accurate, because it involves both dependence and compulsion, as explained by Goodman (1990).

COMMITMENT VERSUS ADDICTION

Glasser (1976, 2012) used the term *positive addiction* to highlight the personally and socially beneficial aspects of regular exercise, in contrast to some self-destructive behaviours, such as drug or alcohol abuse. The 'positive' connotation led to a widespread and *weightless* use of the term *addiction* within both athletic and scholastic circles. For example, runners who claimed that they were *addicted* to their running referred to their *very high level of commitment*. Morgan (1979) has realized this key dilemma. Therefore, to discuss the negative aspects of exaggerated exercise behaviour, he has introduced the term *negative addiction* as an antonym to Glasser's positive addiction. The fact is, however, that all addicted behaviours represent a dysfunction and, therefore, they are *always* negative (Rozin and Stoess, 1993; Szabo, 2010).

Positive addiction is a synonym for *commitment to exercise* (Carmack and Martens, 1979; Pierce, 1994). However, when commitment to exercise is used as a synonym for *addiction* or to *dependence* (Sachs, 1981; Conboy, 1994; Thornton and Scott, 1995), a major conceptual problem is emerging. For example, Thornton and Scott (1995) reported that they could classify 77 per cent of a sample of forty runners as moderately or highly addicted to running. Such a figure is enormous if one considers that, among thousands of runners in a marathon race, more than three-quarters may be addicted! The figure is obviously exaggerated (Szabo, 2000, 2010). Therefore, scholars have realized that this is a problem and have attempted to draw a borderline between commitment and addiction to exercise (Summers and Hinton, 1986; Chapman and De Castro, 1990; Szabo *et al.*, 1997; Szabo, 2000, 2010).

Commitment to exercise is a measure of how devoted a person is to her/his activity. It is an index of the strength of adherence to an adopted, healthy or beneficial activity that is a part of the daily life of the individual. For committed people, satisfaction, enjoyment and achievement derived from their activity are the incentives that motivate them to stick to their sport or exercise (Chapman and De Castro, 1990). Sachs (1981) believed that commitment to exercise results from the intellectual analysis of the rewards, including social relationships, health, status, prestige or even monetary advantages, gained from the activity. Committed exercisers, in Sachs' view: (1) exercise for extrinsic rewards; (2) view their exercise as an important, but not the central, part of their lives; and (3) may not experience major withdrawal symptoms when they cannot exercise for some reason (Summers and Hinton, 1986). Perhaps the key point is that committed exercisers *control* their activity (Johnson, 1995), rather than being controlled by the activity. In contrast to committed exercisers, addicted exercisers: (1) are more likely to exercise for intrinsic rewards, (2) are aware that exercise is the central part of their lives, and (3) experience severe deprivation feelings when they are prevented from exercising (Sachs, 1981; Summers and Hinton, 1986).

ACTIVITY 8.1

Read the following quote:

> I moved to a new town and decided to join a health club as a way of meeting people. Soon, exercise began to become a focal part of my life and I became more determined to keep fit and improve my physique. Gradually, the 3 hours a day I was doing increased to 6 hours and I started to become totally obsessive about exercise. I wouldn't miss a day at the gym. I just lost sight of my body really – I just had to do my workout, come what may, and get my fix.

Does this quote reveal addiction or commitment to exercise? Elaborate on your response.

FOCUS 8.2

A *high* level of commitment to sport or exercise – which has no negative effect on the athlete or exerciser – is not the same as addiction.

APPLYING THE SCIENCE 8.1

Coaches and exercise leaders should monitor the behaviour of athletes, along with their motivation and their attitudes towards sports and exercise, to recognize at an early stage the signs of maladaptive exercise or training patterns.

RESEARCH METHODS 8.1

Only well-researched and validated tools should be used in assessing vulnerability to exercise addiction. Currently, there are two known questionnaires that fulfil the criteria: one is the exercise dependence scale (EDS; Hausenblas and Symons Downs, 2002) and the other is the exercise addiction inventory (EAI; Terry *et al.*, 2004).

INCENTIVES IN EXERCISE ADDICTION

The motive(s) for exercise is another distinguishing characteristic between commitment and addiction to exercise. People exercise for a unique reason. The reason is often an intangible reward, such as being in shape, looking good, being with friends, staying healthy, building muscles, maintaining body weight, etc. The subjective experience of the reward strengthens the exercise behaviour. Scholars known as *behaviourists*, adhering to one of the most influential schools of thought in the field of psychology, postulate that behaviour can be understood and explained via reinforcement and punishment. Accordingly, the *operant conditioning theory* postulates that there are three principles of behaviour: *positive reinforcement, negative reinforcement* and *punishment* (Bozarth, 1994). Positive reinforcement is an incentive for doing something to *gain* a reward, such as bigger muscles. The experienced reward increases the likelihood of that behaviour recurring. In contrast, negative reinforcement is an incentive for exercising to *avoid* something unpleasant, such as feeling fat. The actual avoidance of the feeling then increases the probability of that behaviour recurring in the future. It should be stressed that both positive and negative reinforcers *strengthen* the behaviours (Bozarth, 1994). In contrast, punishment refers to situations in which exposure to a noxious or unpleasant event, or alternatively removal of a pleasant event, reduces the chance of the behaviour recurring. In contrast to reinforcers, punishers *weaken* one's behaviours, and, therefore, exercise or physical activity should not be used as punishment.

People addicted to exercise may be motivated by negative reinforcement (e.g. to avoid withdrawal symptoms), as well as positive reinforcement (e.g. '*runners' high*'; Pierce, 1994; Szabo, 2010). However, negative reinforcement, or avoidance behaviour, is not a characteristic of the committed exercisers (Szabo, 2010). Indeed, committed exercisers maintain their exercise regimen in order to benefit from the activity. On the other hand, addicted exercisers *have to do it*, or else something will happen to them. Their exercise may become an *obligation* that needs to be fulfilled, or otherwise an unwanted life event could occur, such as the inability to cope with stress, or gaining weight, becoming angry or moody, etc. Every time a person engages in a behaviour to avoid something negative or unpleasant, the motive behind that behaviour can be classified as negative reinforcement. In these situations, the person involved *has to do it* rather than *wants to do it*. There are several examples in other sport areas where a behaviour initially driven by positive reinforcement may turn into negatively reinforced behaviour. For example, a skilled football player who starts playing the game for fun, after being discovered as a talent and being offered a contract in a team, becomes a professional player. After the signing of the contract, he *is expected* to perform. Although the player may still enjoy playing the game (especially when all goes well), the pressure due to expectation to perform is the '*has to do*' new facet of football playing and the negatively reinforcing incentive of the sport behaviour. Activity Box 8.2 illustrates the major differences between the underlying motives in behaviours guided by negative and positive reinforcement.

Although positive reinforcement such as runners' high – which is a euphoric feeling after a strenuous workout – and brain reward systems were adopted in explaining exercise addiction, the motivational incentive in addiction may be more closely connected to prevention, escape and/or avoidance of something bad or unwanted, as in several

---

ACTIVITY 8.2

Behaviours driven by positive and negative reinforcement

Provide several examples in which the behaviour or action is motivated by positive or negative reinforcement.

Positive reinforcement	Negative reinforcement
Origin: behaviouristic school of thought	Origin: behaviouristic school of thought
Definition: positive reinforcement strengthens a behaviour because a tangible or intangible gain is secured as a result of the behaviour	Definition: negative reinforcement strengthens a behaviour because a negative condition is stopped and/or avoided as a consequence of the behaviour
Examples:	Examples:
– 'I like the fresh and energizing feeling after exercise' (*gains* good feeling)	– 'I run *to avoid* circulatory problems that my parents had' (avoids illness)
– 'I like running shorter and shorter times on the same distance' (*gains* skill and confidence)	– 'I go to the gym *to avoid* getting fat' (avoids fatness)
– 'I run to be in good shape' (*gains* physical benefits, good shape)	– 'I have to run my 10 miles every day, or else I feel guilty and irritated' (*avoids* feeling of guilt and irritation)

---

models of addiction (Baker *et al.*, 2004). Therefore, the process of addiction is more likely motivated by negative reinforcement, where the affected individual has to exercise to avoid an unwanted consequence. Six symptoms, which are common or 'universal' in exercise addiction, are presented below.

SYMPTOMS OF EXERCISE ADDICTION

Six common symptoms of behavioural addictions were identified through the systematic observation of several behaviours, such as exercise, sex, gambling, video games and also use of the Internet. Based on Brown's (1993) general components of addictions, Griffiths (1996, 1997, 2002) has reiterated them as the following six components:

Salience

This symptom is present when the physical activity or exercise becomes the most important activity in the person's life and dominates their thinking (preoccupation and cognitive distortions), feelings (cravings) and behaviour (deterioration of social behaviours). For instance, even if the person is not actually engaged in exercise, they will be thinking about the next time they will be. The mind of the addicted individual wanders off to exercise during driving, meals, meetings and even between conversations with friends. The closer the planned time for exercise, the greater the urge to exercise, and even anxiety or fear of not starting on time. The addicted exerciser is obsessed with exercise and, regardless of the time of the day, place or activity performed, her or his mind revolves around exercise during most of the awake hours.

Mood modification

This symptom refers to the subjective experiences that people report after exercise and could be seen as a coping strategy (i.e. they experience an arousing 'buzz' or a 'high', or, paradoxically, a tranquil feeling of 'escape' or 'numbing'). Most people report positive feelings and pleasant exhaustion after exercise. However, the addicted person may seek mood modification, not only for the positive mental benefits of exercise, but also for control over the negative psychological feeling states that would occur if the exercise session were missed.

Tolerance

Tolerance is a symptom that manifests itself in the progressively increased amounts of exercise necessary to experience the same effects that were previously felt with less exercise. The runner needs to run longer distances to experience the *runners' high* (Stoll, 1997). Similarly, the addicted exerciser needs larger and larger volumes of exercise to experience the benefits, or the reward, previously achieved with a lower volume of exercise. Tolerance is the main reason why individuals addicted to exercise progressively and continuously increase the frequency, duration and even intensity of the workouts. (Please read Activity Box 8.1 again.)

Withdrawal symptoms

These symptoms are common to all addictions. They are very unpleasant psychological and physical feeling states that occur when exercise is discontinued or largely reduced. Common withdrawal symptoms are guilt, irritability, anxiety, lack of energy, bad mood and feeling fat. Their intensity is severe in people affected by exercise addiction, to the extent that they feel really miserable when the need for exercise is not fulfilled. The manifestation of these withdrawal symptoms in addicted exercisers is largely different from those experienced by committed exercisers. The latter may simply feel a void, or that something is missing, when exercise is not possible for a reason. They look forward to the next opportunity, while prioritizing their obligations. Addicted exercisers, on the other hand, have to exercise to overcome highly distressing withdrawal symptoms, even at the cost of missing other important life obligations.

Conflict

This symptom represents the conflicts between the exercise addicts and others around them (interpersonal conflict), conflicts with other daily activities (job, social life, hobbies and interests) or from within the individual themselves (intra-psychic conflict) that are

ACTIVITY 8.3

Provide several (at least two) examples of interpersonal conflict, conflict in daily activities and intra-psychic conflict that you – or a friend of yours – have experienced in the past. If you have never encountered such conflicts and are unaware of others who have, think of real-life situations in which the three forms of conflict may co-occur. Write down and also elaborate on the examples that you provide.

ACTIVITY 8.4

Using the Internet, find literature on and/or documentation of withdrawal symptoms. Differentiate between physical and psychological withdrawal symptoms and compare the withdrawal symptoms associated with substance (drugs, alcohol, tobacco) and behavioural (gambling, sex, exercise, TV watching, video-game plying) addictions.

concerned with the particular activity. Interpersonal conflict usually results from neglect of relationships with friends or family because of the exaggerated time devoted to exercise. Conflict in daily activities arises because of the abnormally high priority given to exercise, in contrast to activities such as cleaning, taking care of bills, working or studying for exams. Intra–psychic conflict occurs when the addicted person has realized that fulfilling the need to exercise takes a toll on other life endeavours, but she or he is unable to cut down or to control the exercise behaviour.

Relapse

Relapse is the tendency for repeated reversions to earlier patterns of exercise after a break, whether that is voluntary or involuntary. Relapse may be observed after injury or after planned reduction in exercise volume, as a consequence of a decision to manage the unhealthy pattern of exercise or as a consequence of professional or medical advice. Upon resumption of the activity, addicted people could soon end up exercising as much as before the reduction in their volume of exercise, or even more. This is similar to other substance and behavioural addictions in which, for example, the smoker who smokes a packet of cigarettes a day may quit smoking for a period and then start over again, smoking more than a packet per day.

DO WITHDRAWAL SYMPTOMS IMPLY ADDICTION?

Sachs (1981) described addiction to running as, 'addiction of a psychological and/or physiological nature, upon a regular regimen of running, characterized by withdrawal symptoms after 24 to 36 hours without participation' (p. 118). This definition has

---

FOCUS 8.3

Withdrawal symptoms alone are insufficient for suspecting the presence of exercise addiction. The *severity* of withdrawal symptoms and the behavioural incentives aimed at dealing with withdrawal symptoms are the crucial factors that need to be considered.

---

been used by many scholars (e.g. Sachs and Pargman, 1984; Morris, 1989; Furst and Germone, 1993). However, there is a problem with this definition, because withdrawal symptoms, although marking, are only one of several symptoms of addictive behaviours (Brown, 1993; Griffiths, 1997). Incorrectly, many studies have simply assessed the mere presence, rather than type, frequency and intensity, of withdrawal symptoms (Szabo, 1995; Szabo *et al.*, 1997). Yet negative psychological symptoms are reported by almost all habitual exercisers (or hobby makers) for the times when exercise or a hobby activity is prevented for an unexpected reason (Szabo *et al.*, 1996, 1997). Indeed, Szabo *et al.* (1996), conducting a research survey on the Internet, have shown that even participants in physically *light-effort* types of exercise, such as bowling, reported withdrawal symptoms when the activity (in this case, bowling) was prevented. However, the *intensity* of the symptoms reported by this group was lower than that reported by aerobic dancers, weight trainers, cross-trainers or fencers (Szabo *et al.*, 1996).

Consequently, it must be appreciated that the presence of withdrawal symptoms alone is insufficient for the diagnosis of exercise addiction. The intensity of these symptoms is a crucial factor in separating committed from addicted exercisers. Some of the researchers (Cockerill and Riddington, 1996) did not even mention withdrawal symptoms in their listing of the symptoms associated with exercise addiction. In fact, the mere presence of withdrawal symptoms, in many forms of physical activity, suggests that exercise has a positive effect on people's psychological well-being. This positive effect is then missed, obviously, when an interruption to the habitual activity is necessary for some reason. Therefore, withdrawal symptoms do not necessarily imply the presence of addiction. It is not the experience or lack of experience of withdrawal symptoms that should be considered, but rather their severity or intensity when they occur.

ASSESSMENT OF EXERCISE ADDICTION

Before the development of psychometrically validated instruments for gauging exercise addiction, the condition was studied via interviews (Sachs and Pargman, 1979) and a non-specific *commitment to running scale* (CR; Carmack and Martens, 1979). However, using the CR scale has been criticized (Szabo *et al.*, 1997; Szabo, 2010), because, as discussed earlier in this chapter, commitment and addiction are two different concepts.

The negative addiction scale (NAS; Hailey and Bailey, 1982) is a relatively old scale that has been primarily used with runners. It measures psychological, rather than physiological, aspects of compulsive running. Owing to its mediocre psychometric properties, it is hard to make an inference about scores that define a person as addicted to running.

The obligatory exercise questionnaire (OEQ; Pasman and Thompson, 1988) was the first reliable measure aimed at the assessment of exercise addiction. It was modified from the obligatory running questionnaire (Blumenthal *et al.*, 1984). Later, the OEQ was modified to a version that is a more general measure of exercise activity (Thompson and Pasman, 1991). The new version of the questionnaire consists of twenty items evaluating one's exercise habits, rated on a 4-point frequency scale: 1 = never, 2 = sometimes, 3 = usually, 4 = always. Ackard *et al.* (2002) have found that the OEQ (1991 version) has three subscales. These are: (1) exercise fixation (items associated with missed exercise and exercise to compensate for perceived overeating); (2) exercise frequency (addressing frequency and type of exercise); and (3) exercise commitment (indicating a sense of routine that cannot be missed). Ackard *et al.* believe that these subscales highlight the multifaceted nature of excessive exercise.

The exercise dependence questionnaire (EDQ; Ogden *et al.*, 1997) has twenty-nine items in total and eight subscales: (1) interference with social/family/work life, (2) positive reward, (3) withdrawal symptoms, (4) exercise for weight control, (5) insight into problem, (6) exercise for social reasons, (7) exercise for health reasons and (8) stereotyped behaviour. The EDQ was found to have moderate-to-good internal reliability. Some items measure attitudes and social practices, rather than addiction. Consequently, the EDQ has been used only on relatively few occasions in researching exercise addiction.

The exercise beliefs questionnaire (Loumidis and Wells, 1998) assesses personal assumptions in exercise via four factors: (1) social desirability, (2) physical appearance, (3) mental and emotional functioning and (4) vulnerability to disease and ageing. The scale has acceptable-to-good psychometric properties, but it was not widely used in exercise addiction research.

The bodybuilding dependency scale (BDS; Smith *et al.*, 1998) was used specially to assess excessive exercise in bodybuilders. The instrument contains three subscales: (1) social dependence (individual's need to be in the weightlifting environment), (2) training dependence (individual's compulsion to lift weights) and (3) mastery dependence (individual's need to exert control over his/her training schedule). Because of its sport specificity, the BDS has a restricted range of employability in sport and exercise psychology.

Currently, there are two psychometrically valid, widely used tools for the assessment of exercise addiction. These tools have been translated and validated in several languages. One is the EDS (Hausenblas and Symons Downs, 2002). It was designed on the basis of the *Diagnostic and Statistical Manual of Mental Disorders* (*DSM-IV*) criteria for substance dependence (APA, 1994). The EDS is able to identify people: (1) at risk, (2) non-dependent symptomatic and (3) non-dependent asymptomatic. It can also specify whether individuals have physiological dependence (evidence of withdrawal) or no physiological dependence (no evidence of withdrawal). On the EDS, twenty-one items are rated on a 6-point frequency scale, ranging from 1 = never to 6 = always. Evaluation is made in reference to the *DSM-IV* criteria (APA, 1994), with screening for the presence of three or more of the following symptoms: (1) tolerance, (2) withdrawal, (3) intention effects (exercise is done in larger amounts or over a longer period than was intended), (4) loss of control, (5) time (a great deal of time is spent in activities conducive to the obtainment of exercise), (6) conflict and (7) continuance (exercise is continued despite knowledge of persistent or recurrent physical or psychological problems that are likely to have been caused or exacerbated by exercise). A total score and subscale scores can be calculated for the EDS. The higher the score, the higher the risk for exercise addiction. The EDS has good psychometric properties.

The other popular instrument is the exercise addiction inventory (EAI; Terry *et al.*, 2004). It is based on the six common symptoms of addiction (Brown, 1993; Griffiths, 1996, 1997, 2002) that were elaborated above. The tool's brevity renders it suitable for quick and easy assessment of the common symptoms of exercise addiction. The six items are rated on a 5-point scale, from *strongly disagree* (1) to *strongly agree* (5). The EAI cut-off score for individuals considered at risk of exercise addiction is 24. This cut-off value classifies the individuals whose scores are in the top 15 per cent of the total-scale score. The EAI has good psychometric properties in several languages. Activity Box 8.5 illustrates the individual items of the EAI.

Exercise addiction questionnaires could only be used for *screening the risk*, but not for medical *diagnosis*. Therefore, the questionnaire method of assessment estimates the likelihood of addiction in the respondent. Even people scoring above critical values may not necessarily be addicted to exercise. Nevertheless, a score that is close to the maximum may suggest that there is a possibility, or a high risk, of addiction and should

ACTIVITY 8.5

Match each statement on the EAI (left-hand column) with one of the common symptoms of behavioural addiction listed in the middle column, writing the corresponding statement's number to the right of the symptom, in the right-hand column. (The first – tolerance – is done for you, as an example!)

1 Exercise is the most important thing in my life	Tolerance	4
2 Conflicts have arisen between me and my family and/or my partner about the amount of exercise I do	Withdrawal symptoms	
3 I use exercise as a way of changing my mood (e.g. to get a buzz, to escape, etc.)	Relapse	
4 Over time I have increased the amount of exercise I do in a day	Salience	
5 If I have to miss an exercise session I feel moody and irritable	Conflict	
6 If I cut down the amount of exercise I do, and then start again, I always end up exercising as often as I did before	Mood modification	

APPLYING THE SCIENCE 8.2

Although only a very small fraction of exercisers appear to be affected by exercise addiction, the severity of the disorder warrants serious consideration. Consequently, fitness professionals, coaches, orthopaedic doctors, general practitioners, spouses, parents, and even friends, should pay attention to one's exercise habits. If the disorder is recognized at an early stage, *early intervention* becomes possible, and the negative consequences may be reduced.

be followed up with an in-depth interview led by a qualified professional. In formal settings such as schools and sport and leisure facilities, exercise addiction scales may be useful for screening, but many addicted exercisers perform their activity according to need, in an informal setting, by simply going out for a run on their own. In fact, it may be that most exercise addicts are loners in a sense, because no structured physical activity classes or exercising friends could keep up with their workout and busy schedule of exercise in which they engage on a daily basis. Assuming that only about 1–3 per cent of the exercising population may be affected by exercise addiction (Terry *et al.*, 2004; Szabo, 2010; Mónok *et al.*, 2012), and that the majority of exercise addicts may be 'lone wolves', the use of paper-and-pencil questionnaires in researching the morbidity may have further limited value.

MODELS OF ADDICTION

There are several models for exercise addiction. One of the earlier ones is the sympathetic arousal hypothesis (Thompson and Blanton, 1987), which is a physiological model suggesting how adaptation of organisms to regular exercise may lead to addiction. Briefly, adaptation to exercise lowers the body's sympathetic arousal. Low arousal may be inadequate for various daily activities and it may be experienced as a lethargic physical state. This feeling prompts the person to do something about it, or to increase her/his arousal. One means to do that is exercise. However, the effects of exercise in increasing arousal are only temporary, and, therefore, more, longer bouts of exercise may be needed to trigger an optimal state of arousal (Figure 8.1).

Another earlier model is the cognitive appraisal hypothesis (Szabo, 1995), which takes into consideration life stress – which requires challenge beyond one's perceived resources – in the addiction model. Some exercisers may try to escape from major stress by resorting to exercise as a means of coping. Once exercise moderates the stress response, the person depends on it to function well. However, when exercise conflicts with other life obligations, and the individual reduces the volume of exercise, psychological hardship emerges in the form of withdrawal symptoms. Loss of exercise also means the loss of it as a coping mechanism. Therefore, the exerciser loses control, which triggers greater vulnerability to stress by amplifying the negative feelings associated with the lack of exercise. The problem can be resolved only through resuming the previous pattern of exercise, often at the expense of missing other obligations in daily life (Figure 8.2).

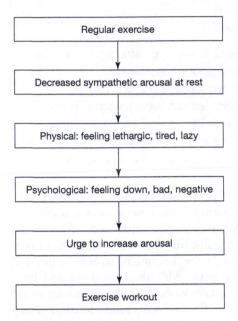

FIGURE 8.1 The sympathetic arousal hypothesis

Source: Data from Thompson and Blanton, 1987. Figure reprinted from Egorov and Szabo, 2013, with permission

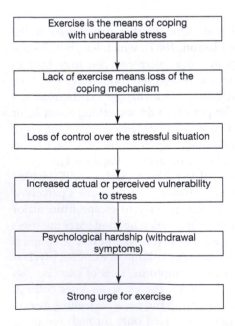

FIGURE 8.2 The cognitive appraisal hypothesis

Source: Data from Szabo, 1995. Figure reprinted from Egorov and Szabo, 2013, with permission

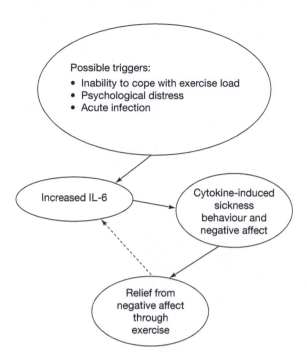

FIGURE 8.3 The IL=6 model for exercise addiction

Source: Data from Hamer and Karageorghis, 2007. Figure reprinted from Egorov and Szabo, 2013, with permission

A theoretical model accentuating the possible role of the hormone interleukin 6 (IL-6) in exercise addiction has been proposed by Hamer and Karageorghis (2007). According to the model, an unidentified trigger causes IL-6 levels to rise and generate cytokine-induced sickness behaviour that is linked to negative affect. In individuals affected by psychological hardship, an elevated level of IL-6 could yield an even more negative mental state. However, the IL-6 hypothesis may not account for the possibility that some individuals will resort to exercise, whereas others may reach for chemical means of escape. The low prevalence of exercise addiction is ascribed to possible adaptations to exercise, whereas the lack of adaptation may increase vulnerability to exercise addiction (Figure 8.3).

A 'four-phase' model for exercise addiction was proposed by Freimuth *et al.* (2011). The first phase represents the pleasurable physical activity that is under control. In the second phase, the mental benefits of exercise are substantiated, and the mood-modifying gains may be used for coping with adversity. Addiction is likely to start when exercise becomes the key means of coping with stress. Subsequently, the third phase is characterized by strict or rigid organization of daily tasks around exercise, negative consequences due to exaggerated exercise, and use of several forms of exercise, either for replacing or complementing the habitual mode of exercise. Further, exercise is performed at self-scheduled intervals and individually, rather than in a group. The fourth stage encompasses the typical symptoms of fully manifested addiction, such as salience, tolerance, conflict, mood modification, withdrawal symptoms and relapse (Figure 8.4).

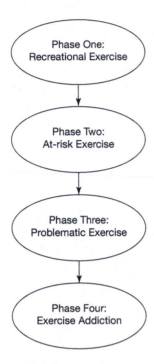

FIGURE 8.4 The four-phase model for exercise addiction

Source: Data from Freimuth *et al.*, 2011

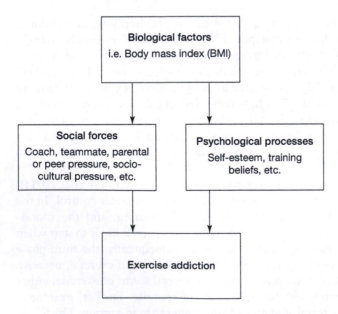

FIGURE 8.5 The biopsychosocial model for exercise addiction

Source: Data from McNamara and McCabe, 2012. Figure reprinted from Egorov and Szabo, 2013, with permission

A 'biopsychosocial' model for exercise addiction in elite athletes was proposed recently (McNamara and McCabe, 2012). The authors found that elite athletes who could be classified as addicted to exercise had higher BMI and manifested extreme as well as maladaptive exercise beliefs, compared with other athletes. They also felt pressure from coaches and teammates and perceived lower social support than their peers. The model (Figure 8.5) suggests that exercise addiction has a biological factor (e.g. BMI) at its route of origin in the elite athletes. Social and psychological processes may interact to determine whether exercise addiction will occur or not.

An interactional model for exercise addiction was recently proposed by Egorov and Szabo (2013). Briefly, the model stresses that interactions between personal and social values, past exercise experience and current life situations may jointly determine whether one will use exercise for coping or resort to other means of dealing

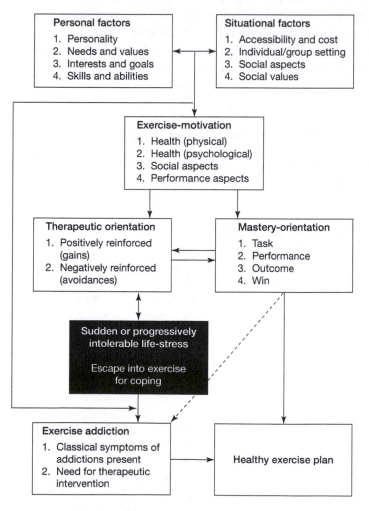

FIGURE 8.6 The interactional model for exercise addiction

Source: Figure reprinted from Egorov and Szabo, 2013, with permission

ACTIVITY 8.6

Describe how the six models forwarded for the explanation of exercise addiction may complement each other to yield a fuller insight into the morbidity.

RESEARCH METHODS 8.2

Nomothetic research on exercise addiction is virtually impossible, as diagnosed (idiographic) cases are only seen in clinics or hospitals. These cases can be studied retrospectively; however, sufferance and hardship during the addiction period may strongly bias one's memory or interpretation during or after treatment. Survey- or questionnaire-based studies could only pinpoint extreme scores of symptoms of addiction that warrant further examination by a qualified medical professional. The key point to remember is that *questionnaires are not diagnosis tools*.

with a toll-taking life stress. The authors speculate that the number of interactions between personal and situational factors is so large that each case is *idiographic*, resembling a mind-locked 'black box' (illustrated in black in Figure 8.6) that could only be unlocked through a person-specific diagnosis by a mental health professional.

CORRELATES OF EXERCISE ADDICTION

Researchers have looked at the correlates of exercise addiction, but have been unable to identify when, how or why a transition takes place from healthy to unhealthy exercise behaviour (Johnson, 1995). Exercise addiction appears to be positively related to anxiety (Morgan, 1979; Rudy and Estok, 1989) and negatively correlated with self-esteem (Estok and Rudy, 1986; Rudy and Estok, 1989). Further, the length of experience with a particular physical activity appears to be positively correlated with exercise addiction scores (Hailey and Bailey, 1982; Thaxton, 1982; Furst and Germone, 1993). In accordance with Egorov and Szabo (2013), if past experience is related to exercise addiction, it is reasonable to suspect that a stressful life event may trigger addiction that is manifested through 'revolutionary' rather than evolutionary changes in the habitual physical activity pattern of the individual. The affected person may see this form of coping as healthy in light of mass knowledge and media information about the positive aspects of exercise.

It is well known that the media play an important role in what people think and believe about regular physical activity. Their beliefs influence their expectations from their exercise. The media–propagated positive image of the habitual exerciser provides a mental defence known as rationalization, behind which a few exercisers with severe emotional problems may hide. Thus, the media-projected positive image concerning regular exercise could be used to deny the existence of the problem (a characteristic defence in most addictive behaviours) and to delay the detection of the problem to the advanced stage, when all symptoms of addiction are vividly present. Because of denial, only a few case studies reported in the literature may present genuine cases of exercise addiction. Their number and case-specificity delay the accumulation of scientific knowledge about this dysfunction. In a random sample of habitual exercisers, only a few cases – if any! – of exercise addicts may be identified (Morris, 1989). As such, the nomothetic (group) approach to studying exercise addiction is inappropriate. The interactional model (Egorov and Szabo, 2013) stresses the need for the idiographic (case-specific) approach for the better understanding of the disorder. Further, if exercise addiction manifests itself as a means of coping with a psychological problem, it should be treated as a symptom of that problem. The psychological problem itself needs to diagnosed and treated by qualified mental health professionals – tasks beyond the scholastic mission of sport scientists.

PREVALENCE OF EXERCISE ADDICTION

Screening for risk of exercise addiction is carried out using psychometrically validated questionnaires. These tools do not convey accurate information about the *actual prevalence of exercise addiction*, as they are screening, not diagnosis, instruments. Indeed, the estimates based on questionnaires should be interpreted as symptomatic or at risk for exercise addiction, as also noted by the developers of the tools (e.g. Hausenblas and Symons Downs, 2002; Terry *et al.*, 2004).

A number of enquiries were conducted on convenience samples of university students. Hausenblas and Symons Downs (2002) reported that between 3.4 and 13.4 per cent of their samples were at high risk for exercise addiction. The lower figure was also confirmed by Griffiths *et al.* (2005), who reported that 3.0 per cent of university students could be at risk of exercise addiction. Later, Szabo and Griffiths (2007) confirmed that the prevalence of risk for exercise addiction is about 3.6 per cent in the general exercising population, whereas the figure is nearly double (6.9 per cent) in British sport science undergraduates. The study by Hausenblas and Symons Downs (2002) was conducting using the EDS, whereas the other two used the EAI. Nevertheless, the two instruments yielded comparable results in American and British samples. Recently, in the first population-wide study (Mónok *et al.*, 2012) of exercise addiction, the proportion of people found to be at risk for addiction was 1.9 per cent among habitual exercisers and 0.3 per cent in the general population, as gauged with the EDS. However, in the same study, the use of EAI yielded higher figures: 3.2 per cent in habitual exercisers and 0.5 per cent in the general population. Mónok *et al.* attributed the discrepancy to the lack of an empirically established cut-off point for the EAI. In spite of the slight discrepancy between the EDS and EAI, they appear to reflect a 'close estimation' of the *prevalence of risk for exercise addiction* in committed exercisers (Sussman *et al.*, 2011). Several investigations that used instruments other than the EDS and EAI in the scrutiny of the risk for exercise addiction have found exaggerated or unlikely figures for the morbidity, as summarized in Table 8.1.

TABLE 8.1 Prevalence of exercise addiction according to various reports in the scholastic literature

Year	Author(s)	Sample studied	Measure(s) used	Prevalence
1995	Thornton and Scott	Runner	CR scale (Carmack and Martens, 1979)	77%
1998	Slay et al.	Runners	obligatory running questionnaire (Blumenthal et al. 1984)	26.2% of male runners, 25% of female runners
2000	Bamber et al.	Mixed exercisers and university students	EDQ (Ogden et al., 1997)	14.8%, and 9% also suffering eating disorders
2002	Ackard et al.	Female university exercisers	OEQ (Pasman and Thompson, 1988)	8.0%
2002	Blaydon and Lindner	Triathletes	EDQ	30.4% primary and 20.6% secondary exercise addiction
2002	Hausenblas and Symons Downs	University students	EDS (Hausenblas and Symons Downs, 2002)	3.4% and 13.4% in two studies
2004	Downs et al.	University students	EDS-Revised (EDS-R; Downs et al., 2004)	3.6% and 5.0% in two studies
2005	Griffiths et al.	University students	EAI (Terry et al., 2004)	3.0%
2007	Allegre et al.	Ultra-marathoners	EDS-R (French)	3.2%
2007	Szabo and Griffiths	Habitual exercisers and sport science students	EAI (Terry et al., 2004)	3.6% in habitual exercisers, 6.9% in sport science undergraduates
2007	Youngman	Triathletes	EAI	19.9%
2008	Lejoyeux et al.	Fitness centre attendees	Interview and own questionnaire	42%

Year	Authors	Sample	Instrument	Prevalence
2009	Modolo et al. (cf. Modolo et al., 2011)	Various amateur athletes	NAS (Hailey and Bailey, 1982)	32%
2010	Smith et al.	Competitive runners	EDS and running addiction scale (Chapman and De Castro, 1990)	50%
2011	Grandi et al.	Habitual exercisers	EDQ (Italian)	40.5%
2011	Villella et al.	High-school students	EAI (Italian)	8.5%
2012	Costa et al.	Fitness centre attendees	EDS-R (Italian)	6.6%
2012	Lejoyeux et al.	Fitness centre attendees	EAI (French) and own questionnaire	29.6%
2012	McNamara and McCabe	Elite athletes	The exercise dependence and elite athletes scale (McNamara and McCabe, 2013)	34.8%
2012	Mónok et al.	Population-wide study	EDS and EAI (Hungarian)	0.3% on EDS and 0.5% on EAI in general population; 1.9% on EDS and 3.2% on EAI in regular exercisers
2012	Lichtenstein et al.	Exercisers and soccer players	EAI (Danish)	5.8%
2013	Menczel et al.	Fitness centre attendees	EDS & EAI (Hungarian)	1.8% + 1.8% who exhibited both exercise addiction and eating disorders

Source: Egorov and Szabo, 2013; used with permission

FOCUS 8.4

Note the high variability in the detected prevalence of exercise addiction in Table 8.1. The psychometric reliability of the adopted questionnaires may be one factor contributing to the wide spectrum of findings. Another factor may be linked to the population or sample studied, and cultural or gender-related interpretations of the items on the screening tools may also add to the high variability in the results.

Although researchers have stressed that actual cases of exercise addiction are rare (De Coverley Veale, 1995; Szabo, 2000), especially when compared with other addictions (Sussman *et al.*, 2011), figures of above 40 per cent prevalence, published in the past few years, suggest that the psychopathology is not well understood among scholars. The diversity in the instruments used, samples and methods of enquiry – as well as some possible cross-cultural issues that have not been addressed to date – may all contribute to the inconsistencies seen in Table 8.1. Further, as noted earlier, the questionnaire-based studies could only estimate the preponderance of the 'at-risk' exercisers, rather than actual clinical cases. Consequently, the latter may be even lower than the estimates based on the population-wide results reported recently (Mónok *et al.*, 2012).

WHAT COULD AN AFFECTED INDIVIDUAL DO?

Physically active people should keep their exercise in perspective. The person who feels that she or he is at risk may wish to evaluate the statements in Activity Box 8.5 using a 5-point rating scale (1 = strongly disagree, 2 = disagree, 3 = uncertain, 4 = agree, 5 = strongly agree). The six statements are based on the most common symptoms of behavioural addiction. If one scores 24 or above on the scale, then there is a likely problem (risk). To avoid negative consequences, the exercise behaviour needs to be discussed with an independent health professional familiar with exercise addiction. Denial of dysfunctional exercise delays any intervention and results in the augmentation of the problem. At this stage, it may be important to admit the fact that too much exercise may have detrimental and irreversible effects. If others' opinions suggest that there is a problem, the root(s) of it (i.e. the reason for over-exercise) should be identified. The mere self-acknowledgement of the problem is already a significant step towards coming back on to a healthy exercise track. Remember, the problem is always other than exercise per se!

WHAT COULD HEALTH PROFESSIONALS DO?

Individuals affected by exercise addiction frequently visit orthopaedic and physiotherapy clinics with injuries caused by exercise that is sustained in spite of contrary medical advice (Wichmann and Martin, 1992). These injuries become more severe with time and force the individual to seek medical help. Therefore, general practitioners, orthopaedic specialists or surgeons, occupational therapists and physiotherapists should be familiar with the main symptoms of exercise addiction. The EAI, which could be completed by patients in less than 1 minute, could be a reinforcing aid in the detection of addiction. Upon recognizing the symptoms in a patient, medical and health professionals should attempt to convince the affected individual that talking over the problem with an impartial specialist may be in their interest. Subsequently, they should refer the patient to a psychologist or psychiatrist colleague who specializes in the area of behavioural addictions. Exercise addiction, like other behavioural addictions, should be considered a serious dysfunction. Therefore, its identification must be positive. Once such a positive diagnosis has emerged, the principal concern should be to find the source or root of addiction. Then, the treatment should be geared towards the cause, not the symptoms, of exercise addiction (Szabo, 2000, 2010). In light of a recently presented interactional model for exercise addiction (Egorov and Szabo, 2013), each *diagnosed case* of exercise addiction may be the result of a number of individual-specific interactions between the person and her/his life situation.

BEYOND THE FRONTIER

Long ago, Szabo (2001) proposed a 'pyramid' approach for the advancement of knowledge about exercise addiction (Figure 8.7). Unfortunately, this approach requires major collaboration at several professional levels, which is difficult to establish. Only focused/directed effort, modelling Szabo's proposal, could be fruitful in better understanding and dealing with exercise addiction. According to Szabo, scholars with research training could do the surface screening ('population' in Figure 8.7). After the screening, professionals with clinical training could then follow up individuals with high scores using in-depth interviews and then separate those who exercise in high volumes but maintain control over their exercise from those who have lost control over their exercise behaviour ('group' in Figure 8.7). The primary incentive for exercise, with special attention to 'wants to do it' and 'has to do it' should be kept in perspective. Once separation at group level has taken place, professionals with clinical training should engage in the treatment of the positively identified individuals, while – with the patients' consent – maintaining a confidential record about the causes and consequences of their addiction ('person' in Figure 8.7). Data from several case studies, then, could be compiled and analysed with qualitative methods to promote the better understanding of exercise addiction. Indeed, perhaps the greatest obscurity in the exercise addiction literature is a confounding interpretation of the results from nomothetic research that do not accentuate clearly that their findings only represent the likely risk, instead of clinically established morbidity. The latter are unique to the person and, therefore, idiographic. This approach would also take into consideration the recently proposed interactional model for exercise addiction (Egorov and Szabo, 2013).

FROM RESEARCH AND CLINICAL INTERVENTION

Research should treat exercise addiction as a symptom of a serious psychological problem. Owing to the fact that only a fraction of the exercising population is affected by exercise addiction (Morris, 1989; Pierce, 1994; Szabo, 2000; Mónok *et al.*, 2012), individual *clinical cases* should be accepted to be the framework of research on exercise addiction. A very high dose of exercise, whether conceptualized in terms of high frequency, intensity, duration or history, is insufficient for the diagnosis of exercise addiction (Szabo, 2010; Freimuth *et al.*, 2011). If physically active individuals have not experienced substantial negative life events directly related to exercise, and they have not jeopardized personal health and social relationships, then they are only committed to their exercise, without risk for exercise addiction. Further, because existing tools for measuring exercise addiction are primarily questionnaires aiming to quantify exercise addiction, they yield a score of addiction ranging from low to high. Graded scales may be effective in the evaluation of tendencies for exercise addiction, which represents a useful surface screening of the problem, but they are inadequate in the diagnosis of the morbidity. People who score on the upper end of these scales should have a further follow-up with qualified mental health professionals who are able to diagnose exercise addiction and then also identify the psychological problem behind it. This method could also allow researchers to identify the life event(s) that trigger exercise addiction.

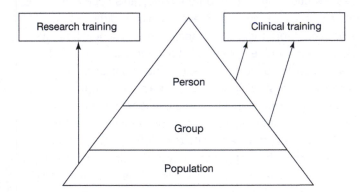

FIGURE 8.7 The interdisciplinary, collaboration-requiring 'pyramid' approach for the better understanding and treatment of exercise addiction

Source: Szabo, 2001

CONCLUSIONS

Exercise addiction is a relatively rare dysfunction within the exercising population that is manifested though obsessive, compulsive and excessive exercise patterns. It results in negative consequences to the affected individual and her or his social environment. The maintenance of the behaviour is most often driven by negative reinforcement that is an incentive by which the exerciser tries to avoid an unpleasant event by regularly engaging in exaggerated amounts of exercise. Many symptoms characteristic of other behavioural addictions are present in exercise addiction as well. Scales or questionnaires developed around the common symptoms are useful in the screening, but not the diagnosis, of exercise addiction. Only case studies are promising for advancing knowledge about this exercise-related dysfunction. The detection of more cases could be expedited through population-wide surface screening, conducted by researchers who have to share the data from such studies with clinically trained professionals for positive diagnosis. The treatment of exercise addiction should be aimed at the psychological problem that triggered the maladaptive behaviour.

KEY CONCEPTS AND TERMS

Commitment to exercise
A high level of devotion or dedication to habitual exercise.

Compulsive exercise
See 'Exercise addiction'.

Exercise abuse
See 'Exercise addiction'.

Exercise addiction
A behavioural process that could provide either pleasure or relief from internal discomfort, characterized by repeated failure to control the behaviour (or powerlessness) and maintenance of the behaviour in spite of major negative consequences (Goodman, 1990).

Exercise dependence
See 'Exercise addiction'.

Negative reinforcement
Motivational incentive for doing something to *avoid* something noxious or unpleasant.

Obligatory exercising
See 'Exercise addiction'.

Operant conditioning theory
Explains how the consequences of a particular behaviour are used to modify the occurrence and the form of that behaviour.

Opioid receptors

A group of G-protein coupled receptors with opioids as ligands. They are widely distributed in the brain and the gut. The endogenous opioids are dynorphins, enkephalins, endorphins, endomorphins and nociceptin/orphanin FQ.

Positive addiction

An activity or hobby that is viewed as personally and socially beneficial, in contrast to destructive or harmful behaviours such as substance abuse.

Positive reinforcement

Motivational incentive for doing something to *gain* or to obtain something pleasant or desirable.

Punishment

A situation where presentation of a noxious stimulus or removal of a pleasant stimulus, following an inappropriate or unacceptable behaviour, decreases the probability of recurrence of that behaviour.

Runners' high

A pleasant feeling associated with positive self-image, sense of vitality, control and a sense of fulfilment, reported by runners as well as by other exercisers after a certain amount and intensity of exercise. The feeling has been associated with increased levels of endogenous opioids and catecholamines observed after exercise.

Staleness

Mental fatigue and loss of enthusiasm, often associated with overtraining or unimaginative, repetitive training sessions.

Volume of exercise

The frequency, duration and intensity or effort of exercise.

RECOMMENDED FURTHER READING

Internet

Titles and web pages were all functioning on 16 July 2014.

Compulsive exercise: http://kidshealth.org/parent/emotions/behavior/compulsive_exercise.html

Confessions of an exercise addict: www.dailymail.co.uk/femail/article-1215705/Im-addicted-exercise-How-fitness-regime-ruined-holidays-social-life-marriage--I-just-stop.html

Exercise addiction: www.nodependence.com/addictions/exercising-addiction/exercise-addic tion.html

Exercise addiction and eating disorders: www.mclean.harvard.edu/pdf/news/fitnessmanage 0704.pdf

Exercise addiction as described on Wikipedia: http://en.wikipedia.org/wiki/Exercise_addiction

Exercise addiction in British sport science students: www.springerlink.com/content/x8460707 wj28kp71/fulltext.pdf

Exercise addiction in eating problems: www.eatingproblems.org/epsexer.html

Exercise addiction in men: http://men.webmd.com/features/exercise-addiction

Exercise addiction in sport: www.thesportinmind.com/articles/exercise-addiction-in-sport/

Passion or problem? (media article): http://greatist.com/fitness/exercise-addiction

Signs of exercise addiction: www.active.com/articles/know-the-signs-of-unhealthy-exercise-addiction

The exercise addiction inventory (EAI): www.hawaii.edu/hivandaids/The_Exercise_Addiction _Inventory__A_New_Brief_Screening_Tool.pdf

The exercise dependence scale (EDS): www.personal.psu.edu/faculty/d/s/dsd11/EDS/

Too much of a good thing: www.acefitness.org/fitfacts/pdfs/fitfacts/itemid_353.pdf

Books

Currie-McGhee, L. K. (2011). *Exercise Addiction (Diseases and Disorders)*. San Diego, CA: Lucent Books.

Friedman, P. (2009). *Diary of an Exercise Addict*. Guilford, CT: Globe Pequot Press.

Kaminker, L. (1998). *Exercise Addiction: When fitness becomes an obsession*. New York: Rosen Publishing.

Kerr, J. H., Lindner, K. J. and Blaydon, M. (2007). *Exercise Dependence*. New York: Routledge. (Based on Google scholar information, currently freely available from: http://dualibra.com/ wp-content/uploads/2011/06/Exercise-Dependence.pdf)

Richardson, S. O., Andersen, M. B. and Morris, T. (2008). *Overtraining Athletes: Personal journeys in sport*. Champaign, IL: Human Kinetics.

Szabo, A. (2010). *Addiction to Exercise: A symptom or a disorder?* New York: Nova Publishers.

Journals

Berczik, K., Szabo, A., Griffiths, M. D., Kurimay, T., Kun, B., Urbán, R. and Demetrovics, Z. (2012). Exercise addiction: Symptoms, diagnosis, epidemiology, and etiology. *Substance Use & Misuse*, *47*(4), 403–17.

Davis, C. (2000). Exercise abuse. *International Journal of Sport Psychology*, *31*, 278–89.

De Coverley Veale, D. M. W. (1987). Exercise Dependence. *British Journal of Addiction*, *82*, 735–40.

Egorov, A. Y. and Szabo, A. (2013). The exercise paradox: An interactional model for a clearer conceptualization of exercise addiction. *Journal of Behavioral Addictions*, *2*(4), 199–208.

Griffiths, M. D. (1997). Exercise addiction: A case study. *Addiction Research & Theory*, 5(2), 161–8.

SAMPLE ESSAY QUESTIONS

1 What are the similarities and difference between high volumes of training in elite sports vs. exercise addiction?

2 Identify issues related to the objective aspect and subjective nature of exercise addiction.

3 Describe the importance of timely recognition of maladaptive exercise patterns in the gym.

4 Describe and discuss the consequences of undiagnosed and untreated exercise addiction.

5 Discuss the importance of unveiling the reinforcers in the maintenance of exercise addiction.

REFERENCES

Ackard, D. M., Brehm, B. J. and Steffen, J. J. (2002). Exercise and eating disorders in college-aged women: Profiling excessive exercisers. *Eating Disorders*, 10(1), 31–47.

Allegre, B., Therme, P. and Griffiths, M. (2007). Individual factors and the context of physical activity in exercise dependence: A prospective study of 'ultra-marathoners'. *International Journal of Mental Health and Addiction*, 5(3), 233–43.

American Psychiatric Association (APA) (1994). *Diagnostic and Statistical Manual of Mental Disorders* (4th edn). Washington, DC: APA.

Baker, T. B., Piper, M. E., McCarthy, D. E., Majeskie, M. R. and Fiore, M. C. (2004). Addiction motivation reformulated: An affective processing model of negative reinforcement. *Psychological Review*, 111, 33–51.

Bamber, D., Cockerill, I. M. and Carroll, D. (2000). The pathological status of exercise dependence. *British Journal of Sports Medicine*, 34(2), 125–32.

Blaydon, M. J. and Lindner, K. J. (2002). Eating disorders and exercise dependence in triathletes. *Eating Disorders*, 10, 49–60.

Blumenthal, J. A., O'Toole, L. C. and Chang, J. L. (1984). Is running an analogue of anorexia nervosa? An empirical study of obligatory running and anorexia nervosa. *Obstetrical & Gynecological Survey*, 40(2), 94–5.

Bozarth, M. A. (1994). Pleasure systems in the brain. In Warburton, D. M. (ed.) *Pleasure: The politics and the reality*, pp. 5–14. New York: John Wiley.

Brown, R. I. F. (1993). Some contributions of the study of gambling to the study of other addictions. In Eadington, W. R. and Cornelius, J. A. (eds) *Gambling Behavior and Problem Gambling*, pp. 241–72. Reno, NV: University of Nevada Press.

Carmack, M. A. and Martens, R. (1979). Measuring commitment to running: A survey of runners' attitudes and mental states. *Journal of Sport Psychology*, *1*, 25–42.

Chapman, C. L. and De Castro, J. M. (1990). Running addiction: Measurement and associated psychological characteristics. *The Journal of Sports Medicine and Physical Fitness*, *30*, 283–90.

Cockerill, I. M. and Riddington, M. E. (1996). Exercise dependence and associated disorders: A review. *Counselling Psychology Quarterly*, *9*, 119–29.

Conboy, J. K. (1994). The effects of exercise withdrawal on mood states of runners. *Journal of Sport Behavior*, *17*, 188–203.

Costa, S., Cuzzocrea, F., Hausenblas, H. A., Larcan, R. and Oliva, P. (2012). Psychometric examination and factorial validity of the Exercise Dependence Scale-Revised in Italian exercisers. *Journal of Behavioral Addictions*, *1*(4), 186–90.

Davis, C. (2000). Exercise abuse. *International Journal of Sport Psychology*, *31*, 278–89.

De Coverley Veale, D. M. W. (1987). Exercise dependence. *British Journal of Addiction*, *82*, 735–40.

De Coverley Veale, D. M. W. (1995). Does primary exercise dependence really exist? In *Exercise Addiction: Motivation for participation in sport and exercise*, pp. 1–5. Leicester, UK: The British Psychological Society.

Downs, D. S., Hausenblas, H. A. and Nigg, C. R. (2004). Factorial validity and psychometric examination of the exercise dependence scale–revised. *Measurement in Physical Education and Exercise Science*, *8*(4), 183–201.

Eberle, S. G. (2004). Compulsive exercise: Too much of a good thing? National Eating Disorders Association. Available online at: www.uhs.berkeley.edu/edaw/CmpvExc.pdf (accessed 23 October 2007).

Egorov, A. Y. and Szabo, A. (2013). The exercise paradox: An interactional model for a clearer conceptualization of exercise addiction. *Journal of Behavioral Addictions*, *2*(4), 199–208.

Estok, P. J. and Rudy, E. B. (1986). Physical, psychosocial, menstrual changes/risks and addiction in female marathon and nonmarathon runners. *Health Care for Women International*, *7*, 187–202.

Freimuth, M., Moniz, S. and Kim, S. R. (2011). Clarifying exercise addiction: Differential diagnosis, co-occurring disorders, and phases of addiction. *International Journal of Environmental Research and Public Health*, *8*(10), 4069–81.

Furst, D. M. and Germone, K. (1993). Negative addiction in male and female runners and exercisers. *Perceptual and Motor Skills*, *77*, 192–4.

Glasser, W. (1976). *Positive Addiction*. New York: Harper & Row.

Glasser, W. (2012). Promoting client strength through positive addiction. *Canadian Journal of Counselling and Psychotherapy/Revue Canadienne de Counseling et de Psychothérapie*, *11*(4), 173–5.

Goodman, A. (1990). Addiction: Definition and implications. *British Journal of Addiction*, *85*, 1403–8.

Grandi, S., Clementi, C., Guidi, J., Benassi, M. and Tossani, E. (2011). Personality characteristics and psychological distress associated with primary exercise dependence: An exploratory study. *Psychiatry Research*, *189*(2), 270–5.

Griffiths, M. D. (1996). Behavioural addiction: An issue for everybody? *Journal of Workplace Learning*, 8(3), 19–25.

Griffiths, M. D. (1997). Exercise addiction: A case study. *Addiction Research*, 5, 161–8.

Griffiths, M. D. (2002). *Gambling and Gaming Addictions in Adolescence*. Leicester, UK: British Psychological Society/Blackwell.

Griffiths, M. D., Szabo, A. and Terry, A. (2005). The exercise addiction inventory: A quick and easy screening tool for health practitioners. *British Journal of Sports Medicine*, 39(6), e30.

Hailey, B. J. and Bailey, L. A. (1982). Negative addiction in runners: A quantitative approach. *Journal of Sport Behavior*, 5, 150–3.

Hamer, M. and Karageorghis, C. I. (2007). Psychobiological mechanisms of exercise dependence. *Sports Medicine*, 37(6), 477–84.

Hausenblas, H. A. and Symons Downs, D. (2002). How much is too much? The development and validation of the exercise dependence scale. *Psychology and Health*, 17, 387–404.

Johnson, R. (1995). Exercise dependence: When runners don't know when to quit. *Sports Medicine and Arthroscopy Review*, 3, 267–73.

Lejoyeux, M., Avril, M., Richoux, C., Embouazza, H. and Nivoli, F. (2008). Prevalence of exercise dependence and other behavioral addictions among clients of a Parisian fitness room. *Comprehensive Psychiatry*, 49(4), 353–9.

Lejoyeux, M., Guillot, C., Chalvin, F., Petit, A. and Lequen, V. (2012). Exercise dependence among customers from a Parisian sport shop. *Journal of Behavioral Addictions*, 1(1), 28–34.

Lichtenstein, M. B., Christiansen, E., Bilenberg, N. and Støving, R. K. (2012). Validation of the exercise addiction inventory in a Danish sport context. *Scandinavian Journal of Medicine & Science in Sports*. DOI: 10.1111/j.1600-0838.2012.01515.x

Loumidis, K. S. and Wells, A. (1998). Assessment of beliefs in exercise dependence: The development and preliminary validation of the exercise beliefs questionnaire. *Personality and Individual Differences*, 25(3), 553–67.

McNamara, J. and McCabe, M. P. (2012). Striving for success or addiction? Exercise dependence among elite Australian athletes. *Journal of Sports Sciences*, 30(8), 755–66.

McNamara, J. and McCabe, M. P. (2013). Development and validation of the Exercise Dependence and Elite Athletes Scale. *Performance Enhancement & Health*, 2(1), 30–6.

Menczel, Z., Kovacs, E., Farkas, J., Magi, A., Eisinger, A., Kun, B. and Demetrovics, Z. (2013). Prevalence of exercise dependence and eating disorders among clients of fitness centres in Budapest. *Journal of Behavioral Addictions*, 2(Suppl 1), 23–4.

Modolo, V. B., Antunes, H. K., Gimenez, P. R., Santiago, M. L., Tufik, S. and Mello, M. T. D. (2011). Negative addiction to exercise: Are there differences between genders? *Clinics (Sao Paulo)*, 66(2), 255–60.

Mónok, K., Berczik, K., Urbán, R., Szabó, A., Griffiths, M. D., Farkas, J., Magi, A., Eisinger, A., Kurimay, T., Kökönyei, G., Kun, B., Paksi, B. and Demetrovics, Z. (2012). Psychometric properties and concurrent validity of two exercise addiction measures: A population wide study in Hungary. *Psychology of Sport and Exercise*, 13, 739–46.

Morgan, W. P. (1979). Negative addiction in runners. *The Physician and Sportmedicine*, 7, 57–71.

Morris, M. (1989). Running round the clock. *Running*, 104(Dec), 44–5.

Ogden, J., De Coverley Veale, D. and Summers, Z. (1997). The development and validation of the Exercise Dependence Questionnaire. *Addiction Research & Theory, 5*(4), 343–55.

Pasman, L. and Thompson, J. K. (1988). Body image and eating disturbance in obligatory runners, obligatory weightlifters, and sedentary individuals. *International Journal of Eating Disorders, 7,* 759–77.

Pierce, E. F. (1994). Exercise dependence syndrome in runners. *Sports Medicine, 18,* 149–55.

Rozin, P. and Stoess, C. (1993). Is there a general tendency to become addicted? *Addictive Behaviors, 18,* 81–7.

Rudy, E. B. and Estok, P. J. (1989). Measurement and significance of negative addiction in runners. *Western Journal of Nursing Research, 11,* 548–58.

Sachs, M. L. and Pargman, D. (1979). Running addiction: A depth interview examination. *Journal of Sport Behavior, 2*(3), 143–55.

Sachs, M. L. and Pargman, D. (1984). Running addiction. In Sachs, M. L. and Buffone, G. W. (eds) *Running as Therapy: An integrated approach,* pp. 231–52. Lincoln, NE: University of Nebraska Press.

Sachs, M. L. (1981) Running addiction. In Sacks, M. and Sachs, M. (eds) *Psychology of Running,* pp. 116–26. Champaign, IL: Human Kinetics.

Slay, H. A., Hayaki, J., Napolitano, M. A. and Brownell, K. D. (1998). Motivations for running and eating attitudes in obligatory versus nonobligatory runners. *International Journal of Eating Disorders, 23*(3), 267–75.

Smith, D. K., Hale, B. D. and Collins, D. (1998). Measurement of exercise dependence in bodybuilders. *The Journal of Sports Medicine and Physical Fitness, 38*(1), 66–74.

Smith, D., Wright, C. and Winrow, D. (2010). Exercise dependence and social physique anxiety in competitive and non-competitive runners. *International Journal of Sport and Exercise Psychology, 8*(1), 61–9.

Stoll, O. (1997). *Endorphine, Laufsucht und Runner's High. Aufstieg und Niedergang eines Mythos. Leipziger Sportwissenschaftliche Beiträge, 38,* 102–21.

Summers, J. J. and Hinton, E. R. (1986). Development of scales to measure participation in running. In Unestahl, L. E. (ed.) *Contemporary Sport Psychology,* pp. 73–84. Sweden: Veje.

Sussman, S., Lisha, N. and Griffiths, M. D. (2011). Prevalence of the addictions: A problem of the majority or the minority? *Evaluation & the Health Professions, 34*(1), 3–56.

Szabo, A. (1995). The impact of exercise deprivation on well-being of habitual exercisers. *The Australian Journal of Science and Medicine in Sport, 27,* 68–75.

Szabo, A. (2000). Physical activity as a source of psychological dysfunction. In Biddle, S. J. H., Fox, K. R. and Boutcher, S. H. (eds) *Physical Activity and Psychological Well-being,* pp. 130–53. London: Routledge.

Szabo, A. (2001). The dark side of sports and exercise: Research dilemmas. Paper presented at the 10th World Congress of Sport Psychology. Skiathos, Greece, 30 May 2001.

Szabo, A. (2010). *Exercise Addiction: A symptom or a disorder?* New York: Nova Science.

Szabo, A., Frenkl, R. and Caputo, A. (1996). Deprivation feelings, anxiety, and commitment to various forms of physical activity: A cross-sectional study on the Internet. *Psychologia, 39,* 223–30.

Szabo, A., Frenkl, R. and Caputo, A. (1997). Relationships between addiction to running, commitment to running, and deprivation from running. *European Yearbook of Sport Psychology, 1*, 130–47.

Szabo, A. and Griffiths, M. D. (2007). Exercise addiction in British sport science students. *International Journal of Mental Health and Addiction, 5*(1), 25–8.

Terry, A., Szabo, A. and Griffiths, M. D. (2004). The exercise addiction inventory: A new brief screening tool. *Addiction Research and Theory, 12*, 489–99.

Thaxton, L. (1982). Physiological and psychological effects of short-term exercise addiction on habitual runners. *Journal of Sport Psychology, 4*, 73–80.

Thompson, J. K. and Blanton, P. (1987). Energy conservation and exercise dependence: A sympathetic arousal hypothesis. *Medicine and Science in Sports and Exercise, 19*, 91–7.

Thompson, J. K. and Pasman, L. (1991). The obligatory exercise questionnaire. *Behavior Therapist, 14*, 137.

Thornton, E. W. and Scott, S. E. (1995). Motivation in the committed runner: Correlations between self-report scales and behaviour. *Health Promotion International, 10*, 177–84.

Villella, C., Martinotti, G., Di Nicola, M., Cassano, M., La Torre, G., Gliubizzi, M. D. *et al.* (2011). Behavioral addictions in adolescents and young adults: Results from a prevalence study. *Journal of Gambling Studies, 27*(2), 203–14.

Wichmann, S. and Martin, D. R. (1992). Exercise excess. *The Physician and Sportsmedicine, 20*, 193–200.

Youngman, J. D. (2007). Risk for exercise addiction: A comparison of triathletes training for sprint-, Olympic-, half-ironman-, and ironman-distance triathlons. Open Access Dissertations, Paper 12. Available online at: http://scholarlyrepository.miami.edu/cgi/viewcontent.cgi?article=1011&context=oa_dissertations (accessed 28 October 2013).

How can sport and exercise psychology professionals help people manage their inner states?

9 Applied sport psychology

Enhancing performance using psychological skills training

Richard Thelwell

CHAPTER SUMMARY

As you will see from the chapters within this book, athletes at the top of the sporting ladder have a number of challenges put before them: these take the form of opponents, environmental conditions and their own mindset, to name but a few. One excellent example of this comes from Usain Bolt, the six-time Olympic champion who, until the Diamond League meeting in Rome on 6 June 2013, had remained unbeaten at major international meetings since his false-start disqualification at the World Championships in South Korea in August 2011. Having been placed second in the Diamond League event, Bolt was quoted as saying, 'I would say that my determination is not as much as it used to be . . . you have to try to find things to motivate you and push yourself harder'. Further to his reflections on his first 'major' defeat, and given the new world acclaim that he has received since winning three gold medals at the London Olympics, Bolt commented that:

> *Starting the season was the roughest part for me – trying to drive myself . . . it has been really crazy since the Olympics. It has been hard for me to get everything together because there are more demands, it is tough.*

Of course, even the most talented of athletes, ones who can be categorized as truly elite, have varying demands placed upon them, and, although one does not know the extent to which Bolt engaged with a sport psychologist, or whether he employed psychological skills, what we do know, from varying laboratory and empirically based peer-reviewed research, is that employing psychological skills increases the chances of going into competition in a positive mindset, and, if this coincides with being physically ready, then positive performance experiences tend to follow.

With this in mind, the purpose of this chapter is to explore how sport psychologists can help athletes enhance their performance via the use of psychological skills training (PST), which, for this chapter, will primarily focus on the skills of self-talk, imagery, relaxation and goal setting. Throughout, we will explore the concept of PST with a specific focus on whether it appears to enhance performance. However, it is worth reminding oneself that psychological skills can affect psychological concepts such as emotion, coping, mood, self-efficacy and anxiety, topics covered in other chapters in this book. Psychological skills have pervasive effects, but this chapter will attempt to delimit itself to focusing on research that looked at their influence on performance. To enable this to be achieved, we will commence the chapter by reviewing literature that has supported the use of PST in sport and provide suggestions to propose why performers have been resistant to the use of such skills. We will then turn our attention to some of the models associated with PST development that link the assessment process to the integration and implementation of psychological skills.

After reviewing the models, the final section of the chapter will focus on the different research approaches that have examined the impact of PST on performance. In addition to the above, throughout this chapter, readers will be asked to reflect on their own experiences as an athlete, or a coach, or a spectator, with reference to the material presented.

LEARNING OUTCOMES

When you have studied this chapter, you should be able to:

1   Evaluate the literature that has suggested PST to be of benefit to the sports performer
2   Evaluate some of the models of PST delivery and appraise how such skills can be implemented
3   Critically evaluate the contemporary approaches to researching PST and performance

LEARNING OUTCOME 1

Evaluate the literature that has suggested PST to be of benefit to the sports performer

Before exploring the benefits of employing psychological skills, we first need to define what we mean by the term psychological skills. Weinberg and Gould (2011), a commonly used textbook in sport and exercise psychology, refer to psychological skills as a systematic and consistent practice of mental or psychological skills for the purpose of enhancing performance, increasing enjoyment or achieving greater sport and physical activity self-satisfaction. This is not a contentious definition, and so using a textbook definition is appropriate, although researchers usually cite peer-refereed journal articles as the authoritative source.

It is suggested that research into psychological skills should be guided by examination of relationships with the three outcomes cited above, and applied sport psychologists should be able to use interventions that are grounded in a scientific evidence base. In

ACTIVITY 9.1

Reflect on your sporting experiences and the psychological skills that you either do, or could, employ to benefit your performance. As you work through the skills, consider whether you do, or could, use them in training as well as competition. Also, consider how such skills have enhanced your performance when you have used them, compared with when you have not.

Skill employed	Training /competition	Impact of using the skill

I would imagine that you, like many athletes, tend to employ psychological skills in a competition environment as opposed to in a training environment. This seems strange, given that it is the training environment where the competition habits are created. Also, I suspect that, when you use the psychological skills, you have greater perceptions of success, possibly because you feel in control, more confident and more focused, compared with when you do not use such skills.

Having considered your own experiences using psychological skills, now read Frey *et al.* (2003) to see how they reported the use of psychological skills and associated perceptions of success in collegiate athletes. Read how they collected their data, how they analysed their data and what they found, and then compare this with what you do.

Should you do anything differently?

an attempt to respond to the questions directed towards whether PST interventions are effective, three meta-analyses have been conducted. A meta-analysis is a powerful way of reviewing the literature. It takes results from research articles and re-analyses them to produce a summary of the key findings. Meta-analyses tend to be conducted when lots of studies have been conducted to examine a similar question. Each of these included intervention studies that were well controlled and based on performance changes in competitive environments (so as to protect against any reductions in the ecological validity of the studies).

The first meta-analysis, conducted by Greenspan and Feltz (1989), reviewed nineteen studies that examined the impact of PST on performance in competitive environments. Even though a variety of sports were studied, the results suggested that such interventions positively influenced performance in over 80 per cent of the studies. A further meta-analysis, by Vealey (1994), reported that PST studies continued to report the positive impact on performance, with in excess of 75 per cent resulting in performance enhancement in both individual and team sports. Finally, Weinberg and Comar (1994) advanced Vealey's study by reporting ten additional intervention-based studies where, once again, positive effects on performance were reported. Taken together, prior to 1994, there was an approximate success rate of 85 per cent reported in studies that examined the impacts of PST on performance, suggesting that PST is of benefit to the performer. Unfortunately, although systematic reviews of specific skills have been presented in the literature, there is no up-to-date meta-analysis of PST intervention studies, despite there being a marked increase in the number of such studies conducted within the past 20 years. Clearly, given the fact that researchers and practitioners alike continue to investigate the effects of PST on performance, a new meta-analysis is required.

In the interim, the effectiveness of PST has been documented within the emerging research area of mental toughness, which is now widely regarded as a fundamental prerequisite for successful performance (Gucciardi *et al.*, 2008; Coulter *et al.*, 2010). The argument is that employing PST improves the mental toughness of the individual, and mentally tough athletes are likely to perform better. However, mental toughness is an area not without its issues. Although, to date, the definitions of mental toughness have been varied, researchers (e.g. Thelwell *et al.*, 2005; Jones *et al.*, 2007) have contended that it includes attributes such as an athlete's ability to recover from setbacks, persistence when faced with failure, maintaining focus despite performance (and other) distractions, and an ability to cope with excessive pressure. Further to this, recent research by Connaughton *et al.* (2010) examining the *development* and *maintenance* of mental toughness in the world's best performers has indicated the use of PST to be critical for both aspects. Therefore, with mental toughness contributing to the attainment of sporting success and PST enabling the development of mental toughness, this provides further justification for the benefits of employing such skills. Given the evidence-based argument for PST enhancing performance, it seems somewhat strange that there are many athletes who choose not to practise such skills. The following provides an insight into why this might be the case.

First, although many athletes use some form of psychological skills, it is often the case that they do not train them deliberately. For example, most people manage to self-regulate without any specific training, and others report their usage of psychological skills via the 'Test of performance strategies' (Thomas *et al.*, 1999) without having received any formal training. Despite the perceived, implicit use of psychological skills, many athletes neglect PST owing to simple misunderstanding of it. This is a concern on a number of levels, with the first being that many athletes perceive PST (and, as such, mental toughness) to be inherent rather than developed. This is an awkward assumption, given that even the most talented individuals in the sporting world spend endless hours practising their skills, even though they may have been blessed with a high level of innate talent. Another misunderstanding is that many athletes expect immediate success following the implementation of an intervention and so do not understand that, like physical skills, psychological skills require a great deal of time and practice to develop.

A further reason why athletes may neglect psychological skills has to do with time. Specifically, many athletes struggle with not being able to devote enough time to the development of physical skills, let alone psychological skills. That is, athletes report that they do not have enough time, which, of course, could be a perceptual issue – they prioritize their time for other things and thus cannot find time. However, it seems clear that, if an athlete does not prioritize PST, then it is not likely to be done, when there are so many competing demands on time. This was one of the key findings reported by Gould *et al.* (1999), who examined some of the roadblocks to the development of psychological skills from the perceptions of junior tennis coaches. This does, however, seem somewhat contradictory, given that many of the reasons provided for performance failure are attributed to psychological factors. For example, how many times have you finished a performance and then said, 'I felt too tense before the shot' or 'I just bottled it, just couldn't get it right at that crucial time . . . my confidence had gone'. As a result, one could suggest that, even though psychological skills may impact quite significantly on performance, they do not appear to be salient to athletes in terms of the time allocated; hence, they become neglected. A possible explanation for athletes' not valuing psychological skills is a failure of academic findings demonstrating their value to be transferred to practice. Or, athletes are not being sold the benefits of using PST as a means of improving performance.

There are also some myths that pervade athletes' use of PST, as outlined in the seminal paper by Gould and Eklund (1991). Included in such myths are suggestions that psychological skills are for 'athletes with problems' or only for 'elite athletes'. However, the vast majority of athletes use a sport psychologist for educational rather than clinical purposes. Despite this, it still remains that there is sometimes a negative stigma associated with consulting a sport psychologist. The main issue here is the view that, if you need to see a sport psychologist, then you are unable to cope with the climate and demands of elite sport. This exact point was reinforced via former Australian cricketer and fast bowler Glenn McGrath, who, prior to the 2006–7 Ashes series, heard that the then new English spin bowler Monty Panesar was seeing a sport psychologist. McGrath commented that it was ridiculous that Panesar was seeking such support prior to the series and that he must be 'soft'. Conversely, former England football goalkeeper David James argues that the benefits of seeing a sport psychologist outweigh any negative public perception. James contends that psychology is one of the building bricks for being a top athlete, and so it should be normal for athletes to use such expert support. In James' experience, developing athletes should work with psychologists.

With regard to PST being for elite athletes only, then, yes, it may be that support is available owing to funding (i.e. through governing bodies, bursaries, etc.), but this is not to say that young, recreational athletes or athletes with disabilities are not able to seek such support. A further myth associated with PST is that it provides 'overnight' performance solutions. Although there will always be examples where athletes have had rapid success after seeing a sport psychologist, the longevity of the success needs to be viewed with caution. It is plausible for an athlete to see a consultant and come away feeling inspired and confident. The consultant might have helped him or her see sport differently, or establish a goal that is meaningful and realistic, or the consultant might have encouraged the athlete to tune up his or her self-talk, emphasizing the use of positive descriptions. However, the pathway or route to psychological skills being effective is through regular practice and by making their use almost autonomous and done effortlessly. Therefore, the achievement of this accelerated success is not possible, owing to the time required to develop the skills in a variety of pressurized environments, prior to their being employed within competition. It is important for sport psychologists to encourage athletes, coaches and sports managers alike to establish a realistic time frame for any intervention work.

LEARNING OUTCOME 2

Evaluate some of the models of PST delivery and appraise how such skills can be implemented

Although we are aware of the potential benefits of PST and some of the reasons why athletes neglect its use, or neglect using the skills in a systematic way, preferring to use them on an ad hoc basis, and possibly not getting the most out of them, the debate about how best to deliver and integrate such skills remains. As such, this section will review some of the key models of psychological-skill delivery, while also providing an insight into how each approach might impact on sports performance.

A model developed by Sinclair and Sinclair (1994) encourages athletes to develop their psychological skills alongside physical and technical skills. The basic premise for the model stemmed from the authors' experiences with a number of athletes. They recognized that, although effective psychological skills were beneficial for enhancing performance, they were only developed when athletes started to experience performance difficulties (similar to the notion of brief contact interventions put forward by Giges and Petitpas, 2000). As a consequence, they contended that athletes are then placed in a position of 'crisis management', where a sport psychologist is brought in and expected to bring about a change in the athletes' psychological condition immediately (which we know from Learning outcome 1 is highly unlikely). In respect of this approach, it could be construed that the development of psychological skills is seen as an 'add-on', rather than inclusive, feature of performance.

In an attempt to resolve the 'add-on' issue, Sinclair and Sinclair (1994) developed their 'mental management' model, which incorporated Norman's (1988) 'action cycle', where the two key aspects of *execution* (doing something) and *evaluation* (where someone is now, and where they want to get to) were central to the process. These two aspects are then split into seven action stages: setting goals, perceiving current situation, interpreting the situation, evaluating interpretations, making intentions to act, selecting a sequence of actions and executing the action sequence. Norman contends that, as with many sporting situations, the whole process is driven by a goal. The goal then requires the individual to develop a set of internal commands that can be completed to achieve it. As such, Norman suggests that the whole process is, in essence, a mental process, given that the action sequence comes into play at the final stage.

In transferring the process to the sporting environment, where athletes are able to develop their psychological skills alongside their physical and technical skills in the training and competition environment, Sinclair and Sinclair (1994) advocate a seven-step approach. Each step will now be worked through prior to Activity Box 9.2, where you will have an opportunity to develop the seven steps for a skill of your choice.

Step 1: Goal setting

Before any action takes place, an objective that is being targeted needs to be identified. To benefit this, goal setting is required where specific, realistic, measurable goals are necessary.

Step 2: Identifying relevant cues

Focusing skills

For any skill that athletes perform, there will be a number of cues that they may focus on. Unfortunately, many of the cues may be irrelevant, and, accordingly, this step is about trying to select the appropriate cue. For example, when working on bowling in cricket, the coach may demonstrate the skill and verbalize some of the key cues that players need to focus on. Some of the cues might include 'smooth run-up', 'nice approach to the wicket', 'high bound', 'head up and looking at the batter', 'drive through with the arms' and 'follow through'. As the bowlers become more proficient at bowling, the cues will become more refined, to a point at which only a couple of 'key words' are used.

Refocusing skills

In addition to focusing skills, *refocusing skills* may also be developed. For example, if a bowler has bowled a poor delivery or has not achieved the intended goal, each delivery will require a refocus to consistently achieve the desired outcome. If task–irrelevant cues are being focused on, an appropriate prompt from the coach can make the player aware of how their attention has shifted inappropriately.

Step 3: Developing a motor plan

Having set a goal and become aware of the cues that will facilitate achievement of this goal, the player must make an appropriate performance plan. This may require the development of imagery skills, wherein the athlete can develop all sensory modalities to recreate the experience. Here, the bowler would think through the execution of a successful delivery while also using the cues established in Step 2. For a full review of imagery theory and research, see Smith and Wright (this issue).

Step 4: Executing the skill

Having set the goal, identified relevant cues and imaged him- or herself performing, this step requires the athlete to have a go at the skill. Inevitably, there will be occasions when the skill is not performed to the aspired level. For example, the ball may be a 'short delivery' rather than a 'good-length delivery', which may be attributed to tension. Here, focus may be directed towards self-awareness and how the athlete felt (both physically and emotionally) before and during the delivery.

Step 5: Evaluation and feedback

Having attempted the skill, the next step is to evaluate the degree to which success was achieved. Often, this process commences with athletes being very negative and evaluating in a dysfunctional manner. However, through appropriate guidance, the development of self-awareness and rationalization skills can be developed. Also, in this stage, athletes may become more aware of the self-talk that they engage in. We know from much of the recent self-talk literature that positive self-talk is more effective than negative self-talk (see Hardy, 2006), but being able to transfer negative into positive self-talk is a skill that requires attention and time. For example, although it is not uncommon for a bowler to berate him- or herself following a poor delivery, it is not always the case that the athlete will know the potential debilitating effect of the self-talk. Therefore, facilitating increased self-awareness of what they are saying will be of use.

Step 6: Revising the motor plan

Here, the procedures advocated in Step 3 would be encouraged.

Step 7: Execute the skill (again and again)

Here, the athlete would be encouraged to execute the procedures advocated in Step 4, followed by the remainder of the cycle, before going back to Step 3 and so on.

As indicated herein, the mental-management approach advocated by Sinclair and Sinclair (1994) enables performers to develop all aspects of performance in a formal and systematic manner. Importantly, the development of fundamental psychological skills (goal setting, focusing, arousal regulation, imagery, self-talk) are embedded within the overall skill development/learning process. Although a brief insight into the mental-management model is presented here, you are encouraged to read Sinclair and Sinclair's work for a fuller description of how psychological skills can be continually reinforced and developed throughout the learning process.

A second approach to the development and integration of PST comes from the conceptual model of Taylor (1995). Taylor posits that the development of PST interventions and subsequent delivery of the skills will depend on the integration of the demands of the sport and the athletes' needs. Specifically, all sports have varying physical, logistical and technical demands that influence the psychological needs for success in the sport. Sport psychologists should be aware of these demands and develop appropriate psychological skill interventions. Take, for example, the 10,000 m run and golf. Although both events are relatively long in duration, they have very different physical demands. They also have very different skill requirements, where golf is a sport requiring precision, whereas a 10,000 m run requires gross motor movements. Alternatively, you could consider a 100-m swimmer who requires explosive power. Evidently, each sport has contrasting demands, especially in terms

ACTIVITY 9.2

Think of a physical/technical skill that you employ that would benefit from additional psychological skills. Consider how you learned the skill and how you would have developed it if you had worked on your psychological skills at the same time. When thinking about the skill, work through the seven steps and identify the psychological skills you would attempt to develop and how they would fit into the overall development of the skill.

Step	Psychological skill	Reason for developing skill
1		
2		
3		
4		
5		
6		
7		

of its duration and physical and technical characteristics, which, according to Taylor, will influence the psychological demands placed on the athletes. For example, with the 10,000 m run being long in duration, involving gross motor movements and being aerobic in nature, the psychological priorities may be to overcome low motivation, pain and boredom-related issues. As such, the psychological skills may include key words (motivational/focus/instructional), relaxation strategies and goal setting, each of which is specific to the demands of the sport. The golfer, for example, may have psychological priorities that are driven by the need to maintain concentration and intensity levels, possibly owing to the length of a round, where the performance time is minimal and the idle periods between shots can be lengthy. Accordingly, skills such as arousal regulation and imagery and a variety of skills put together to develop pre- and post-shot routines would be of benefit.

Of course, although the above psychological priorities and advocated skills represent only a guide, it is the responsibility of the practitioner to assess the demands of the sport and the athlete's needs, prior to developing any ensuing intervention. That said, Taylor's (1995) work is appropriate in suggesting that not all individuals and sports can be addressed with the same skills, in the same manner.

In addition to the two previously discussed consulting models for PST delivery are two further approaches that are worthy of consideration. The first model is the six-phase youth sport consulting model (YSCM; Visek *et al.*, 2009), which is an educational framework for practitioners to follow when delivering sport psychology services to young athletes. The YSCM also outlines some of the key considerations for working with this population, with practitioners being made aware that, to be effective, they need to recognize the specific modifications that must be made, compared with when working with their adult counterparts. Inevitably, this means that practitioners need to be cognizant of any necessary requirements and adjustments throughout the consultation process, and that the stage of development of their client needs to be considered prior to any further engagement. Although the benefits of providing such support to the youth population are widely acknowledged, primarily owing to the opportunity

---

ACTIVITY 9.3

Consider three sports of your choice and work through Taylor's (1995) conceptual model. In doing so, consider the physical demands of each sport, the psychological priorities and the psychological skills that will be most appropriate. To enable you to complete this task you may wish to read the associated paper.

Sport	Physical demands	Psychological priorities	Psychological skills
1			
2			
3			

Having worked through the three sports, you should now be able to see that it is not advisable to approach all three sports in the same manner, especially given that we have not considered the specific needs of the athletes.

to educate them about the purposes and principles of PST and how it can complement varying life skills, there are relatively few resources to support delivery. Further to this, and in keeping with the thoughts of Sinclair and Sinclair (1994), it is accepted that individuals who receive psychological support at a 'youth' level are more likely to use such support later on in their athletic careers (Blom *et al.*, 2003), or will have longer to apply and benefit from the support they receive (Orlick and McCaffrey, 1991). Despite the many perceived similarities between working with 'youth' and 'adult' athletes (e.g. gaining entry, delivering and implementation), there are several key considerations that will influence effectiveness and, possibly, the adopted consulting philosophy. For example, one might consider whether to adopt more of a personal development philosophy, rather than a performance enhancement approach to service provision, given that, for the 'youth' population, a personal development philosophy may promote a variety of lifestyle components, such as motivation and attitude development, self-perception awareness and enhanced self-esteem and confidence management, each of which having the capability to transfer to alternative life domains.

Inherent in the YCSM is guidance as to how practitioners should develop their awareness of the key physical, cognitive, emotional and social development characteristics for this population, and how this development may affect their delivery. For example, although many team sports group performers together by age, this does not cater for the potential physical differences that may subsequently affect confidence levels, potential for injury, self-consciousness or general group integration and social acceptance. Similarly, there are likely to be stark contrasts in the cognitive and emotional capabilities of individuals within a group. In particular, the level of 'coachability' that a player has may well be influenced by their ability to process, interpret and act on information. An inability to respond may result in emotional disturbance and fluctuation, a withdrawn persona or a reduced level of relatedness to those trying to enhance development. Of course, this is also going to be very much influenced by the sporting environment in which the athletes operate, given that the climate is likely to affect their general engagement, perceptions of competence and overall levels of self-esteem.

In addition to encouraging practitioners to consider the physical, cognitive, emotional and social differences that exist across an athlete's development, the YSCM also details the varying development phases that athletes progress through. Specifically, practitioners are encouraged to consider the likely development characteristics for a performer in the mid-childhood (about 6–11 years), early-adolescence (about 10–14 years) and mid-adolescence (about 15–17 years) stages, and how they may affect their approach to working with such groupings. By adopting more of a 'staged' approach to the development process, practitioners can better consider the characteristics that their athletes are likely to possess. For example, if we consider emotional characteristics, it may be that athletes in the mid-childhood stage are starting to experience complex emotions (e.g. shame, anger), while also becoming more sensitive in nature, compared with those in the early-adolescence stage, who may be more emotional and have short, sporadic emotional outbursts, and those in the mid-adolescence stage, who have developed an ability to manage their emotions and express feelings. Each stage, therefore, presents a varying set of considerations for the practitioner, given that the

ACTIVITY 9.4

Imagine that you are working with a number of youth athletes. Consider some of the characteristics that athletes may present across the varying developmental phases.

Stage	Example characteristics			
	Physical	*Cognitive*	*Emotional*	*Social*
Mid childhood (6–11 years)	Becoming more agile	Limited attention	Becoming more sensitive	Peer pressure
Early adolescent (10–14 years)	Onset of puberty	Starting to challenge beliefs	Experiencing emotional outbursts	Needing popularity
Mid adolescent (15–17 years)	Nearing physical maturity	Generally thinking more abstractly	Ability to express feelings	May require independence

Source: Adapted from YSCM

development characteristics (i.e. emotional, physical) seldom operate in isolation, meaning that they must be acknowledged prior to any further progression through the six stages. Although, of course, not all individuals will progress in a similar fashion, and given the fact that groups of athletes will likely include individuals at varying developmental stages for each characteristic, the YSCM provides practitioners with a set of considerations and a useful framework for working with this population.

A final model that is referred to here for the consideration of interested readers is that of the holistic sport psychology model (Friesen and Orlick, 2010). Although many of the PST delivery models have been focused primarily on performance enhancement, there are many practitioners who, through reflection, have recognized that performance improvements are often facilitated by the growth and improvement of an athlete as a human being. In response, a number of consultants have now reviewed their intervention delivery to include strategies for improving the athlete's quality of life, as well as their athletic performance. Although the actual practice of 'holistic sport psychology' remains a little unclear, there is now a consensus position that suggests that a holistic service delivery attempts to manage the psychological effects from non-sport domains on the athlete's performance, develops an individual's core beyond their athletic personality, and recognizes the interaction between an athlete's thoughts, feelings, physiology and behaviour. A detailed review of the research findings associated with the holistic sport psychology model is beyond the scope of this chapter, but it is worth noting that, to be an effective 'holistic sport psychologist', practitioners are encouraged to be personable and to have a good working alliance with the client. Therefore, to be a successful holistic practitioner, a firm grounding in a counselling model of practice may be advisable.

FOCUS 9.1

There are differing approaches to how PST can be delivered and implemented. Despite the contrasts in the models discussed, the key messages can be summarized as follows:

1 Psychological skills are best developed alongside physical and technical skills.
2 Psychological skills need to be evaluated and developed over time.
3 Sports have varying physical and technical demands; therefore, we need to be aware of the differing psychological demands.
4 Practitioners need to be aware of the athlete's needs when developing PST.

LEARNING OUTCOME 3

Critically evaluate the contemporary approaches to researching PST and performance

We will now explore how researchers are examining the PST–performance relationship. Understanding such approaches and the subsequent findings is vital for the applied practitioner, given that our work is based on sound theoretical and research evidence.

What we do know is that, in recent years, the applied sport psychology literature has seen an increase in the number of experimental studies examining the impacts that PST can have on performance. We also know that, although there are many skills and strategies that have been employed, the four most commonly researched are self-talk, imagery, relaxation and goal setting. Among the studies examining the four skills, there have been debates regarding whether psychological skills should be examined singularly or within a package, and developments in the experimental designs employed.

Taking the first point, although Tod *et al.* (2011), in their recent systematic review, have commented that negative self-talk does not always impede performance and that there is inconsistent evidence for the differential effects of motivational and instructional self-talk based on varying task characteristics, several researchers have advocated that, to fully understand the impact of psychological skills on performance, they should be examined individually. Similarly, studies focusing on the effectiveness and frequency of imagery (e.g. Wakefield and Smith, 2011; Post *et al.*, 2012) have reported its varying forms (instructional, motivational, facilitative, debilitative) and how they influence sporting performance. Studies examining goal setting have been less common, with examples here including the now-dated work by Swain and Jones (1995), who examined the impact of a goal-setting intervention on specific basketball components, and the more recent O'Brien *et al.* (2009) study that examined goal-setting effects in boxing. Although the single-skill studies examining self-talk, imagery and goal setting have become commoner in recent years, studies examining the effectiveness of relaxation strategies on performance are less frequent.

The above represent some studies that have adopted a single-skill approach. Together, they have undoubtedly provided practitioners with a wealth of knowledge regarding the merits of developing a single skill over time to enhance performance. However, there are also a number of potential pitfalls in the adoption of such approaches. For example, it is common to find that several skills benefit each other. This has been reported on numerous occasions, where important, yet dated, work by Rushall (1984), Zeigler (1987) and Rushall et al. (1988) concluded that self-talk, when combined with imagery, enhanced performance in rowing, tennis and cross-country skiing. Ostensibly, self-talk allowed performers to focus on relevant and correct cues during the imagery session. Other researchers (e.g. Kirschenbaum and Bale, 1984; Hamilton and Fremouw, 1985) have acknowledged the success of relaxation and self-talk when combined with other mental skills, such as imagery, modelling, attentional focus, game plans and feedback mechanisms. In addition, more recent studies have demonstrated the combination of skills to have positive performance effects (e.g. Rogerson and Hrycaiko, 2002; Cumming et al., 2006).

A further potential shortfall of single-skill interventions is that many sports require multiple skills, and this was clearly articulated earlier in the discussion of both Sinclair and Sinclair's (1994) and Taylor's (1995) models of psychological skill delivery and implementation, and, in response, much of the PST research now tends to adopt a 'package' approach (e.g. Barwood et al., 2007; Thelwell et al., 2010), which brings with it a different set of concerns. The most notable are the uncertainty surrounding the order in which skills should be developed and how they interact with each other to provide an 'additive' effect towards performance improvement. It is clear that the 'jury is still out' with regard to this matter, and, although this remains a challenge for future research, one thing that practitioners can argue with some confidence is that individual differences here will often determine the effectiveness of certain skills.

The second development within application-based research revolves around experimental designs. Although a historical account is not provided here, it is important to note that researchers several years ago foresaw possible changes and, as such, were prepared to accept alternative methods when assessing real-world research. For example, when writing about the development of sport psychology, Alderman (1984) stated that, 'In the field of sport psychology over the next 20 years, research will become more applied, clinical, and technique-oriented' (p. 53). This statement has now become reality, with several researchers tending to prefer the use of single-subject designs as opposed to the more traditional group designs. There are benefits of using single-subject designs, as they enable identification of influential factors at the individual level and, thereby, are helpful for practitioners and athletes alike when they are considering whether to use the intervention tested. This is even more the case given that, within group designs, the exact effects of interventions may be masked and the statistics may suggest no differences, when in fact, for some individuals, the intervention may have been very effective. On this point, it is also important to note that, at an elite level, performance changes may be very subtle and, as such, not shown within a group design. Also, even though the performance changes may be relatively small, at the higher level of performance, the small changes are mostly significant. Finally, the role of applied sport psychologists is to provide an intervention based on the person and sport in question, rather than a group of people. To facilitate this, research designs have progressed to enable practitioners to link research to practice, which itself was commented on more than 25 years ago by Frank (1986), who stated, 'nomothetic science can never escape the individual . . . its findings must [eventually] be applied to the individual' (p. 24).

BEYOND THE FRONTIER

Much of the research examining PST and subsequent effects on performance has been athlete focused, but future work may wish to consider others who have an important role within the sporting domain. For example, there has been recent interest regarding the psychological states of coaches and parents, but, to date, this has largely been limited to descriptive accounts as opposed to being more intervention driven. The literature clearly indicates that these 'significant others' have a profound effect on the athlete (in areas ranging from performance to broader esteem, engagement, adherence and well-being issues), and, although there is now a burgeoning interest in enhancing athlete performance, perhaps a greater focus on enhancing, for example, 'coach' and 'sport-parent' performance, via PST and associated strategies, is worthy of consideration.

In short, the benefits of the single-subject design are that a participant's behaviour is observed prior to any experimental condition, which means that each participant has their own 'control' and 'treatment' condition. There are a number of single-subject design approaches, and, although only the multiple-baseline-across-participants approach will be mentioned here, interested readers are directed towards a special edition of the *Journal of Applied Sport Psychology* (volume 25, 2013) for a detailed review of the approach. An important aspect of this discussion is the fact that applied researchers have sought to use rigorous methods.

A further development in the recent research is related to the fact that the majority of applied studies have focused on the measurement of performance outcomes alone and have neglected performance subcomponents. Although it is acknowledged that this is not always appropriate, there are a number of sports where a more detailed insight into performance subcomponents may give a better understanding of overall performance achievement. One such study was conducted by Thelwell *et al.* (2006), who examined the impact of a soccer, midfielder-specific psychological skills intervention on position-specific performance measures (first touch percentage, pass completion percentage and tackle success percentage). In this particular study, a total of five participants had their performances monitored across nine competitive matches where each, in turn, received the intervention. The results indicated that the intervention, designed with specific positional roles in mind, enabled at least small improvements on the three performance measures for each participant. In discussing the findings, the authors reinforced the potential benefits of using, not just sport-, but position-specific, interventions that examine position-specific measures.

CONCLUSIONS

We have seen that there is a wealth of literature suggesting that psychological skills can be beneficial to athletic performance. Evidence is drawn from studies using successful professional and Olympic athletes, combined with experimental research examining either single-skill or package interventions. It is also evident that there is no exact way in which psychological skills should be delivered, and, although there are more 'desirable' approaches, practitioners are encouraged to employ the most appropriate method, depending on their delivery philosophy, the situation in which they are operating, the clients with whom they are working, and the available underpinning research evidence. We have outlined the proposed benefits of psychological skills, the models for their development and the contemporary research that has demonstrated the efficacy of such skills. The tasks that have been set were designed to reinforce each of the three learning outcomes, while also enabling a more detailed understanding of the psychological skills–performance relationship. It is hoped that this will facilitate an enhanced understanding of applied sport psychology, with specific reference to psychological skills and, in particular, to their effectiveness, their delivery and how they are researched.

RESEARCH METHODS 9.1

A researcher wanting to assess anxiety is faced with a difficult choice. The CSAI-2 has been the most commonly used scale, and the addition of frequency and direction scales has allowed knowledge to be generated about the frequency and perceived helpfulness of these feelings. A limitation of the cognitive anxiety scale is based on the use of 'concern' as the term to describe situations where athletes report anxiety. In addition, given that anxiety research tends to involve assessing anxiety shortly before competition, brevity is important.

With reference to arguments made in relation to measures of anxiety, what scale would you use, and why? The following task has been designed to help you make a choice. There is no one right answer to this task. You will find that researchers continue to use the CSAI-2, despite others pointing out some limitations. Researchers argue that there are strengths and limitations of each approach. And so, with that thought in mind, consider some of the questions you might consider when selecting a scale to use.

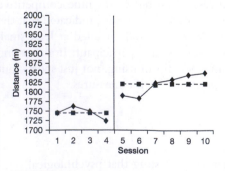

FIGURE 9.1

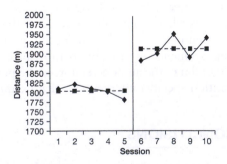

FIGURE 9.2

The single-subject, multiple-baseline-across-individuals research design has been used increasingly within applied research in recent years. The basic premise of the design is that each participant has their baseline (control) data collected concurrently, before receiving the intervention (treatment) in a staggered fashion. This normally takes place when a stable baseline of the dependent variable is achieved, or when performance moves in a direction opposite to that expected following the intervention.

In Figure 9.1, we can see data for two participants who had their 5-minute running performance assessed over a ten-session-per-week period (the blocked line reports actual performance, and the dotted line is the average performance). The first participant had their baseline period for Sessions 1–4, when they then received the intervention. The post-intervention period for Participant 1 was from Sessions 5 to 10, where it can be seen that the intervention enabled an improvement in performance (denoted by actual and average performance). The second participant received the intervention after five baseline sessions, and again the post-intervention performance effects were positive.

To understand the findings fully, we need to be aware of how single-subject data are analysed. Martin and Pear (2003) have suggested that visual inspection of data should look for the following: the number of overlapping data points between pre- and post-intervention phases (the fewer the number, the greater the intervention effect); the immediacy of the effect; the size of the effect after intervention; the number of times the findings are replicated across participants (the greater the number, the greater chance that the intervention will work irrespective of when it is delivered, thus giving some external validity); and the consistency around the mean. Although the first four approaches to visual inspection of data are critical, the final approach is important for the practitioner in a different way. For example, it may be that, although there is no discernable improvement in average performance, the actual performance may become more consistent and closer to the mean scores. Ideally, we would like to see improvements in actual performance, average performance and consistency of performance, post-intervention. However, for some performers, achieving greater consistency is often a difficult hurdle, and practitioners should be encouraged to monitor this.

KEY CONCEPTS AND TERMS

Definition of psychological skills training

Weinberg and Gould (2011, p. 250) defined psychological skills as, 'systematic and consistent practice of mental or psychological skills for the purpose of enhancing performance, increasing enjoyment, or achieving greater sport and physical activity self-satisfaction'.

Sinclair and Sinclair's (1994) mental management
Mental management is where the psychological components of performance are developed alongside the physical, technical and tactical components, rather than being viewed as an 'add-on' that occurs when athletes experience performance difficulties.

Taylor's (1995) conceptual model
Taylor advocated that every sport has a specific set of physical, technical, logistical and psychological demands. As such, the psychological priorities will vary across sports, meaning that the psychological skills necessary to enhance performance will also vary.

Visek et al.'s (2009) youth sport consulting model
The YSCM has been proposed as an educational framework for guiding and supporting practitioners who are providing sport psychology services to young athletes. The YSCM outlines a number of key considerations regarding athletic development across physical, cognitive, emotional and social characteristics.

Friesen and Orlick's (2010) holistic sport psychology model
The holistic sport psychology model provides a framework for practitioners to expand their intervention services, from focusing solely on athletic performance to enhancing the quality of life for the athlete. The model outlines the key characteristics for intervention effectiveness, while outlining athlete–consultant considerations.

Single-subject designs
These are studies that track a performer's performance both pre- and post-intervention. They are designed to detect small changes in performance that may otherwise be 'masked' in group designs. The majority of such studies in sport are multiple-baseline designs, where a small number of participants will be in the study but have the intervention delivered at staggered time points.

RECOMMENDED FURTHER READING

Barker, J. B., Mellalieu, S. D., McCarthy, P. J., Jones, M. V. and Moran, A. (2013). A review of single-case research in sport psychology 1997–2012: Research trends and future directions. *Journal of Applied Sport Psychology*, *25*, 4–32.

Connaughton, D., Hanton, S. and Jones, G. (2010). The development and maintenance of mental toughness in the world's best performers. *The Sport Psychologist*, *24*, 168–93.

Friesen, A. and Orlick, T. (2010). A qualitative analysis of holistic sport psychology consultants' professional philosophies. *The Sport Psychologist*, *24*, 227–44.

Sinclair, G. D. and Sinclair, D. A. (1994). Developing reflective performers by integrating mental management skills with the learning process. *The Sport Psychologist*, *8*, 13–27.

Taylor, J. (1995). A conceptual model for integrating athletes' needs and sport demands in the development of competitive mental preparation strategies. *The Sport Psychologist*, *9*, 339–57.

Thelwell, R. C., Greenlees, I. A. and Weston, N. (2006). Using psychological skills training to develop soccer performance. *Journal of Applied Sport Psychology*, *18*, 254–70.

Visek, A. J., Harris, B. S. and Blom, L. C. (2009). Doing sport psychology: A youth sport consulting model for practitioners. *The Sport Psychologist*, *23*, 271–91.

SAMPLE ESSAY QUESTIONS

1 Critically examine the role that psychological skills have in the development and maintenance of mental toughness.

2 With reference to appropriate examples, critically appraise the effectiveness of two models of psychological skills delivery and implementation.

3 Using relevant literature, discuss the respective merits of single-skill and multiple-skill intervention strategies.

4 Evaluate the development of experimental designs for the study of psychological skills training. Use relevant literature to support your answer.

REFERENCES

Alderman, R. B. (1984). The future of sport psychology. In Silva, J. M. and Weinberg, R. S. (eds) *Psychological Foundations for Sport*, pp. 45–54. Champaign, IL: Human Kinetics.

Barwood, M. J., Datta, A., Thelwell, R. and Tipton, M. J. (2007). Breath-hold performance during cold-water immersion: Effects of habituation with psychological skills training. *Aviation, Space and Environmental Medicine*, *78*, 1029–34.

Blom, L., Hardy, C., Burke, K. and Joyner, A. (2003). High school athletes' perceptions about sport psychology and preferences for service. *International Sports Journal*, *7*, 18–24.

Connaughton, D., Hanton, S. and Jones, G. (2010). The development and maintenance of mental toughness in the world's best performers. *The Sport Psychologist*, *24*, 168–93.

Coulter, T. J., Mallett, C. J. and Gucciardi, D. F. (2010). Understanding mental toughness in Australian soccer: Perceptions of players, parents, and coaches. *Journal of Sports Sciences*, *28*, 699–716.

Cumming, J., Nordin, S., Horton, R. and Reynolds, S. (2006). Examining the direction of imagery and self-talk on dart-throwing performance and self-efficacy. *The Sport Psychologist*, *20*, 257–74.

Frank, I. (1986). Psychology as a science: Resolving the idiographic–nomothetic controversy. In Valsiner, J. (ed.) *The Individual Subject and Scientific Psychology*, pp. 17–36. New York: Plenum Press.

Frey, M., Laguna, P. L. and Ravizza, K. (2003). Collegiate athletes' mental skill use and perceptions of success: An exploration of the practice and competition settings. *Journal of Applied Sport Psychology*, *15*, 115–28.

Friesen, A. and Orlick, T. (2010). A qualitative analysis of holistic sport psychology consultants' professional philosophies. *The Sport Psychologist*, *24*, 227–44.

Giges, B. and Petitpas, A. (2000). Brief contact interventions in sport psychology. *The Sport Psychologist*, *14*, 176–87.

Gould, D. and Eklund, R. (1991). The application of sport psychology for performance optimizations. *Journal of Sports Sciences*, *1*, 10–21.

Gould, D., Medbury, R., Damarjian, N. and Lauer, L. (1999). An examination of mental skills training in junior tennis coaches. *The Sport Psychologist*, *13*, 371–95.

Greenspan, M. J. and Feltz, D. L. (1989). Psychological interventions with athletes in competitive situations: A review. *The Sport Psychologist*, *3*, 219–36.

Gucciardi, D. F., Gordon, D. F. and Dimmock, J. A. (2008). Towards an understanding of mental toughness in Australian Football. *Journal of Applied Sport Psychology*, *20*, 261–81.

Hamilton, S. A. and Fremouw, W. J. (1985). Cognitive-behavioral training for college basketball free-throw performance. *Cognitive Therapy and Research*, *9*, 479–83.

Hardy, J. (2006). Speaking clearly: A critical review of the self-talk literature. *Psychology of Sport and Exercise*, *7*, 81–97.

Jones, G., Hanton, S. and Connaughton, D. (2007). A framework of mental toughness in the world's best performers. *The Sport Psychologist*, *21*, 243–64.

Kirschenbaum, D. S. and Bale, R. M. (1984). Cognitive behavioral skills in sports: Applications to golf and speculations about soccer. In Straub, W. F. and Williams, J. M. (eds) *Cognitive Sport Psychology*, pp. 275–8. Lansing, NY: Sport Science.

Martin, G. and Pear, J. (2003). *Behavior Modification: What it is and how to do it* (7th edn). Englewood Cliffs, NJ: Prentice-Hall.

Norman, D. A. (1988). *The Psychology of Everyday Things*. New York: Basic.

O'Brien, M., Mellalieu, S. D. and Hanton, S. (2009). Goal setting effects in elite and non-elite boxers. *Journal of Applied Sport Psychology*, *21*, 293–306.

Orlick, T. and McCaffrey, N. (1991). Mental training with children for sport and life. *The Sport Psychologist*, *5*, 322–34.

Post, P., Muncie, S. and Simpson, D. (2012). The effects of imagery training on swimming performance: An applied investigation. *Journal of Applied Sport Psychology*, *24*, 323–37.

Rogerson, L. J. and Hrycaiko, D. W. (2002). Enhancing competitive performance of ice-hockey goaltenders using centering and self-talk. *Journal of Applied Sport Psychology*, *14*, 14–26.

Rushall, B. S. (1984). The content of competition thinking. In Straub, W. F. and Williams, J. M. (eds) *Cognitive Sport Psychology*, pp. 51–62. Lansing, NY: Sport Science.

Rushall, B. S., Hall, M., Roux, L., Sasseville, J. and Rushall, A. C. (1988). Effects of three types of thought content instructions on skiing performance. *The Sport Psychologist*, *2*, 283–97.

Sinclair, G. D. and Sinclair, D. A. (1994). Developing reflective performers by integrating mental management skills with the learning process. *The Sport Psychologist*, *8*, 13–27.

Swain, A. and Jones, G. (1995). Effects of goal-setting interventions on selected basketball skills: A single-subject design. *Research Quarterly for Exercise and Sport, 66*, 51–63.

Taylor, J. (1995). A conceptual model for integrating athletes' needs and sport demands in the development of competitive mental preparation strategies. *The Sport Psychologist, 9*, 339–57.

Thelwell, R. C., Greenlees, I. A. and Weston, N. (2006). Using psychological skills training to develop soccer performance. *Journal of Applied Sport Psychology, 18*, 254–70.

Thelwell, R. C., Weston, N. J. V. and Greenlees, I. A. (2005). Defining and understanding mental toughness within soccer. *Journal of Applied Sport Psychology, 17*, 326–32.

Thelwell, R. C., Weston, N. J. V. and Greenlees, I. A. (2010). Examining the use of psychological skills throughout soccer performance. *Journal of Sport Behaviour, 33*, 109–27.

Thomas, P. R., Murphy, S. M. and Hardy, L. (1999). Test of performance strategies: Development and preliminary validation of a comprehensive measure of athletes' psychological skills. *Journal of Sports Sciences, 17*, 697–711.

Tod, D., Hardy, J. and Oliver, E. (2011). Effects of self-talk: A systematic review. *Journal of Sport and Exercise Psychology, 33*, 666–87.

Vealey, R. (1994). Current status and prominent issues in sport psychology interventions. *Medicine and Science in Sport and Exercise, 26*, 495–502.

Visek, A. J., Harris, B. S. and Blom, L. C. (2009). Doing sport psychology: A youth sport consulting model for practitioners. *The Sport Psychologist, 23*, 271–91.

Wakefield, C. and Smith, D. (2011). From strength to strength: A single-case design of PETTLEP imagery frequency. *The Sport Psychologist, 25*, 305–20.

Weinberg, R. S. and Comar, W. (1994). The effectiveness of psychological interventions in competitive sports. *Sports Medicine Journal, 18*, 406–18.

Weinberg, R. S. and Gould, D. (2011). *Foundations of Sport and Exercise Psychology*. Champaign, IL: Human Kinetics.

Zeigler, S. G. (1987). Effects of stimulus cueing on the acquisition of ground strikes by beginning tennis players. *Journal of Applied Behavioral Analysis, 20*, 405–11.

10 Imagery in sport

Dave Smith and Caroline Wakefield

CHAPTER SUMMARY

Imagery is one of the most frequently investigated techniques and commonly used in sport psychology. This chapter tries to explain what imagery is, and how athletes use it to try to enhance performance. We explain why imagery is such a potent tool for enhancing sports performance and provide guidelines based on research from sport psychology and neuroscience aimed at making imagery the most effective it can be.

LEARNING OUTCOMES

When you have studied this chapter, you should be able to:

- Define imagery and explain how athletes commonly use it
- Identify the different imagery types and understand how these may be used in different situations with a view to improving sports performance
- Explain the key mechanisms and processes that increase the effectiveness of imagery and how these impact on the imagery experience
- Name and describe elements of the PETTLEP (physical, environment, task, timing, learning, emotion and perspective) model and explain how these could be integrated into an imagery intervention

WHAT IS IMAGERY?

Imagery can be defined as, 'using all the senses to recreate or create an experience in the mind' (Vealey and Walter, 1993, p. 201). Imagery is not a modern concept, and the idea that people perform tasks through images created mentally can be traced back thousands of years. One of the first reported references to imagery was by Virgil, in 20 BC. He wrote in a poem, '*possunt quia posse videntur*', which translates as 'they can because they see themselves as being able'. The idea of imagining that something happens is something we expect children to do, and, as a result, imagery as an idea is something many people appear to latch on to naturally. Therefore, it should not be surprising that, more recently, many studies have focused on imagery, the ways in which it can improve performance, the target population that would benefit most, and different types of imagery that can be used. Indeed, almost all the popular sport psychology textbooks and self-help books include material on imagery, and many recent reviews in academic journals have focused on this topic (for example, Weinberg, 2008; McCarthy *et al.*, 2012; Smith and Wakefield, 2013; Wakefield *et al.*, 2013).

In terms of the historical development of imagery research, a study by Vandell *et al.* in 1943, on free-throw shooting and dart throwing, found that mental practice was beneficial in improving performance; importantly, they found that it was almost as effective as physical practice. Many other studies have shown that mental practice – which is typically the term used to describe what was done, but, using contemporary definitions, we are suggesting that it could be described as imagery – produces better performance than people in a control group or a no-practice group, but worse performance than physical practice (Mendoza and Wichman, 1978; MacBride and Rothstein, 1979). However, many studies that included combination groups found that combinations of physical and mental practice can be as effective as physical practice alone (see Oxendine, 1969).

In order to try to clarify the effect of imagery on performance, several authors have completed meta-analyses on the topic. Richardson (1967a, 1967b) reported on twenty-five mental-practice studies and concluded that this technique was effective in improving motor performance. In 1983, a meta-analysis of sixty studies, carried out by Feltz and Landers, found an average effect size of 0.48 (indicating a large effect on performance), and another meta-analysis (Hinshaw, 1991) revealed an average effect size of 0.68. A further meta-analysis within this area compared thirty-five studies and used strict selection criteria (Driskell *et al.*, 1994). Driskell *et al.* concluded that their analysis points to a view that mental practice is an effective way to enhance performance, and they found that the effects of mental practice were stronger when cognitive elements were contained within the task.

It appears, therefore, that a wealth of research evidence shows that using imagery is an effective strategy for improving sports performance. The mechanisms behind imagery and how this effect on performance can be improved were unclear at the time. However, we are now beginning to understand these issues, and these will be explored later in the chapter.

HOW DO ATHLETES USE IMAGERY?

Imagery training is commonly used among elite and aspiring athletes to try to improve performance: at least, that is the reason provided by athletes. This is owing to the number of benefits that can be gained from its use. Imagery training can increase self-awareness, facilitate skill acquisition and maintenance, build self-confidence, help regulate emotions, relieve pain, regulate arousal and enhance preparation strategies (Moran, 2012).

Currently, imagery is used with the specific aim of improving athletic performance. It is arguably the most widely practised psychological skill used in sport (Gould *et al.*, 1989; Jowdy *et al.*, 1989; Moran, 2012). For example, Jowdy *et al.* (1989) found that imagery techniques were used regularly by 100 per cent of consultants, 90 per cent of athletes and 94 per cent of coaches sampled. Athletes, especially elite athletes,

APPLYING THE SCIENCE 10.1

Imagery ability is used as a basic assumption for many scientific studies. Typically, participants are tested for their imagery ability, and those with low imagery ability are either placed in control groups or are distributed evenly among the intervention groups. In other studies, imagery ability is used as a mediator for performance effects from imagery. However, imagery ability is a self-report measure, with participants reporting how easy or difficult they find it to see or feel an action, in the absence of overt movement. Results can assist with research studies, but can also form the basis of advice, when one is working as an applied practitioner, with regard to whether imagery should be more visual or kinaesthetic in nature. Try completing the Movement Imagery Questionnaire – Revised (Hall and Martin, 1997) and see whether your results match your predicted ability/preferred style.

ACTIVITY 10.1

Consider your preferred imagery style and imagery ability. The Movement Imagery Questionnaire – Revised (Hall and Martin, 1997) is a measure of imagery ability. This involves conducting a number of short physical tasks and rating how easy or difficult these are to see or feel. For example, one action is standing on one leg while lifting the other knee up in front of you to form a 90° angle with the hip. You then resume a standing position, before rating, on a scale of 1–7, how easy or difficult this was to recreate in your mind. Although you need to complete the full questionnaire to get an accurate reading, this may give you an idea of whether you prefer visual or kinaesthetic imagery and of your imagery ability. Please note that 7 = very easy to see or feel, and 1 = very difficult to see or feel.

use imagery extensively and believe that it benefits performance (Hall *et al.*, 1997). Imagery is traditionally practised by athletes in the training phases of sports performance to aid with competition. However, it can also be used during the competition phase.

IMAGERY TYPES

As noted above, imagery can be used to obtain various outcomes. Hall *et al.* (1997), in developing a questionnaire to measure imagery use – the Sport Imagery Question-naire – noted that there are at least five basic types of imagery that athletes can perform. These are as follows:

- cognitive specific (CS): imagery of specific sport skills (e.g. taking a basketball free throw);
- cognitive general (CG): imagery of strategies and routines (e.g. a golfer's pre-putt routine, a football team's defensive strategy);
- motivational specific (MS): imagery of specific goals and goal-oriented behaviour (e.g. a weightlifter lifting a record weight, holding up the winner's trophy);
- motivational general arousal (MGA): imagery of emotions associated with performance (e.g. excitement felt when competing in front of a large crowd);
- motivational general mastery (MGM): imagery of mastering sport situations (e.g. a footballer keeping focused while being barracked by opposition fans).

Research has shown that all five types of imagery are used by athletes, but motivational imagery is used more than cognitive imagery (Nordin and Cumming, 2005). However, Hall *et al.* (1998) did not claim that their five imagery types represented all the imagery used by athletes, and, indeed, researchers have uncovered other types of imagery used in sport that do not fall easily into one of the above categories. For example, Nordin and Cumming (2005) found that competitive dancers often use imagery of body posture. Also, dancers reported imaging characters and roles related to their dance pieces. Metaphorical imagery, where athletes image movements, sensations or pictorial images that are not necessarily possible, is also commonly used by aesthetic sport athletes such as dancers and bodybuilders. According to a study by Dreidiger *et al.* (2006), injured athletes use physiological images of their injuries healing.

Therefore, depending on the particular aim of the athlete, it appears that various types of imagery can be used. Not surprisingly, CS imagery can enhance performance of the specific skill being imaged, as per the studies mentioned in the 'What is imagery?' section. However, as mentioned previously, there can be other benefits too. For example, studies have shown that CS imagery can lead to greater motivation to prac-tise and increase confidence. CG, MS and MGM imagery can also be effective in enhancing confidence, and MGA imagery can be very useful in psyching up or calming down athletes, getting their arousal to an optimal level so that they can perform their best. For a review of the effects of the different imagery types, see Murphy *et al.* (2008). Athletes should consider using a combination of imagery types, depending upon their specific preferences and goals. However, if improved skill is the aim, CS imagery is usually the most appropriate type to focus on primarily.

> Whatever type of imagery is being used, it appears that athletes with a greater imagery ability (i.e. who find it easier to image clearly) will benefit most from imagery use. However, using structured and theoretically based imagery techniques (such as those described in the section on PETTLEP imagery below) will help athletes achieve vivid imagery.

HOW IMAGERY WORKS

The positive effect that imagery has on performance has been investigated in the neuroscience literature (see, for example, Jeannerod, 1994, 1997). Through using a number of different research methods, discussed below, researchers have concluded that a 'functional equivalence' exists between imagery and actual performance. That is, some of the same neural processes that occur during physical performance of an action or skill occur in the brain during motor imagery (Jeannerod, 1994).

> Neuroscience is a field in which concepts of neuroscience and cognitive psychology are combined (Decety, 1996).

Different areas of the brain appear to contribute towards movement (Kolb and Whishaw, 2008). Therefore, if a 'functional equivalence' exists, some of the same neural areas working during imagery would be expected to be activated during actual performance. Scientists have developed a number of methods to discover whether this is the case, including measuring cerebral activity, mental chronometry, electroencephalography and using the autonomic system.

One method of testing is to measure cerebral activity. When areas of the brain are being specifically used, the blood flow to these areas will increase. This can then be mapped during imagery and actual performance to assess whether the same areas are being activated. A study that examined this, using a technique known as functional magnetic resonance imaging (fMRI), was performed by Kuhtz-Buschbeck et al. (2003). These researchers asked participants to imagine performing finger movements and found that some of the same motor-related brain areas were active during both real and imaged movements, notably the left dorsal and ventral premotor areas and the supplementary motor area. This and other studies have also used a technique known as transcranial magnetic stimulation (TMS), in which a magnetic field is used to cause activity in parts of the brain. In the TMS part of their study, the excitation of task-relevant muscles increased during imagery of complex, but not simple, finger movements. Li (2007), also using TMS, found that the excitability of the nervous system increased during imagery, with responses to TMS being greater in four fingers during imagery of finger movement than when at rest.

Mental chronometry can also be used to measure imagery. This technique is based on the comparison of time taken to complete an activity and the time taken to imagine it. Many studies have found a strong relationship between these two variables; however, possibly the most notable is the classic, much-cited study by Decety and Michel (1989). They compared the times needed to complete actual and imagined movements on two tasks: drawing a cube and writing a sentence. Participants were required to do both of these tasks twice, once using their dominant hand and once using their non-dominant hand. Results showed that participants were slower when completing the tasks with their non-dominant hand, but that this was also reflected in the length of time needed to imagine the tasks. Interestingly, Malouin et al. (2008) found that, in 'non-stroke' participants, the timing of imagery was quite consistent, but that it was much more variable in individuals affected by stroke, suggesting that the damage suffered by the motor system was reflected in their imagery too.

Within the sports setting, Moran and MacIntyre (1998) completed a study focusing on the kinaesthetic imagery experiences of elite canoe-slalom athletes. As part of this study, the athletes were required to image themselves completing a recent race. The time taken to image the race was then compared with the actual race completion time. The resultant positive correlation between the two times indicates support for this approach. This study indicates that a central mechanism is responsible for the timing of motor imagery.

Another method used to establish the relationship between imagery and actual performance focuses on the autonomic system. If actual movement and imagery use the same neural mechanisms, this should also be apparent within the body's responses. Involuntary responses, such as heart rate and respiration, have been found to increase without delay during the onset of actual or imagined exercise (Decety et al., 1991, 1993; Wuyam et al., 1995).

Finally, EEG has been used to examine the similarities in the electrical activity of the cerebral cortex during imagery and actual movement and has tended to find very similar movement-related neural activity in the brain, prior to and during actual and imagined movements (Naito and Matsumura, 1994; Smith and Collins, 2004).

> EEG involves measuring the level and location of electrical currents within the brain by placing electrodes on the skull and measuring the trace of the current.

The studies cited above have found support for the idea that a functional equivalence exists between imagery and overt movement. There is evidence that imagery shares a common mechanism (mental chronometry), utilizes some similar areas of the brain (EEG and fMRI) and produces similar physiological responses (autonomic system). However, to date, this research has not been considered fully within the sports setting. This is unfortunate, because an understanding of the neural mechanisms through which imagery enhances performance may be of value to those designing and carrying out imagery interventions. Without an understanding of how imagery works, such interventions are based on guesswork rather than a solid theoretical foundation.

HOW SHOULD IMAGERY BE PERFORMED?

Many sport psychology publications promote imagery as an important psychological intervention and give advice on how it should be implemented to provide the most effective results. However, such advice is often provided with little in the way of theoretical justification or empirical support. One reason for this may be because the field is relatively narrow, and sport psychology has not made effective use of theories from other fields (Murphy, 1990). In an attempt to rectify this, Holmes and Collins (2001) developed a model (for an update and review of this, see Wakefield *et al.*, 2013) based on the cognitive neuroscience research findings noted above, aiming to produce effective mental simulation: the PETTLEP model. PETTLEP is an acronym, with each letter standing for an important practical issue to consider when implementing imagery interventions. These are: physical, environment, task, timing, learning, emotion and perspective. It is thought that, if the behavioural matching between imagery and physical practice is increased, maximized functional equivalence will also be achieved.

PETTLEP aims to closely replicate the sporting situation through imagery, including physical sensations associated with performance and the emotional impact that the performance has on the athlete. The PETTLEP model comprises seven key elements, and each one of these needs to be considered and implemented as fully as possible for the imagery to be most effective.

The physical component of the model is related to the athlete's physical responses in the sporting situation. Research (e.g. Cabral and Crisfield, 1996) has claimed that athletes are able to imagine a skill or movement vividly if they are in a completely relaxed and undisturbed state. However, most studies have not found any significant benefits from combining imagery and relaxation, and it seems unlikely that this approach would be beneficial. Holmes and Collins (2002) point out that the physical effect of relaxation is in complete contrast to the physical state of the athlete during performance.

Smith and Collins (2004) found that imagery is more effective when it includes all of the senses and kinaesthetic sensations experienced when the task is performed. The inclusion of these sensations will lead to the imagery being more individualized and may increase the behavioural matching between imagery and actual movement. Holmes and Collins (2002) describe various practical ideas that can be used to enhance the physical dimension of an athlete's imagery. These include using the correct stance, holding any implements that would usually be held and wearing the correct clothing.

The environment component of the model refers to the environment in which imagery is performed. In order to achieve the behavioural matching advocated by the model, the environment when imagining the performance should be as similar as possible to the actual performing environment. In one of our studies (Smith *et al.*, 2007), hockey players were required to complete their imagery standing on a hockey pitch. Results revealed that this intervention, which also included wearing hockey kit during imagery, had a strong positive effect on hockey penalty flick performance. If a similar environment is not possible, photographs of the venue or audio tapes of crowd noise can be used. Hecker and Kaczor (1988) conducted a study and reported that physiological responses to imagery occurred consistently when the scene was familiar. By using photographs or video tapes of venues, athletes can become more familiar with them prior to the competition, and, therefore, the imagery will be more effective.

The task component is an important factor, as the imagined task needs to be closely matched to the actual one. According to Holmes and Collins (2002), authors who are also part of our research group, the content of the imagery should be different for elite and non-elite performers. This is primarily because difference in skill level could influence the type and quality of imagery being conducted. When the non-elite performers improve and begin to display characteristics of elite performers, it is then necessary for the imagery script to be altered in accordance with this change. The task should be closely related and specific to the performer, focusing on individual emotions.

The timing component refers to the pace at which the imagery is completed. Some researchers advocate using imagery in slow motion to experience the action fully (see Guillot *et al.*, 2012, for an excellent review of this issue). However, precise timing is often very important in actual game situations and in the execution of specific skills. It would clearly match the desired behaviour more closely if the imagery was completed at the same pace at which the action would be completed.

The learning component of the model refers to the adaptation of the imagery content in relation to the rate of learning. As the performer becomes more skilled at a movement, the imagery script should be altered in order to reflect this. Morris *et al.* (2004) explained that the complexity of the imagery may change as the athlete improves his or her performance of a skill, and Holmes and Collins (2001) suggested that regularly reviewing the content of the imagery is essential, so that a realistic image is retained.

The emotion component refers to the emotions included within the imagery, which should be closely related to those experienced during actual performance. During the imagery the athlete should try to experience all of the emotion and arousal associated with the performance, to aid the athlete in dealing with the emotions prior to and during competition.

Finally, the perspective component refers to the way imagery is viewed. Imagery can be internal (first person) or external (third person). Internal perspective refers to the view that an athlete would have when he/she was actually performing, whereas external perspective would be like watching yourself performing on a video tape. From a functional equivalence perspective, internal imagery would appear preferable, as it more closely approximates the athlete's view when performing. However, some studies have shown external imagery to be beneficial when form-based skills are being learned, such as gymnastic moves (White and Hardy, 1995; Hardy and Callow, 1999). Research indicates that the more advanced performers will be able to switch from one perspective to another (cf. Smith *et al.*, 1998) and, in doing so, gain advantages from

ACTIVITY 10.2

Think of an action that you complete regularly in your own sport. Try imaging this, in a vivid and controllable manner, from a first-person perspective (through your own eyes) and a third-person perspective (as if viewing yourself on a television screen). Note your preference and any challenges you experience in creating each of these images.

both perspectives, optimizing the imagery experience and enhancing the athlete's performance.

Since the PETTLEP model was developed, several studies have been performed to test it explicitly, either as a whole or in part. For example, Smith *et al.* (2007) compared the use of PETTLEP imagery with more traditional, primarily visual imagery of a full turning gymnastics jump. They found that, over 6 weeks spent performing the interventions, the PETTLEP imagery group improved, but the 'traditional' imagery group did not. Also, the PETTLEP imagery group improved to the same extent as a group who physically practised the skill. This supports the use of an individually tailored PETTLEP approach when an imagery intervention is produced. The PETTLEP imagery group also completed their imagery while standing on the beam in their gymnastics clothing, which may have led to improved behavioural matching and a subsequent performance benefit.

In a follow-up study by the same authors, PETTLEP interventions were employed with a hockey penalty flick task. The study compared a sport-specific group (incorporating the physical and environment components of the PETTLEP model, wearing their hockey strip and doing their imagery on the hockey pitch) with a clothing-only group (who also wore their hockey strip while doing their imagery, but did their imagery at home) and a traditional-imagery group (who did their imagery sitting at home, in their everyday clothing). They found that the sport-specific group improved by the largest amount, followed by the clothing-only group and then the traditional-imagery group. This supports the PETTLEP model, as, when components of the PETTLEP model were added to the intervention, a greater improvement in performance was apparent.

A study by Smith *et al.* (2008) tested the effects of combining PETTLEP imagery and physical practice on golf bunker shot performance. Here, county- or international-level golfers were split into four groups: PETTLEP imagery, physical practice, PETTLEP imagery plus physical practice and a control group. The PETTLEP imagery group completed its imagery wearing golf clothing and standing in a tray of sand to mimic the necessary bunker shot. Results showed that the group combining PETTLEP imagery and physical practice exhibited the largest performance improvements. However, despite both also improving performance, there was no apparent difference in the usefulness of PETTLEP imagery and that of physical practice.

Furthermore, we conducted a longitudinal study examining the effect of PETTLEP imagery on bicep curl strength over a period of 22 weeks (Wakefield and Smith, 2011). The multiple-baseline, single-case design aimed to assess the effectiveness of various frequencies of imagery interventions (i.e. completing imagery either once, twice or three times per week). We wanted to examine the effects of different frequencies of

ACTIVITY 10.3

Choose a sport that you are familiar with but that is not a sport that you play personally. Go through each of the elements of the PETTLEP model and note what you would advise for each of the components.

imagery, but using the same participants in each of the conditions. Also, rather than using a group-based design, where individual differences between participants in the same group are often averaged out and ignored, we were interested in examining each individual's progress in great depth. This was a challenging study to design, organize and complete, as it required a long-term commitment from a small number of participants. Results indicated that, as the frequency of imagery increased, so too did the associated performance effect. Therefore, the authors recommended that, although completing imagery once a week can be useful, more effective results will be apparent from conducting imagery more frequently (three times per week). Little research has been conducted using imagery in a longitudinal manner over this length of time. However, if you are willing to invest time over a number of weeks and have the commitment of the participants, then we believe it is a worthy pursuit.

EXAMPLE OF IMAGERY STUDY

Traditionally, studies into imagery and mental practice consist of a pre-test in a specific motor skill, followed by an intervention period, a post-test in the same skill and possibly a follow-up retention test after a period of time when the intervention has been withdrawn. Groups typically include a physical practice group, an imagery group, a control group and, often, a group that combines physical practice with the imagery intervention. This allows each intervention to be tested to establish its effectiveness and provides a structured way in which to assess changes/differences in performance. A downside of such studies is, as mentioned in the previous section, that sometimes differences in individuals' responses to the imagery are largely ignored, with researchers interested in overall levels of change that occur within the group. Single-case designs, on the other hand, can examine interindividual differences more effectively, but lack the larger numbers of participants necessary to generalize findings to the population as a whole. In the example below, therefore, we use a traditional group-based design.

A study was completed by Smith and Collins (2004) to assess the effect of including stimulus and response propositions in imagery on the performance of two tasks. Stimulus propositions are units of information relating to the content of a scene, whereas response propositions are units of information relating to the individual's response to being in that situation. For example, if a footballer was imaging performing in an important match, stimulus propositions would include the sight of the other players and the sound of the crowd, and response propositions would include increased heart rate, sweating and feelings of butterflies in the stomach. Smith and Collins (2004) compared groups using physical practice, stimulus and response proposition and stimulus proposition only interventions. The task used was a contraction of the abductor digiti minimi (the muscle responsible for moving the little finger away from the hand). Smith and Collins (2004) also measured the late CNV (a negative shift that occurs in the EEG waveform prior to movement) to assess any differences between the groups during the movement. They found that the physical practice group, stimulus and response proposition group and the stimulus proposition only group all improved significantly from pre-test to post-test. However, there was no significant difference in the magnitude of their improvement. The CNV waves were also apparent in all conditions (see Figure 10.1).

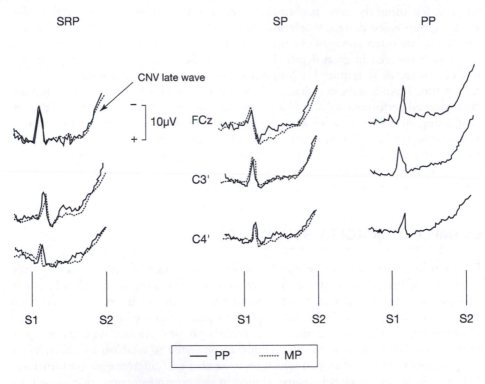

FIGURE 10.1 The late CNV prior to physical and mental practice of the finger strength task. PP = physical practice; MP = mental practice; SRP = stimulus and response proposition imagery; SP = stimulus proposition imagery; S1 = warning stimulus (instruction to get ready to move); S2 = imperative stimulus (instruction to move)

Source: Journal of Sport and Exercise Psychology, 26, 419. Reprinted by kind permission of Human Kinetics Publishers

The second of this series of studies compared similar groups on a barrier knock-down task, which involved clicking a computer mouse to knock down barriers on a computer screen in a pre-prescribed order. Smith and Collins (2004) found that the stimulus and response imagery group and physical practice group improved their performance significantly from pre-test to post-test, whereas the stimulus-only group did not. Additionally, the late CNV was observed preceding real or imagined movement in the physical practice and stimulus and response imagery groups, but not in the stimulus-only group (see Figure 10.2).

This has strong implications for imagery interventions, as it appears that physical practice is more accurately mimicked by the inclusion of response propositions. The inclusion of these propositions may also enhance the functional equivalence of the intervention (at least in the case of more 'cognitive' motor tasks), which would explain the larger increase in performance for the stimulus and response group with the barrier knock-down task.

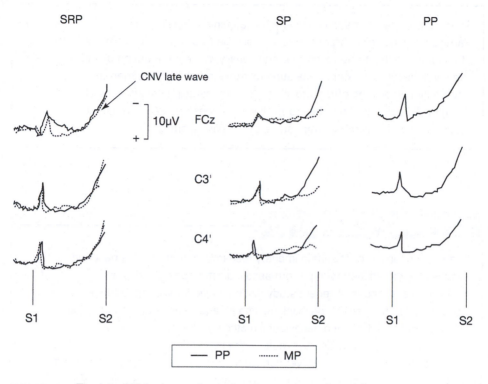

FIGURE 10.2 The late CNV prior to physical and mental practice of the barrier knock-down task

Source: Journal of Sport and Exercise Psychology, 26, 422. Reprinted by kind permission of Human Kinetics Publishers

ACTIVITY 10.4

Think of a sporting situation that you have recently experienced. Note the stimuli present in that situation, including what you could see and hear within that environment. Next, note your responses to that situation. These may be psychological, including elation or anxiety, and physiological, including experiences such as tension within the muscle.

With strength tasks, the inclusion of response propositions in the intervention may be less important, although further research in more ecologically valid settings, as in the gym-based study of Wakefield and Smith (2011) mentioned earlier, is necessary to explore this issue further.

There are ethical issues to consider when administering any intervention. Participants must give informed consent and be free to withdraw from the studies at any time, without repercussions. Additionally, if the intervention used can benefit the participant (from exam preparation to stroke rehabilitation), then the intervention should be offered to all of the other participants, after the study has finished. This ensures that the group allocation does not lead to a useful intervention being withheld from some of the participants.

BEYOND THE FRONTIER

There has been a recent shift in imagery research, with scientists becoming increasingly dissatisfied with performance indicators being used as a measure of imagery effectiveness. A recent study distinguished between the functional equivalence of the central mechanisms and an equivalence of the actions and process completed, named behavioural matching (Wakefield *et al.*, 2013). Research focus is now on investigating the mechanisms behind imagery, in order to further understand the efficacy of interventions and how these can be developed and maximized. Psychophysiology research will lead the way in this regard. We believe that extending research in this area, through the use of equipment such as TMS and EEG, will enhance knowledge in this field and assist in understanding the link to practice. Further areas to be developed include exploration of potential collaboration with other psychology topic areas and investigation into how these central imagery mechanisms work in those with impaired visuomotor skills.

CONCLUSION

Imagery can be a very effective intervention for athletes to use when trying to find ways to perform better. Although it is very commonly used by athletes, often they may not get the most out of it, as it is often performed in an unstructured and unrealistic (not behaviourally matched) way. There are several different types of imagery that can be used by athletes, all of which may have different effects on performance and self-confidence. To make the most of the various kinds of imagery that can be performed, imagery needs to be practised consistently, in a purposeful and structured way, and it also need to be as realistic as possible. Use of the guidelines of the PETTLEP model can be very helpful in achieving these goals for imagery training.

KEY CONCEPTS AND TERMS

Imagery

Imagery is commonly used as a performance-enhancing technique.

Many studies have shown imagery to have strong positive results on sporting performance.

There are many different benefits of using imagery, and these can be linked to the imagery types.

Recently, the concept of functional equivalence has led to the development of the PETTLEP model: a model aiming to give guidelines on behavioural matching to optimize the positive effects of imagery interventions.

The mechanisms occurring during imagery are still unclear, and research is continuing into this area.

RECOMMENDED FURTHER READING

Books

Jeannerod, M. (1997). *The Cognitive Neuroscience of Action*. Oxford, UK: Blackwell.

Weinberg, R. S. and Gould, D. (2011). *Foundations of Sport and Exercise Psychology* (5th edn). Champaign, IL: Human Kinetics.

Journals

Driskell, J. E., Copper, C. and Moran, A. (1994). Does mental practice improve performance? *Journal of Applied Psychology*, *79*, 481–92.

Feltz, D. L. and Landers, D. M. (1983). The effects of mental practice on motor skill learning and performance: A meta-analysis. *Journal of Sport Psychology*, *5*, 25–57.

Hall, C., Mack, D., Paivio, A. and Hausenblas, H. (1998). Imagery use by athletes: Development of the sport imagery questionnaire. *International Journal of Sport Psychology*, *29*, 73–89.

Holmes, P. S. and Collins, D. J. (2001). The PETTLEP approach to motor imagery: A functional equivalence model for sport psychologists. *Journal of Applied Sport Psychology*, *13*(1), 60–83.

Jeannerod, M. (1994). The representing brain: Neural correlates of motor intention and imagery. *Behavioral and Brain Sciences*, *17*, 187–245.

Murphy, S. M. (1990). Models of imagery in sport psychology: A review. *Journal of Mental Imagery*, *14*, 153–72.

Nordin, S. M. and Cumming, J. (2005). Professional dancers describe their imagery: Where, when, what, why, and how. *The Sport Psychologist*, *19*, 295–416.

Smith, D., Wright, C. J., Allsopp, A. and Westhead, H. (2007). It's all in the mind: PETTLEP-based imagery and sports performance. *Journal of Applied Sport Psychology*, *19*, 80–92.

Wakefield, C. J. and Smith, D. (2011). Frequency of PETTLEP imagery and strength gains: A case study. *The Sport Psychologist, 25*(3), 305–20.

Wakefield, C. J., Smith, D., Moran, A. and Holmes, P. (2013). Functional equivalence or behavioural matching? A critical reflection on 15 years of research using the PETTLEP model of motor imagery. *International Review of Sport and Exercise Psychology, 6*, 105–21.

SAMPLE ESSAY QUESTIONS

1 There are many different positive effects that imagery can have on performance. Choose one imagery type and describe how implementing it may benefit performance.

2 Describe how functional equivalence can be strived for by behaviourally matching imagery, using the example of a golf tee shot.

3 Explain how a study could be organized to compare different interventions and give the benefits of including each of the interventions.

REFERENCES

Cabral, P. and Crisfield, P. (1996). *Psychology and Performance*. Leeds. UK: National Coaching Foundation.

Decety, J. (1996). Do imagined and executed actions share the same neural substrate? *Cognitive Brain Research, 3*, 87–93.

Decety, J., Jeannerod, M., Durozard, D. and Baverel, G. (1993). Central attraction of autonomic effectors during mental simulation of motor actions. *Journal of Physiology, 461*, 549–63.

Decety, J., Jeannerod, M., Germain, M. and Pastène, J. (1991). Vegetative response during imagined movement is proportional to mental effort. *Behavioural Brain Research, 42*, 415–26.

Decety, J. and Michel, F. (1989). Comparative analysis of actual and mental movement times in two graphic tasks. *Brain Cognition, 11*, 87–97.

Dreidiger, M., Hall, C. and Callow, N. (2006). Imagery use by injured athletes: A qualitative analysis. *Journal of Sports Sciences, 24*, 261–71.

Driskell, J. E., Copper, C. and Moran, A. (1994). Does mental practice improve performance? *Journal of Applied Psychology, 79*, 481–92.

Feltz, D. L. and Landers, D. M. (1983). The effects of mental practice on motor skill learning and performance: A meta-analysis. *Journal of Sport Psychology, 5*, 25–57.

Gould, D., Tammen, V., Murphy, S. and May, J. (1989). An examination of the US Olympic sport psychology consultants and the services they provide. *The Sport Psychologist, 3*, 300–12.

Guillot, A., Hoyek, N., Louis, M. and Collet, C. (2012). Understanding the timing of motor imagery: Recent findings and future directions. *International Review of Sport and Exercise Psychology, 5*, 3–22.

Hall, C., Mack, D., Paivio, A. and Hausenblas, H. (1998). Imagery use by athletes: Development of the Sport Imagery Questionnaire. *International Journal of Sport Psychology, 28*, 1–17.

Hall, C. R. and Martin, K. A. (1997). Measuring movement imagery abilities: A revision of the movement imagery questionnaire. *Journal of Mental Imagery, 21*, 143–54.

Hardy, L. and Callow, N. (1999). Efficacy of external and internal visual imagery perspectives for the enhancement of performance on tasks in which form is important. *Journal of Sport and Exercise Psychology, 21*, 95–112.

Hecker, J. E. and Kaczor, L. M. (1988). Application of imagery theory to sport psychology: Some preliminary findings. *Journal of Sport and Exercise Psychology, 10*, 363–73.

Hinshaw, K. E. (1991). The effects of mental practice on motor skill performance: Critical evaluation and meta-analysis. *Imagination, Cognition and Personality, 11*, 3–35.

Holmes, P. S. and Collins, D. J. (2001). The PETTLEP approach to motor imagery: A functional equivalence model for sport psychologists. *Journal of Applied Sport Psychology, 13*(1), 60–83.

Holmes, P. S. and Collins, D. J. (2002). Functional equivalence solutions for problems with motor imagery. In Cockerill, I. (ed.) *Solutions in Sport Psychology*, pp. 120–40. London: Thompson.

Jeannerod, M. (1994). The representing brain: Neural correlates of motor intention and imagery. *Behavioral and Brain Sciences, 17*, 187–245.

Jeannerod, M. (1997). *The Cognitive Neuroscience of Action*. Oxford, UK: Blackwell.

Jowdy, D. P., Murphy, S. M. and Durtschi, S. (1989). *An Assessment of the Use of Imagery by Elite Athletes: Athlete, coach and psychological perspectives*. Colorado Springs, CO: United States Olympic Committee.

Kolb, B. and Whishaw, I. Q. (2008). *Fundamentals of Human Neuropsychology* (6th edn). New York: W.H. Freeman.

Kuhtz-Buschbeck, J. P., Mahnkopf, C., Holzknecht, C., Siebner, H., Ulmer, S. and Jansen, O. (2003). Effector-independent representations of simple and complex imagined finger movements: A combined fMRI and TMS study. *European Journal of Neuroscience, 18*, 3375–87.

Li, S. (2007). Movement-specific enhancement of corticospinal excitability at subthreshold levels during motor imagery. *Exprimental Brain Research, 179*, 517–24.

MacBride, E. R. and Rothstein, A. L. (1979). Mental and physical practice and the learning and retention of open and closed skills. *Perceptual and Motor Skills, 49*, 359–65.

McCarthy, P., Wilson, M., Keegan, R. and Smith, D. (2012). Three myths about applied consultancy work. *Sport and Exercise Psychology Review, 8*, 3–16.

Malouin, F., Richard, C. L., Durand, A. and Doyon, J. (2008). Reliability of mental chronometry for assessing motor imagery ability after stroke. *Archives of Physical Medicine and Rehabilitation. 89*, 311–19.

Mendoza, D. W. and Wichman, H. (1978). 'Inner' darts: Effects of mental practice on the performance of dart throwing. *Perceptual and Motor Skills, 47*, 1195–9.

Moran, A. (2012). *Sport Psychology: A critical introduction*. London: Routledge.

Moran, A. P. and MacIntyre, T. (1998). 'There's more to an image than meets the eye': A qualitative study of kinaesthetic imagery and elite canoe-slalomists. *The Irish Journal of Psychology*, *19*, 406–23.

Morris, T., Spittle, M. and Perry, C. (2004). Mental imagery in sport. In Morris, T. and Summers, J. (eds) *Sport Psychology: Theory, applications and issues*, pp. 344–83. New York: Wiley.

Murphy, S. M. (1990). Models of imagery in sport psychology: A review. *Journal of Mental Imagery*, *14*, 153–72.

Murphy, S. M., Nordin, S. M. and Cumming, J. (2008). Imagery in sport, exercise and dance. In Horn, T. (ed.) *Advances in Sport Psychology* (3rd edn), pp. 297–324. Champaign, IL: Human Kinetics.

Naito, E. and Matsumura, M. (1994). Movement-related slow potentials during motor imagery and motor suppression in humans. *Cognitive Brain Research*, *2*, 131–7.

Nordin, S. M. and Cumming, J. (2005). Professional dancers describe their imagery: Where, when, what, why, and how. *The Sport Psychologist*, *19*, 295–416.

Oxendine, J. B. (1969). Effect of mental and physical practice on the learning of three motor skills. *Research Quarterly*, *40*, 755–63.

Richardson, A. (1967a). Mental practice: A review and discussion (Part 1). *Research Quarterly*, *38*, 95–107.

Richardson, A. (1967b). Mental practice: A review and discussion (Part 2). *Research Quarterly*, *38*, 263–73.

Smith, D. and Collins, D. (2004). Mental practice, motor performance, and the late CNV. *Journal of Sport and Exercise Psychology*, *26*, 412–26.

Smith, D., Collins, D. and Hale, B. (1998). Imagery perspectives and karate performance. *Journal of Sports Sciences*, *16*, 103–4.

Smith, D. and Wakefield, C. (2013). A timely review of motor imagery: A commentary on Guillot *et al.* (2012). *Frontiers in Human Neuroscience*, 7. DOI: 10.3389/fnhum.2013.00761

Smith, D., Wright, C. J., Allsopp, A. and Westhead, H. (2007). It's all in the mind: PETTLEP-based imagery and sports performance. *Journal of Applied Sport Psychology*, *19*, 80–92.

Smith, D., Wright, C. J. and Cantwell, C. (2008). Beating the bunker: The effect of PETTLEP imagery on golf bunker shot performance. *Research Quarterly for Exercise and Sport*, *79*, 385–91.

Vandell, R. A., Davis, R. A. and Clugston, H. A. (1943). The function of mental practice in the acquisition of motor skills. *Journal of General Psychology*, *29*, 243–50.

Vealey, R. S. and Walter, S. M. (1993). Imagery training for performance enhancement and personal development. In Williams, J. M. (ed.) *Applied Sport Psychology: Personal growth to peak performance* (2nd edn), pp. 200–21. Mountain View, CA: Mayfield.

Wakefield, C. J. and Smith, D. (2011). Frequency of PETTLEP imagery and strength gains: A case study. *The Sport Psychologist*, *25*(3), 305–20.

Wakefield, C. J., Smith, D., Moran, A. and Holmes, P. (2013). Functional equivalence or behavioural matching? A critical reflection on 15 years of research using the PETTLEP model of motor imagery. *International Review of Sport and Exercise Psychology*, *6*, 105–21.

Weinberg, R. (2008). Does imagery work? Effects on performance and mental skills. *Journal of Imagery Research in Sport and Physical Activity*, *3*(1). DOI: 10.2202/1932-0191.1025

White, A. and Hardy, L. (1995). Use of different imagery perspectives on the learning and performance of different motor skills. *British Journal of Psychology*, *86*, 169–80.

Wuyam, R., Moosari, S. H., Decety, J., Adams, L., Lansing, R. W. and Guz, A. (1995). Imagination of dynamic exercise produced ventilatory responses which were more apparent in competitive sportsmen. *Journal of Physiology*, *482*, 713–24.

11

The application and impact of performance profiling in sport

Neil J. V. Weston

CHAPTER SUMMARY

This chapter provides a comprehensive overview of the performance profiling technique (Butler and Hardy, 1992). Performance profiling is a client-centred assessment procedure that encourages athletes to identify qualities they deem important to performance and then rate their ability on each of those qualities. This process helps athletes to increase their self-awareness as to their strengths and weaknesses and thus provides an ideal basis from which to set goals and develop future training interventions. The chapter begins by describing how the traditional profiling procedure can be delivered with individual athletes, coaches and teams, in addition to outlining the sporting and theoretical origins of the technique. Variations to the original procedure will then be presented, followed by a critical evaluation of the profiling research, including a summary of the uses, benefits, impacts and limitations of the technique. A case study provides a creative use for profiling within an applied setting. The chapter should provide the reader with an insight as to the usefulness of performance profiling within sports settings.

LEARNING OUTCOMES

When you have studied this chapter, you should be able to:

1 Describe the traditional performance profiling technique and adaptations to this procedure
2 Describe and explain the theoretical roots of performance profiling
3 Critically evaluate the profiling literature and outline the uses, impacts and limitations of the technique
4 Understand how to use the performance profile in a variety of ways to suit the sporting context

ACTIVITY 11.1

In relation to the sport you are currently playing, identify the key attributes or skills that help you to perform in that sport. What are the physical, technical, attitudinal, mental and tactical skills that enable you to play well?

It may help to reflect on a recent best performance. What skills/qualities helped you to perform to a high standard during that performance? Alternatively, reflect on an elite athlete in your sport/position. What skills/qualities/attributes do they possess that enable them to consistently perform at the highest level? It may help to watch some video clips of this athlete to help formulate your ideas about the qualities that make them so competent within their sport.

Write down these qualities in Table 11.1.

TABLE 11.1 List of performance qualities

Performance qualities			
Technical	Tactical	Physical	Psychological

One thing that strikes many athletes when they are completing this task is how difficult it is to identify accurately the qualities that enable them to perform well, perhaps because they are rarely asked to consider what it takes to be good in their sport. Second, the list of qualities that you have identified in this first attempt is rarely a definitive list. Invariably, you will need to reflect over time and add to the list of qualities, before you can be sure that it closely resembles those required for elite performance in your sport. This process of self-reflection and self-awareness is at the heart of Butler's (1989) performance profiling technique and is discussed in more detail in the next section.

BUTLER AND HARDY'S (1992) PERFORMANCE PROFILING TECHNIQUE

The origins of performance profiling

The performance profiling technique was developed and used by Dr Richard Butler while he was working with the British Olympic boxing team in the lead-up to the 1988 Seoul Olympics. Butler (1989) surmised that, in order to succeed with any intervention, a sport psychologist must empathize and understand the athletes' perception of themselves. He interviewed the boxers to understand what they perceived were the essential qualities required to perform successfully and then brought the boxers together as a group to agree upon the twenty most important qualities. Each boxer was finally asked to rate themselves on a scale of 1–7, to help identify their perceived strengths and weaknesses. Butler called the final product a 'self-perception map', later termed the *performance profile* (Butler and Hardy, 1992). Following reflection and several years spent consulting with the British Olympic boxing team, in 1992 he formalized the performance profiling procedure, detailing specifically how the procedure can be employed within individual and team settings, in addition to defining its theoretical roots.

Performance profiling procedure

The traditional approach to performance profiling follows three simple phases that can be adapted to suit the athlete(s). In the first phase, performance profiling is introduced as a way of helping athletes to become more aware of the attributes necessary for successful performance in their sport and their perceived strengths and weaknesses. The athlete is instructed that there are no right or wrong answers, and that an honest appraisal of their ability on the identified qualities can help to design training programmes to improve any areas of weakness. It may also help to present an example of a completed profile (see Figures 11.1 and 11.2), so that the athlete gets an idea of the types of quality that have been identified and the end product that they will produce. It is important at this stage that the consultant or coach introducing the performance profile to the athlete provides a solid rationale for the procedure, so that the athlete fully understands what the technique is, what is required of them and, importantly, how it can benefit their development. Two main methods of presenting the completed profiles have been adopted in the literature. The first is the circular target (as seen in Figure 11.1), and the second is a tabular format (as seen in Figure 11.2).

In the second phase, when the qualities to form the basis of the profile are generated, the procedure differs for group and individual settings. In a group setting, the qualities are developed through brainstorming in small groups that are typically based on positions within the team. A soccer squad, for example, would be split into goalkeeper, defender, midfielder and attacker groups. Each group is then asked to consider, 'What in your opinion are the qualities or characteristics of an elite athlete in your sport?' (Butler and Hardy, 1992, p. 256). Each group would then spend 10–20 minutes discussing and recording (typically on flipchart paper) the qualities they think are essential for elite performance in their chosen position. Each group then presents its findings to the whole team, with discussion where appropriate. Athletes are then

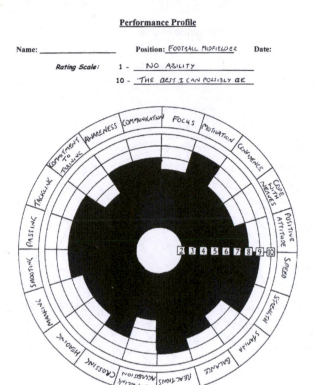

FIGURE 11.1 Circular performance profile of a soccer player

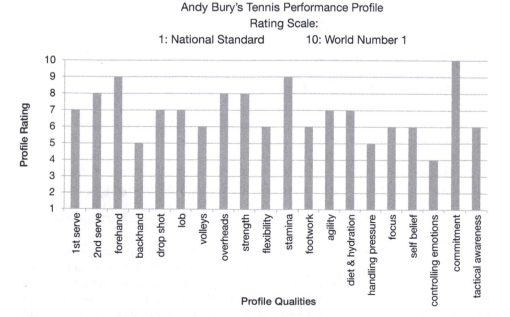

FIGURE 11.2 Tabular performance profile of a tennis player

Performance Profile

Name: _____   Sport/Position: _____
Rating Scale: 1 –   10 –

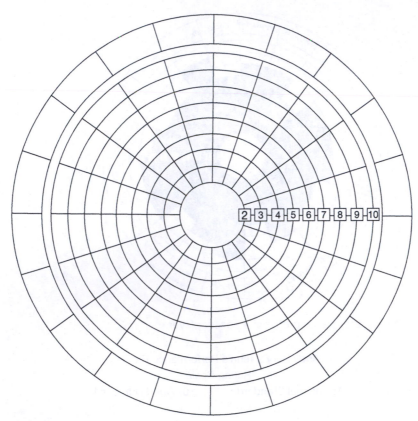

FIGURE 11.3 Blank performance profile template

provided with a blank performance profile (see Figure 11.3) and asked to identify, from all the qualities presented by the groups, the twenty most important qualities related to their position and style of play.

It is important at this stage that athletes are asked to define each of the qualities. This is particularly important to make sure that any future ratings of profile attributes (by athlete and/or coach) are based on the same definition. As a result, consultants can be more confident in the accuracy of any comparison of profile ratings over time or between athlete and coach.

In an individual setting, the athlete elicits the attributes on a one-to-one basis with the help of the sport psychologist. As this process invariably sits within a wider initial assessment process, I tend to introduce the profiling procedure towards the end of a client meeting, with a view to producing the profile in the next session. As part of this introduction, I give a rationale for engaging in profiling and also provide a completed profile from another sport, to show the athlete what we are attempting to produce. I then provide the athlete with a take-away task (see Table 11.1) to complete for the next session, which asks the athlete to consider the technical, tactical, psychological and physical qualities/attributes that they think are essential to their performance. I give them about a week to do so and ask that they watch videos of themselves or their sporting idols to help generate the qualities. I also encourage them to sit down and discuss their list of qualities with their coach to obtain their input and advice. When the athlete returns for the next session, we discuss their list of qualities, and, where relevant, I ask questions to help tease out any remaining qualities. These questions could relate to getting them to reflect on the qualities required to achieve a recent best performance, or getting them to reflect on their recent training sessions and identifying what they did and what attributes they think their coaches were trying to develop in these training drills. Having exhausted the quality-generation process, we then identify the twenty most important qualities, define them and then insert them into a blank profile (see Figure 11.3).

The third and final profiling phase involves assessment of the qualities chosen by the athlete(s) on a scale of 1 (lowest possible ability) to 10 (ideal level for each quality). The rating scale (i.e. what constitutes a 1 and a 10) is determined by the athlete and must be meaningful to them. The ratings the athlete assigns to each quality are in relation to the athlete's current perception of their ability on each of the qualities. The completed profile provides a useful visual display of the athlete's strengths and weaknesses that can then be used as a basis for identifying specific goals and training programmes to enhance those areas requiring improvement. It is important to emphasize the need for the athlete to continue to reflect upon their profile and modify/update the profile qualities, until they feel certain that those chosen are an accurate list of qualities required to fulfil their sport/position. At this stage, it is imperative that the athlete is encouraged to sit down with their coach and discuss the profile findings in detail, in order to ensure that the athlete and coach are on the same page with regard to their understanding of the qualities required by the athlete to fulfil their potential. As part of this discussion, it is important that the coach and athlete work together in setting goals and training programmes to improve those areas of weakness and maintain and/or further improve those strengths.

ACTIVITY 11.2

Having identified the list of qualities for your sport in Activity Box 11.1, now choose the twenty most important qualities from that list. Using the blank profile provided in Figure 11.3, enter your qualities into each segment on the edge of the circular target and then rate yourself on the scale of 1 (lowest possible ability) to 10 (ideal level for each quality).

One of the key benefits of profiling is that it helps to highlight the specific areas that athletes believe they must improve and thus provides an excellent basis from which to determine athlete-centred goal setting and training programme implementation. Therefore, based on your profile, please complete Table 11.2, outlining three key qualities that you need to improve, current profile rating, new rating target, a time frame for improvement and a few strategies that will enable you to achieve that goal.

TABLE 11.2 Performance priorities and plan

Quality to improve	Current profile rating	Profile target rating	Timeline	Strategies to achieve target rating
e.g. Stamina	5	8	1 Sept–1 Dec	1 Arrange meeting with my strength and conditioning coach in the next week
				2 Identify a training programme for next 3 months
				3 Buy a diary to record my training and progress towards goals
				4 Identify monthly rewards for achieving my goals

Commonly, athletes will dwell on areas of weakness and fail to emphasize their strengths. It is important that we encourage athletes to be aware of their strengths as much as those areas that they need to improve, in order that their confidence is maintained. Therefore, in Table 11.3, please record the top three strengths that you have identified, and their ratings, and provide a brief statement, in the final column, to explain what you are going to do to maintain and/or improve these strengths.

TABLE 11.3 Performance strengths and plan

Area of strength	Current profile rating	Strategies to achieve target rating
e.g. Strength	8	To reassess current strength and conditioning levels with coach and identify new targets for next 3 months

THE THEORETICAL ROOTS OF PERFORMANCE PROFILING

Kelly's (1955) personal construct theory

Butler and Hardy (1992), in introducing and describing performance profiling, stated that the technique was based on Kelly's (1955) *personal construct theory* (PCT). Kelly's theory of personality attempts to explain the way in which people interpret and thus behave in the world. Essentially, Kelly believed that people attempt to understand the world by continually developing personal theories. These theories – or constructs, as he later termed them – help an individual to anticipate events in their life and are based on what he termed corollaries (or, more simply, 'effects'). Constructs can be revised based on athletes' experience of those events over time (the experience corollary). For example, over the course of an athlete's career, a number of assumptions (theories) regarding their sport and their ability (perhaps what they believe contributes to success) may be revised.

Kelly (1955) suggested that individuals will differ in the interpretation of events in their lives (the individuality corollary), and that, in order for one to play a role in the 'social process' with another, one must attempt to understand the perceptions of that other person (the sociality corollary). By employing the profiling procedure sport psychologists are able to understand the individual athlete's perception of performance, discuss such issues more effectively as a result of the increased understanding, and tailor training more closely to the athlete's perceived needs.

Thomas (1979) attempted to extend Kelly's (1955) PCT with the introduction of a self-awareness corollary. He suggested that a person will become more aware of themselves as a result of actively seeking to understand their own thought processes regarding the construction of events. This concept is closely aligned to the performance profiling procedure, which asks athletes to organize their own thought processes and become more aware of the important qualities required to perform successfully in their sport as well as their perceived strengths and weaknesses in relation to those qualities.

In summary, performance profiling provides a direct application of Kelly's (1955) PCT in the sporting environment. The procedure takes account of the fact that each athlete's interpretation of a situation or event will differ (individuality corollary) and provides an opportunity for those alternative views to be displayed to coaches/sport psychologists, thereby helping to improve the social interaction (sociality corollary). In actively getting athletes to evaluate the essential qualities and then rate themselves on those qualities, profiling can help to enhance an athlete's sporting self-awareness (self-awareness corollary). Moreover, as an individual's interpretation is likely to be revised based on experiences of events (experience corollary), repeated employment of the procedure over time will help to record any of these changes in opinion (for a more detailed description of the PCT as it relates to profiling, see Gucciardi and Gordon, 2009).

Deci and Ryan's (1985) cognitive evaluation theory

Besides PCT, Butler and Hardy (1992) cite Deci and Ryan's (1985) *cognitive evaluation theory* (CET) as a theoretical basis for employing the technique. CET proposes that social and environmental factors (e.g. coach behaviour, rewards, etc.) that reinforce an individual's perceptions of autonomy (feelings of personal control), competence (confidence in ability) and relatedness (feeling of belonging in a social setting) will facilitate higher levels of intrinsic motivation. Research evidence has shown such self-determined motivation to result in a number of positive consequences within sport/exercise, including pleasure and enjoyment (Beauchamp et al., 1996), interest (Li, 1999), pleasant emotions and satisfaction (Blanchard et al., 2009) and physical self-perception (Martin-Albo et al., 2012).

Butler and Hardy (1992) proposed that the autonomy-supportive nature of profiling in the initial assessment phase would help to reinforce the athlete's intrinsic motivation for their sport. Furthermore, profiling, when repeated over time, could help to reinforce improvements made on key performance attributes, thereby helping to improve athlete perceptions of competence. Finally, the group nature of the profiling procedure could help facilitate greater perceptions of relatedness, as athletes communicate, interact and discuss performance-related issues with fellow teammates and/or coaching staff.

Despite the evident rationale for profiling being useful in facilitating more self-determined motivation, little research has examined the motivational consequences of profiling within sport settings. Weston et al. (2011b) examined the impact of a profiling intervention on intrinsic motivation in collegiate soccer players over a 6-week period, in comparison with two control conditions. Findings revealed that a single profiling session was insufficient to significantly improve intrinsic motivation in players who had moderate intrinsic motivation at baseline; however, three sessions, delivered over 6 weeks within season, was sufficient to do so (7 per cent improvement). Further research is needed to examine (a) whether profiling can significantly improve athlete perceptions of autonomy, competence and relatedness; (b) how often the procedure needs to be employed to bring about significant improvements; and (c) whether any positive affects, cognitions and behaviours accompany these motivational changes.

VARIATIONS IN THE PROFILING PROCEDURE

Since its inception, performance profiling has been employed in a wide variety of both individual and team sports (Weston *et al.*, 2012). This has resulted in the original procedure being modified to suit the demands of the particular consultancy situation. The majority of studies (e.g. Butler *et al.*, 1993; Dale and Wrisberg, 1996; Doyle and Parfitt, 1999) have used the basic group profiling procedure outlined by Butler and Hardy (1992), in which a group brainstorming session is followed by the production of individual athlete performance profiles. However, variation in the generation of profile qualities, in profile scoring and in the implementation of performance profiles has occurred.

Dale and Wrisberg (1996), in their consultancy with a female collegiate volleyball team, produced both coach and team performance profiles, in addition to the traditional individual athlete profiles. Whereas the individual athlete profiles adhered to Butler and Hardy's (1992) group profiling approach, the team and coach profiling procedures differed slightly. The authors asked the athletes to generate and then come to a consensus as to the qualities reflective of a successful team and ideal coach. Following this, each athlete was asked to rate the team and coach independently on the qualities of each profile, on a scale of 1–10. A mean score for each attribute was established to determine the team's consensus regarding perceived strengths and weaknesses. At this point, the coach was asked to independently rate each of the profiles to provide a comparison between athlete and coach opinions. This was subsequently used as a discussion tool for addressing the key athlete, team and coach performance-related issues.

A synthesis of literature suggests that comparing coach and athlete profile attributes can occur in two different ways (Butler, 1989, 1995; Butler and Hardy, 1992; Butler *et al.*, 1993). The coach and athlete can independently identify the qualities for the athlete, come together and agree upon the twenty most important, separately rate the qualities and then discuss the rating similarities and/or differences. Alternatively, the athlete can determine the qualities and then give them to their coach to rate, before coming together to discuss the profile findings. There are a number of potential benefits and pitfalls with this coach/athlete comparison approach. First, consultants should be wary of how much disparity there is between ratings before getting athlete and coach to discuss the findings. Clearly, if there is already a conflict or clash of personalities between the coach and athlete, getting them to compare ratings may be problematic. Therefore, consultants need to use their judgement in determining the suitability of adopting this profiling approach and look for circumstances where such comparisons will facilitate a positive influence on the athlete's performance development. Indeed, in situations where you have a particularly under-confident athlete, getting the coach to rate their profile's attributes can provide a valuable mechanism to boost the athlete's confidence as they see their coach ratings exceed their own.

Jones (1993) provided a useful application of the performance profile when produced in a one-to-one setting. Using a completed profile example and prompts, where appropriate, the athlete produced a list of twenty-five constructs from which to rate her ability. Jones (1993) then employed a variation of the basic rating procedure by asking the athlete to rate each quality on an importance scale of 1 ('not important at all') to 10 ('of crucial importance'). In keeping with the traditional approach (Butler and Hardy, 1992), Jones asked the athlete to determine her ideal score (typically 10) and her current level (C) on each of the qualities, on a scale of 1 ('couldn't be any worse') to 10 ('couldn't be any better'). Taking the C away from the ideal (I) and multiplying it by the importance rating (IR) produced a discrepancy score (D): D = (I − C) × IR. This provided an indication of the areas requiring the most improvement. Based on this procedure, Jones was able to identify, not only areas of weakness, but also the most important areas that required immediate attention (see also Doyle and Parfitt, 1996, 1997).

More recently, Gucciardi and Gordon (2009) have presented arguably the most significant variation to Butler and Hardy's (1992) original procedure. Drawing upon a wider range of the tenets of Kelly's (1955) PCT, the authors assert that their procedure helps to derive more information from the performer and, thus, provides a greater insight into the athlete's perspective. The alterations to the profiling procedure fall into three broad changes. The first variation is aligned with the importance rating adopted by Jones (1993) and takes into consideration the organizational corollary of PCT. This corollary asserts that there is an interrelated, but hierarchical, structure to one's construct system, where some constructs are more important than others, in order to make our lives more manageable. In acknowledging this proposal, Gucciardi and Gordon's (2009) extended profiling procedure asks athletes to rank the order of importance of each of their attributes to one another (i.e. the most important is ranked 1, second most important 2, and so on, until all attributes are ranked). The second addition to the traditional approach draws upon the dichotomy corollary of PCT, where the authors introduce a bipolar classification for each profile attribute. Therefore, instead of a singular term being used to describe an attribute (e.g. concentration), the authors encourage athletes to identify two bipolar categories for each attribute (e.g. fully focused, totally lacking focus), thus enabling a greater and clearer understanding of the athlete's perspective. Indeed, I believe that this approach does help athletes to identify their rating for each attribute more clearly, as they see the bipolar extremes at each end of the attribute rating–scale continuum. The third and final modification to the profiling approach draws upon the range corollary of PCT, where athletes are asked to identify the contexts in which each attribute is most applicable (e.g. in training, pre-competition, during certain competition contexts, etc.). The authors assert that each profile attribute is likely to be restricted to a certain range of convenience (i.e. a certain number of situations in which it will be applicable), and that the more contexts an attribute is applicable to, the more important that attribute is to the athlete's development and, thus, performance.

In summary, there have been some useful adaptations of Butler and Hardy's traditional profiling approach. Some of these have centred on modifying the generation of profile attributes (Dale and Wrisberg, 1996; Butler, 1997), whereas others have attempted to devise innovative approaches to the profile ratings procedure (Jones, 1993; Doyle and Parfitt, 1996, 1997). The extended profile proposed by Gucciardi and Gordon (2009) represents the most recent and, arguably, the most radical extension of the profiling procedure and requires further use and research to examine its efficacy, from athlete, coach and sport psychology practitioner perspectives.

ACTIVITY 11.3

Based on the profile you produced as part of Activity 11.2, it would now be useful to examine how the addition of an importance rating, as used by Jones (1993), influences the priority of qualities requiring improvement. Using Table 11.4, first record your qualities and their current ratings (C) in the first two columns. Then determine an ideal rating (I) for each quality (in most instances, this is likely to be 10) and rate the quality as to how important (IR) it is for performance (from 1 = not important at all, to 10 = extremely important). In the final column, take your current rating away from the ideal and then multiply by the importance rating: the higher the score, the greater the priority for improving the quality.

TABLE 11.4 Profile importance ratings

Profile quality	Current rating (C)	Ideal rating (I)	Importance-rating (IR)	Discrepancy score D = (I – C) × IR
e.g. Focus	6	10	8	32

THE PROFILING LITERATURE: USES, IMPACTS AND LIMITATIONS OF THE TECHNIQUE

Research examining the performance profile has been dominated by descriptive accounts of practitioner experiences of using the profile with their clients. Experimental research has tested the construct (Doyle and Parfitt, 1997) and predictive validity (Doyle and Parfitt, 1996) of profiling, in addition to examining the impact of mood state on profile responses (Doyle and Parfitt, 1999) and of repeated profiling on intrinsic motivation (Weston *et al.*, 2011b). Despite the profile's widespread use, there remains very little published research examining the efficacy of the technique. This lack of experimental research is surprising, given the numerous uses and impacts of profiling that have been proposed in the literature.

Uses and impacts of performance profiling

Figure 11.4 provides a summary of the various impacts and uses of profiling that have been proposed in the literature, some of which will now be discussed.

Enhanced self-awareness

Butler and Hardy (1992), in introducing the performance profile, suggest that the technique increases the athlete's self-awareness by encouraging the athlete to explore the qualities that define a successful performer in their own sport. In an examination of national under-21 netball player perceptions of the profiling procedure, the majority of players indicated that profiling was useful, citing an increase in self-awareness as a reason for its usefulness (Palmer *et al.*, 1996). Furthermore, Weston *et al.* (2010) found that fifty-six sport psychology practitioners, accredited by the British Association of Sport and Exercise Sciences (BASES), strongly believed profiling to be useful in raising

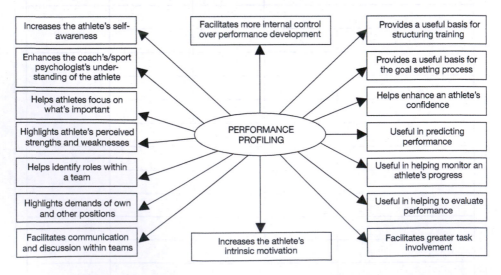

FIGURE 11.4 A summary of the proposed impacts and uses of performance profiling as suggested in the literature

athlete self-awareness. Two of the key facilitators come in the identification of the athlete's perceived strengths and also those areas that they need to improve (Butler and Hardy, 1992; Butler et al., 1993).

Profiling, specifically within a group environment, provides an additional opportunity to raise athlete awareness of the role of their fellow teammates. If players are split up into positional groups and asked to brainstorm qualities and then present those qualities to their team, they can become more aware of the various positional demands within the team (cf. Dale and Wrisberg, 1996; Weston et al., 2010, 2011a).

Developing intrinsic motivation

As described earlier, the performance profiling technique provides athletes with a more dominant role in the decision-making process regarding their future development and, in doing so, helps to maintain or increase athlete intrinsic motivation. Descriptive research has suggested a possible increase in motivation as a result of profiling interventions (Jones, 1993; D'Urso et al., 2002). Furthermore, recent research examining British collegiate athlete perceptions of profiling indicated that they believed the procedure could help to motivate them to improve and train (Weston et al., 2011a), findings supported by BASES-accredited sport psychology practitioners, who believed the profile would help to enhance athlete intrinsic motivation (Weston et al., 2010). Despite this research and a strong theoretical rationale to suggest profiling could enhance athlete motivation, there has only been one experimental investigation into the impact of profiling on intrinsic motivation (Weston et al., 2011b). In this study, forty collegiate soccer players in season were randomly assigned to three conditions (performance profiling, sports science educational presentation and control), each delivered on three occasions for approximately 1 hour, 3 weeks apart. The sport motivational scale (Pelletier et al., 1995) was completed on four occasions (pre-intervention and then after each session) to examine the impact of each condition on athlete intrinsic motivation. Findings revealed that a single profiling intervention was insufficient to significantly improve intrinsic motivation; however, three sessions were sufficient. Further research examining the characteristics (i.e. type, duration, frequency, length) of profiling that leads to significant and sustained improvements in intrinsic motivation would be worthwhile.

Facilitating task involvement

Task-involved goal perspectives, where athletes orient themselves more towards skill mastery and self-referent performance evaluation (Nicholls, 1984, 1989), have been linked with more self-determined behaviour (Deci and Ryan, 1985). This is in contrast to ego-oriented perspectives, where athletes focus upon comparing themselves with others and thus, in failure situations, are likely to avoid challenges, exert low effort, lack persistence in the face of failure and ultimately drop out from their sport, should the failures persist (Duda and Hall, 2001). Such goal perspectives are, however, modifiable by virtue of the situational factors within the context in which the athlete operates. Greenlees (2009) suggests that performance profiling could provide a useful strategy to encourage more task-involved goal perspectives, in that the strategy asks athletes to focus upon controllable skills and qualities required for successful performance, in addition to getting athletes to rate themselves in a self-referent way. This proposition was examined by Weston et al. (2010), who asked fifty-six BASES-accredited sport psychology practitioners to rate, on a 5-point Likert scale (1 = not at all, to 5 = very), how effective the production of an athlete perform-ance profile, within a group setting, was in relation to a number of possible impacts. The findings revealed that practitioners believed profiling in this way to be beneficial in promoting task involvement (mean = 3.67); however, further experimental research is needed to investigate this suggestion.

Developing confidence

Bandura (1997) outlines four sources of efficacy information: performance accomplish-ments, vicarious experience, verbal persuasion and interpretation of physiological/ emotional arousal. The use of performance profiling as a monitoring and evaluation technique (see below) could help reinforce a perception of performance accomplish-ment. For example, Butler et al. (1993, p. 61) suggest that using the performance profile to monitor performance improvements could improve athlete confidence, 'in that improvement reinforces a belief in the preparation'. The authors do warn, however, that using the profile to monitor progress could negatively influence an athlete's confidence if their profile ratings fail to improve, particularly in the lead-up to competitions.

Verbal persuasion refers to the use of persuasive techniques by self or other people (such as coaches, parents, peers, etc.) to influence perceptions of self-efficacy. Examples of such techniques include self-talk, evaluative feedback, attributions, expectations of others, and pre-, during or post-game speeches (Feltz et al., 2008; Short and Ross-Stewart, 2009). Profiling could provide an alternative method to help coaches' feedback and/or reinforce perceptions of an athlete's current ability. By employing the procedure of comparing coach/athlete profile ratings (Butler and Hardy, 1992), the coach can reinforce their belief in the ability of the athlete in the integral attributes required for successful performance.

Useful basis for goal setting

Goal setting has frequently been shown to be a highly consistent and effective strategy in helping to enhance performance across a wide range of general and sport-related tasks (Burton and Weiss, 2008). Kingston and Wilson (2009), drawing upon the meta-analytic findings of Kyllo and Landers (1995), assert that athlete autonomy in the process of goal setting is likely to facilitate greater intrinsic motivation and thus further enhance the effectiveness of the goals set. The profiling procedure of identifying key performance attributes, and then rating the strengths and weaknesses of those attributes, provides a useful template from which performance-related, autonomy-supportive goal setting can start (Butler, 1997). The choice corollary of Kelly's (1955) PCT suggests that a person is likely to choose an avenue or alternative that will best facilitate a particular outcome. Thus, athletes will choose those goals that they believe will result in the greatest improvements in their performance. Butler (1997) does, however, warn practitioners that the goals chosen and set by athletes may not always be the most appropriate. Hence, although it may be important to get athletes involved in setting goals for themselves, psychologists and coaches should attempt to steer athletes towards choosing more appropriate goals when necessary.

Performance monitoring

The monitoring of performance is an important component in helping athletes to develop and improve. Repeated profiling over time has been suggested as a beneficial way of monitoring the progress of an athlete (Butler and Hardy, 1992; Doyle and Parfitt, 1997). Doyle and Parfitt (1997) experimentally investigated the usefulness of the performance profile in monitoring progress over time, in their examination of the construct validity of the performance profile. The authors suggested that the construct validity of the profile would be shown if a significant decrease in the area of perceived need (ideal score minus current score) related to a significant increase in performance over time. Twelve track and field athletes devised and completed their performance profile five times over the course of a training and competitive indoor season. The athletes completed their profile as close to the training session or competition as possible. Other measures assessed included the actual performance score (time or distance) and perceptions of performance from the athlete and the coach. Partial support was found for the construct validity of performance profiling. A significant increase in the mean actual performance measure was evident, in accordance with a significant decrease in the mean areas of perceived need profile scores. However, no significant difference was found for either the athletes' or coaches' perception of performance in relation to the perceived need changes. Doyle and Parfitt (1997) concluded that practitioners employing the performance profile as a monitoring tool should be aware that it may only be useful when large changes in performance are likely, either during intense training periods or when recovering from injury. Further research is warranted to examine the profile's utility in these situations over longer time periods and across various sporting populations.

Performance evaluation

Performance profiling has been proposed as a useful technique to help athletes evaluate their performance (Butler and Hardy, 1992; Butler et al., 1993; Weston et al., 2010). An inherent and important part of any such evaluation is to determine one's reasons for the success or failure. Weiner's (1986) model of achievement attributions has populated our understanding of the reasons, causes or attributions that athletes give for their performances. Weiner asserts that athlete attributions fall into three complementary dimensions: locus of causality (whether the reason is internal (e.g. effort) or external (e.g. referee decision)), stability (whether it is changeable (e.g. luck) or relatively stable (e.g. ability)) and controllability (whether it is within the athlete's control (e.g. preparation) or not (e.g. weather)). The attributions are also categorized into functional or dysfunctional attributions. A functional attribution following success is one that is internal and controllable (e.g. good technique), whereas a dysfunctional attribution is external, uncontrollable and stable (e.g. opposition ability). Alternatively, following failure, a functional attribution would be internal, controllable and likely to change (e.g. effort), whereas a dysfunctional attribution in such situations is generally uncontrollable and unlikely to change (e.g. either an opponent's or the athlete's ability). Examination of the profiling strategy suggests the procedure could be useful in helping athletes to evaluate their performances in relation to internal, controllable and changeable qualities. Getting athletes to focus their performance evaluation upon such qualities would encourage athletes to develop a more functional attributional mindset, irrespective of whether they were to win or lose. Despite this assertion, no research has examined whether performance profiling is useful as an attribution retraining strategy in moving athletes from a dysfunctional to a more functional attribution state of mind.

Improving team-related functioning

The nature of the group-based approach to profiling introduces the potential for the technique to positively impact upon team cohesion (Butler and Hardy, 1992). Inspection of the descriptive research suggests that the procedure could be useful in facilitating communication and discussion within teams (Dale and Wrisberg, 1996; Weston *et al.*, 2010) and between athletes and their coaches (Butler and Hardy, 1992; Butler *et al.*, 1993; Dale and Wrisberg, 1996; Weston *et al.*, 2011a), in addition to helping identify roles within a team (Mellalieu and Juniper, 2006) and improving team dynamics (Weston *et al.*, 2010). Despite these observations, more empirical research is needed to establish the characteristics of profiling (i.e. duration, frequency, type) that can bring about significant, positive improvements in team functioning.

Limitations of performance profiling

It is important that practitioners are aware of the limitations of profiling in order to employ the technique in a balanced and appropriate manner. One limitation centres on the identification of the qualities for an athlete's profile. Given that athletes predominantly identify their qualities, problems may emerge in relation to the appropriateness of those qualities produced. In particular, athletes who have low self-awareness, are new to the sport or are young in age may struggle to produce a list of attributes that are fully representative of the sport and/or position (Weston *et al.*, 2012). In these instances, the practitioner must facilitate coach involvement to enable sufficient breadth and depth in the generation of profile attributes. Furthermore, with young athletes, with whom brainstorming the key qualities may prove difficult, it would be worthwhile providing them with a predetermined list of appropriate qualities from which they can then choose (D'Urso *et al.*, 2002; see Case Study). Although not entirely adhering to Butler and Hardy's (1992) suggestions, this process still enables the athletes to feel that they have been involved in the process of developing their profile. A secondary issue relating to profile quality identification is that an athlete's profile rarely captures the true essence of an individual's personal constructs after the first attempt. Indeed, several additional reflections on the profile are needed before an athlete can be reasonably sure that the profile fully represents the necessary qualities needed for successful performance in their sport/position. This can result in the profiling procedure being perceived as too time consuming and thus can potentially result in a lack of engagement from both athlete and coach.

Limitations in the profile can also be found in the rating of profile attributes. First, the subjective nature of athlete rating can result in issues with regard to the accuracy of attribute ratings. There may also be issues with athletes being dishonest or self-serving in their ratings. Furthermore, continued rating of the profile over time may result in a decrease in profile ratings, adversely affecting the athlete's confidence. Finally, athletes have voiced concern at rating profiles in pre-season or early season, when they have little playing experience from which to judge their ability on each quality

(Weston, 2005). In light of these concerns, it is important that practitioners are wary of when (and when not) to profile athletes throughout a season in order that accurate ratings can be produced. It is also important to encourage athletes to choose a rating scale that is meaningful and easily understood, so as to increase the accuracy of ratings. Finally, it is critical that athletes are clearly instructed as to the benefits that they will gain through profiling and the confidential nature of the findings, so as to encourage greater honesty in profile ratings.

Doyle and Parfitt (1999), in examining the association between mood state and profile ratings, provide an important consideration when one is attempting to use the technique. The authors found that a happy mood state (the subject listening to an imagery-based relaxation tape and visualizing themselves watching the National Lottery draw and winning £10,000) prior to profile rating would result in elevated responses to profile constructs, whereas sad or neutral mood states did not affect profile responses. Although this is not necessarily a limitation of the profiling procedure, it is important that consultants and coaches are aware that pleasant mood states prior to profile completion can result in athletes' overestimating their ability on profile qualities.

CONCLUSIONS

Initial assessment within sport psychology is fundamental to allow the consultant to correctly ascertain an athlete's key strengths and weaknesses and thus determine intervention strategies to aid improvements in performance. Performance profiling has been successfully employed across a range of ages, abilities and sports, providing a useful method of assessment that places the athlete at the centre of the decision-making process regarding their future development. Given the flexible nature of the procedure, it can be employed with individual athletes, coaches, teams and units within teams. Based on the selected principles of Kelly's (1955) PCT, profiling helps to raise athlete awareness of the qualities essential to elite performance, in addition to their perceived strengths and weaknesses. It provides a useful basis for goal setting and has been found to be useful in evaluating and monitoring performance and facilitating coach–athlete communication, in addition to enhancing communication, interaction and discussion within teams.

The descriptive research that has dominated the examination of the efficacy of performance profiling (e.g. Butler and Hardy, 1992; Jones, 1993; Dale and Wrisberg, 1996; Weston et al., 2010, 2011a) has suggested that the technique is beneficial in a number of ways (e.g. improving confidence, intrinsic motivation, task involvement, self-awareness, etc.). The next key step in validating these suggestions is to empirically investigate them in a variety of sport populations. Although athlete and sport psychology consultant perceptions of the profile's usefulness have been examined as part of this descriptive research, little research has examined coaches' perspective on the technique. Given their crucial role in developing athletes, teams and fellow coaching staff, a wider investigation into coach perspectives of the most effective ways of utilizing performance profiling to improve athlete, team and coach performance development, is an important priority.

More generally, the literature to date has primarily been restricted to examining the efficacy of profiling in the short term. More longitudinal evaluative research, employing during, post and retention measures, is needed to ascertain the efficacy of the technique in order to enhance its credibility. Indeed, the use of longitudinal single-case-study designs (see Barker *et al.*, 2011) could provide a useful, practical, applied-research approach. Furthermore, with the introduction of Gucciardi and Gordon's (2009) extended profile, research is necessary to examine the efficacy of this approach and provide in comparison to the original Butler and Hardy (1992) approach.

CASE STUDY: WORKING WITH YOUNG PERFORMERS

One of the key benefits of performance profiling, especially with children, lies in the technique's simplicity, as well as the visual nature of the information derived, which helps to represent pictorially where the athlete is strong and where they need to improve. Despite the advancement in our understanding of the benefits of autonomy-supportive and athlete-centred coaching, junior athletes are very rarely asked to sit down and reflect upon their performance and what it takes to be a great performer in their sport/position. Hence, the simple, visual and reflective nature of performance profiling provides an ideal strategy to facilitate junior-athlete awareness of the qualities essential for their sport, in addition to their strengths and weaknesses in relation to those qualities. The present case study highlights the use of profiling with a junior rugby union team.

The coach of an under-14s male county rugby union squad requests that their team could experience five sport psychology sessions to improve their understanding of how their mind influences their performance. Examination of the work of Potter and Anderson (1998) reveals that profiling may provide a useful starting point to improve athlete self-awareness and help to prioritize the content of the remaining four sessions. In other words, identifying the common areas of psychological weakness across players that emerge from the initial profiling activity could help to prioritize the content of the remaining sessions. In such situations, where time is at a premium and, thus, must be used wisely, adopting the pro-active approach of observing the team's training a week before the first group session is a worthwhile activity. This helps the consultant to familiarize him/herself with the coach and playing staff, get a feel for their ability, maturity and professionalism, and meet with the players and brief them on their upcoming sessions. Another important function of this activity is to initiate the start of the profiling activity, in advance of the session, by handing the players a profiling activity sheet (see Table 11.1). The players are then asked, between then and the first session, to list all the qualities or skills that they feel are important for playing in their position. A table with four columns is provided whereby the players can list the technical, tactical, psychological and physical skills or qualities that they feel make an elite player in their position. Players are provided with a completed profile of a soccer player to give them an indication as to what they are trying to accomplish. Furthermore, they are asked to watch videos of their elite rugby idols to help generate the qualities. As a precursor to the profiling session, the team members are asked to provide some examples of their role models there and then.

A final incentive ('bribe') is provided whereby the three players with the longest list of qualities will each receive a prize at the start of the upcoming profiling session.

The profiling session begins approximately a week later, in a spacious room filled with tables and chairs to create an ideal environment to facilitate player engagement and interaction. The session is introduced as per Butler and Hardy's (1992) recommendations, whereby it is communicated that the purpose of the session is to raise athlete awareness of the qualities essential for elite performance in their sport, in addition to highlighting their perceived strengths and weaknesses; that there will be no right or wrong answers; and that the profile produced can provide an ideal basis from which to set goals and discuss their performance development with the coaching staff. A completed profile from another sport can again be provided to reinforce what each athlete should be aiming to produce.

In planning for any eventuality, it is important to assume the athletes will not bring their list of qualities with them. Hence, it is a good idea to prepare a list of attributes for each of the key areas in advance of the session, informed by rugby union coaching books, checked by the team's coaching staff and inclusive of definitions. This approach of a prepared list of qualities draws upon the fixed profile approach adopted by Butler (1997) and D'Urso *et al.* (2002). Although not strictly adhering to Butler and Hardy's (1992) profile quality generation procedure, it still allows players the opportunity to select those qualities that they deem are essential for their position from a large bank of relevant qualities and, thus, maintains a sense of autonomy in the process. The squad is then split into positional groups (e.g. front row, second row, back row, half-backs, centres, back three) and provided with a bag of laminated qualities, Blu-tack and an A0 poster, tailored to the position of each group and covered with pictures of the role models they had communicated the previous week and other well-known players in their position. The players are then asked to identify 'the most important qualities or skills of an elite athlete in their position' from the examples provided and those that they have brought with them. A useful activity to employ immediately prior to the group work, to get the players into the right mindset, is to play a brief montage of video footage of the elite performers in their sport. This helps to focus and motivate the mind, in addition to stimulating ideas around the qualities that make an elite athlete in their sport and position. When this video finishes, the groups are given approximately 20 minutes to achieve the task (by sticking the qualities to the poster using the Blu-tack) and told that they can select no more than twenty-five qualities.

An integral part of this discussion process is to ensure that the coaching staff are fully engaged in the discussion of these qualities. Hence, the coaches are asked to interact with the groups and, where possible, facilitate discussion and reflection upon their recent training and competitive experiences. It is also important for the consultant to wander around and interact with each group to stimulate discussion.

When each group has identified its qualities, each poster is positioned at the front of the room, visible to all. A representative from each group is asked to summarize their findings, with comments and questions invited from the other groups and coaching staff. Upon completion of this activity, the players are then provided with blank profiles and asked to select the twenty most important qualities that are essential for their position. These qualities can be selected from any of the groups' posters. They are then instructed to rate each profile quality on a scale from 1 ('the worst I could be') to 10 ('the best I can be'), to identify their strengths and weaknesses. On completion of the session, players are advised to discuss their profiles with their coaches, to help identify priority areas to improve as part of their future training programmes. Each player's profile is photocopied, so that an analysis of the common areas of strength and weakness in each of the key areas (e.g. technical, tactical, psychological, physical) can be conducted. The coaches can then be notified of the findings, to inform their future training sessions. Furthermore, the findings provide the consultant with the common psychological areas requiring improvement, which can then be targeted in the remaining workshop sessions.

BEYOND THE FRONTIER

Initial assessment and then subsequent regular monitoring of athlete performance are high priority for any sporting organization. Athletes come and go, but performance targets and ambitions remain, and so accurately assessing an athlete's strengths and weaknesses and then identifying a plan to develop the athlete to realize their full potential are together an essential focus for coaches and performance directors alike. There is now a clear and understandable focus on attending to, and developing, all the key components of performance (e.g. physical, technical, tactical, psychological, etc.) to achieve such outcomes. Aligned with this is the use of specialist professionals to attend to all of these requirements (e.g. nutritionists, massage therapists, physiologists, biomechanists, physiotherapists, psychologists, technical coaches, performance analysts, etc.). Indeed, a multispecialist approach to performance development is clearly an important component of high-level sports performance; however, what is less clear is how this is operationalized in order to bring about timely maximal improvements in athlete performance. Butler and Hardy's (1992) performance profile provides a useful resource that can examine the strengths and weaknesses of an athlete across a variety of performance indices. Although simple in nature, it can provide an athlete-centred, specialist-involved approach to performance assessment and subsequent monitoring. Indeed, the profile could be used by multiple specialists, as part of an athlete's support team, to develop a specific and detailed picture of the requirements of an athlete's sport in order to inform discussions around the priorities for the athlete's development.

From a practical point of view, Butler and Hardy's (1992) performance profiling procedure has been confined to a paper-and-pencil delivery approach. Although this has its benefits, it does restrict the ongoing practicality of using the profiling procedure with athletes and their coaches. Given the global nature of sports participation and the proliferation of computerized applications, it would make sense to develop a computer application for this procedure, whereby the athlete and consultant/coach could create, store and share profiles electronically. This would allow athletes and consultants/coaches, in the same or different countries, to review, discuss, evaluate and/or monitor performance development through an e-profile. Although this is not currently available for profiling, a software package called Goalscape is (www.goalscape.com) and it closely aligns with the profiling procedure, albeit its central focus is on helping individuals set, communicate and achieve their goals. The production of an e-profile application focusing on the core principles of Butler and Hardy's (1992) performance profiling procedure (and possibly Gucciardi and Gordon's extended profile, 2009) would provide a very valuable resource for athletes, coaches and sport psychology practitioners alike.

KEY CONCEPTS AND TERMS

Butler and Hardy's (1992) performance profile
This is a client-centred assessment procedure that encourages athletes to identify qualities they deem important to performance and then rate their ability on each of those qualities.

Kelly's (1955) personal construct theory
Kelly's theory of personality attempts to explain the way in which people interpret and, thus, behave in the world. Essentially, Kelly believed that people attempt to understand the world by continually developing personal theories. These theories, or constructs as he later termed them, help an individual to anticipate events in their life and can be revised based on their experience of those events over time.

Deci and Ryan's (1985) cognitive evaluation theory
Cognitive evaluation theory proposes that social and environmental factors that reinforce an individual's perceptions of autonomy (feelings of personal control), competence (confidence in ability) and relatedness (feeling of belonging in a social setting) will facilitate higher levels of intrinsic motivation.

RECOMMENDED FURTHER READING

Books and book chapters

Butler, R. (1997). Performance profiling: Assessing the way forward. In Butler, R. J. (ed.) *Sports Psychology in Performance*, pp. 33–48. Oxford, UK: Butterworth-Heinemann.

Butler, R. J. (1989). Psychological preparation of Olympic boxers. In Kremer, J. and Crawford, W. (eds) *The Psychology of Sport: Theory and practice*, pp. 74–84. Belfast, Northern Ireland: BPS Northern Ireland Branch.

Journals

Butler, R. J. and Hardy, L. (1992). The performance profile: Theory and application. *The Sport Psychologist*, 6, 253–64.

Dale, G. A. and Wrisberg, C. A. (1996). The use of a performance profile technique in a team setting: Getting the athletes and coach on the 'same page'. *The Sport Psychologist*, 10, 261–77.

Doyle, J. M. and Parfitt, G. (1997). Performance profiling and constructive validity. *The Sport Psychologist*, 11, 411–25.

Gucciardi, D. F. and Gordon, S. (2009). Revisiting the performance profile technique: Theoretical underpinnings and application. *The Sport Psychologist*, 23, 93–117.

Jones, G. (1993). The role of performance profiling in cognitive behavioral interventions in sport. *The Sport Psychologist*, 7, 160–72.

Weston, N. J. V., Greenlees, I. A. and Thelwell, R. C. (2012). A review of Butler and Hardy's (1992) performance profiling procedure within sport. *International Review of Sport and Exercise Psychology*, 5, 1–21.

SAMPLE ESSAY QUESTIONS

1   Critically evaluate the use, impacts and limitations of Butler and Hardy's (1992) performance profiling procedure.

2   Provide a critical discussion of the evidence base to justify the use of Butler and Hardy's (1992) performance profiling technique.

3   Critically evaluate the following statement: 'Butler and Hardy's (1992) performance profiling technique is a beneficial strategy for athletes to engage in'.

4   'Performance profiling fails to provide a valid and reliable method of performance assessment.' Critically evaluate this statement with reference to appropriate literature.

REFERENCES

Bandura, A. (1997). *Self-efficacy: The exercise of control.* New York: Freeman.

Barker, J., McCarthy, P., Jones, M. and Moran, A. (2011). *Single-case Research Methods in Sport and Exercise Psychology.* London: Routledge.

Beauchamp, P. H., Halliwell, W. R., Fournier, J. F. and Koestner, R. (1996). Effects of cognitive-behavioural psychological skills training on motivation, preparation and putting performance of novice golf players. *The Sport Psychologist*, 10, 157–70.

Blanchard, C., Amiot, C., Perreault, S., Vallerand, R. J. and Provencher, P. (2009). Cohesiveness, coach's interpersonal style, and psychological needs: Their effects on self-determination and athletes' subjective well-being. *Psychology of Sport and Exercise, 10,* 545–51.

Burton, D. and Weiss, C. (2008). The fundamental goal concept: The path to process and performance success. In Horn, T. (ed.) *Advances in Sport Psychology* (3rd edn), pp. 339–75. Champaign, IL: Human Kinetics.

Butler, R. (1995). Athlete assessment: The performance profile. *Coaching Focus, 29,* 18–20.

Butler, R. (1997). Performance profiling: Assessing the way forward. In Butler, R. J. (ed.) *Sports Psychology in Performance,* pp. 33–48. Oxford, UK: Butterworth-Heinemann.

Butler, R. J. (1989). Psychological preparation of Olympic boxers. In Kremer, J. and Crawford, W. (eds) *The Psychology of Sport: Theory and practice,* pp. 74–84. Belfast, Northern Ireland: BPS Northern Ireland Branch.

Butler, R. J. and Hardy, L. (1992). The performance profile: Theory and application. *The Sport Psychologist, 6,* 253–64.

Butler, R. J., Smith, M. and Irwin, I. (1993). The performance profile in practice. *Journal of Applied Sport Psychology, 5,* 48–63.

Dale, G. A. and Wrisberg, C. A. (1996). The use of a performance profile technique in a team setting: Getting the athletes and coach on the 'same page'. *The Sport Psychologist, 10,* 261–77.

Deci, E. L. and Ryan, R. M. (1985). *Intrinsic Motivation and Self-determination in Human Behavior.* New York: Plenum Press.

Doyle, J. and Parfitt, G. (1996). Performance profiling and predictive validity. *Journal of Applied Sport Psychology, 8,* 160–70.

Doyle, J. M. and Parfitt, G. (1997). Performance profiling and constructive validity. *The Sport Psychologist, 11,* 411–25.

Doyle, J. and Parfitt, G. (1999). The effect of induced mood states on performance profile areas of perceived need. *Journal of Sports Sciences, 17,* 115–27.

Duda, J. L. and Hall, H. (2001). Achievement goal theory in sport: Recent extensions and future development. In Singer, R. N., Hausenblas, H. A. and Janelle, C. M. (eds) *Handbook of Sport Psychology,* pp. 417–43. New York: Wiley.

D'Urso, V., Petrosso, A. and Robazza, C. (2002). Emotions, perceived qualities, and performance of rugby players. *The Sport Psychologist, 16,* 173–99.

Feltz, D. L., Short, S. E. and Sullivan, P. J. (2008). *Self-efficacy in Sport.* Champaign, IL: Human Kinetics.

Greenlees, I. (2009). Enhancing confidence in a youth golfer. In Hemmings, B. and Holder, T. (eds) *Applied Sport Psychology: A case study approach,* pp. 89–105. New York: Wiley.

Gucciardi, D. F. and Gordon, S. (2009). Revisiting the performance profile technique: Theoretical underpinnings and application. *The Sport Psychologist, 23,* 93–117.

Jones, G. (1993). The role of performance profiling in cognitive behavioral interventions in sport. *The Sport Psychologist, 7,* 160–72.

Kelly, G. A. (1955). *The Psychology of Personal Constructs* (Vols 1 and 2). New York: Norton.

Kingston, K. M. and Wilson, K. M. (2009). The application of goal setting in sport. In Mellalieu, S. D. and Hanton, S. (eds) *Advances in Applied Sport Psychology: A review*, pp. 75–123. Abingdon, UK: Routledge.

Kyllo, L. B. and Landers, D. M. (1995). Goal-setting in sport and exercise: A research synthesis to resolve the controversy. *Journal of Sport and Exercise Psychology*, *17*, 117–37.

Li, F. (1999). The Exercise Motivation Scale: Its multifaceted structure and construct validity. *Journal of Applied Sport Psychology*, *11*, 97–115.

Martin-Albo, J., Nunez, J. L., Dominguez, E., Leon, J. and Tomas, J. M. (2012). Relationships between intrinsic motivation, physical self-concept and satisfaction with life: A longitudinal study. *Journal of Sports Sciences*, *30*, 337–47.

Mellalieu, S. D. and Juniper, S. W. (2006). A qualitative investigation into experiences of the role episode in soccer. *The Sport Psychologist*, *20*, 399–418.

Nicholls, J. G. (1984). Achievement motivation: Conceptions of ability, subjective experience, task choice, and performance. *Psychological Review*, *91*, 328–46.

Nicholls, J. G. (1989). *The Competitive Ethos and Democratic Education*. Cambridge, MA: Harvard University Press.

Palmer, C., Burwitz, L., Collins, D., Campbell, E. and Hern, J. (1996). Performance profiling: Construct validity and utilization. *Journal of Sport Sciences*, *14*, 41–2.

Pelletier, L. G., Fortier, M. S., Vallerand, R. J., Tuson, K. M., Briere, N. M. and Blais, M. R. (1995). Toward a new measure of intrinsic motivation, extrinsic motivation, and amotivation in sports: The Sport Motivation Scale (SMS). *Journal of Sport and Exercise Psychology*, *17*, 35–53.

Potter, C. L. and Anderson, A. G. (1998). Using performance profiles with a regional junior table tennis squad. In Lees, A., Maynard, I., Hughes, M. and Reilly, T. (eds) *Science and Racket Sports II*, pp. 142–7. London: E & FN Spon.

Short, S. and Ross-Stewart, L. (2009). A review of self-efficacy based interventions. In Mellalieu, S. D. and Hanton, S. (eds) *Advances in Applied Sport Psychology: A review*, pp. 221–80. Abingdon, UK: Routledge.

Thomas, L. F. (1979). Construct, reflect and converse: The conventional reconstruction of social realities. In Stringer, P. and Bannister, D. (eds) *Constructs of Sociality and Individuality*, pp. 49–72. London: Academic Press.

Weiner, B. (1986). *An Attributional Theory of Motivation and Emotion*. New York: Springer-Verlag.

Weston, N. J. V. (2005). *The Impact of Butler and Hardy's (1992) Performance Profiling Technique in Sport*. Unpublished doctoral dissertation. University of Southampton, UK.

Weston, N. J. V., Greenlees, I. A. and Thelwell, R. C. (2010). Applied sport psychology consultant perceptions of the usefulness and impacts of performance profiling. *International Journal of Sport Psychology*, *41*, 360–8.

Weston, N. J. V., Greenlees, I. A. and Thelwell, R. C. (2011a). Athlete perceptions of the impacts of performance profiling. *International Journal of Sport and Exercise Psychology*, *9*, 173–88.

Weston, N. J. V., Greenlees, I. A. and Thelwell, R. C. (2011b). The impact of a performance profiling intervention on athlete intrinsic motivation. *Research Quarterly for Exercise and Sport*, *82*, 151–5.

Weston, N. J. V., Greenlees, I. A. and Thelwell, R. C. (2012). A review of Butler and Hardy's (1992) performance profiling procedure within sport. *International Review of Sport and Exercise Psychology*, *5*, 1–21.

12

The scientific application of music in exercise and sport

Towards a new theoretical model

Costas I. Karageorghis

CHAPTER SUMMARY

This chapter provides a comprehensive update on the science and application underlying the effects of music in exercise and sport. Recent theoretical advances are briefly discussed, and relevant literature is critically appraised. The first half of the chapter leads towards the presentation of a new theoretical model that draws on the latest empirical evidence and provides an impetus for future research and evidence-based practice. To aid practitioners, an instrument is presented that can be used to assess the motivational qualities of music in exercise and sport: the Brunel Music Rating Inventory-3. The chapter is peppered with examples of how music can be applied in exercise and sport contexts using a scientific approach.

LEARNING OUTCOMES

When you have studied this chapter, you should be able to:

1 Describe the main constituents of music and its psychological, psychophysical, psychophysiological and ergogenic effects
2 Explain the conceptual/theoretical models that have been advanced to account for the effects of music in the domain of exercise and sport

> 3 Apply an objective method to the selection of music that is appropriate for both exercise and sport contexts
> 4 Design some music-related interventions for exercise participants or athletes using the evidence base and a theoretical underpinning

INTRODUCTION: AN OVERVIEW OF MUSIC IN EXERCISE AND SPORT

History books reveal that, from the very dawn of civilization, ancient cultures combined sounds in ways that influenced the human psyche. With the passage of time, primitive forms of music evolved into ever-more artistically pleasing arrangements. Accordingly, music came to be used for highly diverse purposes: as an integral part of worship, as a stimulus for manual workers, as a form of entertainment, as a healing aid, as a talisman to lead soldiers into battle and as a sonic backdrop to our civil ceremonies.

A musical composition entails the organization of three primary elements: *melody*, *harmony* and *rhythm*. Melody is the tune of a piece of music – the part you might hum or whistle along to. Harmony entails a simultaneous combination of tones and acts to shape the mood of the music, to make you feel happy, sad, edgy or romantic, through the meshing of sounds. Rhythm concerns the speed of music and the way in which it is accented; essentially, rhythm is the element of music that prompts a physical response in the listener. Wilson and Davey (2002, p. 177) observed that, even when people sit motionless, 'it is often very difficult to suppress the natural urge to tap the feet or strum the fingers along with the beat of the music'. Moreover, musical rhythm relates to the various periodicities of the human functioning, such as respiration, heart beat and walking (Bonny, 1987).

During the last two decades, music has become almost ubiquitous in venues associated with physical exercise, sports training or competition. It is played in gymnasiums, athletic stadiums and even through underwater speakers in swimming pools. Major sporting events have sprung up with music at their core, such as the Run to the Beat series of musical half-marathons (see Karageorghis, 2014). Is such music played in order to promote greater work output, or does it simply make participation in activities such as long-distance running a little more pleasurable? If music does indeed increase work output or enjoyment of an activity, how can we go about maximizing such benefits? These are questions that will be addressed in this chapter, using, in part, the author's own research findings, conceptual frameworks and examples of applied practice.

History, tradition and mythology

During the twentieth century, the Olympic Games helped to formalize the association between music and athletic endeavour that culminated in such a memorable marriage of music and sport at the London 2012 Olympiad. Indeed, the modern Olympics would not possess the majesty and global impact they do without the culturally unifying

FIGURE 12.1 As illustrated by Team GB cyclists Jessica Varnish (left) and Victoria
Pendleton, the London 2012 Olympics represented a watershed moment
for the relationship between music and athletic endeavour

Source: Photo © Stefano Rellandini/Reuters/Corbis

and signifying force of music. Music is woven into several Olympic events, such as
rhythmic gymnastics and synchronized swimming. Musical performances are integral
to the opening and closing ceremonies of the Games. One of the most spectacular
examples of this phenomenon, from the closing ceremony of the London 2012
Olympic Games – billed as *A Symphony of British Music* – entailed the late Freddie
Mercury being projected onto large screens to perform a stirring call-and-response
routine with the 80,000-strong crowd and athletes on the infield. Traditionally, the
national anthem of the winning athlete is played at the medal ceremony for each event,
often reducing seasoned competitors to tears as the emotion associated with the
occasion overwhelms them.

Music and sport seem to go hand in hand at modern-day sporting events, with
professional DJs often hired to make appropriate selections to rouse the players or
engage the crowd. It is rare not to hear music blaring out of soccer stadiums, rugby
grounds and basketball arenas, wherever you might find yourself in the world. Most
professional teams have adopted their own anthems or signature tunes. For example,
at West Ham United FC, it's the classic 'I'm Forever Blowing Bubbles', and the Kop
at Liverpool FC and Celtic Park stadium in Glasgow reverberate to the anthemic
'You'll Never Walk Alone', which was popularized by Gerry and the Pacemakers in
the 1960s.

'Swing Low, Sweet Chariot'

The use of anthemic chanting that reverberates around a rugby stadium can be a tremendous source of inspiration to the players. Most great teams have a signature chant or song. For example, England rugby fans sing the rousing negro spiritual 'Swing Low, Sweet Chariot'. This was spontaneously adopted in March 1988 during a game against Ireland, when Chris Oti, a black player, scored a sensational hat-trick for England. The recital of this hymn, whether in the stands or the players' dressing room, serves to promote feelings of patriotism, unity and pride.

Through a cursory examination of popular myth and folklore, one might reach the conclusion that music has a profound influence on the human psyche. The Pied Piper of Hamlin took revenge on the town's dishonourable officials by entrancing all of the children with his intoxicating melodies. In Homer's *Odyssey*, Odysseus told of the songs of sirens, creatures who were half woman and half bird, that cast a spell on sailors, whose ships were subsequently dashed against the rocks. He insisted that wax be placed in the ears of each of his men, and he himself was tied to the mast of his ship so as not to succumb to the sirens' songs. In the Old Testament, David's harp playing enabled King Saul to overcome a deep state of depression, and David went on to become the second king of Israel. In more recent history, the 12-bar blues emerged through the work songs of enslaved African Americans. Their work movements were made smoother and more efficient by the directing force of group singing (Farnsworth, 1969). Such songs also gave the slaves hope of a future free of oppression and exploitation.

The principal effects of music

In the context of exercise and sport, the extant literature has primarily explored the *psychological, psychophysical, psychophysiological* and *ergogenic* effects of music. *Psychological* effects entail the impact music has on mood, emotion, affect (feelings of pleasure or displeasure), cognition (thought processes) and behaviour. The *psychophysical* effects of music concern the psychological perception of one's physical state – a branch of psychology known as *psychophysics*. In the context of music and physical activity, the measure that is most often used in this regard is that of rating of perceived exertion (RPE; e.g. Edworthy and Waring, 2006; Bacon *et al.*, 2012; Hutchinson and Karageorghis, 2013; Lim *et al.*, 2014). *Psychophysiological* effects of music have to do with the impact of music on physiological functioning: typical dependent measures in experimental work include heart rate (HR), oxygen uptake and exercise lactate. Music has an *ergogenic* effect when it enhances work output or engenders higher than expected power output, endurance or productivity.

MUSIC IN EXERCISE AND SPORT: PAST CONCEPTUAL APPROACHES

Scientific studies into the effects of music in exercise and sport contexts have reported more modest reactions than those documented in mythology. Nonetheless, it has been demonstrated that music has the potential to make a meaningful difference to performance in the hotbed of competition, where skills and abilities are often closely matched. Moreover, music can have a profound effect on exercise performance and could play a major role as part of the solution to the nation's growing inactivity and obesity problem (Karageorghis et al., 2009; Karageorghis and Priest, 2012a, 2012b). The notion of *joint action*, which entails coordinated and synchronized actions performed by a number of people who share common goals (Sebanz et al., 2006), has begun to garner considerable interest in the psychomusicology literature (e.g. Kirschner and Tomasello, 2010; Van Dyck et al., 2013). This notion underlies the exercise-to-music class phenomenon, first witnessed in the USA in the 1970s, and now popular in a variety of formats throughout the world (e.g. aqua aerobics, step aerobics, Boxercise, Zumba, etc.).

Much of the early experimental work in this area was blighted by an atheoretical approach that yielded largely equivocal findings (e.g. Uppal and Datta, 1990; Copeland and Franks, 1991; Dorney et al., 1992). The review of Karageorghis and Terry (1997) highlighted several methodological weaknesses that may have accounted for such findings and set the scene for future conceptual developments. The main weaknesses evident in past research were: (a) the failure to consider the sociocultural background of experimental participants; (b) the imprecise approach to musical selection or failure to report the music played; (c) inconsistencies regarding the temporal factors, such as the duration of music exposure and when it was played relative to the experimental task; (d) inaccurate use of musical terminology by exercise and sport researchers; and (e) the use of performance measures that were either inappropriate or difficult to control.

In nearly two decades since the review of Karageorghis and Terry (1997), there has been a marked increase in the number of studies examining the effects of music in exercise and sport. This is evidenced by the small number of related studies ($k = 13$) cited in Karageorghis and Terry's review, which covered research conducted over the 25-year period since the review of Lucaccini and Kreit (1972). In the subsequent 17-year period, at least 100 related studies have been published. As well as an increase in the quantity of studies, there has also been a marked increase in the quality. This is corroborated by the attention researchers have given to the selection of music programmes, greater internal validity in the design of experimental studies, power analyses to determine appropriate sample sizes, more sophisticated analytical methods, better interpretation of findings and publications in higher-impact journals. The present chapter will consider conceptual advances and research conducted in the period since the 1997 review paper, with a primary focus on the last 6 years (2008–14).

The first conceptual model (1999)

To address the paucity of theory, the author and his collaborators published a number of conceptual frameworks over the last two decades. The original conceptual framework for predicting psychophysical effects of asynchronous (background) music in exercise and sport (Karageorghis *et al.*, 1999) held that four factors contribute to the motivational qualities of a piece of music – rhythm response, musicality, cultural impact and association. These factors emerged from an earlier review (Karageorghis and Terry, 1997) and were subject to empirical examination using both exploratory and confirmatory factor analyses (Karageorghis *et al.*, 1999).

Rhythm response relates to innate human responses to musical rhythm, especially tempo, which is the speed of music as measured in beats per minute (bpm). Musicality refers to pitch-related elements such as melody and harmony. Cultural impact concerns the pervasiveness of music within society or a particular subcultural group; exposure to music increases familiarity, which has an important role in terms of aesthetic response. Finally, association pertains to the extra-musical associations that music may evoke in the listener, such as those linking 'Eye Of The Tiger' with the feats of the fictional boxer Rocky Balboa in the *Rocky* film series. Such associations are built up by repetition and powerful images in which cinema, television, radio and social media play an important role.

In the 1999 model, these factors are subgrouped into *internal factors* (rhythm response and musicality) that concern aspects of the musical composition, and *external factors* (cultural impact and association) that relate to how music is interpreted by the listener. The factors and their grouping are presented hierarchically, representing a prediction that the internal factors are more salient in determining one's response to music in an exercise or sport context. This proposition has been supported by a number of independent researchers (e.g. Atkinson *et al.*, 2004; Crust, 2008; Hutchinson *et al.*, 2011). The implication is that, when one is choosing music for a group with different musical experiences, it is possible to select tracks with motivational properties, as careful attention can be given to the internal factors. The relationship between internal and external factors, the motivational qualities of music and potential benefits can be seen in Figure 12.2.

The *asynchronous* use of music occurs when there is no conscious synchronization between one's movement and the rhythmical qualities of music (Karageorghis and Terry, 1997). For this reason, asynchronous music has often been described in the literature

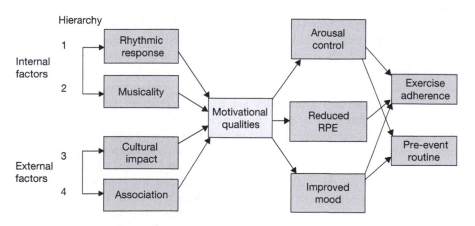

FIGURE 12.2 Conceptual framework for the prediction of responses to motivational asynchronous music in exercise and sport

Source: Adapted with permission from Karageorghis *et al.*, 1999

as *background* music (e.g. Copeland and Franks, 1991; Kämpfe *et al.*, 2011), although it is not *necessarily* playing 'in the background'. On occasion, the playing of asynchronous music can result in synchronous movement that does not arise from conscious effort. For example, the Brazilian football team has a large contingent of percussion players among its supporters. Many observers have noted that the Brazilian style of play often appears to emulate the lilting swing of the samba, a rhythm synonymous with Brazilian culture. Indeed, the national team is commonly referred to as the 'Samba Boys'.

Researchers have comprehensively investigated the psychological, psychophysical, psychophysiological and ergogenic effects of asynchronous music (e.g. Yamashita *et al.*, 2006; Birnbaum *et al.*, 2009; Karageorghis *et al.*, 2013). The main benefit of listening to asynchronous music is that it can act as a stimulant or sedative to influence arousal levels. In general terms, loud, upbeat music will function as a stimulant (increases arousal), whereas soft, slow music will function as a sedative (reduces arousal). Music can reduce RPE, but only during submaximal work intensities, because, during high-intensity activity, physiological cues predominate attention, and so music has a negligible effect on RPE (Rejeski, 1985; Tenenbaum, 2001; Ekkekakis, 2003). Music can enhance positive affective states and reduce negative affective states (Karageorghis *et al.*, 2009; Hutchinson *et al.*, 2011; Karageorghis and Jones, 2014). In turn, these benefits can impact upon adherence to exercise through making the exercise experience more pleasurable, or be used as part of a pre-event routine in sport to engender an optimal mindset (arousal control and improved mood; cf. Thelwell, this edition).

Motivational and oudeterous music

Alongside their conceptual framework, Karageorghis *et al.* (1999) developed an associated measure of the motivational qualities of music known as the Brunel Music Rating Inventory (BMRI). The main characteristics of *motivational music* are that it has a fast tempo (> 120 bpm) and strong rhythm, and it increases energy and induces bodily action. Karageorghis *et al.* also operationalized the term *oudeterous music* to refer to music that is neither motivating nor demotivating. This was necessary owing to the confusion that might have ensued through using the term *neutral music*, which has connotations that transcend the motivational qualities of music (cf. neutral colours, neutral emotions, neutral point of view, etc.). Many subsequent studies used the BMRI and its derivatives to rate objectively the motivational qualities of music used in experimental conditions (e.g. Lin and Lu, 2013; Karageorghis and Jones, 2014; Lim *et al.*, 2014).

Through their research into, and application of, the BMRI, Karageorghis and his collaborators found certain limitations in terms of its psychometric properties and applicability in exercise and sport. This led them to redesign and revalidate the instrument (Karageorghis *et al.*, 2006a). The process began with an extensive qualitative appraisal of the scale by exercise participants using an interview protocol. The results of this analysis contributed to a new item pool, and each of these items was structured to refer to an *action*, a *time*, a *context* and a *target* (cf. Azjen and Fishbein, 1977). The action concerned motivation, the time reference was *during* exercise, the context was exercise, and the target was a property of the music such as melody or tempo. Hence, the generic form of each item was: 'The *property* [e.g. melody] of this music would motivate me during exercise'. For the purposes of this chapter, there is a slightly modified version of the BMRI-2 (the BMRI-3) included, which can be used to rate the motivational qualities of music for both exercise and sport contexts: see Activity Box 12.1.

ACTIVITY 12.1

The BMRI-3

This questionnaire is designed to assess the extent to which the piece of music you are about to hear would motivate you during [*insert activity here*]. For our purposes, the word 'motivate' means music that would make you want to either pursue [*insert activity here*] with greater intensity or to stick at it for longer, or both. As you listen to the piece of music, indicate the extent of your agreement with the six statements listed below by circling *one* of the numbers to the right of each statement. You should provide an honest response to each statement. Give the response that *best* represents your opinion, and avoid dwelling for too long on any single statement.

	Strongly disagree		In-between			Strongly agree	
1 The rhythm of this music would motivate me during [*insert activity here*]	1	2	3	4	5	6	7
2 The style of this music (e.g. rock, dance, jazz, hip-hop, etc.) would motivate me during [*insert activity here*]	1	2	3	4	5	6	7
3 The melody (tune) of this music would motivate me during [*insert activity here*]	1	2	3	4	5	6	7
4 The tempo (speed) of this music would motivate me during [*insert activity here*]	1	2	3	4	5	6	7
5 The sound of the instruments used (e.g. guitar, synthesizer, saxophone, etc.) would motivate me during [*insert activity here*]	1	2	3	4	5	6	7
6 The beat of this music would motivate me during [*insert activity here*]	1	2	3	4	5	6	7

BMRI-3 scoring instructions

Add the items for a score between 6 and 42. A score in the range of 36–42 indicates high motivational qualities in the piece of music; a score in the range of 24–35 indicates moderate motivational qualities; and a score below 24 indicates that the track lacks motivational qualities.

A cautionary note on use of the BMRI-3

The authors of the BMRI-2 indicated that there are limitations in rating the multitudinous facets of the musical response using solely a psychometric-type approach. Some aspects of aesthetic experience, such as personal meaning and association, transcend scientific evaluation; therefore, to elicit optimum selection of music in exercise and sport settings, it may be necessary to use the BMRI-3 in tandem with qualitative methods. The BMRI-3 can be used as a wide filter to identify music pieces that can then be considered on additional grounds, such as the optimal tempo for a given exercise/training intensity, extra-musical associations and lyrical content. Karageorghis *et al.* (2006a, p. 907) presented a framework of criteria for music selection that you may wish to refer to.

The second conceptual model (2006)

Terry and Karageorghis (2006) further developed the conceptual framework, primarily by postulating an extended list of benefits that became evident through empirical work that was published during the period 1999–2006. The full set of benefits that they

FIGURE 12.3 Assessing the motivational qualities of music

Source: Photograph courtesy of Brunel University London photographer, Sally Trussler

---

Football's coming home

When England football fans hear the chant 'It's coming home, football's coming home', from the song 'Three Lions', performed by popular TV comedians Baddiel and Skinner, they immediately think of the 1996 European Football Championships, hosted by England, and are reminded of the sense of optimism and expectation that surrounded this event. The lyrics alluded to the fact that England, the spiritual home of football, had not won a major championship since the World Cup it hosted in 1966. Unfortunately, it wasn't to be for England on this occasion. However, the catchy refrain served to bridge the gap between a mere soccer tournament and a stage for the nation's hopes and dreams.

Listen to the track on YouTube,[1] close your eyes and contemplate the imagery that it conjures up.

---

identified were as follows: (a) increased pleasant moods and reduced unpleasant moods, (b) pre-event activation or relaxation, (c) dissociation from unpleasant feelings such as pain and fatigue, (d) reduced RPE, (e) increased work output through audio–motor synchronization of musical tempo with movement, (f) enhanced acquisition of motor skills when rhythm or association is matched with required movement patterns, (g) increased likelihood of athletes/exercisers achieving flow states and (h) enhanced performance levels via combinations of the above mechanisms. These benefits, in tandem with findings that have entered the public domain over the last decade, are embraced in the new theoretical model that is presented later and forms the focal point of this chapter.

In the brief review of literature that follows, the material is organized in accordance with the time period when researchers introduced music in relation to an exercise- or sport-related task: *pre-task*, *in-task* and *post-task*.

PRE-TASK MUSIC

A small number of studies have investigated music use as a means by which to manipulate exercisers' or athletes' mindset prior to physical performance. Most often, such studies centre on the stimulative or sedative qualities of music and how they might enhance or impair subsequent motor performance (e.g. Eliakim *et al.*, 2007; Chtourou *et al.*, 2012). Collectively, such studies have shown that stimulative music can increase psychomotor arousal, motivational imagery and the incidence of both positive self-talk and flow (e.g. Bishop *et al.*, 2007, 2013; Pain *et al.*, 2011). Music can also be used effectively in manipulating emotional states that bear influence on performance. For example, Bishop *et al.* (2009) demonstrated that musically induced emotions influenced athletes' subsequent choice reaction time (CRT) performance. Faster music tempi elicited pleasanter and more aroused emotional states in fifty-four young tennis players, and higher music intensity yielded both higher levels of arousal and faster subsequent CRT performance.

Olympic 800-metre finalist Andrew Osagie

Andrew Osagie, from Harlow in Essex, is one of the finest British middle-distance runners of his generation. In London 2012, he made the 800-metre final – the only male Team GB representative to reach a middle-distance final at those Games. His time of 1:43.77 minutes, a new lifetime best, would have won him the gold medal at the three preceding Olympic Games. During the 2013 track season, a song by the US rap trio Migos caught Osagie's ear. The title was 'Versace', but all the track star could hear in the track was a long chorus of 'Osagie, Osagie, Osagie, Osagie'. The near homophone gave Osagie a psychological boost, and so the track became a staple part of his pre-event routine. After competing at the 2013 IAAF World Championships in Moscow, where he came fifth, Osagie told the press, 'Everyone was walking past me going "Osagie, Osagie, Osagie, Osagie" which was a bit different!'

Listen to the track on YouTube to hear the famous 'Osagie' chorus.[2]

Both Yamamoto *et al.* (2003) and Eliakim *et al.* (2007) investigated the effects of pre-task stimulative music on maximal cycle sprinting on a stationary bike. Yamamoto *et al.*'s participants heard either slow or fast music for 20 minutes before completing the task. Neither condition influenced performance, which was measured in terms of power output. The music did, however, exert an influence on the neurotransmitter norepinephrine, which is known to play a pronounced role in the fight–or–flight response. The Japanese researchers reasoned that the slower music lowered arousal during the listening period, whereas the faster music elevated it. By way of contrast, Eliakim and his co-workers employed only a stimulative music condition that did not lead to an ergogenic effect. Nonetheless, the music did raise HR measured immediately before the task, which indicates an elevation in physiological arousal.

Although the physiological effects reported in the aforementioned studies, and others like them, are integral to preparing the body for a physical task, such as a bout of exercise, there is some inconsistency pertaining to subsequent effects on motor performance. The inconsistency arises most often from a lack of assessment pertaining to what participants' optimal level of activation is for a given motor task (e.g. Eliakim *et al.*, 2007). Thus, the protocols that researchers have employed are predicated on a series of assumptions relating to what constitutes optimal activation for a given task (e.g. that a highly motoric task requires high levels of activation), without due consideration for personal factors, such as personality or attentional style. The new model, which is presented later in this chapter, addresses this potential limitation by placing considerable emphasis on the moderating influence of a range of personal factors in the music–performance relationship.

Summary of findings relating to pre-task music

Collectively, research has shown that pre-task music can be used to: (a) manipulate emotional states and enhance subsequent motor performance through its arousal control qualities, (b) facilitate task-relevant imagery, (c) promote flow, and (d) enhance perceptions of self-confidence. There is a paucity of research in this area, creating considerable scope for examination of music's role in priming individuals for bouts of exercise or eliciting optimal pre-performance states in athletes.

IN-TASK MUSIC

Asynchronous music

The asynchronous application of music has, by a wide margin, attracted the most research interest, with some ninety published studies to date. Researchers have used in-task music to stimulate participants during short bouts of high-intensity exercise and demonstrated that they endure longer or work harder in the presence of music, when compared with control (e.g. Crust and Clough, 2006; Rendi et al., 2008; Razon et al., 2009; Hutchinson et al., 2011; Tate et al., 2012; Karageorghis et al., 2013).

Uniquely in the exercise domain, Crust and Clough (2006) assessed whether personality traits had a role in moderating responses to music. Their findings indicated that there were associations between trait liveliness and rhythm response, and between trait sensitivity and musicality response (i.e. response to the melodic and harmonic properties of music; cf. Karageorghis et al., 1999). In studies of very high-intensity exercise that give inadequate attention to music selection, music has proven ineffectual in terms of increasing work output (e.g. maximal repetitions using circuit-type exercises; Doiron et al., 1999). In some of the studies that reported performance increases, there were concomitant positive influences on affect and/or self-reported task motivation (e.g. Hutchinson et al., 2011; Karageorghis et al., 2013).

The majority of studies using low-to-moderate-intensity endurance tasks have shown marked improvements in endurance associated with music use (e.g. Elliott et al., 2004; Yamashita et al., 2006; Lane et al., 2011). Moreover, both preferred (e.g. Yamashita et al., 2006) and arbitrarily selected (e.g. Szmedra and Bacharach, 1998) music reduces perceived exertion, although preferred/motivational music has been shown to engender more positive affective states (e.g. Shaulov and Lufi, 2009; Hutchinson and Karageorghis, 2013). Findings pertaining to RPE generally support the posits of Rejeski's (1985) parallel processing model, which holds that, as exercise intensity increases, physiological cues predominate attentional processes. Notably, the benefits of music to endurance and perceived exertion appear to be magnified when it is delivered in tandem with video (e.g. Barwood et al., 2009).

A number of studies have examined the effects of music on high-intensity endurance tasks (e.g. Nakamura et al., 2010; Tate et al., 2012; Dyer and McKune, 2013; Hutchinson and Karageorghis, 2013; Karageorghis et al., 2013). The intensity of human effort is often set at a percentage of maximal oxygen uptake, or $\dot{V}O_2$ max as it is otherwise known; this represents the maximal volume of oxygen that the body is able to utilize per kilogram of body weight per minute. It appears that, up to approximately 75 per cent of maximal oxygen uptake, music reduces perceived exertion, but its effects are sharply diminished beyond this intensity (e.g. Tenenbaum et al., 2004; Hutchinson and Karageorghis, 2013). Despite the consistent finding that even well-selected music does not reduce perceived exertion at very high intensities, it does appear to positively

APPLYING THE SCIENCE 12.1

Antoinette, the triathlete

Antoinette is an outstanding cyclist and runner, but a relatively weak swimmer. This 'chink in her armour' has prevented her from enjoying international success in her sport. She makes a concerted effort to improve by swimming at least 15 miles in training each week. This is often a lonely and physically challenging task, with little variation. Her coach aims to make Antoinette a more competent swimmer. To achieve this, Antoinette needs to relax and avoid wasting energy through excessive muscular tension. To aid her improvement, she uses a specially designed waterproof MP3 player in her swimming cap.[3] Antoinette listens to soulful ballads and soft, relaxing music. In particular, she enjoys listening to the indie rock track 'What The Water Gave Me', by Florence and the Machine. She associates the ebb and flow of the music with the graceful, submarine movements that she is striving to maintain. The harmonies within the music create a positive mood, and the four-beat rhythm and moderate tempo help her to relax and maintain an efficient and regular stroke. The music also becomes a focus on long-distance swims and distracts her from the negative bodily sensations associated with fatigue. In fact, the effects of the track's vocal content can be quite hypnotic, and, after a while, she feels as though she is gliding effortlessly through the water.

FIGURE 12.4 The Speedo Aquabeat 2.0 Underwater MP3 player

Source: Philip North-Coombes.[4] Reproduced with permission

influence affective states (e.g. Tenenbaum *et al.*, 2004; Hutchinson *et al.*, 2011; Hutchinson and Karageorghis, 2013; Karageorghis and Jones, 2014). In terms of performance measures, music use is associated with prolonging the onset of volitional exhaustion in ergometer trials (e.g. Atkinson *et al.*, 2004; Bharani *et al.*, 2004), although the evidence is equivocal, with some of the studies employing high–intensity tasks showing no performance benefits (e.g. Crust, 2004; Atan, 2013; Hagen *et al.*, 2013).

There is quantitative and qualitative evidence to suggest that foreknowledge of which segment of an exercise bout will be accompanied by music influences participants' pacing strategy (Priest and Karageorghis, 2008; Lim *et al.*, 2009; Lima–Silva *et al.*, 2012). Even the anticipation of music can serve a *priming* or stimulating function, and this sense of anticipation can also apply to preferred segments of musical works (e.g. a chorus). Moreover, physically untrained participants appear to derive greater benefit from music than trained participants, regardless of the exercise intensity (e.g. Brownley *et al.*, 1995; Mohammadzadeh *et al.*, 2008). In particular, music has a more potent effect on perceived exertion and affective valence among the untrained or recreationally active (e.g. Hutchinson *et al.*, 2011).

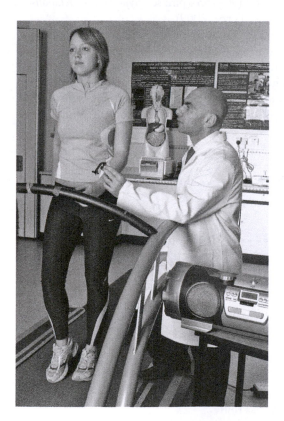

FIGURE 12.5 Assessing tempo preference at different exercise intensities

Source: Photograph courtesy of Brunel University London photographer, Sally Trussler

There is a clear trend to indicate that, when exercise tasks are self-paced, both performance and psychological states appear to be enhanced by the presence of asynchronous music (e.g. Barwood *et al.*, 2009; Waterhouse *et al.*, 2010; Fritz *et al.*, 2013; Karageorghis *et al.*, 2013). Another trend in the literature pertains to the relationship between heart rate and preference for music tempo during exercise. In contrast to previous suggestions (e.g. Iwanaga, 1995), the relationship between exercise heart rate and music tempo preference has been shown to take a nonlinear trajectory (Karageorghis *et al.*, 2006b, 2008, 2011).

Karageorghis *et al.* (2011) examined preference for music tempo over a wide range of exercise intensities, and the exercise heart rate–music tempo preference relationship that they observed exhibited a linear trendline at lower exercise intensities of 40–50 per cent maximal heart rate reserve (max HRR); in simple terms, increases in exercise intensity were matched by increasing preferences for faster music. At moderate intensities (60–70 per cent max HRR), a plateau was observed whereby further elevations in HR were not accompanied by preferences for faster music. Thereafter, a slight dip or attenuation in preference for faster music was observed at very high intensities (> 80 per cent max HRR; see the *actual relationship* trendline in Figure 12.6). Notably, exercise participants reported preferences for a much narrower band of tempi (125–40 bpm) than was previously expected (90–155 bpm; see *hypothesized relationship* trendline in Figure 12.6; Karageorghis and Terry, 2009).

The relationship exhibited in Figure 12.6 can only be applied to cycle ergometry, given that, when its stability was tested using a different exercise modality (treadmill running), it was found to be unstable (Karageorghis and Jones, 2014). This latest study in the series was bolstered by the inclusion of psychological outcome variables (e.g. state attention and affective valence) and post-experiment interviews. Results did not support the expected cubic relationship (two points of inflection on the plotted line),

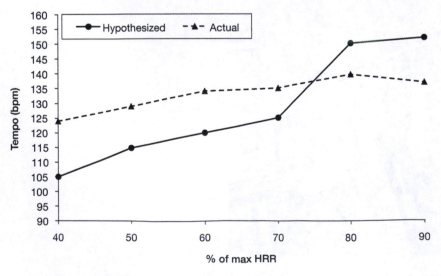

FIGURE 12.6 Superimposition of hypothesized and actual relationship between exercise heart rate and preference for music tempo

but rather a quadratic one (with one point of inflection), and there was a weak association between the optimal choice of music tempo and positive psychological outcomes. Moreover, the range of preferred tempi for treadmill exercise (123–31 bpm) appeared to be even narrower than that for cycle ergometry (125–40 bpm).

Should the reader wish to find out the tempo of any given piece of music, this detail can often be located online: there are an increasing number of websites dedicated to presenting various characteristics of music, including tempo. The use of Google search terms such as 'music tempo list' or 'DJ music bpm' returns dozens of helpful websites.[5] Music platforms such as iTunes are also becoming capable of adding bpm information; although the algorithms they use are not entirely foolproof, they work for most popular selections. Finally, there are phone apps such as Audioshift that not only calculate tempo but can alter it without affecting pitch (how high or low the music sounds), so that you can manage the speed of your music as would a professional DJ.

Table 12.1 shows the tempi of a range of music selections that have proved popular in the domain of exercise and sport. There is also Activity Box 12.2, which encourages you to create a music programme to accompany a typical exercise or training session. You might use the Internet sites presented above to complete this exercise.

Szabo et al. (1999) found that a switch from slow- to fast-tempo music yielded an ergogenic effect during cycle ergometry. The practical implication of this finding is that a change of music tempo from slow to fast may enhance participants' motivation and work output, especially when work level plateaus or in the latter stages of an exercise bout. Similarly, Atkinson et al. (2004) indicated that the careful application of asynchronous music during a simulated 10-km cycle time trial could be used to regulate work output. The music was particularly effective in the early stages of the trial, when perceived exertion was relatively low. Using the BMRI to rate the motivational qualities of accompanying music, participants supported the prediction that rhythmic components of music contribute more to its motivational qualities than melodic or harmonic components (Karageorghis et al., 1999).

Synchronous music

People exhibit a strong tendency to respond to the rhythmical qualities of music. This tendency sometimes results in synchronization between the tempo or speed of music and an exercise participant's or athlete's movements. When movement is consciously performed in time with music, then the music is said to be used *synchronously*. Scientists also commonly use the term *auditory–motor synchronization* in reference to this phenomenon, and there is emerging evidence to demonstrate the degree to which auditory cues can enhance movement consistency (e.g. Bood et al., 2013).

Synchronous music is used in sports such as figure skating, rhythmic gymnastics and dance aerobics contests. Reviewers have explained the synchronization between musical tempo and human movement in terms of the human predisposition to respond to the rhythmical qualities of music (Karageorghis and Terry, 1997; Large, 2000). Ostensibly, musical rhythm can replicate natural movement-based rhythms. Over the last decade, an increasing number of studies have focused on the application of synchronous music (e.g. Simpson and Karageorghis, 2006; Bacon et al., 2012; Terry et al., 2012; Bood et al., 2013).

TABLE 12.1 Music selections widely used in exercise and sport contexts

Track title	Artist(s)	Tempo (bpm)	Style	Length (mins)
'Chariots Of Fire'	Vangelis	62	New age	3:26
'We Are The Champions'	Queen	64	Rock	3:00
'Fix You'	Coldplay	70	Pop/rock	3:46
'Gotta Get Thru This'	Daniel Beddingfield	70	Pop/R&B	4:31
'Roar'	Katy Perry	92	Pop/rock	3:44
'Fancy'	Iggy Azalea, ft Charli XCX	95	Electro hop	3:19
'Mas Que Nada'	Sergio Mendes, ft Black Eyed Peas	102	Pop/hip hop	4:23
'Ghost'	Ella Henderson	105	Pop	3:36
'Gettin' Jiggy Wit It'	Will Smith	108	Hip hop	3:51
'Yeah Yeah'	Willy Moon	108	Alternative hip hop	2:44
'The Monster'	Eminem, ft Rihanna	110	Hip hop	4:10
'The Power'	Snap!	112	Dance/hip hop	4:05
'Everybody Dance Now (Gonna Make You Sweat)'	C & C Music Factory	113	Dance	4:10
'Uptown Funk'	Mark Ronson, ft Bruno Mars	115	Funk	4:29
'Love Never Felt So Good'	Michael Jackson and Justin Timberlake	117	Disco	4:05
'Cheerleader' (Felix Jaehn remix)	OMI	118	Dancehall	3:00
'Sing'	Ed Sheeran	120	Pop	3:55
'Rather Be'	Clean Bandit, ft Jess Glynne	121	House	3:49
'Hideaway'	Kiesza	123	Dance/electronic	4:11
'Need U 100%'	Duke Dumont, ft A*M*E	124	House	3:11
'What About Us'	The Saturdays, ft Sean Paul	124	Electropop	3:41

Song	Artist	BPM	Genre	Time
'La La La'	Naughty Boy, ft Sam Smith	125	UK garage	3:41
'Get Ready For This'	2 Unlimited	125	Dance	3:21
'Stronger'	Clean Bandit	125	Dance	3:41
'Radioactive'	Rita Ora	126	Dance	4:11
'Get Down'	Groove Armada, ft Stush and Red Rat	127	Dance/UK garage	3:28
'Love Me'	Stooshe, ft Travie McCoy	128	R&B	3:05
'Feel My Rhythm'	Viralites	128	Electro dance	3:12
'Moves Like Jagger'	Maroon 5, ft Christina Aguilera	128	Dance/pop	3:22
'Let It Roll'	Flo Rida	128	Hip house	3:14
'Wake Me Up'	Avicii	128	Electro dance	4:08
'Wild'	Jessie J, ft Dizzee Rascal & Big Sean	129	Dance/pop	3:55
'Sexy And I Know It'	LMFAO	130	Hip house	3:19
'Play Hard'	David Guetta, ft Ne-Yo & Akon	130	Electro dance	3:21
'All About That Bass'	Meghan Trainor	134	Pop	3:08
'Jump Around'	House of Pain	134	Hip hop	3:22
'Sandstorm'	Da Rude	135	Dance	5:34
'Feel This Moment'	Pitbull, ft Christina Aguilera	136	Dance/Pop	3:50
'Firestarter'	Prodigy	136	Dance	3:54
'Make U Bounce'	DJ Fresh vs TC	140	Dance	3:11
'Beat It'	Michael Jackson	140	Rock	4:18
'Applause'	Lady Gaga	140	Dance/pop	3:33
'Ace Of Spades'	Motörhead	142	Rock/metal	3:45
'Can't Hold Us'	Macklemore & Ryan Lewis, ft Ray Dalton	146	Alternative hip hop	4:18
'Bang Bang'	Jessie J, Ariana Grande & Nicki Minaj	150	Pop	3:19

ACTIVITY 12.2

An example of how musical selections can be moulded around the components of a typical training session

TABLE 12.2 Musical selections to accompany a workout

Workout component	Title	Artist(s)	Tempo (bpm)
Mental preparation	'Rolling In The Deep'	Adele	101
Warm-up activity	'Move'	Little Mix	121
Stretching	'Breathe, Stretch, Shake'	Ma$e, ft P Diddy	104
Strength component	'Titanium'	David Guetta, ft Sia	125
Endurance component	'Sweat'	Snoop Dogg vs David Guetta	130
Warm-down activity	'Wide Awake'	Katy Perry	82

Now prepare your own version of the above table and use the music programme to give your training sessions a boost.

Musical selections to accompany a workout

Workout component	Title	Artist(s)	Tempo (bpm)
Mental preparation			
Warm-up activity			
Stretching			
Strength component			
Endurance component			
Warm-down activity			

Haile impressive

A classic example of synchronous music having an ergogenic effect came at an athletics invitation meeting at Birmingham's National Indoor Arena in February 1998. The meeting showcased the talents of legendary Ethiopian distance runner Haile Gebrselassie, who broke Eamonn Coughlan's world indoor record in the 2000 m. Gebrselassie made the unusual request to the meeting organizers for his favourite pop song – 'Scatman' by Scatman John – to be played during the race. He took off from the gun at a furious pace, and the pacemakers were soon left trailing in his wake. The Ethiopian contingent in the crowd went wild, their passions fuelled by the pulsating rhythm of the music. Gebrselassie clipped more than 1 s off the existing record, finishing in a time of 4:52.86. When interviewed by *Athletics Weekly* about the race and his unusual request, he said, 'The music gives me a rhythm that fits in with my record pace'. Gebrselassie had consciously synchronized his stride rate with the music tempo to achieve a world record.

FIGURE 12.7 Haile Gebrselassie is famous for using the power of music to break records

Source: Photo © Thierry Orban/Sygma/Corbis

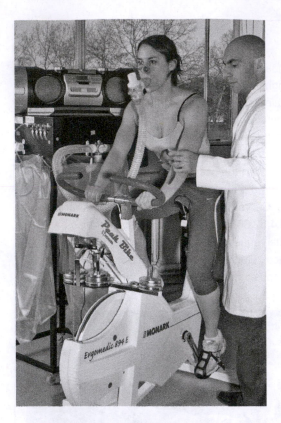

FIGURE 12.8 Assessing oxygen uptake in response to synchronous music

Source: Photograph courtesy of Brunel University London photographer, Sally Trussler

Researchers have consistently shown that synchronous music yields significant ergogenic effects in participants who are not highly trained. Such effects have been demonstrated in bench stepping (Hayakawa *et al.*, 2000), cycle ergometry (Anshel and Marisi, 1978), circuit-type exercises (Karageorghis *et al.*, 2013), callisthenic–type exercises (Uppal and Datta, 1990), treadmill running (Bood *et al.*, 2013) and 400-m track running (Simpson and Karageorghis, 2006). Independent of such research, there has been a wave of commercial activity focused on the development and promotion of walking/running programmes that use synchronous music to enhance fitness and/or performance levels.[6]

One of the earliest studies compared synchronous and asynchronous music using a cycle ergometer endurance task (Anshel and Marisi, 1978). The researchers found that endurance was prolonged by the use of synchronous music, in comparison with asynchronous music and a no–music control condition. In both the non-synchronous conditions, a blinking light was provided with which participants could synchronize their pedalling rate, thus isolating the effect of the music.

It has been proposed that the use of synchronous music elicits a reduction in the metabolic cost of exercise by promoting greater neuromuscular or metabolic efficiency

(Smoll and Schultz, 1978). This proposition was the subject of a study by Bacon *et al.* (2012). Participants performing a submaximal cycle ergometry task were able to maintain a set intensity (60 per cent of their maximal HR) using 7.4 per cent less oxygen when listening to a selection of synchronous music as opposed to music that was asynchronous (slightly slower than the movement tempo).

A follow-up study by Lim *et al.* (2014) examined the degree to which the synchronous application of music moderated the metabolic demands of cycle ergometry at 90 per cent of ventilatory threshold. This threshold represents a shift from moderate-to high-intensity activity, characterized by breathlessness and the production of lactic acid in the working muscles. Lim *et al.*'s physiological data revealed no differences in terms of oxygen uptake between synchronous, asynchronous, auditory metronome and control conditions; however, the task was only 6 minutes in duration, which may have limited the emergence of any efficiency gains. Their findings did show some interesting differences across conditions in the psychological and psychophysical measures. Specifically, affective valence was more positive in the synchronous and asynchronous music conditions, compared with the metronome condition and control, whereas limb discomfort was lower in the synchronous music and metronome conditions when compared with the control.

A similar study (Karageorghis *et al.*, 2009) examined the effects of two experimental conditions, motivational synchronous music and oudeterous synchronous music, and a no-music control, on four dependent measures during treadmill walking at 75 per cent maximal HR: time to exhaustion, RPE, in-task affect and exercise-induced feelings states. The authors hypothesized that the motivational synchronous music condition would yield the most positive outcomes, followed by the oudeterous music condition. It was also expected that RPE during the early stages of the task would be lower with the motivational music condition than with the oudeterous and control conditions. The results indicated that RPE was lowered and in-task affect was enhanced at moderate work intensity (first half of the exercise bout), during the motivational synchronous music condition. This condition also yielded a 14 per cent increase in endurance over a no-music control. Both music conditions yielded more positive outcomes than the no-music control.

Until recently, there had been no research into the effects of synchronous music on the performance of elite athletes, despite the well-documented exploits of Ethiopian distance runner Haile Gebrselassie. This prompted Terry and his co-workers (2012) to embark on a programme of research with triathletes at the Queensland Academy of Sport in Australia. Their findings indicated that the triathletes endured for 19.7 per cent longer when running in synchrony with oudeterous music. However, motivational music produced a very similar result (18.1 per cent). Mood responses and feeling states were more positive with motivational music when compared with either oudeterous music or no music (see Figure 12.9). RPEs were lowest for oudeterous music and highest for the no-music control. In both synchronous music conditions, oxygen consumption was reduced by approximately 1 per cent, and both were associated with better running economy than the no-music control. The degree of benefit that these athletes derived from the synchronous music may be related to the fact that they were tested in relatively sterile laboratory conditions, and so the music provided some relief from the conditions, rather than being influential in absolute terms. For this reason, the findings need to be re-examined in a real-life context, where

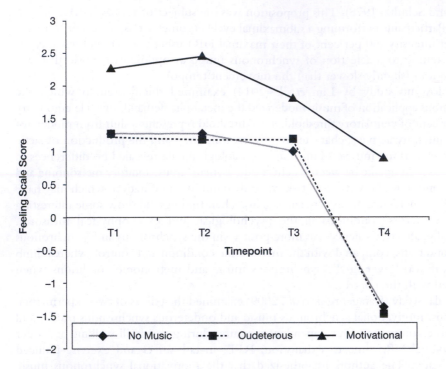

FIGURE 12.9 Feeling Scale scores of elite triathletes under two music conditions and a no-music control condition

Source: Adapted, with permission, from Terry *et al.*, 2012

the observed benefits associated with the musical intervention are likely to be considerably smaller.

Summary of findings relating to in-task music

The main trends emanating from the body of work that has examined in–task music are:

- slow music is inappropriate for exercise or training contexts, unless used solely to limit or reduce the intensity of effort;
- fast-tempo music played during high-intensity activity yields high preference scores and is likely to enhance in-task affect;
- an increase in tempo from slow to fast might engender an ergogenic effect in aerobic endurance activities;
- music played during submaximal exercise reduces RPE by about 10 per cent, but the degree to which this effect is moderated by the motivational qualities of music remains unclear;
- the most sensitive marker of the psychological impact of music appears to be in-task affective valence;

APPLYING THE SCIENCE 12.2

Khalida and the musical pacing method

Khalida is an 800-m runner who has just completed her first season on the European grand prix circuit, following a very successful international career as a junior. While attending her *lycée d'enseignement* (technical school) in Algiers, her training was inconsistent in terms of quality; however, she was able to get by quite comfortably on natural ability. The demands of the grand prix and major championships necessitated a far more structured approach, and she found the transition from the junior to senior ranks very challenging.

While Khalida was growing up in Algeria, she noticed that, on occasions when music was played through the public address system of her local stadium, it made her feel as though she was running on air. Pace judgement was always a problem for Khalida, both in training and competition. Frequently, she would start too fast, but musical accompaniment helped to regulate her stride. Following a consultation with a performance specialist in London, it was suggested that Khalida should apply synchronous music to her interval training – music that would coincide in tempo with her cadence at different running intensities.

Thus, Khalida worked out, using video analysis, that when she was performing 400-m intervals in 60 seconds, she took 200 strides per minute on average. This coincided with musical selections that had a tempo of 100 bpm, as Khalida took two strides to each beat. Appropriate musical selections included the bright dance track 'Crazy In Love' by Beyoncé and the energizing 'Pon De Replay' by Rihanna. Khalida made similar calculations for other common interval distances that she completed in training – 600 m, 800 m, and so on. She used an MP3 player attached to her upper arm to ensure that the audio equipment did not inhibit her smooth style and even adjusted the tempo of some of her favourite tracks, such as 'Beat It' by Michael Jackson.

In competition, the use of music was not permitted, and, therefore, Khalida recalled the musical selection that corresponded with her time goal, and this helped her to pace each race evenly. Also, hearing the music in her mind's ear distracted her from the internal sensations of hard running, while the inspirational lyrics gave her a competitive edge: 'Beat it, no one wants to be defeated'.

- music is, perhaps, less influential on psychological, psychophysical and psycho-physiological responses during very high–intensity activities;
- synchronous music can be applied to aerobic and anaerobic endurance per-formance among exercise participants and athletes with positive psychological, psychophysical and psychophysiological effects; it also yields a meaningful ergogenic effect;

- recent findings indicate that synchronous music applied to submaximal repetitive activity can result in approximately a 7 per cent decrease in oxygen uptake.

POST-TASK MUSIC

To date, only five studies have investigated the post-task application of music. Post-task music is proposed to perform a recuperative role and aid recovery from injury, competition or exercise/training (Terry and Karageorghis, 2011). Recently, two studies by Eliakim and colleagues have examined the influence of motivational music during active recovery from high-intensity training (Eliakim *et al.*, 2012, 2013). In the first study, the music led to superior lactate clearance following exhaustive treadmill exercise, as well as reduced RPE. The second study isolated the effect of rhythm by using a selection of dance tracks (140 bpm), rhythm-only edits of the same tracks and a no-music control. Both experimental conditions expedited recovery relative to control, with the standard dance tracks eliciting the best results overall. The authors did not provide a cogent rationale for the use of such a high-tempo music programme for the purpose of active recovery.

Using a static recovery protocol, Jing and Xudong (2008) applied a sedative instrumental piece to aid the recovery of male students for 15 minutes, following a cycle ergometer trial to a point of volitional exhaustion. Decreases in HR, urinary protein (indicative of post-exercise kidney function) and RPE were greater in the music group compared with a no-music control. Subsequently, Savitha *et al.* (2010) showed that slow music accelerated the haemodynamic (blood pressure and HR) recovery after 5 minutes of intense treadmill running, in comparison with both fast music (17 per cent difference) and a no-music control (32 per cent difference).

Along similar lines, Tan *et al.* (2014) investigated HR recovery and salivary cortisol for a 15-minute period following a 4-minute treadmill protocol that involved walking and running. Given that the experimental task was not particularly demanding in physiological terms (up to 60 per cent of age-predicted maximal HR), it was perhaps unsurprising that relaxing music had no influence on HR recovery. In terms of salivary cortisol, there is a delay of about 20 minutes required to observe a response to a stressful task (Nicolson, 2008), and, therefore, the experiment was of insufficient duration to capture this. The findings of these five studies indicate some initial promise for this line of research and provide tentative evidence that music can enhance both active and static post-exercise recovery.

NEW THEORETICAL MODEL

In this section, a new theoretical model is presented detailing the antecedents, moderators and consequences of music use in exercise and sport. The model incorporates almost all of the key elements that appeared in previous models (e.g. Karageorghis *et al.*, 1999; Terry and Karageorghis, 2006), but takes a far more integrative approach. It provides a blueprint for a series of testable hypotheses to stimulate further research and is intended to inform the music-selection decisions of exercise and sport practitioners.

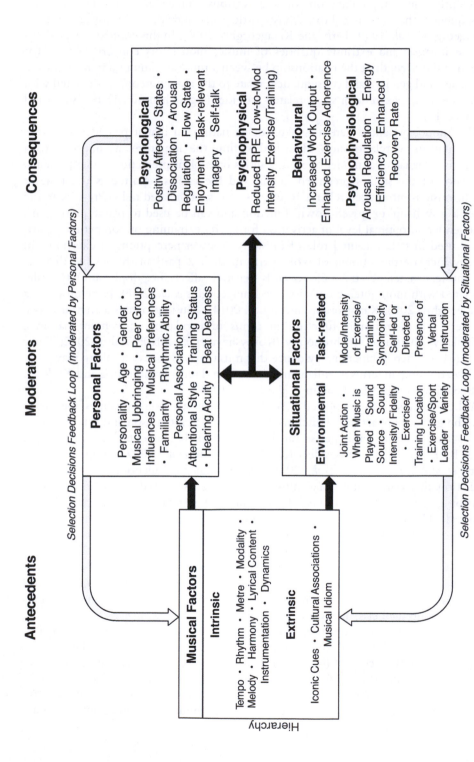

Antecedents

Moderators

Consequences

Selection Decisions Feedback Loop (moderated by Personal Factors)

Selection Decisions Feedback Loop (moderated by Situational Factors)

Musical Factors

Intrinsic

Tempo · Rhythm · Metre · Modality · Melody · Harmony · Lyrical Content · Instrumentation · Dynamics

Extrinsic

Iconic Cues · Cultural Associations · Musical Idiom

Hierarchy

Personal Factors

Personality · Age · Gender · Musical Upbringing · Peer Group Influences · Musical Preferences · Familiarity · Rhythmic Ability · Personal Associations · Attentional Style · Training Status · Hearing Acuity · Beat Deafness

Situational Factors

Task-related

Mode/Intensity of Exercise/ Training · Synchronicity · Self-led or Directed · Presence of Verbal Instruction

Environmental

Joint Action · When Music is Played · Sound Source · Sound Intensity/ Fidelity · Exercise/ Training Location · Exercise/Sport Leader · Variety

Psychological

Positive Affective States · Dissociation · Arousal Regulation · Flow State · Enjoyment · Task-relevant Imagery · Self-talk

Psychophysical

Reduced RPE (Low-to-Mod Intensity Exercise/Training)

Behavioural

Increased Work Output · Enhanced Exercise Adherence

Psychophysiological

Arousal Regulation · Energy Efficiency · Enhanced Recovery Rate

FIGURE 12.10 A theoretical model embracing the antecedents, moderators and consequences of music use in the exercise and sport domain

Redevelopment was needed, as existing models were not thought to provide a sufficiently clear representation of the various antecedents, moderators and consequences that are integral to exercise participants' and athletes' musical responses (Karageorghis *et al.*, 1999; Terry and Karageorghis, 2006). In this context, antecedents are the intrinsic and extrinsic qualities of music, moderators concern factors that influence the strength of the relationship between a musical stimulus and responses to it (e.g. age and gender), and consequences relate to the main outcomes associated with music use during exercise or sport-related activities (e.g. enhanced affective states and lower RPEs).

The model presented herein is heuristic in nature, in that it provides a holistic representation of relationships identified within the literature, as opposed to a mechanistic or factorial model offering a series of explicit predictions. The principal delineator of the studies presented herein and the effects reported is the time at which music is introduced relative to exercise- or sport-related tasks. Pre-task music serves a 'psych-up' or 'psych-down' function and can be used to prime participants or engender an optimal level of activation for exercise/training or competitive sport. When used in task, a central role of music is to lower perceptions of exertion and thereby increase the amount of work performed. It is particularly notable that in-task music can temper the shift towards negative affect (i.e. displeasure) typically associated with more intense exercise (see Karageorghis *et al.*, 2009; Hutchinson and Karageorghis, 2013; Karageorghis and Jones, 2014). Music provides a rhythmic cue that serves a metronomic function in terms of regulating movement patterns, particularly when used synchronously (Kornysheva *et al.*, 2010; Grahn, 2012; Terry *et al.*, 2012). There is emerging evidence that music may also have a role to play post-exercise/training, in terms of enhancing recovery and recuperation (Jing and Xudong, 2008; Savitha *et al.*, 2010; Eliakim *et al.*, 2012, 2013).

Although music that is selected according to its motivational qualities appears to have the greatest impact (e.g. Hutchinson *et al.*, 2011; Hutchinson and Karageorghis, 2013), it is clear that music per se can lead to measurable benefits, both in terms of lower RPE and an ergogenic effect (e.g. Karageorghis *et al.*, 2009; Tate *et al.*, 2012; Terry *et al.*, 2012; Leman *et al.*, 2013). Accordingly, Karageorghis *et al.*'s (1999) prediction that only motivational music is associated with reductions in perceived exertion (Figure 12.2) has not been borne out by the 15 years of research that have followed. The affective impact of music may be key to its positive influence on endurance in high-intensity exercise/training and lead ultimately to the promotion of exercise adherence (e.g. Annesi, 2001; Hutchinson and Karageorghis, 2013). This notion is supported by interview-based evidence (DeNora, 2000, pp. 89–103; Priest and Karageorghis, 2008), which demonstrates that an exercise instructor's musical selections can prove to be a seminal influence on exercise participants' decisions regarding continued class attendance.

The conceptual frame of music research in exercise and sport has broadened to include variables relating to exercisers/athletes themselves, the nature of the task and the exercise/sporting context (see Figure 12.10). A far broader sweep of literature has been considered in the development of this new model than was the case with earlier conceptual frameworks (e.g. Karageorghis *et al.*, 1999; Terry and Karageorghis, 2006), and both individual and group-based exercise and training involving joint action are embraced (cf. Sebanz *et al.*, 2006).

The model also incorporates current thinking in mainstream psychology regarding aesthetics (e.g. North and Hargreaves, 2008; Nieminen *et al.*, 2011). It is more complex than its predecessors, and, therefore, only segments of the model can be tested in any single study. Moreover, the complexity of the relationships that are represented by the model is such that individual hypotheses are not made explicit in pictorial form; rather, these are drawn out in the narrative that follows. The model also has numerous implications for exercise and sport practitioners that will be elaborated upon. It accounts for the findings that have sprung from the last half-century of empirical work and postulates a series of reciprocal interactions and feedback loops among the antecedents, moderators and consequences of music use. The model shares its construction with many other stimulus–response models in psychology (e.g. Rapee and Heimberg, 1997), in that an input (music) is identified, coded and moderated by a range of personal and situational factors.

Whereas the temporal aspects of music – tempo, rhythm and metre (how the listener perceives tempo and rhythm) – exert a strong influence on arousal, aspects such as modality (e.g. major [happy] vs minor [sad] key) and harmony may be particularly salient in terms of evoking an affective response in the listener (Juslin, 2009; van der Zwaag *et al.*, 2011). More specifically, rhythm and tempo will lead to differential responses depending on the age and personality profile of exercisers and the nature of the task (e.g. Crust and Clough, 2006; Clark *et al.*, 2012; Deutsch and Hetland, 2012). Older exercisers (> 50 years) generally prefer slower tempi than their younger counterparts (Priest *et al.*, 2004) and may also *need* slower tempi to facilitate exercise at a lower work rate. Age-congruent music is selected with reference to the artist, musical idiom/style, and age (date of release) of specific tracks (Karageorghis *et al.*, 2006a).

With reference to personality, extroverts may prefer stimulative music (cf. Eysenck, 1967; McCown *et al.*, 1997), which is characterized by a fast tempo, prominent rhythm and exaggerated bass tones. Similarly, the melodic and harmonic qualities of music will lead to differential responses depending on the cultural background of the listener. For example, Westerners typically associate major-scale melodies and harmonies with positive feelings and happiness, whereas, in many Eastern cultures, minor-sounding melodies and harmonies induce the same response, owing to cultural differences in musical composition (Levitin, 2006, p. 31).

The effect of the semantic information contained in lyrics depends, not only on the way it is received by the listener, but also on the relevance of the information to the task: a certain lyric may prove highly emotive for a given individual, may even promote a flow experience, but have no effect whatsoever on a different person (Priest and Karageorghis, 2008; Sanchez *et al.*, 2014). The same piece of music, performed with alternative instrumentation, can also result in entirely different responses: if one imagined listening to the original synthesized version of Vangelis's 'Chariots Of Fire' as a precursor to a run, and then envisaged hearing the piece being played on the steel drums, much of the affective power of the composition would be lost, and it would take on an entirely new identity, with new associations – a Caribbean holiday, perhaps.

The final intrinsic music factor, dynamics, concerns energy transmitted by musicians through touch or breath to influence the volume of their instruments. Take, for example, the dynamics of a heavy metal band, which typically entail a singular *fortissimo* (very loud) dynamic. These dynamics will differ markedly from those of a classical string quartet, which will play *pianissimo* (very soft), *fortissimo* and all the grades in between. Personality type (e.g. extrovert vs introvert), musical upbringing (which embraces cultural background) and hearing acuity are likely to moderate one's response to changes in musical dynamics.

Along the lines of previous conceptualizations (e.g. Karageorghis *et al.*, 1999), the intrinsic properties of music stimuli are separate from extrinsic properties. The former properties are intrinsic to the sound of a musical work (e.g. tempo, rhythm, harmony), whereas the latter relate to contextual associations of the sound (i.e. how they relate to a particular setting, situation or set of circumstances). Among the extrinsic properties, iconic cues concern how structural elements of a musical work relate to the tone of certain emotions: for example, fast/loud music may sound 'lively' because there are commonalities with energy and excitement (see North and Hargreaves, 2008). Given that such cues are grounded in the structure of music, the same music should hold similar 'iconic meaning' for different people. Cultural associations are often propagated by the mass media and are thus also likely to influence large sections of the population, albeit for a different reason. For example, consider the use of the theme music from the 1980s Hamlet cigar TV commercials – a jazzy version of Bach's 'Air on the G String' – to generate a state of happiness and a carefree attitude to life.

The model distinguishes cultural associations from personal associations, and the latter pertain directly to individual experiences of music. For instance, the 'our song' phenomenon describes the way a particular piece of music has special meaning for lovers, as it reminds them of their early courtship (North and Hargreaves, 2008, p. 135). These associations are cultivated at an individual level and may involve the mass media; hence, there is some overlap with cultural associations. Musical idiom concerns the stylistic category into which a work commonly falls (e.g. jazz, pop, reggae, etc.). This idiomatic criterion is often overlooked by exercise practitioners, who have a tendency to be guided by their own preferences rather than those of their clients (e.g. see Priest *et al.*, 2004).

As with the Karageorghis *et al.* (1999) model, it is postulated that the intrinsic factors are more salient than the extrinsic factors, and this hierarchy has been supported by work that tested the posits of the 1999 model (e.g. Atkinson *et al.*, 2004; Crust and Clough, 2006; Crust, 2008; Priest and Karageorghis, 2008; Waterhouse *et al.*, 2010; Hutchinson and Karageorghis, 2013). With reference to intrinsic factors, the aforementioned studies also confirm that the rhythmic qualities of music have the most salient influence in an exercise context. It should be noted, however, that the intrinsic properties of music often make an important contribution to iconic cues. As an illustration of this contribution, the Survivor track 'Eye Of The Tiger' was selected for the film *Rocky III* because of its intrinsic properties (e.g. rousing guitar riff and anthemic chorus), but developed a strong cultural association with boxing owing to its prevalence in an iconic film.

There is a reciprocal relationship between personal and situational factors, given that, in an exercise or training context, the music should be *functional* or carefully coordinated with the tasks and specifics of a session (cf. Kodzhaspirov *et al.*, 1986). Nonetheless, these factors are not arranged in a hierarchical order, given that there is currently insufficient empirical evidence to inform any such hierarchy. Moderators such as personal preferences and attentional style (e.g. associator vs dissociator; whether an individual has a tendency to focus inwardly on bodily processes vs outwardly on environmental stimuli) will interact with the social environment to determine musical response (cf. Hutchinson and Karageorghis, 2013). For example, if the playing of a popular piece results in a surge of enthusiasm within an exercise group that pertains to the influences of joint action (Sebanz *et al.*, 2006), this surge is likely to have a positive effect on an individual who may not necessarily express a liking for that piece, resulting in a behavioural consequence (i.e. more effort expended). Likewise, if a particular piece is highly preferred by an exercise or sport leader, this preference will have a direct influence on exercise/sport participants through the non-verbal communication that the leader will exude (Priest and Karageorghis, 2008). For example, a piece that energizes an exercise-to-music instructor may also influence the effort expended by those in her class in an indirect way, regardless of the direct influence of that piece on class members. The foregoing issue creates an apparent inconsistency within the model, in that two forces oppose each other: the prefer- ences of exercise participants and those of instructors. In practice, this is often a trade-off.

Numerous studies have shown that gender and age moderate one's response to music during exercise or sports training (e.g. McCown *et al.*, 1997; Karageorghis *et al.*, 1999, 2010; Priest *et al.*, 2004; Crust, 2008). For example, females rate the importance of rhythmic qualities and the 'danceability' of music more highly than males do. However, males value the importance of cultural associations to a greater extent than their female counterparts (Karageorghis *et al.*, 1999). In one study that examined health club members, it appeared that the younger strata in the sample generally rated music as being more important to them than their older counterparts, in addition to preferring contemporary and up-tempo selections (Priest *et al.*, 2004); such a finding is consistent with the known role of music in forming a cultural identity during adolescence (Tarrant *et al.*, 2001), but does require further empirical investigation. All age groups consider the churn or variety of music programmes to be an important factor (Priest *et al.*, 2004): over-familiarity with music can lead to a decrement in liking (see Berlyne, 1971, pp. 193–8).

The consequences have been delineated in accordance with the literature reviewed herein. The two strongest and most consistent sets of consequences appear first (psychological and psychophysical), followed by behavioural consequences and, finally, psychophysiological consequences, which are the least consistent. Synchronization does not appear as a behavioural consequence, because it is already present in the model as a moderator, under task-related factors. This decision to omit synchronization was taken to preserve conceptual clarity and parsimony in the model, although it should be noted that auditory–motor synchronization can be considered a behavioural outcome as well as a task-related moderator. In many studies, the consequences appear to have been experienced in unison; for example, appropriate music use can result in more positive affect that is coupled with greater work output (e.g. Elliott *et al.*, 2004; Karageorghis *et al.*, 2009, 2010). We have yet to discover the precise lineage of the processes involved (i.e. whether enhanced affect leads to the ergogenic effect or vice versa) or their neurophysiological correlates. Therefore, when there is a greater body of work to draw upon, the model might be refined accordingly.

There is a feedback loop from the consequences back to the music factors that influences future selection decisions and is moderated by personal factors and contextual/situational factors. The feedback loop relates to the intuitive and reflective appraisal (see Vallerand, 1987) of the outcomes pertaining to music use and also how such outcomes relate to moderators such as personal preferences and exercise/training mode. For example, music liking may dwindle through over-exposure (Berlyne, 1971, pp. 193–8), or the arousal response to a certain piece of music may become conditioned if it is used in conjunction with a specific training task (see Priest and Karageorghis, 2008). The latter example is also an incidence of a personal association. Essentially, the model proposes that the responses to music we experience in an exercise or sport context will be considered by the exerciser/athlete with reference to the moderator factors and shape their future selection decisions.

Pieces of music that lead to positive consequences are more likely to be reselected (and vice versa) and promote the selection of similar pieces (e.g. works by the same artist, in the same idiom or of a similar tempo/rhythmic feel). Moreover, the feedback loop results in the formation of preferences that can be task-specific: for instance, a recuperative musical programme comprising sedative tracks by artists such as Enya or Enigma may be selected for warm-down or stretching activities in order to lower HR towards resting levels and induce muscular relaxation (cf. Jing and Xudong, 2008; Savitha et al., 2010).

Hypotheses emanating from the model and directions for future work

Figure 12.10 provides a fisheye depiction of the principal hypotheses emanating from the model, which are, in turn, based on the previously introduced trends that are evident within the body of empirical work. The model suggests that age-congruent music should be the most desirable in an exercise context, particularly when people of the same age group are exercising together (i.e. there is joint action). This proposed preference for congruence serves to explain the inevitable tension relating to music selection that ensues when people from different age groups engage in joint action in an exercise or training context (e.g. see Priest et al., 2004; Clark et al., 2012). Also, in concert with models of information processing and attention in the exercise domain (Rejeski, 1985; Tenenbaum, 2001), music will not moderate RPEs beyond the anaerobic threshold, when physiological cues tend to predominate. When a differentiated or multidimensional approach is taken in the measurement of perceived exertion (e.g. Hutchinson and Tenenbaum, 2006), it appears likely that well-selected music (e.g. motivational music) can influence the motivational–affective component of perceived exertion beyond the anaerobic threshold, even if it cannot alter gestalt perceptions of exertion at such intensities. Such a measurement approach has considerable potential to further our understanding of music's perceptual effects during exercise.

The model predicts that the beneficial consequences associated with music use are maximized when preference for the music programme is high, it is appropriate for a particular exercise or training task, and it is congruent with the personal character-istics of the exerciser(s)/athlete(s). In long-duration, repetitive tasks, such as cycle or treadmill ergometry, individuals will derive a larger ergogenic effect from the synchronous application of music, and this effect is not moderated by gender. Contrastingly, females are likely to derive greater benefit from the synchronous use of music when performing motor tasks with relatively complex patterns or during the joint action that characterizes aerobic dance exercise (cf. Karageorghis *et al.*, 2010). Nonetheless, individuals with higher rhythmic ability will find it easier to engage in auditory–motor synchronization (Roerdink, 2008, p. 13). The work of Large (2000) can be taken to imply that perception of a beat and metrical structure in music is an inherent process within rhythm response behaviours. Accordingly, individuals who are able readily to perceive such features should prove more adept in the level of entrainment that they achieve.

The model predicts that extroverts – those who are socially outgoing and seek stimulation in their environment – are likely to derive greater benefit from loud/ stimulative musical selections than introverts – those who are shy or reticent. Ambiverts, who exhibit a balance of extrovert and introvert features in their personality, should also derive benefit from loud/stimulative music, given contextual influences (i.e. exercise and training environments are associated with 'high-energy' states; cf. North and Hargreaves, 2008), albeit to a lesser degree than extroverts. This prediction is based on an Eysenckian principle and is worthy of more systematic evaluation in the exercise and sport domain; there is a dearth of research that considers the moderating role of personality-related variables (e.g. Crust and Clough, 2006; Hutchinson and Karageorghis, 2013).

Along similar lines, the influence of attentional style on musical response has received scant consideration; the model predicts that dissociators are likely to derive greater benefit from music use than associators or switchers (those with a tendency to shift between the two attentional styles), although this will only hold at moderate work intensities (cf. Hutchinson and Karageorghis, 2013); at low intensities, all will dissociate, and, at high intensities, all will associate (Rejeski, 1985; Tenenbaum, 2001). There is emerging evidence that cognitive strategies change in accordance with the intensity of an exercise task (Hutchinson and Tenenbaum, 2006, 2007; Hutchinson and Karageorghis, 2013), which means that low-intensity tasks leave greater attentional capacity for parallel-processing tasks such as music listening (cf. Tenenbaum, 2001).

There has been a reluctance to assess experiment participants' hearing acuity, although this is a fundamental factor in the aesthetic appreciation of music. Related to the issue of hearing acuity is the rare condition of *beat deafness*, a form of congenital amusia estimated to afflict about 4 per cent of people in Western Europe and North America. The condition is characterized by an inability to perceive or 'hear' the beat in a piece of music (Phillips-Silver *et al.*, 2011). The model posits that exercisers/athletes with significant hearing loss or beat deafness will not derive major benefits from music use. In the latter case, music may actually significantly reduce the quality of the exercise/training experience. An implication for researchers is that they should screen potential experiment participants for hearing acuity and beat deafness.

Applied work involving music applications with elite athletes has led the author to conclude that training status is also an important moderator, and that some highly trained individuals prefer to 'listen to their bodies' (see Karageorghis and Terry, 2011, pp. 197–221); they also tend to work at high intensities. The model predicts that, owing to differences in motivation and the cognitive strategies typically employed (e.g. see Hutchinson and Tenenbaum, 2007), recreationally active participants stand to reap greater rewards from music use than their highly trained counterparts. There is some evidence to support this prediction (Brownley *et al.*, 1995; Mohammadzadeh *et al.*,

2008; Hagen *et al.*, 2013), which is supplemented by earlier work that shows that elite athletes tend to have an associative attentional style (Morgan and Pollock, 1977) and well-established motor rhythms that are less amenable to external manipulation (MacPherson *et al.*, 2007). It might also be argued that highly trained individuals are likely to exhibit higher motivation than their recreational counterparts and would, therefore, have less to gain from the use of music. Nevertheless, even highly trained athletes, under certain circumstances (long-duration, low-intensity activities), stand to benefit from the judicious use of music – an example of interaction between personal and task-related factors (see Laukka and Quick, 2013).

The highly trained might also explore the application of sedative post-task music, which the model predicts will enhance recovery rate. Indeed, post-task music is a subject worthy of systematic investigation, as there are currently only five published studies (Jing and Xudong, 2008; Savitha *et al.*, 2010; Eliakim *et al.*, 2012, 2013; Tan *et al.*, 2014), none of which is particularly strong in methodological terms. Allied to this, and to promote more rigorous future research, there is a need for a sister instrument to the BMRI-3 that will assess the sedative qualities of music to aid its use as an anxiety-control technique (sport) or as a post-task recuperative tool (exercise/training).

Associations are a powerful personal factor that can be exploited in order to maximize the benefits of music use. Such associations are built up by repetition – perhaps in the exercise or sport environment – and the images that music evokes manifest through a process of classical conditioning. Cinema, television, radio and social media play a pivotal role, and the associations formed often interact with the exercise context. As a simple illustration, consider the use of music from the *Rocky* film series applied to a Boxercise class: substantial dynamism is added to the class as the participants associate with Rocky's herculean feats while engaging in boxing-themed

BEYOND THE FRONTIER

The new theoretical model (Figure 12.10) addresses music delivery in the absence of video. Nonetheless, the ecological validity of the music–video combination, as experienced in many health and fitness facilities, suggests a particularly fruitful avenue for future study. It is evident that experimental research is currently out of kilter with the ways in which music is used in real-life settings. Promising initial findings using semi-structured interviews (e.g. Priest and Karageorghis, 2008) and experimental approaches (e.g. Barwood *et al.*, 2009) should be built upon. In addition, research is needed to further address the interactive effects of music and video (e.g. Loizou and Karageorghis, 2009; Lin and Lu, 2013; Jones *et al.*, 2014), and this suggestion is prompted by the prevalence of motivational video use in elite and professional sports teams (e.g. Groom *et al.*, 2011). Moreover, it is envisaged that neurophysiological approaches will play an increasingly important role in the development of this area of study (cf. Nieminen *et al.*, 2011; Bishop *et al.*, 2013). This research channel will be facilitated by the increasing utility and fidelity of functional neuroimaging and near-infrared spectroscopy technologies.

activities. The model predicts that music selections that exploit cultural and personal associations are likely to yield significant benefits, particularly in terms of cognitive and affective consequences (see Bishop *et al.*, 2014). Although the *Rocky* example entails predominantly a cultural association, a personal association can occur when a piece of music reminds an exerciser or athlete about an aspect of their own lives that is emotionally significant (Laukka and Quick, 2013; Priest and Karageorghis, 2008).

The body of work pertaining to in-task music has yielded some fairly robust findings – particularly when it is used as an adjunct for submaximal exercise/training – and it is assuredly time for the work to be extended to more externally valid, 'real-life' environments. In particular, interventions designed to enhance public health could easily be structured around: (a) music programmes that correspond to different ranges of expected HR; (b) the application of the joint action principle; and (c) auditory–motor synchronization, or entraining to the beat. The health benefits and motivation outcomes associated with such programmes should be investigated. Similarly, there is tremendous scope for the use of music in physiotherapy rehabilitation programmes (cf. Clark *et al.*, 2012).

Practical implications of the model

The new theoretical model (Figure 12.10) provides a robust basis for the recommendations of practitioners working with exercise and sport participants (e.g. coaches, facility managers, fitness instructors, health professionals, personal trainers, physical educationalists, strength and conditioning specialists, etc.), as it details the span of variables that need to be taken into account when considering musical response in the exercise and sport domain. In this section, the key implications of the model have been distilled into a series of recommendations.

In line with the new model, music selected as an accompaniment for exercise or sporting endeavour should be congruent with the participants' personal characteristics, the task, the exercise environment and desired consequences. With reference to the participants, the music should be age-appropriate and reflective of sociocultural upbringing. In respect of contextual factors, the tempo of the music should be selected with exercise/training intensity in mind. Other than when warming up, warming down or recovering/recuperating, the appropriate band of tempi for the asynchronous application of music appears to be approximately 120–140 bpm (Karageorghis *et al.*, 2011; Karageorghis and Jones, 2014); this finding can also be taken as evidence that music plays a specialized role in the exercise/training context. Furthermore, the rhythm of the music should approximate the motor patterns enacted where possible (Simpson and Karageorghis, 2006; Leman *et al.*, 2013).

The model has a number of implications that pertain to the application of music during instructor-led exercise or sports training. For example, if verbal instruction is required during the session, the sound intensity should not inhibit participants' hearing and processing of these instructions. This interaction of task-related and environmental factors should also be considered with reference to training status – a personal factor – as highly trained exercisers/athletes will require less concurrent feedback/instruction in the execution of an exercise/training routine (e.g. see McMorris, 2004, p. 220). The motor performance of highly trained participants is unlikely to be inhibited when relatively loud music is used (i.e. 75–80 dB at ear level). Moreover, instructors engaged in one-on-one training are likely to maximize the efficacy of their instruction by restricting their client's use of personal listening devices to periods of cardiovascular training involving simple and repetitive motor tasks (e.g. cycle ergometry or treadmill walking), during which the exerciser or athlete may not require any verbal instruction.

Concerning the consequences of listening, music containing affirmations of exercise/sport or inspirational references to popular culture should be selected in order to promote task-relevant imagery and self-talk. Positive affect is thought to be consequent to the modality of music (e.g. major vs minor key; Juslin, 2009; van der Zwaag et al., 2011) and its melodic/harmonic features, in combination with lyrical content (e.g. Priest and Karageorghis, 2008; Sanchez et al., 2014). In order to stimulate participants, the music should be up-tempo (> 120 bpm) and characterized by pronounced rhythmical features. In order to sedate, a slow tempo (< 80 bpm), simple rhythmical structure, regular pulsation and repetitive tonal patterns based on a limited number of pitch levels are recommended (e.g. see Karageorghis and Terry, 2009). Exercise instructors, sports coaches and participants should routinely reflect upon and evaluate the consequences of their music listening experiences and use this process as a means by which to inform future music selections. This practice is the enactment of the feedback loop, from the consequences to the antecedents via the moderators, that is germane to the new theoretical model (Figure 12.10).

A novel finding that emanated from qualitative work is that music selection for exercise is concerned with the entire programme of music – the combination of multiple musical selections on a 'playlist' that is used to accompany a bout of exercise – rather than just individual pieces (e.g. Priest and Karageorghis, 2008), a perspective not countenanced in the experimental literature (see Karageorghis and Priest, 2012a, 2012b). For example, selectors should consider the congruence of musical pieces that appear in close proximity on a playlist and aim to achieve variety in terms of the music programme; similarly, programmes should be 'churned' over time. Indeed, the music churn is included as an environmental factor in the model (see Figure 12.10), yet has seldom been investigated. The earlier review indicated that, when music is self-selected or participants are offered some degree of autonomy, the benefits associated with music use appear to be enhanced (e.g. Yamashita et al., 2006; Barwood et al., 2009).

In a recent national expert statement for the UK (Karageorghis et al., 2012), it was concluded that, although music is a beneficial accompaniment to exercise or training in most circumstances, it is contraindicated under certain conditions: (a) when it may distract from safety-relevant information (e.g. on public roads); (b) when exercisers/ athletes need to focus their full attention on learning a demanding motor skill; and (c) when exercising or training at high intensities that require an associative attentional style (i.e. 'listening to the body'). It is probable that, as a stimulant, music should be used intermittently (i.e. not all of the time). This tactic will prevent desensitization to its stimulative effects and permit exercisers/athletes to habituate themselves for occasions when they may not be able to use it (e.g. during long-distance running events). Repeated exposure to excessively loud music combined with high-intensity exercise is to be avoided, because of the potential threat to the structures of the inner ear (Alessio and Hutchinson, 1991). A possible mechanism is that blood flow is diverted to the working muscles, leaving the 15,400 hair cells in the cochlea more susceptible to damage from high-intensity music (cf. Lindgren and Axelsson, 1988; Nakashima et al., 2003). Research shows that even moderate-intensity activity accompanied by

---

Strange choices also work, but for strange reasons

Prior to their final test against India in Mumbai, 2006, the England cricket team, led by their charismatic captain Andrew 'Freddie' Flintoff, sang the Johnny Cash classic 'Ring Of Fire' just before stepping out on to the pitch. When asked by an Indian reporter to explain the meaning behind the use of the song, Flintoff could barely keep a straight face: 'It's just a song that the boys like', he pronounced.

Flintoff knew the real connection, but it would have been distinctly impolite to explain that the song's title was an unintended reference to the after-effects of eating spicy food; indeed, most of the team had been dogged by tummy upsets during the test series. It was said that the atmosphere in the England dressing room during the lunch interval on the final day was akin to a rugby match. With 'Ring Of Fire' blaring out at full blast, the players whipped themselves up into a hand-clapping, feet-stomping frenzy.

Similarly, during the 2007 Rugby World Cup in France, England's rugby stars sang Kenny Rogers' song 'The Gambler' to boost morale before matches, after prop Matt Stevens began strumming it on his guitar in their hotel lounge. The song became a staple part of the team's evening social gatherings and their pre-match build-up, as the team made their unexpected progress through the tournament into the final.

Martin Corry, the then England captain, told *The Sunday Telegraph*, on 17 October 2007, that: 'Given where we are as a team, the lyrics seem to have struck a chord with us'. He highlighted the chorus: 'You've got to know when to hold 'em, know when to fold 'em, know when to walk away and know when to run'. Team veteran Mike Catt told the same newspaper that the song had become the squad's 'lucky charm'. The players clearly identified with the underlying message of the song: it's not the hand you have, but the way you play it.

---

very loud music (> 100 dB sound pressure level) can cause temporary hearing loss (Lindgren and Axelsson, 1988); this finding represents an interaction of the personal, environmental and task–related moderators in the model (see Figure 12.10).

SUMMARY

The three conceptual approaches that underlie the study and application of music in exercise and sport contexts, presented herein, represent an evolution over a 15–year period (Karageorghis *et al.*, 1999; Terry and Karageorghis, 2006). Music can be applied to exercise, sports training and competition in many different ways. One of the main benefits of music use is that it enhances certain aspects of the psychological state, which has implications for both performance and enjoyment of exercise and sport. Pre-task music can have a priming effect for exercise participants or athletes (e.g. Bishop *et al.*,

2007; Laukka and Quick, 2013). It is most commonly used to increase activation or as a 'psych-up' tool in the exercise domain, whereas, in the sport domain, it serves both 'psych-up' and 'psych-down' functions, depending on its qualities (tempo, intensity, lyrical content, etc.).

In-task music can boost work output, enhance affective valence and reduce perceived exertion through both synchronous and asynchronous applications (e.g. Bood *et al.*, 2013; Karageorghis *et al.*, 2013). When in-task music is selected in terms of its motivational qualities, it can assuage the sharp decline in affective valence that is observed beyond the ventilatory threshold (cf. Ekkekakis, 2003; Hutchinson and Karageorghis, 2013; Jones *et al.*, 2014). Work on the application of post-task music is currently at a fledgling stage, although initial findings appear promising in terms of how music can expedite the recovery process (e.g. Jing and Xudong, 2008; Savitha *et al.*, 2010).

It is hoped that, through the judicious application of the principles outlined in this chapter, the reader will be able to harness the psychological, psychophysical, psychophysiological and ergogenic effects of music with greater precision. The author anticipates that, in the next decade, music-related exercise interventions will play a prominent role in the battle against inactivity and obesity throughout the developed world. Moreover, music will continue to be used by athletes in ever more sophisticated ways in their attempts to gain an edge over rivals.

> I listen to hip-hop and rap to sort of help me get focussed, to get ready to get up and do what I'm there to do. It helps me to tune everything out, and take one step at a time.
>
> (Michael Phelps, American swimmer who is the most decorated Olympian of all time, with twenty-two medals, in a 2007 interview with Time.com)[8]

ACKNOWLEDGEMENTS

Much of the Brunel-based work presented in this chapter would not have been possible were it not for the author's longstanding collaboration with Professor Peter Terry (University of Southern Queensland, Australia) and Professor Andrew M. Lane (University of Wolverhampton, UK). He is most grateful for their wise counsel, kindness and scholarly perspicacity. The author would also like to thank his graduate students, from whom he has drawn, and continues to draw, much inspiration: Dr David-Lee Priest, Dr Kelly Ashford, Dr Ruth Hewston, Dr Daniel Bishop, Dr Georgios Loizou, Dr Massimo Vencato, Dr Harry Lim, Dr Alessandra Mecozzi Saha and Dr Leighton Jones.

KEY CONCEPTS AND TERMS

Affective valence
This is the hedonic tone of feelings (i.e. whether they are positive or negative).

Asynchronous music

This is used to describe the use of music as a background to exercise- or sport-related activities, without any conscious attempt by the performer to synchronize their movements with musical tempo or rhythm.

Entrainment

Entrainment is an individual's or group's adjustment of their movement pattern so that it synchronizes with the rhythms of the music.

Flow

Flow is a holistic experience associated with total involvement or immersion in an activity. Flow is also associated with peak performance in a sporting context.

Heuristic model

This is a holistic model that serves to indicate or illustrate a series of relationships in order to stimulate interest and promote further investigation.

In-task affect

In-task affect concerns the feelings of pleasure or displeasure experienced during an exercise task and often assessed using an 11-point bipolar measure known as the feeling scale.

Ventilatory threshold

This is the exercise intensity at which the volume of carbon dioxide expelled is larger than the volume of oxygen consumed.

Synchronous music

This is used to describe conscious synchronization between the rhythmical features of music (e.g. tempo) and movement patterns during sport- or exercise-related tasks.

RECOMMENDED FURTHER READING

Books and book chapters

Bishop, D. T. and Karageorghis, C. I. (2009). Managing pre-competitive emotions with music. In Bateman, A. J. and Bale, J. R. (eds) *Sporting Sounds: Relationships between Sport and Music*, pp. 59–84. London: Routledge.

Juslin, P. N. and Sloboda, J. A. (2011). *Handbook of Music and Emotion: Theory, research, applications*. Oxford, UK: Oxford University Press.

Karageorghis, C. I. (2008). The scientific application of music in sport and exercise. In Lane, A. M. (ed.) *Sport and Exercise Psychology*, pp. 109–37. London: Hodder Education.

Karageorghis, C. I. (2016). *Applying Music in Exercise and Sport*. Champaign, IL: Human Kinetics.

Karageorghis, C. I. and Terry, P. C. (2009). The psychological, psychophysical and ergogenic effects of music in sport: A review and synthesis. In Bateman, A. J. and Bale, J. R. (eds) *Sporting Sounds: Relationships between Sport and Music*, pp. 13–36. London: Routledge.

Karageorghis, C. I. and Terry, P. C. (2011). *Inside Sport Psychology*. Champaign, IL: Human Kinetics.

Loizou, G. and Karageorghis, C. I. (2009). Video, priming and music: Effects on emotions and motivation. In Bateman, A. J. and Bale, J. R. (eds) *Sporting Sounds: Relationships between Sport and Music*, pp. 37–58. London: Routledge.

Lucaccini, L. F. and Kreit, L. H. (1972). Music. In Morgan, W. P. (ed.) *Ergogenic Aids and Muscular Performance*, pp. 240–5. New York: Academic Press.

North, A. C. and Hargreaves, D. J. (2008). *The Social and Applied Psychology of Music*. Oxford, UK: Oxford University Press.

Journals

Anshel, M. H. and Marisi, D. Q. (1978). Effects of music and rhythm on physical performance. *Research Quarterly*, *49*, 109–13.

Bishop, D. T., Karageorghis, C. I. and Loizou, G. (2007). A grounded theory of young tennis players' use of music to manipulate emotional state. *Journal of Sport & Exercise Psychology*, *29*, 584–607.

Bishop, D. T., Wright, M. J. and Karageorghis, C. I. (2013). Tempo and intensity of pre-task music modulate neural activity during reactive task performance. *Psychology of Music*, *42*, 714–727.

Hutchinson, J. C. and Karageorghis, C. I. (2013). Moderating influence of dominant attentional style and exercise intensity on responses to asynchronous music. *Journal of Sport & Exercise Psychology*, *35*, 625–43.

Hutchinson, J. C., Karageorghis, C. I. and Jones, L. (2015). See hear: Psychological effects of music-video in exercise. *Annals of Behavioural Medicine*, *49*, 199–211.

Jones, L., Karageorghis, C. I. and Ekkekakis, P. (2014). Can high-intensity exercise be more pleasant? Attentional dissociation using music and video. *Journal of Sport & Exercise Psychology*, *36*, 528–41.

Karageorghis, C. I. (2014). Run to the beat: Sport and music for the masses. *Sport in Society*, *17*, 433–47.

Karageorghis, C. I., Hutchinson, J. C., Jones, L., Farmer, H. L., Ayhan, M. S., Wilson, R. C., Rance, J., Hepworth, C. J. and Bailey, S. G. (2013). Psychological, psychophysical, and ergogenic effects of music in swimming. *Psychology of Sport and Exercise*, *14*, 560–8.

Karageorghis, C. I. and Jones, L. (2014). On the stability and applicability of the exercise heart-rate music tempo preference relationship. *Psychology of Sport and Exercise*, *15*, 299–310.

Karageorghis, C. I., Mouzourides, D., Priest, D. L., Sasso, T., Morrish, D. and Walley, C. (2009). Psychophysical and ergogenic effects of synchronous music during treadmill walking. *Journal of Sport & Exercise Psychology*, *31*, 18–36.

Lim, H. B. T., Karageorghis, C. I., Romer, L. and Bishop, D. T. (2014). Psychophysiological effects of synchronous versus asynchronous music during cycling. *Medicine & Science in Sport & Exercise*, *46*, 407–13.

Sanchez, X., Moss, S. L., Twist, C. and Karageorghis, C. I. (2014). On the role of lyrics in the music–exercise performance relationship. *Psychology of Sport and Exercise*, *15*, 132–8.

Terry, P. C., Karageorghis, C. I., Saha, A. M. and D'Auria, S. (2012). Effects of synchronous music on treadmill running among elite triathletes. *Journal of Science and Medicine in Sport*, *15*, 52–7.

SAMPLE ESSAY QUESTIONS

1   What evidence is there to suggest that structured music use might contribute to exercise or training adherence?

2   Discuss the evolution of conceptual frameworks that have been advanced to explain the effects of music in the domain of exercise and sport.

3   How can sport psychologists harness the power of music to enhance the potency of psychological interventions?

4   'Music is a wholly ineffective auditory stimulus at high exercise intensities.' Discuss with reference to relevant theories and empirical evidence.

5   Using a suitable theoretical framework, explain how pre-task music might be used to enhance a sports skill of your choice for an athlete of your choice. Detail specific tracks that might be applied to the individual performing the skill, and why you think they might be appropriate.

6   Explain how music could be coordinated in a synchronous manner with the training activities associated with three different sports. Include an appraisal of the potential benefits of synchronous music within each sport.

NOTES

1   www.youtube.com/watch?v=RjqimlFcJsM
2   www.youtube.com/watch?v=rF-hq_CHNH0
3   Speedo Aquabeat 2.0 Underwater MP3 player.
4   www.philipnorthcoombes.com
5   These include www.tempotap.com, www.songbpm.com and www.djcity.com
6   For example, www.run2r.com, www.rockmyrun.com or www.jogtunes.com
7   See e.g. www.youtube.com/watch?v=T0klExG8s0c
8   See http://content.time.com/time/arts/article/0,8599,1612765,00.html

REFERENCES

Alessio, H. M. and Hutchinson, K. M. (1991). Effects of submaximal exercise and noise exposure on hearing loss. *Research Quarterly*, *62*, 413–19.

Annesi, J. J. (2001). Effects of music, television, and a combination entertainment system on distraction, exercise adherence, and physical output in adults. *Canadian Journal of Behavioural Science*, *33*, 193–201.

Anshel, M. H. and Marisi, D. Q. (1978). Effect of music and rhythm on physical performance. *The Research Quarterly*, *49*, 109–13.

Atan, T. (2013). Effect of music on anaerobic exercise performance. *Biology of Sport*, *30*, 35–9.

Atkinson, G., Wilson, D. and Eubank, M. (2004). Effects of music on work-rate distribution during a cycling time trial. *International Journal of Sports Medicine*, *25*, 611–15.

Azjen, I. and Fishbein, M. (1977). Attitude–behavior relations: A theoretical analysis and review of empirical research. *Psychological Bulletin*, *84*, 888–918.

Bacon, C. J., Myers, T. R. and Karageorghis, C. I. (2012). Effect of music–movement synchrony on exercise oxygen consumption. *Journal of Sports Medicine and Physical Fitness*, *52*, 359–65.

Barwood, M. J., Weston, N. V. J., Thelwell, R. and Page, J. (2009). A motivational music and video intervention improves high-intensity exercise performance. *Journal of Sports Science and Medicine*, *8*, 435–42.

Berlyne, D. E. (1971). *Aesthetics and Psychobiology*. New York: Appleton-Century-Crofts.

Bharani, A., Sahu, A. and Mathew, V. (2004). Effect of passive distraction on treadmill exercise test performance in healthy males using music. *International Journal of Cardiology*, *97*, 305–6.

Birnbaum, L., Boone, T. and Huschle, B. (2009). Cardiovascular responses to music tempo during steady-state exercise. *Journal of Exercise Physiology Online*, *12*, 50–7.

Bishop, D. T., Karageorghis, C. I. and Kinrade, N. P. (2009). Effects of musically-induced emotions on choice reaction time performance. *The Sport Psychologist*, *23*, 59–76.

Bishop, D. T., Karageorghis, C. I. and Loizou, G. (2007). A grounded theory of young tennis players' use of music to manipulate emotional state. *Journal of Sport & Exercise Psychology*, *29*, 584–607.

Bishop, D. T., Wright, M. J. and Karageorghis, C. I. (2014). Tempo and intensity of pre-task music modulate neural activity during reactive task performance. *Psychology of Music*, *42*(5), 714–727, 2014, http://bura.brunel.ac.uk/handle/2438/9047

Bonny, H. L. (1987). Music, the language of immediacy. *Arts in Psychotherapy*, *14*, 255–61.

Bood, R. J., Nijssen, M., van der Kamp, J. and Roerdink, M. (2013). The power of auditory–motor synchronization in sports: Enhancing running performance by coupling cadence with the right beats. *PLos ONE*, *8*, e70758.

Brownley, K. A., McMurray, R. G. and Hackney, A. C. (1995). Effects of music on physiological and affective responses to graded treadmill exercise in trained and untrained runners. *International Journal of Psychophysiology*, *19*, 193–201.

Chtourou, H., Chaouachi, A., Hammouda, O., Chamari, K. and Souissi, N. (2012) Listening to music affects diurnal variation in muscle power output. *International Journal of Sports Medicine*, *33*, 43–7.

Clark, I. N., Taylor, N. F. and Baker, F. A. (2012). Music interventions and physical activity in older adults: A systematic literature review and meta-analysis. *Journal of Rehabilitation Medicine*, *44*, 710–19.

Copeland, B. L. and Franks, B. D. (1991). Effects of types and intensities of background music on treadmill endurance. *The Journal of Sports Medicine and Physical Fitness*, *31*, 100–3.

Crust, L. (2004). Carry-over effects of music in an isometric muscular endurance task. *Perceptual and Motor Skills*, *98*, 985–91.

Crust, L. (2008). Perceived importance of components of asynchronous music during circuit training. *Journal of Sports Sciences, 26,* 1547–55.

Crust, L. and Clough, P. J. (2006). The influence of rhythm and personality in the endurance response to motivational asynchronous music. *Journal of Sports Sciences, 24,* 187–95.

DeNora, T. (2000). *Music in Everyday Life.* Cambridge, UK: Cambridge University Press.

Deutsch, J. and Hetland, K. (2012). The impact of music on pacer test performance, enjoyment and workload. *Asian Journal of Physical Education & Recreation, 18,* 6–18.

Doiron, B. A. H., Lehnhard, R. A., Butterfield, S. A. and Whitesides, J. F. (1999). Beta-endorphin response to high intensity exercise and music in college-age women. *Journal of Strength and Conditioning Research, 13,* 24–8.

Dorney, L., Goh, E. K. M. and Lee, C. (1992). The impact of music and imagery on physical performance and arousal: Studies of coordination and endurance. *Journal of Sport Behavior, 15,* 21–33.

Dyer, B. J. and McKune, A. J. (2013). Effects of music tempo on performance, psychological, and physiological variables during 20 km cycling in well-trained cyclists. *Perceptual and Motor Skills, 117,* 484–97.

Edworthy, J. and Waring, H. (2006). The effects of music tempo and loudness level on treadmill exercise. *Ergonomics, 49,* 1597–610.

Ekkekakis, P. (2003). Pleasure and displeasure from the body: Perspectives from exercise. *Cognition and Emotion, 17,* 213–39.

Eliakim, M., Bodner, E., Eliakim, A., Nemet, D. and Meckel, Y. (2012). Effect of motivational music on lactate levels during recovery from intense exercise. *The Journal of Strength and Conditioning Research, 26,* 80–6.

Eliakim, M., Bodner, E., Meckel, Y., Nemet, D. and Eliakim, A. (2013). Effect of rhythm on the recovery from intense exercise. *The Journal of Strength and Conditioning Research, 27,* 1019–24.

Eliakim, M., Meckel, Y., Nemet, D. and Eliakim, A. (2007). The effects of music during warm-up on consecutive anaerobic performance in elite adolescent volleyball players. *International Journal of Sports Medicine, 28,* 321–5.

Elliott, D., Carr, S. and Savage, D. (2004). Effects of motivational music on work output and affective responses during sub-maximal cycling of a standardized perceived intensity. *Journal of Sport Behavior, 27,* 134–47.

Eysenck, H. J. (1967). *The Biological Basis of Personality.* Springfield, IL: Thomas.

Farnsworth, P. R. (1969). *The Social Psychology of Music.* Ames, IA: Iowa State University Press.

Fritz, T. H., Hardikar, S., Demoucron, M., Neissen, M., Demey, M., Giot, O., Li, Y., Haynes, J. D., Villringer, A. and Leman, M. (2013). Musical agency reduced perceived exertion during strenuous physical performance. *Proceedings of the National Academy of Sciences, 110,* 17784–9.

Grahn, J. A. (2012). Neural mechanisms of rhythm perception: Current findings and future perspectives. *Topics in Cognitive Science, 4,* 585–606.

Groom, R., Cushion, C. and Nelson, L. (2011). The delivery of video-based performance analysis by England youth soccer coaches: Towards a grounded theory. *Journal of Applied Sport Psychology, 23,* 16–32.

Hagen, J., Foster, C., Rodriguez-Marroyo, J., de Koning, J. J., Mikat, R. P., Hendrix, C. R. and Porcari, J. P. (2013). The effect of music on 10-km cycle time trial performance. *International Journal of Sports Physiology and Performance, 8*, 104–6.

Hayakawa, Y., Miki, H., Takada, K. and Tanaka, K. (2000). Effects of music on mood during bench stepping performance. *Perceptual and Motor Skills, 90*, 307–14.

Hutchinson, J. C. and Karageorghis, C. I. (2013). Moderating influence of dominant attentional style and exercise intensity on psychological and psychophysical responses to asynchronous music. *Journal of Sport & Exercise Psychology, 35*, 625–43.

Hutchinson, J. C., Sherman, T., Davis, L. K., Cawthon, D., Reeder, N. B. and Tenenbaum, G. (2011). The influence of asynchronous motivational music on a supramaximal exercise bout. *International Journal of Sport Psychology, 42*, 135–42.

Hutchinson, J. C. and Tenenbaum, G. (2006). Perceived effort – can it be considered gestalt? *Psychology of Sport and Exercise, 7*, 463–76.

Hutchinson, J. C. and Tenenbaum, G. (2007). Attention focus during physical effort: The mediating role of task intensity. *Psychology of Sport and Exercise, 8*, 233–45.

Iwanaga, M. (1995). Relationship between heart rate and preference for tempo of music. *Perceptual and Motor Skills, 81*, 435–40.

Jing, L. and Xudong, W. (2008). Evaluation on the effects of relaxing music on the recovery from aerobic exercise-induced fatigue. *Journal of Sports Medicine and Physical Fitness, 48*, 102–6.

Jones, L., Karageorghis, C. I. and Ekkekakis, P. (2014). Can high-intensity exercise be more pleasant? Attentional dissociation using music and video. *Journal of Sport & Exercise Psychology, 36*, 528–41.

Juslin, P. N. (2009). Music (emotional effects). In Sander, D. and Scherer, K. R. (eds) *The Oxford Companion to Emotion and the Affective Sciences*, pp. 269–71. New York: Oxford University Press.

Kämpfe, J., Sedlmeier, P. and Renkewitz, F. (2011). The impact of background music on adult listeners: A meta-analysis. *Psychology of Music, 39*, 424–48.

Karageorghis, C. I. (2014). Run to the beat: Sport and music for the masses. *Sport in Society, 17*, 433–47.

Karageorghis, C. I., Hutchinson, J. C., Jones, L., Farmer, H. L., Ayhan, M. S., Wilson, R. C., Rance, J., Hepworth, C. J. and Bailey, S. G. (2013). Psychological, psychophysical, and ergogenic effects of music in swimming. *Psychology of Sport and Exercise, 14*, 560–8.

Karageorghis, C. I. and Jones, L. (2014). On the stability and relevance of the exercise heart rate–music-tempo preference relationship. *Psychology of Sport and Exercise, 15*, 299–310.

Karageorghis, C. I., Jones, L. and Low, D. C. (2006b). Relationship between exercise heart rate and music tempo preference. *Research Quarterly for Exercise and Sport, 26*, 240–50.

Karageorghis, C. I., Jones, L., Priest, D. L., Akers, R. I., Clarke, A., Perry J., Reddick, B. T., Bishop, D. T. and Lim, H. B. T. (2011). Revisiting the exercise heart rate–music tempo preference relationship. *Research Quarterly for Exercise and Sport, 82*, 274–84.

Karageorghis, C. I., Jones, L. and Stuart, D. P. (2008). Psychological effects of music tempi during exercise. *International Journal of Sports Medicine, 29*, 613–19.

Karageorghis, C. I., Mouzourides, D., Priest, D. L., Sasso, T., Morrish, D. and Walley, C. (2009). Psychophysical and ergogenic effects of synchronous music during treadmill walking. *Journal of Sport & Exercise Psychology, 31*, 18–36.

Karageorghis, C. I. and Priest, D. L. (2012a). Music in the exercise domain: A review and synthesis (Part I). *International Review of Sport and Exercise Psychology*, *5*, 44–66.

Karageorghis, C. I. and Priest, D. L. (2012b). Music in the exercise domain: A review and synthesis (Part II). *International Review of Sport and Exercise Psychology*, *5*, 67–84.

Karageorghis, C. I., Priest, D. L., Terry, P. C., Chatzisarantis, N. L. D. and Lane, A. M. (2006a). Redesign and initial validation of an instrument to assess the motivational qualities of music in exercise: Brunel Music Rating Inventory-2. *Journal of Sports Sciences*, *24*, 899–909.

Karageorghis, C. I., Priest, D. L., Williams, L. S., Hirani, R. M., Lannon, K. M. and Bates, B. J. (2010). Ergogenic and psychological effects of synchronous music during circuit-type exercise. *Psychology of Sport and Exercise*, *11*, 551–9.

Karageorghis, C. I. and Terry, P. C. (1997). The psychophysical effects of music in sport and exercise: A review. *Journal of Sport Behavior*, *20*, 54–68.

Karageorghis, C. I. and Terry, P. C. (2009). The psychological, psychophysical and ergogenic effects of music in sport: A review and synthesis. In Bateman, A. J. and Bale, J. R. (eds) *Sporting Sounds: Relationships between Sport and Music*, pp. 15–46. London: Routledge.

Karageorghis, C. I. and Terry, P. C. (2011). *Inside Sport Psychology*. Champaign, IL: Human Kinetics.

Karageorghis, C. I., Terry, P. C. and Lane, A. M. (1999). Development and initial validation of an instrument to assess the motivational qualities of music in exercise and sport: Brunel Music Rating Inventory. *Journal of Sports Sciences*, *17*, 713–24.

Karageorghis, C. I., Terry, P. C., Lane, A. M., Bishop, D. T. and Priest, D. L. (2012). British Association of Sport and Exercise Sciences expert statement on the use of music in exercise. *Journal of Sports Sciences*, *30*, 953–6.

Kirschner, S. and Tomasello, M. (2010). Joint music making promotes prosocial behavior in 4-year old children. *Evolution and Human Behavior*, *31*, 354–64.

Kodzhaspirov, Y. G., Zaitsev, Y. M. and Kosarev, S. M. (1986). The application of functional music in the training sessions of weightlifters. *Soviet Sports Review*, *23*, 39–42.

Kornysheva, K., von Cramon, D. Y., Jacobsen, T. and Schubotz, R. I. (2010). Tuning-in to the beat: Aesthetic appreciation of musical rhythms correlates with a premotor activity boost. *Human Brain Mapping*, *31*, 48–64.

Lane, A. M., Davis, P. A. and Devonport, T. J. (2011). Effects of music interventions on emotional states and running performance. *Journal of Sports Science and Medicine*, *10*, 400–7.

Large, E. W. (2000). On synchronizing movements to music. *Human Movement Science*, *19*, 527–66.

Laukka, P. and Quick, L. (2013). Emotional and motivational uses of music in sports and exercise: A questionnaire study among athletes. *Psychology of Music*, *41*, 198–215.

Leman, M., Moelants, D., Varewyck, M., Styns, F., Noorden, L. and Martens, J. P. (2013). Activating and relaxing music entrains the speed of beat synchronized walking. *PLoS ONE*, *8*, e67932.

Levitin, D. (2006). *This Is Your Brain on Music*. London: Atlantic Books.

Lim, H. B. T., Atkinson, G., Karageorghis, C. I. and Eubank, M. R. (2009). Effects of differentiated music on cycling time trial. *International Journal of Sports Medicine*, *30*, 435–42.

Lim, H. B. T., Karageorghis, C. I., Romer, L. and Bishop, D. T. (2014). Psychophysiological effects of synchronous versus asynchronous music during cycling. *Medicine & Science in Sports & Exercise, 46*, 407–13.

Lima-Silva, A. E., Silva-Cavalcante, M. D., Pires, F. O., Bertuzzi, R., Oliveira, R. S. F. and Bishop, D. (2012). Listening to music in the first, but not the last 1.5 km of a 5-km running trial alters pacing strategy and improves performance. *International Journal of Sports Medicine, 33*, 813–18.

Lin, J. H. and Lu, F. J. H. (2013). Interactive effects of visual and auditory intervention on physical performance and perceived effort. *Journal of Sports Science and Medicine, 12*, 388–93.

Lindgren, F. and Axelsson, A. (1988). The influence of physical exercise on susceptibility to noise-induced temporary threshold shift. *Scandinavian Audiology, 17*, 11–17.

Loizou, G. and Karageorghis, C. I. (2009). Video, priming and music: Effects on emotions and motivation. In Bateman, A. J. and Bale, J. R. (eds) *Sporting Sounds: Relationships between Sport and Music*, pp. 37–58. London: Routledge.

Lucaccini, L. F. and Kreit, L. H. (1972). Music. In Morgan, W. P. (ed.) *Ergogenic Aids and Muscular Performance*, 235–62. New York: Academic Press.

McCown, W., Keiser, R., Mulhearn, S. and Williamson, D. (1997). The role of personality and gender in preference for exaggerated bass in music. *Personality and Individual Differences, 23*, 543–47.

McMorris, Y. (2004). *Acquisition and Performance of Sports Skills*. New York: Wiley.

MacPherson, A. C., Turner, A. P. and Collins, D. (2007). An investigation of the natural cadence between cyclists and non-cyclists. *Research Quarterly for Exercise and Sport, 78*, 396–400.

Mohammadzadeh, H., Tartibiyan, B. and Ahmadi, A. (2008). The effects of music on the perceived exertion rate and performance of trained and untrained individuals during progressive exercise. *Facta Universitatis Series Physical Education and Sport, 6*, 67–74.

Morgan, W. P. and Pollock, M. L. (1977). Psychologic characterization of the elite distance runner. *Annals of the New York Academy of Sciences, 301*, 382–403.

Nakamura, P. M., Pereira, G., Papini, C. B., Nakamura, F. Y. and Kokubun, E. (2010). Effects of preferred and nonpreferred music on continuous cycling exercise performance. *Perceptual and Motor Skills, 110*, 257–64.

Nakashima, T., Naganawa, S., Sone, M., Tominaga, M., Hayashi, H., Yamamoto, H., Liu, X. and Nuttall, A. L. (2003). Disorders of cochlear blood flow. *Brain Research Reviews, 43*, 17–28.

Nicolson, N. A. (2008). Measurement of cortisol. In Luecken, L. J. and Callo, L. C. (eds) *Handbook of Physiological Research Methods in Health Psychology*, 37–74. Newbury Park, CA: Sage.

Nieminen, S., Istok, E., Brattico, E., Tervaniemi, M. and Huotilainen, M. (2011). The development of aesthetic responses to music and their underlying neural and psychological mechanisms. *Cortex, 47*, 1138–46.

North, A. C. and Hargreaves, D. J. (2008). Music and taste. In North, A. C. and Hargreaves, D. J. (eds) *The Social and Applied Psychology of Music*, 75–142. Oxford: Oxford University Press.

Pain, M. A., Harwood, C. and Anderson, R. (2011). Pre-competition imagery and music: The impact on flow and performance in competitive soccer. *The Sport Psychologist, 25*, 212–32.

Phillips-Silver, J., Toiviainen, P., Gosselin, N., Piche, O., Nozaradan, S., Palmer, C. and Peretz, I. (2011). Born to dance but beat deaf: A new form of congenital amusia. *Neuropsychologia, 49*, 961–9.

Priest, D. L. and Karageorghis, C. I. (2008). A qualitative investigation into the characteristics and effects of music accompanying exercise. *European Physical Education Review, 14*, 347–66.

Priest, D. L., Karageorghis, C. I. and Sharp, N. C. C. (2004). The characteristics and effects of motivational music in exercise settings: The possible influence of gender, age, frequency of attendance, and time of attendance. *Journal of Sports Medicine and Physical Fitness, 44*, 77–86.

Rapee, R. M. and Heimberg, R. G. (1997). A cognitive-behavioral model of anxiety in social phobia. *Behaviour Research and Therapy, 35*, 741–56.

Razon, S., Basevitch, I., Land, W., Thompson, B. and Tenenbaum, G. (2009). Perception of exertion and attention allocation as a function of visual and auditory conditions. *Psychology of Sport and Exercise, 10*, 636–43.

Rejeski, W. J. (1985). Perceived exertion: An active or passive process? *Journal of Sport Psychology, 75*, 371–8.

Rendi, M., Szabo, A. and Szabo, T. (2008). Performance enhancement with music in rowing sprint. *Sport Psychology, 22*, 175–82.

Roerdink, M. (2008). *Anchoring: Moving from theory to therapy*. Amsterdam: IFKB.

Sanchez, X., Moss, S. L., Twist, C. and Karageorghis, C. I. (2014). On the role of lyrics in the music–exercise performance relationship. *Psychology of Sport and Exercise, 15*, 132–8.

Savitha, D., Mallikarjuna, R. N. and Chythra, R. (2010). Effect of different musical tempo on post-exercise recovery in young adults. *Indian Journal of Physiology and Pharmacology, 54*, 32–6.

Sebanz, N., Bekkering, H. and Knoblich, G. (2006). Joint action: Bodies and minds moving together. *Trends in Cognitive Sciences, 10*, 70–6.

Shaulov, N. and Lufi, D. (2009). Music and light during indoor cycling. *Perceptual and Motor Skills, 108*, 597–607.

Simpson, S. D. and Karageorghis, C. I. (2006). The effects of synchronous music on 400-m sprint performance. *Journal of Sports Sciences, 24*, 1095–102.

Smoll, F. L. and Schultz, R. W. (1978). Relationships among measures of preferred tempos and motor rhythm. *Perceptual and Motor Skills, 8*, 883–94.

Szabo, A., Small, A. and Leigh, M. (1999). The effects of slow- and fast-rhythm classical music on progressive cycling to voluntary physical exhaustion. *Journal of Sports Medicine and Physical Fitness, 39*, 220–5.

Szmedra, L. and Bacharach, D. W. (1998). Effect of music on perceived exertion, plasma lactate, norepinephrine and cardiovascular hemodynamics during treadmill running. *International Journal of Sports Medicine, 19*, 32–7.

Tan, F., Tengah, A., Nee, L. Y. and Fredericks, S. (2014). A study of the effect of relaxing music on heart rate recovery after exercise among healthy students. *Complementary Therapies in Clinical Practice, 20*, 114–17.

Tarrant, M., North, A. C. and Hargreaves, D. J. (2001). Social categorization, self-esteem, and the estimated musical preferences of male adolescents. *Journal of Social Psychology*, *141*, 565–81.

Tate, A. R., Gennings, C., Hoffman, R. A., Strittmatter, A. P. and Retchin, S. M. (2012). Effects of bone-conducted music on swimming performance. *Journal of Strength and Conditioning Research*, *26*, 982–8.

Tenenbaum, G. (2001). A social-cognitive perspective of perceived exertion and exertion tolerance. In Singer, R. N., Hausenblas, H. A. and Janelle, C. (eds) *Handbook of Sport Psychology*, pp. 810–22. New York: Wiley.

Tenenbaum, G., Lidor, R., Lavyan, N., Morrow, K., Tonnel, S., Gershgoren, A., Meis, J. and Johnson, M. (2004). The effect of music type on running perseverance and coping with effort sensations. *Psychology of Sport and Exercise*, *5*, 89–109.

Terry, P. C. and Karageorghis, C. I. (2006). Psychophysical effects of music in sport and exercise: An update on theory, research and application. In Katsikitis, M. (ed.) *Proceedings of the 2006 Joint Conference of the APS and the NZPS*, pp. 415–19. Melbourne, Australia: Australian Psychological Society.

Terry, P. C. and Karageorghis, C. I. (2011). Music in sport and exercise. In Morris, T. and Terry, P. C. (eds) *The New Sport and Exercise Psychology Companion*, pp. 359–80. Morgantown, WV: Fitness Information Technology.

Terry, P. C., Karageorghis, C. I., Mecozzi Saha, A. and D'Auria, S. (2012). Effects of synchronous music on treadmill running among elite triathletes. *Journal of Science and Medicine in Sport*, *15*, 52–7.

Uppal, A. K. and Datta, U. (1990). Cardiorespiratory response of junior high school girls to exercise performed with and without music. *Journal of Physical Education and Sport Science*, *2*, 52–6.

Vallerand, R. J. (1987). Antecedents of self-related affects in sport: Preliminary evidence on the intuitive–reflective appraisal model. *Journal of Sport Psychology*, *9*, 161–82.

van der Zwaag, M. D., Westerink, J. H. D. M. and van den Broek, E. L. (2011). Emotional and psychophysiological responses to tempo, mode, and percussiveness. *Musicae Scientiae*, *15*, 250–69.

Van Dyck, E., Moelants, D., Demey, M., Deweppe, A., Coussement, P. and Leman, M. (2013). The impact of the bass drum on human dance movement. *Music Perception*, *30*, 349–59.

Waterhouse, J., Hudson, P. and Edwards, B. (2010). Effects of music tempo upon submaximal cycling performance. *Scandinavian Journal of Medicine & Science in Sport*, *20*, 662–9.

Wilson, E. M. F. and Davey, N. J. (2002). Musical beat influences corticospinal drive to ankle flexor and extensor muscle in man. *International Journal of Psychophysiology*, *44*, 177–84.

Yamamoto, T., Ohkuwa, T., Itoh, H., Kitoh, M., Terasawa, J., Tsuda, T., Kitagawa, S. and Sato, Y. (2003). Effects of pre-exercise listening to slow and fast rhythm music on supramaximal cycle performance and selected metabolic variables. *Archives of Physiology and Biochemistry*, *111*, 211–14.

Yamashita, S., Iwai, K., Akimoto, T., Sugawara, J. and Kono, I. (2006). Effects of music during exercise on RPE, heart rate and the autonomic nervous system. *The Journal of Sports Medicine and Physical Fitness*, *46*, 425–30.

IV | Beliefs versus reality, or beliefs as reality?

13 Beliefs versus reality, or beliefs as reality?

The placebo effect in sport and exercise

*Philip Hurst, Abby Foad
and Chris Beedie*

CHAPTER SUMMARY

The placebo effect is a positive outcome arising from the belief that a beneficial treatment has been received (Clark et al., 2000). A negative belief effect, the 'nocebo effect' (Hahn, 1997), is the opposite: a negative outcome resulting from the belief, either that a desired treatment has not been received, or that a received treatment is harmful.

The inclusion of the placebo-controlled trial in the 'gold' standard of biomedical research, the double-blind randomized trial, has demonstrated that the placebo effect has a central role in science. Researchers gain confidence about the true effects of a treatment when it is compared with a placebo control. Generally, the placebo control is, theoretically at least, indistinguishable from the treatment under examination, meaning that participants are unaware whether they are receiving the placebo or the treatment. This allows the researchers to identify whether any observed effects are the direct result of the biological or mechanical qualities of the treatment or the result of cognitive factors such as expectation, cognitive–behavioural factors such as conditioning, or psychophysiological (emotional) responses such as reduced anxiety.

As well as employing placebo controls in research examining, for example, the effects of ergogenic aids and nutritional supplements on sports performance, sports scientists have gone one step further and investigated the direct effects of placebos. Collectively, these studies demonstrate that, when athletes believe that they have been given a beneficial treatment, the performance of a significant percentage of those athletes is enhanced, even when the treatment is a placebo. Likewise, in exercise research, the belief that an activity is likely to improve mental health has resulted in improvements in these variables.

The placebo effect might be of more significance to sport psychology than at first appears. This chapter will begin by reviewing several empirical investigations of the placebo effect in sport and exercise, with emphasis on the methodologies and implications (this is not a comprehensive review, for which see Beedie and Foad, 2009). Some of the common assumptions related to the placebo effect in sport and exercise research will be addressed. The role and potential impact of placebo effects in the field will be considered, and the ethics surrounding the investigation and use of the placebo effect will be discussed. Perhaps most controversially, the issue of whether some sports psychological interventions are essentially a placebo will be raised. Throughout this chapter, readers will be encouraged to think critically about the role and implications of the placebo effect and, beyond this specific phenomenon, about the wider issue of the relationship between mind and body, for research and practice in sport and exercise.

LEARNING OUTCOMES

When you have studied this chapter, you should be able to:

1 Describe research that has investigated the placebo effect in sport and exercise
2 Evaluate the concept of the placebo effect in research
3 Critically consider the role and implications of the placebo effect for athletes, exercisers and professional practitioners

LEARNING OUTCOME 1

Describe research that has investigated the placebo effect in sport and exercise

Placebo-effect research in sport

Most placebo–effect research in sport has investigated the placebo effects of purported ergogenic aids on sports performance (e.g. Maganaris *et al.*, 2000; Beedie *et al.*, 2006, 2007; Foad *et al.*, 2008). Beedie *et al.* (2006) investigated the effects of placebos on 10-km cycling performance, as well as the possibility of a dose–response relationship. Competitive cyclists were informed that they would receive a placebo, 4.5 mg kg^{-1} and 9.0 mg kg^{-1} in a counterbalanced repeated-measures design. However, they actually received a placebo in each condition. A dose–response relationship was observed, with participants producing 1.4 per cent less power in the placebo condition, and 1.3 per cent and 3.1 per cent more power in the 4.5 and 9.0mg kg^{-1} conditions, respectively (the response in the placebo condition was arguably a nocebo effect). Post hoc semi-structured interviews indicated that five participants believed that they had experienced a placebo effect in one or more of the three experimental trials. Each proposed mechanism, such as lower levels of pain and anxiety, as well as the deliberate modification of pacing strategy, resulted from the belief that they would produce more power as the result of ingesting caffeine. These data suggested that placebo responses may be associated with changes in psychological variables that indirectly affect performance.

The results of the above study indicate how beliefs (positive or negative) could shape the efficacy of an intervention. Beedie *et al.* (2007) examined this phenomenon further and investigated the degree to which positive and negative beliefs about the same nutritional intervention might influence the effects of that intervention on performance. The authors allocated forty-two team sport athletes into two groups. Following 3×30 m baseline sprints, Group 1 was provided with positive information about a hypothetical new ergogenic aid (a placebo), whereas Group 2 was provided with negative information about the same substance. The sprint protocol was repeated. A significant linear trend towards greater speed in experimental trials in Group 1 suggested that positive belief exerted a positive effect on performance. However, performance in experimental trials for Group 2 was significantly slower than baseline (1.7 per cent), suggesting that negative belief exerted a negative effect on performance. The authors concluded that, following an intervention, positive and negative effects on performance might be a function of the beliefs and expectations of the athlete about that intervention. Theoretically, such beliefs and expectations, if negative, could offset some or all of the potential benefits of that intervention.

The majority of placebo-effect research in sport has been conducted in tightly controlled conditions. Its impact may, therefore, be methodological, and the effects may be overridden during competition, where psychological mechanisms such as anxiety, motivation, confidence and perceived pain can mask its magnitude (Beedie, 2007). In an attempt to demonstrate how the placebo effect may operate in real-world settings, Hurst *et al.* (2013) investigated its effect during a competitive 5-km performance time trial. Fifteen athletes, each separated by 1 week, performed two baseline trials and two placebo trials in a randomized order. Participants were told that the placebo was a 'new' ergogenic supplement, purported to improve endurance performance. Compared with mean baseline, administration of a placebo was associated with a mean 1.7 per cent improvement in 5-km performance. The results reveal the possibility that athletes who believe they are taking a beneficial supplement may show improvements in real-life competitions.

Of course, the placebo effects of an intervention (psychological) and true effects of that intervention (e.g. biological or pharmacological) might each contribute to improvements in performance. To investigate this possibility, several authors (McClung and Collins, 2007; Foad *et al.* 2008; Duncan, 2010) have used the 'balanced

ACTIVITY 13.1

The research described demonstrates that presenting athletes with placebos, described as performance-enhancing supplements, may improve performance substantially. Are the improvements related to the placebo drug, or are the effects due to interaction between the athlete and researcher? How would this impact upon a coach–athlete relationship?

TABLE 13.1 The balanced placebo design

	Athlete receives drug	Athlete receives no drug
Athlete is told they will receive drug	A: placebo effect + drug effect	B: placebo effect alone
Athlete is told they will receive no drug	C: drug effect alone	D: baseline

Source: Adapted from Marlatt and Rohsenow, 1980

placebo', or 'double disassociation' design (Table 13.1). This elegant design enables the assessment of each possible combination of what the athlete believes they have taken (i.e. placebo or drug) and what the athlete has actually taken (again, placebo or drug). (Note that, although beyond the scope of this chapter, this design is both ethically and experimentally problematic and requires a great degree of skill and experience on the part of the research team to ensure results are reliable.)

McClung and Collins (2007) used the balanced placebo design to investigate the placebo and pharmacological effects of sodium bicarbonate over a 1,000-m self-paced running time trial. Sixteen male endurance athletes performed the following conditions in a randomized order: (a) informed supplement/received supplement, (b) informed supplement/received placebo, (c) informed placebo/received supplement, and (d) informed placebo/received placebo. The authors reported that, not only did the overt administration of sodium bicarbonate improve performance by a substantial 1.7 per cent over the no-treatment condition, but that the expectation of receiving sodium bicarbonate improved performance in the absence of that substance by a not dissimilar 1.5 per cent. The authors suggest that such an effect could make a significant difference to athletes in competition. More significantly perhaps, they note *the lack of a performance effect when subjects had ingested sodium bicarbonate but believed that they had not*, suggesting what they termed a biochemical 'failure', that is, the possibility – which makes sense, given what we know about placebo effects in sport and elsewhere – that a substance might be far more effective if the athlete knows that they have taken it. McClung and Collins' data also hint at the possibility that certain substances might only be effective if the athlete knows they have taken them and – we must assume, given the data of Beedie *et al.* (2007) – believes that they will be effective.

The above findings were supported by Duncan (2010), who used a similar design, examining the ingestion of 5 mg kg^{-1} of caffeine during a 30-s Wingate test. The positive expectation of receiving caffeine and being informed correctly improved peak power output by 12.8 per cent compared with the told placebo/given placebo condition. Interestingly, the told caffeine/given placebo condition reported an 8.9 per cent improvement in peak power compared with the placebo condition. This effect was greater than that of informed placebo/given caffeine, which showed a 7.3 per cent improvement compared with the placebo/placebo condition.

Collectively, the above results highlight the possible implications for support staff such as managers, coaches, physiotherapists and – as we will return to below – sports psychologists in ensuring that athletes believe that an intervention will be effective.

However, not all athletes respond to a placebo, even in situations in which they expect an intervention to improve performance. Foad *et al.* (2008) used the balanced placebo design to identify the unique psychological and pharmacological effects of caffeine on a laboratory 40-km cycling time trial. Results demonstrated that the average power output increased by 3.5 per cent over baseline when participants received caffeine, regardless of whether the participants *knew* that they were receiving caffeine or not. The belief that caffeine had been received did not improve performance compared with baseline conditions; however, a substantial interaction between belief and pharmacology indicated that caffeine exerted a greater effect on performance when participants were informed they had not ingested it. The nocebo effect was evidenced in the told placebo/given placebo condition and indicated a 1.9 per cent decrease in performance. Further qualitative analyses of the fourteen cyclists sampled (Beedie *et al.*, 2008) indicated that only two demonstrated a true placebo response – that is, a consistent effect on performance – whereas seven participants subjectively believed they had taken caffeine when they had, in fact, taken a placebo, but the performance of these athletes did not improve significantly. These results demonstrate that not all athletes will experience improved performance, even when they believe they have ingested a legitimate ergogenic aid and expect that substance to be effective. Although some participants expected the caffeine to work, expectation alone may not produce a marked improvement in performance, but might be manifested in, for example, reduced perception of effort, reduced anxiety and greater confidence.

Findings of studies using the balanced placebo design have suggested the potentially unique roles of expectancy and biology/pharmacology on performance, but have also exposed a range of new questions. Data from studies by McClung and Collins, and Duncan suggest that improvements in performance associated with the ingestion of sodium bicarbonate and caffeine, respectively, are heightened when an athlete believes they are taking the substance. However, the results of Foad *et al.* perhaps reveal the difficultly of conducting placebo-effect research.

The research described above has provided interesting data relating to the direction, magnitude and frequency of the placebo effect, and these data arguably have implications for research and practice. For example, over and above the finding that belief that a beneficial treatment has been received might significantly enhance performance or performance-related factors, such as pain sensation or perceived exertion, this research has demonstrated that:

* placebo and experimental effects may interact (i.e. placebo effects in control and experimental conditions may not always be equivalent in magnitude);
* beliefs can have both positive (placebo) and negative (nocebo) effects;
* placebo effects may be experienced both objectively and subjectively;
* not all participants are placebo responsive.

These findings have implications for practitioners seeking to optimize the effects of an intervention, an individual's experience of physical activity or an athlete's performance, and for researchers seeking to obtain valid and reliable estimates of treatment effects. The following section examines the potential impact of beliefs on the outcome of the placebo-controlled trial, the experimental design from which much of our knowledge regarding treatment effects in sport and exercise science is derived.

LEARNING OUTCOME 2

Evaluate the concept of the placebo effect in research

The placebo–control condition is a fundamental part of research in sport and exercise where it is used to 'control' for the effects of beliefs on the outcome of an intervention. By subtracting the mean effect observed in the placebo condition from the mean effect observed in the experimental condition, an estimate of the 'true' mean effect is calculated.

Several assumptions are implicit within the above model:

1 the placebo control is an 'inactive' condition;
2 placebo effects are always positive in direction; and
3 placebo and experimental effects are additive, not interactive.

If these assumptions are correct, valid approximations of experimental effects may be obtained. However, if these assumptions are incorrect, interpretation of both placebo and experimental effects becomes problematic.

Assumption 1: The placebo control is an 'inactive' condition

The notion of the placebo control as an inactive condition is understandable, given that placebos and placebo effects are so often associated with words such as 'inert', 'sham' and 'non-specific'. What is often overlooked, however, is that the placebo condition represents an active psychological treatment that, as has been demonstrated above, may in itself elicit significant effects. These effects are likely of significance to sports performers and practitioners, but are all too often overlooked in research, in which a null finding is often described in terms such as 'the experimental treatment performed no better than a placebo control'. As has been suggested many times, just because a treatment works no better than a placebo doesn't mean that it doesn't work. It simply suggests that the mechanisms might be more psychological than biological.

Assumption 2: Placebo effects are always positive in direction

Given common definitions of the placebo effect as a 'positive outcome', it is not surprising that the effects of individuals' beliefs in the placebo-controlled trial are often assumed to be positive in relation to baseline or no-treatment conditions. Beedie *et al.*'s (2007) findings (described in Learning outcome 1 above) indicate that, in a placebo-controlled trial, negative beliefs about an intervention may elicit a negative or 'nocebo' effect, whereby performance drops below baseline. If this phenomenon is translated to the research setting, and assuming the intervention under examination is effective, performance in the experimental condition would likely still be above baseline, but probably lower among athletes who had negative expectations than among those who had high expectations. Although the reported experimental effect would remain the same as when subjects held positive beliefs about the intervention, it would, however, represent an overestimate of the true increase over baseline. Inclusion of a baseline measure or no-treatment control condition in the standard placebo-controlled design is therefore essential, if valid approximations of both placebo and experimental effects are to be made.

Assumption 3: Placebo and experimental effects are additive, not interactive

An important assumption made when evaluating the results of a placebo-controlled trial is that the effects of the experimental treatment and the placebo are separable, additive, linear and stable. However, this model may be too simplistic, because it does not account for the possibility of interactions between experimental and placebo effects. Research has, in fact, demonstrated that a placebo effect may operate differently in the presence of an active substance from when one is not present, and that an active substance may act differently when subjects believe that they have ingested it from when subjects believe that they have not (McClung and Collins, 2007; Foad et al., 2008; Duncan, 2010). The placebo effect associated with the simple act of ingesting a substance believed by the subject to be ergogenic may potentiate the physio-logical effect of that substance (Benedetti et al., 2011). Different interventions may mobilize different mechanisms (e.g. psychological, biological, pharmacological) to different degrees, and these mechanisms can be additive for only so long as they are truly independent and not constrained by ceiling effects. Thus, it is possible that the magnitude of the true experimental effect may well be constrained by interventions that are particularly effective at mobilizing psychological mechanisms, or in particularly placebo-responsive individuals. Evidence of such complex interactions suggests that deriving true effects by subtracting placebo from experimental effects is much too simple an approach.

Resolving the efficacy conundrum depends almost entirely on our methodological ability to parcel out the different components of treatment. Given the small magnitude of many treatment effects in sport and exercise research, and given the difficulty of obtaining large sample sizes and/or conducting repeated trials that might strengthen the reliability of estimates of effect, any fluctuation in the magnitude and valence of placebo effects between placebo and experimental conditions may significantly confound precise assessments of outcome. A greater understanding of the nature of placebo effects may, therefore, help to strengthen the reliability and validity of research in sport and exercise and better clarify the mechanisms underlying observed effects.

ACTIVITY 13.2

Think of an example in sport or exercise where the placebo effect might impact on performance outcome or a similar dependent variable. Design a study to investigate the placebo effect in this context. Is your study valid and reliable? What problems might you encounter in your design that could confound accurate estimation of the placebo effect?

LEARNING OUTCOME 3

Critically consider the role and implications of the placebo effect for athletes, exercisers and practitioners

The convention of the placebo–controlled trial suggests that sport and exercise scientists recognize the potential for placebo effects to impact on the outcomes of research. Indeed, data from empirical investigations are increasing our knowledge of the magnitude, valence, frequency and variability of this effect in research. However, beyond the scientific interest in understanding how the placebo effect works, it is important that this research is translated into improving an athlete's performance. Just as translational biomedical research moves from basic *in vitro* and *in vivo* science towards applied disease prevention and management, so research into the placebo effect should be conducted to an applied end.

The example of Roger Bannister and the 4–minute mile is a similar illustration of the importance of the relationship between coach and athlete and how beliefs can be manipulated through verbal suggestions. Between 1931 and 1945, the men's mile world

---

APPLYING THE SCIENCE 13.1

The placebo effect has been shown to improve sport performance in controlled scientific environments; it is now time for this research to be translated into the field, where coaches, physiotherapists, nutritionists and psychologists alike might use knowledge of the placebo effect to bring out improvements in performance.

An account written by *soigneur* Willy Vogt (1999) is a vibrant, albeit controversial, example of how the placebo effect might be translated into the field. Vogt tricked the French champion cyclist Richard Virenque into believing he had taken a performance-enhancing substance, as illustrated below:

> That day he rode the time trial of his life, finishing second on the stage to Ullrich. The German started 3 minutes after Richard and caught him, after which the pair had a memorable ding-dong battle all the way to the finish. 'God I felt good! That stuff's just amazing' he babbled. 'We must get hold of it.' Of course his result did have something to do with the magic capsule – but there is one thing he doesn't know, unless he reads this. I had got rid of the fabulous potion and swapped it for one which contained a small amount of glucose. There is no substitute for self belief.
>
> (Vogt, 1999, p. 104)

The false belief Vogt instilled in Virenque is, perhaps, an example of the power coaches might be able to exert over their athletes. Much as the relationship between doctor and patient can be instrumental in health, the relationship between an athlete and their support personnel might be fundamental to that athlete achieving their full potential.

ACTIVITY 13.3

Vogt (1999) reported an instance of the placebo effect in competitive sports performance. What alternative explanations might there be for such apparently placebo-enhanced performance? If a placebo effect was responsible, what do you think was the most likely mechanism?

BEYOND THE FRONTIER

So, there is arguably much more to the placebo effect than the administration of an inert capsule in a scientific study: it is as much about beliefs, both false and, as was perhaps the case with Bannister, true. Data attesting to the placebo effect might, as a result, be used in a number of ways.

---

record had improved by in the order of 5 s, to 4:01(min:s) and stood for 9 years. Running 1 mile in 4 min or less was, according to many scientists, physically impossible, and many attempts by other athletes had failed. On 6 May 1954, Roger Bannister was set to break the world record for the mile, but felt it was too windy and cold for a world-record attempt. Bannister's coach (Franz Stampfl) informed Bannister that he was able to run 1 mile in 3:56 and should be able to run under 4 min. Bannister ran 3:59 and later explained that his coach's suggestion of being able to run a mile in 3:56 gave him the belief he needed to break the world record (Noakes, 2012).

Beliefs and performance outcomes

Research addressing the placebo effect is arguably a demonstration of what the placebo effect *can* do. The placebo effect is now in a position to be used as an intervention to educate and provide knowledge to athletes, as well as athlete support personnel, about how beliefs can truly influence performance.

Anti-doping interventions

This may have an impact from an anti-doping perspective, where athletes are choosing not to use performance-enhancing supplements. Maganaris *et al.* (2000) examined how placebos, deceptively disguised as anabolic steroids, improved the performance of eleven competitive powerlifters from national standard to international standard. The findings corresponded with those of Ariel and Saville (1972). Maganaris *et al.* reported that the placebo effect could be a potential anti-doping intervention. Theoretically, if we can demonstrate to athletes and coaches that the power to improve their performance is as much in the mind as in the bottle or syringe, we could help reduce drug use in sport. This, in turn, might improve the confidence of the public – especially the parents of aspiring athletes – in sport. More importantly, it could reduce the often negative health effects of drug use. Research currently under way at Canterbury Christ Church University tests this idea by evaluating attitudes to drug use before and after an athlete has experienced the type of 'sports placebo effect' described above.

Sport and exercise psychology interventions and the placebo effect

Many of the key constructs of sport and exercise psychology are beliefs: self-confidence is the belief we have in our own or our team's ability; anxiety is the belief that we might not have the resources to meet an upcoming challenge. Furthermore, confidence and anxiety are often catalysed by beliefs about our opponent's ability or similar environmental factors (see both chapters by Uphill and Hays *et al.* elsewhere in this book). Likewise, in exercise, many people participate because they believe that it makes them feel better, or because they believe that they are unhealthy. Sport psychologists often have to modify the beliefs of their clients to enable those clients to perform to a higher level. For example, an under-confident athlete who, perhaps, suffers from tunnel vision might require a confidence-boosting strategy, whereas an over-confident athlete who is, perhaps, not sufficiently focused on the task in hand might need reminding of the seriousness of the challenge ahead and of the potential threat that the opponent poses. It could be argued that, by modifying organic (that is, naturally occurring) levels of confidence or anxiety, a sport psychologist is actually catalysing a false belief to bring about a positive outcome. Does this sound familiar? In other words, many interventions in sport and exercise psychology might operate via a placebo effect.

Surprising though this might sound, the issue has been the subject of research in clinical and counselling psychology for many years. In fact, the charge that psychotherapy might exert its effect via a placebo mechanism is not the worst to be aimed at it: it has been suggested, not only that many forms of psychotherapy are no better than a placebo, but that they may even be no better than no treatment (see Evans, 2003, chapter 8, for discussion). Research elsewhere in medicine has demonstrated that the beliefs of the practitioner about a treatment might be a significant factor in the success of that treatment. That is, in any therapeutic setting, the magnitude of any placebo effect might be driven by the beliefs of both practitioner and patient/client. This has often been cited as the mechanism underlying many examples of 'faith healing'.

ACTIVITY 13.4

Using research evidence, suggest what might happen should an athlete be referred to a sport psychologist, but believes that the sport psychologist is likely to have a negative effect on their performance. Describe the possible mechanisms underlying the outcome and suggest what a sport psychologist could do to prevent any negative response.

The idiosyncrasies of the supplement or treatment can, in turn, influence its outcome also. The participants' belief concerning a supplement can be affected by its physical characteristics. Szabo *et al.* (2013) revealed how perceptual properties of sports supplements (e.g. shape, size, colour) influence its perceived effectiveness, and that effects can be quite specific. For example, athletes perceived a white powder to be more effective for strength, compared with endurance or concentration, whereas a green gel was perceived to be more effective for endurance than for strength and concentration. It could be speculated that, even before an athlete has been given information about the supplement, just having looked at the supplement, the athlete has already made up his/her mind on whether it will be effective or not.

It is fair to say that, in many respects, whether an intervention operates via what we term 'real' or what we term 'placebo' mechanisms is not important. If it works, it works. If an athlete runs faster because they believe that they have ingested 450 mg of caffeine when they have not, or if the same athlete runs faster because they believe that their sport psychologist has resolved their anxiety issue, the athlete is *still running faster*. Perhaps the placebo effect and many sport psychology interventions operate in the same gap between what is currently being achieved and what is achievable.

IMPLICATIONS OF PLACEBO RESPONSIVENESS FOR THE ATHLETE/EXERCISER AND PRACTITIONER

Mechanisms by which an individual's beliefs might impact upon the outcome of research findings are described above, but what are the implications of placebo responsiveness for the athlete or exerciser themselves, and for practitioners working with these individuals? The following sections describe how placebo responsiveness may manifest itself in sport and exercise settings and suggest ways in which such responsiveness may be identified by the practitioner to optimize the athlete's or exerciser's experience.

Placebo effects are traditionally viewed as a positive phenomenon. Indeed, the common-sense model of the placebo effect is one in which an individual benefits from false information such as, 'The tablet I am about to give you will enhance your power output in the upcoming competition'. However, experiential data from Beedie *et al.* (2006) revealed that enhanced performance in placebo trials was often coupled with positive changes in psychological factors, such as confidence, motivation and arousal. These findings suggest that the placebo effect may be reflective of a suboptimal psychological status, whereby the belief that a beneficial treatment has been received optimizes psychological variables, subsequently enabling the athlete to perform to their full potential. If this is in fact the case, then sport and exercise practitioners would perhaps do better to address such deficiencies, as opposed to attempting to bridge the gap by means of a false belief. This is particularly germane, given the evidence that an individual susceptible to a false positive belief may be equally susceptible to a false negative belief (Beedie *et al.*, 2006, 2007), and, therefore, there is the potential for belief effects to impact both positively and negatively on performance.

IDENTIFICATION OF PLACEBO-RESPONSIVE ATHLETES

Although not all individuals will be placebo responsive in all situations, the understanding and prevention of placebo/nocebo responses should be the concern of sport and exercise practitioners. But how does the practitioner know if their athlete/exerciser is placebo responsive? Is placebo responsiveness a function of personality? Is it more of a contextual situational phenomenon, or a genetic predisposition?

Early attempts to identify a relationship between placebo effects and personality indicated that certain psychological variables such as anxiety (Shapiro and Shapiro, 1984), extraversion (Lasagna, 1986), self-esteem (Gelfand, 1962) and agreeableness (McNair et al., 1979) could be related to placebo responding. These findings were, however, equivocal, and the general consensus of early research was that the placebo effect was more a contextual situational phenomenon than an enduring personality trait. However, research in social psychology (e.g. Geers et al., 2005) suggests that personality characteristics may predispose an individual to respond to a placebo, but that situational factors are likely to interact with these traits to determine the degree of response exhibited. For instance, in medicine, saline solutions and sugar pills may fail as placebos if the psychosocial context is absent. The establishment of a placebo effect is susceptible to the practitioner's clothing, the instruments used, the appearance of the room or laboratory, the words communicated to the patient and the relationship between the practitioner and patient (Benedetti and Amanzio, 2011). All of these characteristics play an important role in developing the placebo effect and must be considered to establish whether an individual is placebo responsive.

Interestingly, recent research has suggested that placebo responsiveness is predetermined by genetics. A study investigating the placebo effect for irritable bowel syndrome discovered that participants who possessed a specific gene were more placebo responsive than participants who had a variation of the genetic factor (Hall et al., 2012). Although it would be irregular and costly for sport scientists to conduct this procedure on athletes, it can offer an explanation as to why some individuals are placebo responsive. Psychometric assessment of personality to identify potentially placebo-responsive traits such as anxiety or extraversion, and assessment of beliefs and expectations regarding a particular intervention, may help to alert sport and exercise practitioners to the potential for placebo responsiveness and facilitate appropriate counsel.

PSYCHOLOGICAL MECHANISMS

The placebo effect is an outcome involving psychological, physiological, neurophysiological and social changes and can be associated with expectations, desires, hopes and rewards. The placebo effect results from psychological and socio-environmental influences, suggesting that it does not operate within a vacuum but as a consequence of a host of elements. Of the mechanisms posited, classical conditioning and expectancy theory have been traditionally cited as the key contenders. The two mechanisms have often been disputed and may not be mutually exclusive, but both play an important role in producing the placebo effect.

Classical conditioning, originally demonstrated by Ivan Pavlov (1927), demonstrated how associative learning was considered to be a combination of two stimuli. The first by itself produces no response and is called the conditioned stimulus (CS), whereas the second typically produces a response and is termed the unconditioned stimulus (US). The CS becomes a guide that delivers information to the US to produce a conditioned response (CR). In Pavlov's study, the repeated association of ringing a bell (CS) when delivering the dog food (US) resulted in the dog salivating (CR). The ringing of the bell formed a learning response, and the dog, upon hearing the bell, anticipated food and began salivating. Translating this into sport, the sight, smell, touch and taste associated with performance-enhancing supplements can become CSs through the repeated association of using such substances. Placebos provided to athletes with the same perceptual characteristics, but without the US, may elicit a CR similar to the performance-enhancing supplement.

Expectations have been related to the placebo effect directly. A placebo produces an effect because the recipient expects it to. Expectations can be generated by many factors, such as verbal suggestions (as mentioned in the Bannister and Vogt examples), environmental prompts, emotional arousal, interaction with professional practitioners and previous experiences. When an athlete expects a particular outcome – for example, that caffeine will improve performance – a set of cognitions and behaviours may be produced to create that outcome. An athlete who ingests caffeine to improve performance may have a decrease in anxiety and an increase in self-confidence and may persist in difficult situations. If the athlete improves, the success is misattributed to the caffeine and not to the psychological process that occurred (Michael *et al.*, 2012). Athletes who are given a placebo, with the belief that it is an ergogenic substance, should expect to improve performance. Placebos have, therefore, been described as an expectancy manipulation (Stewart-Williams and Podd, 2004) and have a direct influence upon producing a placebo effect.

Expectancy and classical conditioning are the two protagonists explaining the placebo effect. However, to understand the mechanisms fully, it is important to consider the source of learning involved in shaping placebo effects. Classical conditioning is often produced through learning, and expectations are often the product of a learned response. Understanding the athlete's previous experience from what has been learned is of great interest for practitioners considering using the placebo effect as a direct intervention on sports performance.

ETHICS OF THE USE OF DECEPTION IN RESEARCH AND IN THE FIELD

The placebo effect is complex to investigate and represents something of a paradox to researchers. Harnessing its full power and translating the outcome into an improvement in sports performance should be done in correspondence with professional norms and ethical guidelines. Support personnel handing out placebos and informing athletes that they are performance-enhancing supplements are promoting deception and dishonesty, contrary to the ethos of sport.

The ethical codes governing research are in place to ensure that the mental and physical health, as well as the dignity, of subjects participating in such research are not in any way undermined. Research ethics committees scrutinize research proposals to ensure that ethical guidelines will be followed in research studies. Deception, although unlikely to undermine physical or mental health, could be seen to undermine the dignity of subjects and, thus, is likely to concern an ethics committee. However, several areas of human behaviour, including the placebo effect, are highly problematic to investigate empirically without some form of deception. In such cases, ethics committees generally require that the researcher provide a strong rationale for the use of such procedures. Specifically, the researcher must demonstrate: first, that they are aware of the ethical issues surrounding the use of deception in research; second, that they have carefully considered these issues in relation to their own research question; third, that the possible benefits of their research outweigh any risks to participants; and, finally, that effective, non-deceptive procedures are not feasible. (Specific guidelines aimed at reconciling the use of deception with the ethical norms of human participant research are provided by the American Psychological Association, 2002.)

As has previously been mentioned, the placebo response can impact expectations, beliefs, trust and hope. The placebo effect in sport has regularly involved using deceptive methods to initiate a response. The act of an athlete trusting a practitioner, or coach, and believing in the methods they use may trigger a set of cognitions and biological events that influence the perception or course of an outcome. The existence of this relationship raises a number of ethical concerns as to the application of the placebo effect and the use of deception. The placebo effect can change a person's mind and behaviour and opens the door for a practitioner to influence an athlete's mindset to gain positive effects (Benedetti, 2013). Australian swim coach Harry Gallagher (1970), for example, described how he used to doctor the watches and clocks at swimming pools to provide athletes with false-negative feedback, ensuring that they swam 'faster' in competition than in training, and provided a sense of psychological momentum at competitive events. However, this application could easily backfire, as shown by Seligman et al. (1990), who used similar methods to Gallagher's. During training sessions, Seligman would falsely state negative times to swimmers and give them an opportunity to improve. However, the impact this had on certain swimmers was detrimental to performance, although in others it improved performance. Seligman et al. concluded that swimmers who reported a pessimistic personality would swim even more slowly, whereas optimists tried harder and swam faster. The deliberate use of false feedback to produce a placebo effect could, therefore, be seen as unethical, largely unrepeatable over time and likely to be counter-productive. If coaches begin to paternalistically lie to athletes, regardless if intentions are moral, then the trust and honesty of the athlete–coach relationship may be damaged. An athlete falsely led to believe that they have ingested a powerful ergogenic aid might produce a better performance than usual; however, that athlete – upon being either debriefed or inadvertently finding out – might have less trust in their coach in future. Instead of deceit, placebo research conveys how important beliefs are to the efficacy of interventions. Sport coaches, psychologists, leaders, and so on, have such a power they can harness to bring the best out of their athletes through positive expectations. Coaches could, therefore, promote the training athletes undertake, through encouraging positive adaptions and enhancing self-belief. The ergogenic effects of ice baths, altitude chambers and compression garments, for example, can become heightened when a positive expectation is attached to them. Deception and untruthful anecdotes are unethical, but we can still promote positive expectations through encouraging verbal suggestions.

Deceptive methods are rarely used in sports research, but this is perhaps more owing to the lack of a perceived need than any specific ethical objections. However, what is and what is not acceptable is not just a function of law and guidelines, but of what ethics committees and journal editors deem appropriate methods for addressing often increasingly complex questions. Historical trends in research ethics suggest that, owing to changes in law, culture or knowledge, practices considered legitimate at one point in time may not be so at a later date (and, arguably, vice versa). For example, several years ago, the elimination of placebo-responsive participants from clinical drug trials might have been deemed unethical, as such a practice constituted a self-selecting sample, deprived participants of potentially effective treatment and inflated observed drug effects. However, the practice has become increasingly widespread, as drug companies strive to derive ever less ambiguous findings from increasingly expensive and time-consuming drug trials. The ethics of research will, to a certain extent, always be guided by the shifting balance between the need to protect participants, on the one hand, and the need to provide society with reliable information about the effects of interventions, on the other.

SUMMARY

The placebo effect has been recognized as a factor in medicine for several centuries. During that time, its status has evolved from that of a superstitious and mercurial phenomenon, through experimental artefact to be controlled for, to that of a legitimate psychological construct in its own right. This process has recently been reflected in sport and exercise, where, after many years of being widely acknowledged but little understood, it is finally the focus of systematic research. Recent research in sport and exercise has demonstrated that the placebo effect can elicit substantial and significant positive and negative effects on a number of dependent variables. Pharmacological effects of ergogenic aids give marginal improvements in performance in the order of

1–3 per cent, but these improvements are rarely additive. When ergogenic aids are combined together, greater improvements are rarely shown (Bellinger et al., 2012; Kilding et al., 2012; Price and Cripps, 2012). Ergogenic aids simply allow us to 'give a little more', but these improvements have been shown to be matched with a placebo, or the belief we have ingested a potential beneficial supplement (Beedie et al., 2006; McClung and Collins, 2007; Duncan, 2010).

The placebo effect is, however, not simply an interesting and potentially useful psychological construct. Although it has much in common with other complex sports psychological processes, such as flow states or automaticity, the placebo effect presents the sport psychologist with practical and ethical questions: for example, to what extent can the placebo effect be utilized to enhance performance? If it is possible to enhance performance via placebo mechanisms, is it ethical to do so? If an athlete is highly placebo responsive, are they likely to be nocebo responsive also? Is placebo responsiveness desirable or undesirable for an athlete? Can placebo/nocebo responsiveness be modified via sport psychology interventions? Answers to these questions will require, not only a substantial and systematic research initiative, but – as is arguably required in contemporary medicine also – a concurrent and equally systematic interrogation of the ethical implications of that research.

Over and above the questions, however, the placebo effect presents perhaps a greater challenge to practitioners. It is quite likely, as has been the case in medicine and psychotherapy, that a substantial number of interventions used in sport psychology might operate, at least in part, via placebo mechanisms. With the increased scientific and ethical scrutiny of such professions that characterizes contemporary medical and related professional practice, such mechanisms will need to be investigated, and either discounted or acknowledged and addressed accordingly.

Sport and exercise science is increasingly an evidence-based practice. With the increasing emphasis in medicine, science and the media on mind–body interactions, the placebo effect, together with related research and therapeutic approaches such as psychoneuroimmunology (e.g. Ader and Cohen, 1993), has become the focus of medical research, academic enquiry and media speculation. Greater knowledge of the placebo effect per se resulting from this process will not only enhance our understanding of the interaction between mind and body – possibly increasing our understanding of the therapeutic effects of processes such as hypnosis and even exercise – but will likely enhance our understanding of the findings of the clinical trials and experimental studies that form the basis of the evidence base alluded to above. This will allow researchers in a wide range of scientific and academic disciplines to make more reliable estimates of the effects of the interventions under investigation.

Despite the attempts of many scientists to argue otherwise (e.g. Hróbjartsson and Gøtzsche, 2010), the placebo effect is probably, perhaps like many other aspects of human psychology, an evolved adaptive mechanism. As with many other adaptive mechanisms, evidence suggests that we, or those from whom we seek help or advice, may be able to 'tap in' to these mechanisms when a certain set of environmental conditions are met. Such a set of environmental conditions might be, for example, when there is a desired state (e.g. a certain level of health or performance), a difference between our current state and that desired state (an illness or low level of performance), a mechanism we believe may enhance our chances of reaching the desired state (e.g. a course of antibiotics or a sport psychology intervention) and the belief that the intervention has been received. This does not discount any of the effectiveness of either antibiotics or sport psychology interventions, it merely highlights that a treatment in which an individual holds a strong and positive belief is more likely to elicit a positive placebo response. Whether this placebo response only operates in the absence of the intervention in question (the classic placebo effect), or whether it can also add to a legitimate biological or psychological intervention, is a question for future research.

FUTURE DIRECTIONS

Research to date in sport and exercise has used the placebo as a demonstration, rather than as an intervention. Understanding the specific psychosocial characteristics of the environment and how this can be adapted to specific individuals is the primary aim for future research. Using multi-method and –disciplinary approaches is almost certainly required to achieve this aim. Finally, understanding the impact the placebo effect has upon athletes' knowledge and how this affects decisions about using performance-enhancing supplements is also an intriguing area worth investigating.

KEY CONCEPTS AND TERMS

Placebo effect

A positive outcome arising from the belief that a beneficial treatment has been received.

Nocebo effect

A negative outcome arising from the belief either that a negative treatment has been received or that a beneficial treatment has been withheld.

Placebo-controlled clinical trial

An empirical exploration of the experimental effects of an intervention in which the potential psychological effects (placebo effects) are controlled for by use of a placebo control.

RECOMMENDED FURTHER READING

Books

Evans, D. (2003). *Placebo: The belief effect*. London: HarperCollins.

Journals

Beedie, C. J. and Foad, A. (2009). The placebo effect in sports performance: A brief review. *Sports Medicine*, *39*(4), 313–29.

Benedetti, F., Maggi, G., Lopiano, L., Lanotte, M., Rainero, I., Vighetti, S. and Pollo, A. (2003). Open versus hidden medical treatments: The patient's knowledge about a therapy affects the therapy outcome. *Prevention and Treatment*, *6*(1), 1–16.

Colloca, L. and Miller, F. G. (2011). Harnessing the placebo effect: The need for translation research. *Philosophical Transactions of the Royal Society B: Biological Sciences*, *366*, 1922–30.

Howick, J., Friedemann, C., Tsakok, M., Watson, R., Tsakok, T., Thomas, J., Perera, R., Fleming, S. and Heneghan, C. (2013). Are treatments more effective than placebos? A systematic review and meta-analysis. *PLoS One*, *15*(8). Available online at: www.plosone.org/article/info%3Adoi%2F10.1371%2Fjournal.pone.0062599 (accessed 8 April 2015).

Kaptchuk, T. J. (2001). The double-blind, randomized, placebo-controlled trial. Gold standard or golden calf? *Journal of Clinical Epidemiology*, *54*(6), 541–9.

Kirsch, I. and Weixel, L. J. (1988). Double-blind versus deceptive administration of a placebo. *Behavioural Neuroscience*, *102*(22), 319–23.

SAMPLE ESSAY QUESTIONS

1   With reference to theory and research, discuss the contention that the placebo effect is a resource that might be exploited by sport psychologists.

2   The placebo control has been fundamental to empirical research in medicine, psychology and sports science for more than 50 years. Describe a hypothetical placebo-controlled experiment and highlight why the placebo control is necessary. Provide a detailed example of how a placebo control could be used in a study of a sport psychology intervention.

3   The placebo effect represents a problem for sport psychology: discuss.

4   It has been suggested that the placebo effect might account for a significant percentage of the observed effects of psychotherapy (e.g. Evans, 2003). Using ethical and scientific principles as guides, discuss the contention that, if the same is true of applied sport psychology, the end still justifies the means.

REFERENCES

Ader, R. and Cohen, N. (1993). Psychoneuroimmunology: Conditioning and stress. *Annual Review of Psychology*, *44*, 53–85.

American Psychological Association (2002). *Ethical Principles of Psychologists and Code of Conduct.* Available online at: www.apa.org/ethics/code2002.pdf (accessed 8 April 2015).

Ariel, G. and Saville, W. (1972). Anabolic steroids: The physiological effects of placebos. *Medicine and Science in Sports and Exercise*, *4*, 124–6.

Beedie, C. J. (2007). The placebo effect in competitive sport: Qualitative data. *Journal of Sport Science and Medicine, 6,* 21–8.

Beedie, C. J., Coleman, D. A. and Foad, A. J. (2007). Positive and negative placebo effects resulting from the deceptive administration of an ergogenic aid. *International Journal of Sports Nutrition and Exercise Metabolism, 17,* 259–69.

Beedie, C. J. and Foad, A. (2009) The placebo effect in sports performance: A brief review. *Sports Medicine, 39*(4), 313–29.

Beedie, C. J., Foad, A. J. and Coleman, D. A. (2008). Identification of placebo responsive participants in 40km laboratory cycling performance. *Journal of Sports Science & Medicine, 7*(1), 166–75.

Beedie, C. J., Stuart, E. M., Coleman, D. A. and Foad, A. J. (2006). Placebo effects of caffeine in cycling performance. *Medicine and Science in Sport and Exercise, 38,* 2159–64.

Bellinger, P. M., Howe, S. T., Shing, C. M. and Fell, J. W. (2012). Effect of combined A-alanine and sodium bicarbonate supplementation on cycling performance. *Medicine and Science in Sports and Exercise, 44*(8), 1545–51.

Benedetti, F. (2013). Placebo and the new physiology of the doctor–patient relationship. *Physiological Reviews, 93*(3), 1207–46.

Benedetti, F. and Amanzio, M. (2011). The placebo response: How words and rituals change the patient's brain. *Patient Education and Counseling, 84*(3), 413–19.

Benedetti, F., Carlino, E. and Pollo, A. (2011). How placebos change the patient's brain, *Neuropsychopharmacology, 36*(1), 339–54.

Clark, V. R., Hopkins, W. G., Hawley, J. A. and Burke, L. M. (2000). Placebo effect of carbohydrate feeding during a 40-km cycling time trial. *Medicine and Science in Sports and Exercise, 32,* 1642–7.

Duncan, M. J. (2010). Placebo effects of caffeine on anaerobic performance in moderately trained adults. *Serbian Journal of Sports Sciences, 4*(1–4), 99–106.

Evans, D. (2003). *Placebo: The belief effect.* London: HarperCollins.

Foad, A. J., Beedie, C. J. and Coleman, D. A. (2008). Pharmacological and psychological effects of caffeine ingestion in 40-km cycling performance. *Medicine and Science in Sports and Exercise, 40*(1), 158–65.

Gallagher, H. (1970). *On Swimming,* pp. 33–8. London: Pelham.

Geers, A. L., Helfer, S. G., Kosbab, K., Weiland, P. E. and Landry, S. J. (2005). Reconsidering the role of personality in placebo effects: Dispositional optimism, situational expectations, and the placebo response. *Journal of Psychosomatic Research, 58,* 121–7.

Gelfand, D. M. (1962). The influence of self-esteem on rate of verbal conditioning and social matching behaviour. *Journal of Abnormal Social Psychology, 65,* 259–65.

Hahn, R. A. (1997). The nocebo phenomenon: Concept, evidence, and implications for public health. *Preventative Medicine, 26,* 607–11.

Hall, K. T., Lembo, A. J., Kirsch, I., Ziogas, D. C., Douaiher, J., Jensen, K. B., Conboy, L. A., Melley, J. M., Kokkotou, E. and Kaptchuk, T. J. (2012). Catechol-O-methyltransferase val158met polymorphism predicts placebo effect in irritable bowel syndrome. *PloS One, 7*(10), e48135.

Hróbjartsson, A. and Gøtzsche, P. C. (2010). Placebo interventions for all clinical conditions. *The Cochrane Library*. Available online at: www.rima.org/web/medline_pdf/Placebointer ventions.pdf (accessed 16 April 2015).

Hurst, P., Board, L. and Roberts, J. (2013). Expectancy effects on competitive 5 km time-trial performance. *British Journal of Sports Medicine*, 47(17), e4.

Kilding, A. E., Overton, C. and Gleave, J. (2012). Effects of caffeine, sodium bicarbonate and their combined ingestion on high-intensity cycling performance. *International Journal of Sport Nutrition and Exercise Metabolism*, 10(4), 464–75.

Lasagna, L. (1986). The placebo effect. *Journal of Allergy and Clinical Immunology*, 78, 161–5.

McClung, M. and Collins, D. (2007). 'Because I know it will!': Placebo effects of an ergogenic aid on athletic performance. *Journal of Sport and Exercise Psychology*, 29, 382–94.

McNair, D. M., Gardos, G., Haskell, D. S. and Fisher, S. (1979). Placebo response, placebo effect and two attributes. *Psychopharmacology*, 63, 245–50.

Maganaris, C. N., Collins, D. and Sharp, M. (2000). Expectancy effects and strength training: Do steroids make a difference? *Sport Psychologist*, 14, 272–8.

Marlatt, G. A. and Rohsenow, D. J. (1980). Cognitive processes in alcohol use: Expectancy and the balanced placebo design. In Mello, N. (ed.) *Advances in Substance Abuse* (1), pp. 159–99. Greenwich, CT: JAI Press.

Michael, R. B., Garry, M. and Kirsch, I. (2012). Suggestion, cognition, and behavior. *Current Directions in Psychological Science*, 21(3), 151–6.

Noakes, T. (2012). *The mindset to succeed*. Available online at: http://tedxcapetown.org/video/ tim-noakes-mindset-succeed (accessed 16 April 2015).

Pavlov, I. P. (1927). *Conditioned Reflexes: An investigation of the physiological activities of the cerebral cortex*. Available online at: http://psychclassics.yorku.ca/Pavlov/ (accessed 17 April 2015).

Price, M. J. and Cripps, D. (2012). The effects of combined glucose–electrolyte and sodium bicarbonate ingestion on prolonged intermittent exercise performance. *Journal of Sports Sciences*, 30(10), 975–83.

Seligman, M. E., Nolen-Hoeksema, S., Thornton, N. and Thornton, K. M. (1990). Explanatory style as a mechanism of disappointing athletic performance. *Psychological Science*, 1(2), 143–6.

Shapiro, A. K. and Shapiro, E. (1984). Patient–provider relationships and the placebo effect. In Matarazzo, J. D., Weiss, S. M., Heird, J. A. and Miller, N. E. (eds) *Behavioural Health: Handbook of health enhancement and disease prevention*, pp. 371–83. New York: Wiley.

Stewart-Williams, S. and Podd, J. (2004). The placebo effect: Dissolving the expectancy versus conditioning debate. *Psychological Bulletin*, 130(2), 324–40.

Szabo, A., Bérdi, M., Köteles, F. and Bárdos, G. (2013). Perceptual characteristics of nutritional supplements determine the expected effectiveness in boosting strength, endurance, and concentration performances. *International Journal of Sport Nutrition and Exercise Metabolism*, 23(6), 624–8.

Vogt, W. (1999). *Breaking the Chain: Drugs and cycling, the true story* (trans. William Fotherington). London: Random House.

Index